Macroeconomic Modelling and Monetary and Exchange Rate Regimes

Macroeconomic Modelling and Monetary and Exchange Rate Regimes

PAUL R. MASSON
Weatherstone Consulting, Canada

World Scientific

NEW JERSEY · LONDON · SINGAPORE · BEIJING · SHANGHAI · HONG KONG · TAIPEI · CHENNAI · TOKYO

Published by

World Scientific Publishing Co. Pte. Ltd.

5 Toh Tuck Link, Singapore 596224

USA office: 27 Warren Street, Suite 401-402, Hackensack, NJ 07601

UK office: 57 Shelton Street, Covent Garden, London WC2H 9HE

Library of Congress Cataloging-in-Publication Data

Names: Masson, Paul R., author.

Title: Macroeconomic modelling and monetary and exchange rate regimes / by
Paul R. Masson (Weatherstone Consulting, Canada).

Description: New Jersey : World Scientific, [2019]

Identifiers: LCCN 2019014023 | ISBN 9789811200953 (hc)

Subjects: LCSH: Monetary policy--Econometric models. | Foreign exchange--
Econometric models. | Macroeconomics--Econometric models.

Classification: LCC HG230.3 .M379 2019 | DDC 339.5/3011--dc23

LC record available at https://lccn.loc.gov/2019014023

British Library Cataloguing-in-Publication Data

A catalogue record for this book is available from the British Library.

Copyright © 2019 by World Scientific Publishing Co. Pte. Ltd.

*All rights reserved. This book, or parts thereof, may not be reproduced in any form or by any means,
electronic or mechanical, including photocopying, recording or any information storage and retrieval
system now known or to be invented, without written permission from the publisher.*

For photocopying of material in this volume, please pay a copying fee through the Copyright Clearance
Center, Inc., 222 Rosewood Drive, Danvers, MA 01923, USA. In this case permission to photocopy
is not required from the publisher.

For any available supplementary material, please visit
https://www.worldscientific.com/worldscibooks/10.1142/11297#t=suppl

Desk Editors: Anthony Alexander/Lum Pui Yee

Typeset by Stallion Press
Email: enquiries@stallionpress.com

About the Author

Dr. Paul R. Masson has published numerous articles and books in various areas of economics, including macroeconomic modelling, monetary and fiscal policy, international finance, exchange rate regimes, and regional integration. His books include **The Monetary Geography of Africa** with Catherine Pattillo (Brookings, 2005) and **Topics in International Finance** (World Scientific, 2008). Until recently, he taught international finance at the University of Toronto, after careers at the Bank of Canada, the OECD, and the IMF, where he worked in the Research, European, and African departments. Since then, he has served as Special Adviser to the Governor of the Bank of Canada and Monetary Union Advisor for the government of Rwanda, and worked as an economic consultant. Masson is currently Research Affiliate with the National Bureau of Economic Research (U.S.A.), Research Fellow at the C.D. Howe Institute (Canada), and Principal at Weatherstone Consulting. He lives in Niagara-on-the-Lake, Ontario, Canada.

Contents

About the Author   v

Chapter 1. Introduction   1

Part I. Macroeconomic Modelling   15

Chapter 2. Macroeconomic Effects of Projected
Population Aging in Industrial Countries   17

Paul R. Masson and Ralph W. Tryon

Chapter 3. Models of Inflation and the Costs of
Disinflation   57

Bankim Chadha, Paul R. Masson
and Guy Meredith

Chapter 4. German Unification: What Have We
Learned from Multi-Country Models?   101

Joseph E. Gagnon, Paul R. Masson
and Warwick J. McKibbin

Part II. Exchange Rate Regimes and International Currencies   141

Chapter 5. Exchange Rate Regimes of Developing Countries: Global Context and Individual Choices   143

Esteban Jadresic, Paul R. Masson and Paolo Mauro

Chapter 6. Should African Monetary Unions Be Expanded? An Empirical Investigation of the Scope for Monetary Integration in Sub-Saharan Africa   195

Xavier Debrun, Paul R. Masson and Catherine Pattillo

Chapter 7. Currency Unions in Africa: Is the Trade Effect Substantial Enough to Justify Their Formation?   243

Paul R. Masson

Chapter 8. Fiscal Asymmetries and the Survival of the Euro Zone   263

Paul R. Masson

Chapter 9. The Euro at 20: Lessons for Africa   297

Paul R. Masson

Part III. Monetary Regimes   329

Chapter 10. The Scope for Inflation Targeting in Developing Countries   331

Paul R. Masson, Miguel A. Savastano and Sunil Sharma

Contents

Chapter 11. Are Bygones Not Bygones? Modeling Price-Level Targeting with an Escape Clause and Lessons from the Gold Standard   385

Paul R. Masson and Malik D. Shukayev

Chapter 1

Introduction

The papers in this volume represent a selection from the papers I wrote during several decades, while working first at the International Monetary Fund and then teaching at the University of Toronto — many with co-authors. Broadly speaking, all of these papers use models as a way of informing the choice of macroeconomic policies. While some of the papers are technical, they were all written to address real-world economic policy problems. Moreover, these economic problems and consideration of appropriate policy responses continue to be relevant today, as is the economic analysis used to address them.

Part I includes papers that analyse the effects of major international developments affecting the global economy, using a multi-country global model — MULTIMOD — developed by myself and collaborators at the IMF. In each case, the appropriate response of macroeconomic policy (fiscal or monetary) is discussed. The papers here use MULTIMOD to look at three specific issues of great importance for economic policy choice. Those issues are as follows:

- the effects of a transition to an older population on output, capital stocks, factor prices, and current account balances (among other variables);
- how the economic costs of reducing the rate of inflation can be minimized;
- the domestic and global effects of the unification of East and West Germany.

1

2   *Macroeconomic Modelling and Monetary and Exchange Rate Regimes*

These are issues that obviously continue to be relevant, especially the first two. It is also true, moreover, of German unification, since its effects, for instance, the stresses it imposed on the European Monetary System in the early 1990s, may recur in other situations. This paper not only reports MULTIMOD simulation results but also compares them to two other state-of-the-art multi-country models of that vintage, evaluating the success of these models in capturing the main implications of unification.

Parts II and III consider the interrelated choices of a monetary/exchange rate regime. As is now widely accepted, economies that are exposed to highly mobile capital flows cannot choose their exchange rate regime independently of their monetary policy. Part II considers the policy choice from the perspective of the advantages and disadvantages of various exchange rate regimes that imply differing degrees of commitment to a fixed rate. Part III, in contrast, discusses issues with regard to using monetary policy to target either the rate of inflation or the price level, with the exchange rate assumed able to adjust in order to permit those targets to be achieved. In both cases, the papers argue that it is essential to take into account the specificities of a country's level of development, its financial markets, and the size and orientation of its trade with the rest of the world before coming to a conclusion concerning its appropriate monetary/exchange rate regime.

The monetary/exchange rate regime choice is a cornerstone of economic policy, not just for advanced countries but also emerging market and less-developed economies, and the papers in Parts II and III span the range of countries and issues involved. For the more advanced economies that have sophisticated capital markets and no barriers to capital inflows and outflows, several prominent economists have argued that the choice is essentially between a freely flexible exchange rate and (if regional exchange rate stability is judged to be essential) a single currency (see, for instance, Obstfeld and Rogoff, 1995). For other countries, however, the policy choice may not be that stark, and the first paper in Part II argues that it is important to take into account differences in economic structures and levels of development. In particular, countries that trade primarily with a larger neighbor may be able to peg to the neighbor's currency in a credible fashion. Other countries may want to use the exchange rate as an intermediate target given its visibility as a key price in the economy, provided that there is a clear commitment to adjust other policies to be consistent with the targeted exchange rate level.

The idea that policy regimes need to be chosen with regard to a country's specificities recurs in Part III. A survey of the prerequisites for inflation targeting (IT) to work well concludes that IT may not be appropriate for all countries, given widely differing economic institutions, degrees of consensus on the objectives of monetary policy, and extent of wage/price flexibility. Thus, the papers in this volume eschew the "one size fits all" approach to economic policy.

In what follows, a more in-depth discussion of the various papers in the book is provided. The reader can refer to the Table of Contents for details concerning titles, authors, and publication details. Reference is made to the papers using the ordering of the Table of Contents, from Chapters 2–11 (this introduction is Chapter 1). In all but two cases (Chapters 9 and 10), these papers have previously been published in academic journals. The first one of the unpublished papers, Chapter 9, on the lessons for Africa from the euro zone, has evolved from a conference paper. The second, on prerequisites for IT (Chapter 10), though widely cited in its working paper form, has not been published. It has continued relevance, given the large number of countries that have adopted or are considering IT. The version presented here is an abridged version of that working paper.

Part I: Macroeconomic Modelling

The three papers in Part I present simulations of the global macroeconomic model then in use at the IMF, MULTIMOD (see Masson *et al.* 1990). The model includes each of the G7 countries separately, the remaining industrial countries as a bloc, and developing countries divided into capital importing and capital exporting countries. The model embodies stock/flow equilibrium, optimizing consumers and firms with rational expectations, and high capital mobility among the industrial countries.

4   *Macroeconomic Modelling and Monetary and Exchange Rate Regimes*

The generalised aging of the populations in the industrial countries, linked to the post-world-war-two baby boom, is studied in Chapter 2. This was one of the first attempts to quantify the effects of an older population in an empirical general-equilibrium global model. An older population has a number of important economic effects. They include the following:

- fewer active members of the labour force, hence lower output per capita (other things equal);
- greater government expenditures on health care and pensions;
- higher consumption from a given household disposable income, or equivalently, a lower aggregate savings rate, for a given interest rate and aggregate wealth.

The implications for such variables as output, interest rates, capital stocks, exchange rates and current account balances are complex, and a quantitative assessment (or even a qualitative one) requires an empirical general-equilibrium model. The country-specific effects, moreover, depend on the extent of aging in one country relative to that in other countries. The overall effects could be expected to be large, in any case, given that projections of elderly dependency ratios (those over 65 divided by those between 15–64) were projected to increase from 20% in 1985 to 35% in 2025 in the average G7 country.

The simulation results depend importantly on an estimated consumption equation that has both life-cycle and liquidity-constrained elements, plus a positive effect of the old age dependency ratio. They do not assume that all consumers can implement a lifetime plan, but rather rely on the statistical relationship between dependency ratios and saving. The projections of population and government spending were taken from other sources. They project a larger and earlier increase in dependency ratios in Japan and Germany than in the other G7 countries, and this differential has a strong influence on simulation results.

Looking first at the effect of aging on consumption, and ignoring effects on labour supply and government expenditure, both Japan and Germany have lower saving and these countries run current

Introduction 5

account deficits, while the United States runs surpluses and accumulates net foreign assets. The labour supply effect, in contrast, lowers GDP in all countries, by 2020 when dependency ratios have increased significantly in all countries. Government spending effects are more moderate, but tend to go in the same direction as the consumption effects, lowering aggregate saving.

The combined effects of the three channels imply very different impacts on the United States versus Japan and Germany, with the other G7 countries somewhere in between. The relatively less important increase in dependency ratios in the United States produces a real exchange rate depreciation, a fall in the real interest rate and increase in output there (which declines to zero by 2025), associated with current account surpluses relative to the baseline. In contrast, Germany and, especially, Japan experience falls in output, real exchange rate appreciations and current account deficits. Interestingly, real interest rates (which are forward looking in the model) fall initially and then rise, as the demographic effects stabilize toward the end of the simulations.

The simulations highlight some features that are often ignored, namely that different extents of population aging in different countries have a major effect on the results through exchange rate changes. This difference explains why the United States sustains a depreciation and an increase in output (despite a fall in labour supply), as other countries' output falls and consumption increases. While the path of consumption is shown to be sensitive to modelling strategies, the simulations are an antidote to simplistic analysis using a growth model with fully optimising consumers applied to a single country.

A second important issue considered using MULTIMOD is the cost of disinflation, studied in Chapter 3. In the two decades that followed the breakdown of the Bretton Woods system of fixed parities — characterised by sharp increases in oil and other commodity prices — most countries faced the difficult choice of restricting demand through high interest rates in order to contain and eventually reduce the rate of increase of prices. How drastic should the adjustment be — should it be a short, sharp increase in interest

6   *Macroeconomic Modelling and Monetary and Exchange Rate Regimes*

rates, or a more gradual monetary contraction? The answer should depend on the resulting increase in unemployment, and associated decrease in output — the cumulative output loss — in the two cases.

The 1970s, 1980s and 1990s also saw a great deal of research into the dynamics of inflation. It was increasingly recognised that inflation expectations did not just look at past experience of inflation but rather could be influenced by a credible announcement of a policy change. But, the extent of that forward-looking behaviour is important in influencing the output costs of disinflation. If expectations of the future are all that matters, then costless disinflation is possible — contrary to actual experience. The paper shows that there is some critical level for forward-looking behaviour above which costs can be eliminated, while below that value some output losses are unavoidable.

In Chapter 3, a model of inflation is estimated with both forward- and backward-looking expectation elements, whose weights sum to one. The estimation results find a significant effect of output capacity utilisation in boosting inflation, and suggest that the weight on forward-looking expectations is slightly less than one-half. Both of the extremes — purely backward-looking or forward-looking models — are rejected by the data. The model does not imply that a costless disinflation path is possible, and alternative speeds of disinflation are simulated in order to identify those with the lowest cost.

The third paper, in Part I (Chapter 4), reports on the use of three rational expectations, multi-country models to assess the effects of German unification. Appropriately, the paper is co-authored by the heads of the three groups, Joseph Gagnon (the MX3 model, maintained at the Federal Reserve Board), Warwick McKibbin (MSG2 model, at the Brookings Institution) and myself (MULTIMOD, where the work was done in close collaboration with the IMF's European Department in 1990).

German unification was a major shock to the European economy. It involved opening up East Germany to competition (which meant the closing of many uneconomic plants), the restructuring of East German industry, the conversion of Ost marks at a one-to-one rate into deutsche marks, and massive fiscal transfers to East Germany (which amounted to over 40% of East German GDP in each of the first 5 years). The expansionary fiscal policy put upward pressure on interest rates and tended to appreciate the deutsche mark, causing strains within the EMS and leading to a large widening in the margins of fluctuation around central parities as well as an abandonment of their defense by the UK and Italy.

German unification was a major challenge for the modelling groups. None of the models included East Germany explicitly, so that some *ad hoc* changes were necessary. In 1990, data on the competitiveness (or lack of it) of the East German economy were not known, nor was it clear how the process of privatizing the government-owned means of production would proceed. Finally, the size of the fiscal transfers and the effect of the expansion of the German money supply relative to money demand had to be estimated.

Despite these challenges and the fact that the modelling groups were working independently, simulations of the three models got many of the broad effects of unification right. It was correctly anticipated that government spending would put upward pressure on output, inflation, and interest rates, and lead to German current account deficits, facilitated by a real exchange rate depreciation. The possibility of tensions within the EMS was well understood, and some of the modelers simulated realignment scenarios in which the other EMS currencies devalued against the deutsche mark — well before the EMS crisis. All in all, the results of this important exercise highlighted the usefulness of the new generation of rational expectations, multi-country models.

Part II: Exchange Rate Regimes and International Currencies

Part II begins with a discussion of the range of possible exchange rate regimes (Chapter 5), arguing that each may be appropriate for some countries at various stages of development. It then goes on to consider more specifically the case for and against monetary unions, in particular in Africa (Chapters 6 and 7), and an evaluation of the

8 *Macroeconomic Modelling and Monetary and Exchange Rate Regimes*

experience of the prime example of a monetary union among a group of sovereign countries — the euro zone (Chapters 8 and 9).

The creation of European Monetary Union has stimulated interest in creating regional monetary unions in Africa — a continent that already has two monetary unions (the West and Central African CFA franc zones), as well as an hybrid exchange-rate union centered around South Africa's rand. Monetary integration in Europe has inspired a vast literature, much of it following the lead of Robert Mundell, who in a seminal 1961 paper put forward the notion of "optimum currency areas". While this literature focuses on the costs of sharing a common currency in the absence of factor mobility, wage/price flexibility, or fiscal transfers, it provides few insights into the benefits of a common currency, which in principle should include reducing transactions costs and stimulating trade and investment. A more recent strand of literature has attempted to quantify those benefits, in particular the increased trade that results when countries are members of a currency union (see, for instance, Rose, 2000; Glick and Rose, 2015). Estimates of this effect should inform the decision whether or not to proceed with monetary unions in Africa.

Part II includes two papers (Chapters 6 and 7) that evaluate plans for monetary unions in Africa. These include a number of projects at various stages of realization within Regional Economic Communities (RECs) on the continent. Prime among them is a plan (whose timetable has however been postponed several times) to create a common currency for West Africa (ECOWAS) that would subsume the West African CFA franc zone and also include Nigeria, Ghana and several smaller countries in the region. A monetary union has also been agreed among members of the East African Community and is slated to be put in place in 2024.

In joint work (Chapter 6) with Xavier Debrun and Catherine Pattillo,[1] these and other projects were evaluated using a model which embodies some important aspects of the costs and benefits of being a member of a monetary union. A monetary union by

---

[1] See also references in Chapter 6 to related joint work with Debrun and Pattillo.

definition involves sharing a common monetary policy. The common monetary policy imposes costs, since it cannot respond to country-specific shocks, but countries may also benefit from the fact that a common currency prevents neighbouring countries from engineering competitive depreciations of their currencies. This model was calibrated to African data and used to evaluate the regional monetary unions. Important inputs to the evaluation are as follows:

- *The extent of trade among the countries of a region*: Countries with little trade with their neighbours could be expected to benefit little from exchange rate stability with regards to them.
- *Asymmetry of terms of trade shocks*: This would put stress on a monetary union.
- *Asymmetry of fiscal discipline*: Countries that run large deficits would put pressures on the central bank to provide monetary financing. Therefore, more fiscally disciplined countries would not want to share a currency with very undisciplined ones.

Aside from the existing monetary/exchange rate unions (the CFA franc and rand zones) which our welfare analysis suggested are generally beneficial, our analysis reached sceptical conclusions as to whether new monetary unions would be desirable. However, extending the existing ones to a few other countries with similar economic structures might be mutually beneficial.

In another paper (Chapter 7), I considered whether estimates that a common currency could produce a large increase in trade (by a factor of two or three) would overturn these conclusions. In fact, because much of African countries' exports is comprised of primary commodities that go to Asia, Europe or North America, intraregional trade is at present very small. Even such a large increase of intraregional trade would therefore not provide enough in the way of benefits to offset the costs of heterogeneity among the countries concerned, since in most regions there are large differences in fiscal discipline and in terms of trade shocks. In particular, a hypothetical ECOWAS monetary union would include, on the one hand, a large oil exporter lacking fiscal discipline (Nigeria), and, on the other hand, mostly oil importers exhibiting greater fiscal discipline. Thus, the terms of trade of the two would move in opposite directions in response to a global oil price shock. A common currency, by tying them together, would make adjustment to such a shock more difficult for both sets of countries. In addition, the other countries of the region might suffer from the large budget deficits run by Nigeria because they could exert pressures on the central bank to provide monetary financing, producing higher inflation and a depreciating currency.

The same model also sheds light on the tensions within the euro zone, and Chapter 8 considers its implications. The statutes of the European Central Bank (ECB) are designed to insulate it from fiscal dominance, that is, allay concerns that fiscal indiscipline might put pressures on the central bank to pursue an easier monetary policy. What if the ECB were not in fact independent from those pressures? Using the same model as for African monetary unions, calibrated to EU data, Chapter 8 provides a possible answer. Unlike in Africa, where intraregional trade is low and terms of trade shock asymmetries are high, in Europe the reverse is true.

Thus, potential gains from monetary union are large, as long as fiscal asymmetries are not too great. The model simulations conclude that membership in the euro zone is beneficial for most countries relative to their pre-euro zone status, with the major exception of Germany — on the assumption that the Bundesbank, when the deutsche mark was in existence, was independent of fiscal pressures, while the ECB is assumed not to be independent. The paper goes on to consider whether the welfare of remaining euro zone countries would be improved if any of the other countries left the euro zone. In particular, model simulations suggest that France, Greece and Italy are countries whose membership in the zone is problematic because of their lack of fiscal discipline. The departure of any of them individually would improve welfare of the other members. Finally, the paper considers the incentives facing Germany: would a narrower monetary union with only fiscally responsible countries — for instance, the "core ERM" countries which maintained their exchange rates against the deutsche mark during the 1992–1993 ERM crisis (Austria, Belgium, Luxembourg and the Netherlands)

be incentive compatible if it could commit to IT and be free of fiscal pressures? The answer given by the model is "no", because such a narrow monetary union would not internalise much trade, while still preventing the common monetary policy from responding fully to Germany-specific shocks.

Part II concludes with a paper that draws some lessons for other regions from the euro zone experience over the past two decades (Chapter 9). Clearly, despite decades of planning and the expenditure of considerable resources in preparation, the architects of the euro zone did not anticipate the extent that weak government finances and banking crises could feed upon themselves and produce a loss of confidence in the currency. The crisis that the euro zone has faced episodically since 2008 has led the ECB to change drastically the way it intervened in financial markets to prevent the increase in government borrowing costs of weaker member countries. The crisis has also laid bare the failures of community institutions to produce fiscal discipline that the Stability and Growth Pact aimed to correct, and the need to buttress monetary union with other policies to bolster solidarity among member states and to make viable the monetary union. In particular, the elements of a banking union — common supervision and lender of last resort facilities — are now viewed as essential, and are being implemented within the euro zone, as well as greater sharing of risks.

What are the lessons from this for Africa? The paper argues that the requirements for a successful monetary union are more stringent than was previously thought, and they include the need for a high degree of solidarity among countries and the sharing of similar economic philosophies. Unexpected events are likely to threaten the monetary union, and countries must be willing and able to reach agreement among themselves to take the necessary steps to preserve it. The political will to proceed with a monetary union is not sufficient, since that political will is unlikely to survive evidence that continued membership in the monetary union carries with it large economic costs. Finally, the experience of the euro zone suggests caution in committing to such arrangements, and the need for a long lead time to create the necessary institutions to support a monetary union.

Part III: Monetary Regimes

Since the early 1990s, a number of advanced countries have adopted IT as their monetary regime and use a specific numerical target for inflation at some future point as operational guide for monetary policy settings — specifically short-term interest rates. A previously unpublished paper written in 1997 (Chapter 10) considers whether such a regime can and should also be adopted by developing countries.

The paper provides a thorough review of the literature on IT, which was already extensive, concluding that the regime is characterised by two essential requirements as follows:

- It must have a central bank able to conduct its monetary policy with a degree of independence. In particular, it must be free from fiscal dominance, that is, monetary policy must not be subservient to the need to finance government deficits.
- The authorities must not have any firm commitment to target any other nominal variable, such as the exchange rate.

In practice, central banks that operationalize IT need to have a quantitative model that permits them to forecast inflation over a horizon that corresponds to the lags in the effect of monetary policy instruments on inflation. By explaining to the public the basis for their instrument settings, central banks can improve the transparency of monetary policy and anchor the public's expectations. If the transmission mechanism is very uncertain, however, then it is likely that targets frequently will not be met, and the credibility advantages of IT will not accrue.

In discussing the scope for IT among developing countries, Chapter 10 first stresses the great heterogeneity of the countries concerned. For instance, data on seigniorage (that is, the amount of monetary financing), rates of inflation and budget deficits differ widely. Some countries can clearly be ruled out on the grounds that those variables have high values that suggest the central bank would not be able to operate sufficiently independently to be successful in meeting IT objectives.

Introduction 13

As for the second prerequisite, the absence of another nominal target, there was during the 1990s a shift away from pegged exchange rates, largely in response to the crises in emerging markets. Many countries retained some implicit or explicit commitment to an exchange rate level or range that would interfere with IT, however. Furthermore, the monetary linkages were more uncertain than was the case for the advanced countries that had adopted IT.

Thus, the paper concluded that most developing countries were probably not ready for IT, but "... a strengthening of their institutions may ... make IT an attractive option for some developing countries ... In fact, it is quite possible that IT will receive increasing consideration in developing countries as high capital mobility and instability in money demand make alternative nominal anchors less feasible." Indeed, that has proved to be the case, and several dozen developing countries now practice IT in some form.

Another important issue with respect to monetary targeting is the choice between a target for the rate of inflation versus one for the price level (or a fixed upward path for prices). This is the subject of Chapter 11. The main difference between the two regimes is that in the case of overshoots or undershoots of inflation, IT would not reverse them later but price level (or price path) targeting, which we will call PT for short, would. Supporters of PT claim that this would enhance the stabilising properties of PT relative to IT, because if private agents expected implementation errors to be corrected, then they would align their expectations more closely to the official targets. Thus, there would be a credibility advantage to PT.

However, Chapter 11 argues that there is another force at play that could detract from these credibility advantages, namely the increased likelihood that the PT regime would be abandoned in the event of a very large and unanticipated shock to the system. This may occur precisely because PT is more constraining. The experience with the gold standard during the 1930s is instructive. In the face of global loss of confidence and widespread unemployment, countries that were on the gold standard (which included most of the industrialised countries) abandoned the peg of their currencies to gold to pursue more expansionary monetary policies. This could also occur if PT were adopted, and expectations might take this into account, nullifying the credibility enhancement relative to IT. Indeed, simulations of a calibrated global economic model suggest that for a country like Canada, PT is dominated by IT, which is more robust to large shocks.

References

Glick, R. and Rose, A. "Currency Unions and Trade: A Post-EMU Mea Culpa," Paper Presented to a Conference at the Federal Reserve Bank of San Francisco, October 26, 2015.

Masson, P.R., Symansky, S. and Meredith, G. *MULTIMOD Mark II: A Revised and Extended Model*, Occasional Paper 71 (Washington: International Monetary Fund, 1990).

Mundell, R. "A Theory of Optimum Currency Areas", *American Economic Review*, Vol. 51, No. 4, pp. 657–665 (1961).

Obstfeld, M. and Rogoff, K. "The Mirage of Fixed Exchange Rates," *Journal of Economic Perspectives*, Vol. 9, No. 4, pp. 73–96. (Fall 1995).

Rose, A. "One Money, One Market: Estimating the Effect of Common Currencies on Trade," *Economic Policy*, Vol. 30, pp. 9–45, (2000).

Part I
Macroeconomic Modelling

Chapter 2

Macroeconomic Effects of Projected Population Aging in Industrial Countries*

Paul R. Masson and Ralph W. Tryon

The effects of population aging are examined with a theoretical model and simulations of MULTIMOD. An older population will consume more of aggregate disposable income, require higher government expenditure, and decrease labor supply. These effects should raise real interest rates and lower capital stock and output. Effects on current balances will depend on the relative speed and extent of aging. Simulations of projected demographic changes suggest that by 2025, real interest rates would be increased in all countries, and net foreign assets would be increased in the United States and decreased in the Federal Republic of Germany and Japan.

1. Introduction

If current projections prove to be correct, the populations of most industrial countries will experience significant aging in the first few decades of the next century. Birthrates have already declined markedly

---

*This chapter originally appeared in *Staff Papers* (*International Monetary Fund*) (1990), 37(3), 453–485. At time of writing, both authors were staff members of the International Monetary Fund.

from their high levels of the early postwar period, and are projected to decline further. Even though projections that far ahead are obviously subject to considerable uncertainty, a prospective increase in the average age of the population is to a large extent inevitable as the postwar "baby boom" generation moves through the age structure. Aging of the population can be expected to bring about major changes in the economy, associated with an increase in the number of dependents relative to those that are employed (the dependency ratio), and in some countries with very low birthrates, projected declines in the population. An especially large element of uncertainty attaches to birthrate projections and to changes in population due to migration, but in any case, dependency ratios will almost certainly rise in the next three decades; a substantial rise in birthrates would, if anything, increase dependency ratios over this time period.

With the aging of the population, it is plausible to expect a decline in saving rates to the extent that "life-cycle" motives for saving operate — that is, individuals save for retirement during the years in which they are employed and dissave subsequently.[1] In addition, the demand for social services will change toward providing more medical services and pension benefits and away from spending on education. Finally, the presence of fewer individuals of working age will be associated with lower levels of employment and hence of output, other things being equal, than would otherwise be the case. What happens to per capita output will depend on the resulting capital stock per worker, as well as on the proportion of the population in the labor force.

The macroeconomic effects of these changes, which can be expected to be substantial, are the subject of this paper. Changes in saving propensities, government spending, and labor supply have

---

[1]Saving may in fact be "hump-shaped"; that is, saving may be negative in the early years of adulthood, positive in the middle years, and negative again after retirement. Intergenerational transfers complicate the analysis of saving behavior, which should be modeled at the household level. Parents finance consumption for their children when young and may save for their college education. Moreover, the aged may also save in order to make bequests to their children (or to charity).

implications for relative prices, real interest rates, and real exchange rates; these variables in turn feed back onto decisions to spend and produce. The paper is an attempt to gauge the global macroeconomic consequences of generalized aging of the population in industrial countries.

To understand these consequences requires a macroeconomic model. A multicountry context is also important because some of the effects — for example, on real exchange rates and on current account balances — depend crucially on the extent of aging in one country *relative* to that in other countries. In this paper, we use simulations of the International Monetary Fund's multiregion econometric model (MULTIMOD) in order to gauge the effects of the demographic developments described above.

Aging of the population affects macroeconomic variables in the model through three channels.[2] First, aggregate consumption relative to income is increased by a rise in the dependency ratio. Second, higher dependency ratios lower the labor force, which is associated with a decline in potential output. Third, an older population requires larger government expenditures on medical services and on pension benefits; however, these may be partially offset by a decline in education expenditures.

To date, a macroeconomic framework has not been used to capture the general equilibrium, multicountry effects of demographic projections. There are a number of relevant studies of various features of the issue, however. Heller and others (1986) considered the effect of aging on social expenditures in seven major industrial countries (the so-called Group of Seven), and we will use their estimates below as input to our simulations. Heller (1989) examined the impact of aging on private saving, using several estimated consumption models; he also discussed implications for government budgets. The Organization for Economic Cooperation and Development (OECD) has produced several studies of saving behavior, including effects of demographic factors (Dean

---

[2]Another channel, through the rate of population growth, is ignored here; the population is taken to be exogenous in our simulations discussed below.

and others (1989) and Herd (1989)), and has examined implications of aging for public finances (Hagemann and Nicoletti (1989)). In addition, Auerbach and others (1989) studied the dynamics of the effects of aging on the economies of four industrial countries using a general equilibrium, overlapping-generations model; however, that model considered each country in isolation rather than as part of a closed world system. Ritzen and van Dalen (1989) considered the optimal fiscal policy in the transition to an older population, using a single-country theoretical model. Lee and Lapkoff (1988) looked at intergenerational transfer issues in an overlapping-generations context, but did not treat multicountry issues. Horne, Kremers, and Masson (1989) examined the long-run relationship between dependency ratios and net foreign asset positions for the United States, Japan, and the Federal Republic of Germany.

It is important to make clear at the outset the limitations of our study.[3] We do not examine issues related to intergenerational transfers — namely, questions of equity — since this would require a more detailed model. Furthermore, policy questions — for instance, how should increases in government spending be financed, or whether incentives for private saving should be put in place today — are not treated here.

We have not attempted to incorporate projections for aging in developing countries. Finally, we do not take into account effects of the age structure on labor force participation due to endogenous participation or retirement decisions,[4] or to changes in the growth rate of the population.[5]

The plan of the paper is as follows. Section 2 discusses the OECD's demographic projections and presents the projections of expenditures on government services given in Heller and

---

[3]Some of the issues mentioned in what follows are discussed in Bös and Weizsäcker (1989).

[4]However, Table 8 assesses the sensitivity of our results to these factors.

[5]Some theoretical effects of permanent changes in population growth are analyzed in the Appendix; other things being equal, a lower population growth rate would imply lower real interest rates.

others (1986). Section 3 details the model of private consumption that is embodied in MULTIMOD and compares its estimate of the effect of demographic factors to those found in other studies. Section 4 presents simulations of the effects of aging using MULTIMOD; the results are compared to the long-run effects that can be derived from a simple theoretical model that is the prototype for MULTIMOD. (Derivations are detailed in the Appendix.) Finally, Section 5 provides some concluding remarks.

2. Demographic Trends and Projections

In most industrial countries, the decade and a half following the end of World War II saw very high birthrates, which have since moderated. The early postwar generation — often termed the baby boom generation — is now 30–45 years old; as a result, a large fraction of the population is currently employed. However, when the baby boom generation retires in the years 2010–25, there will likely be large declines in the number employed relative to those that depend on them — or on their own savings.

A measure of the age structure of the population is the dependency ratio, which can be calculated in various ways. Table 1 gives historical data and projections for three measures — the ratios of the young and of the old to those of working age (assumed to be between 15 and 64), as well as their combined ratio.[6] The youth dependency ratio declined markedly from 1965 to 1985; that ratio is projected to decline further in some countries (the United States, France), but generally to remain constant through 2025, at least if birthrates do not change substantially. In contrast, the elderly dependency

---

[6]These projections of dependency ratios are substantially the same as those given in the *World Economic Outlook* (International Monetary Fund (1989)), with a few revisions. In particular, Japan's dependency ratio is projected here to be several percentage points higher in the 2010–20 period. However, the simulations discussed below extend the analysis in the *World Economic Outlook* by taking into account induced labor force and government spending changes. In International Monetary Fund (1990), some tax policy issues related to aging are also considered.

Table 1. Selected Demographic Variables, 1965–2025 (In Percent)

Country	1965	1975	1985	Projections			
				1995	2005	2015	2025
Population under 15/population 15–64							
United States	51	39	33	34	29	29	30
Japan	38	36	32	25	28	28	27
Germany, Fed. Rep. of	35	34	22	23	22	19	23
France	41	38	32	31	28	26	28
Italy	—	—	—	25	25	22	24
United Kingdom	36	37	29	31	31	31	31
Canada	57	41	32	30	27	25	28
Population 65 and over/population 15–64							
United States	16	16	18	19	18	21	29
Japan	9	12	15	19	26	33	32
Germany, Fed. Rep. of	18	23	21	24	29	31	37
France	19	22	20	22	24	27	33
Italy	—	—	—	22	25	28	32
United Kingdom	19	22	23	23	22	24	28
Canada	13	13	15	18	19	25	34
Overall dependency ratio							
United States	67	55	51	52	47	50	59
Japan	48	48	47	44	54	61	59
Germany, Fed. Rep. of	54	56	43	47	51	51	60
France	61	60	52	53	52	53	61
Italy[a]	52	54	45	47	50	50	55
United Kingdom	55	59	52	54	53	55	59
Canada	70	54	48	48	46	50	61

Note: [a]Fund staff estimates for 1965–85.

Source: Organization for Economic Cooperation and Development, *Labour Force Statistics, 1964–84, 1967–87;* and OECD Secretariat, Directorate for Social Affairs, Manpower, and Education, Demographic Databank projections.

ratio — roughly constant since 1965 — is projected to rise in all countries by 2025. However, the extent of the rise varies greatly across countries.

A summary statistic of the importance of the age structure is the overall dependency ratio, given in the bottom panel of Table 1. This ratio captures the labor force implications of the fraction of the population that is either too young or too old to work.[7] Whether the increase in the overall dependency ratio occurs because of an increase in the young or the old has implications for other variables, for instance medical care and education, as discussed below. It may also matter for the economy's saving propensity; however, consumption equation estimates reported in Section 3 below use the overall ratio, since there was no significant difference between the effects of youth and elderly dependency ratios.

With the year 1995 as a base (as is done in the simulations in Section 4), changes in the overall dependency ratio to 2025 vary greatly across countries, though dependency ratios end up at similar levels in 2025. Increases of 13–15 percentage points are projected for Japan and the Federal Republic of Germany; moreover, a large part of the increase occurs by 2015 (especially in Japan). In contrast, the ratio for the United States increases by 7 percentage points by 2025, and is actually projected to be lower in 2015 than in 1995; the ratio for the United Kingdom increases by 5 percentage points. Canada is projected to have a large increase, but only in the 2015–25 period. France and Italy have increases on the order of 8 percentage points by 2025, with the changes occurring fairly gradually. Thus, both the extent of aging and the speed with which it occurs differ substantially among the major industrial countries. Projections for the smaller industrial countries (Hagemann and Nicoletti (1989)) also indicate significant increases in dependency ratios.

Heller and others (1986) projected the change of social expenditures by governments on the basis of demographic projections similar to those in Table 1. They included in their study expenditures on education, medical care, pensions, unemployment compensation, and

---

[7]Of course, in many countries secondary education extends beyond age 15, and in addition many students proceed to university before entering the labor force. Also, retirement age may not correspond to age 65; early retirement is possible; conversely, in most professions retirement at 65 is not compulsory. A more precise measure of dependency would adjust the denominator (the working-age population) by the participation rate, to obtain those actually in the labor force (see Hagemann and Nicoletti (1989)).

income maintenance for the poor, at both the general and local government levels.

We focus in this paper on three components of government spending that are closely related to demographic developments: medical expenses, education expenses, and pension benefit payments. We do not attempt to disaggregate *revenues*, however — for instance, by separating social security contributions from other taxes. Whether social security programs are funded or unfunded and the resulting implications for the economy are beyond the scope of this paper. Instead, we simulate the model with a tax-rate reaction function that tends to resist movements away from an exogenous government debt to gross national product (GNP) ratio. This rule prevents a snowballing accumulation of debt leading to eventual government default. Deficits do occur for a number of years as a result of demographic changes, but they are eventually eliminated.

Table 2 summarizes the projections in Heller and others (1986) for government spending on medical care, education, and pensions. The effects of demographic changes are calculated as the difference between the GNP share of spending on each category projected for 2000–25, and its value in 1980 (a more recent year of historical data was not available in their study). The increases in government expenditure on medical care (as a percent of gross domestic product (GDP)) are large but not enormous. Moreover, except in Germany and Japan, they are mostly offset by declines in projected education expenditures. In contrast, pension benefits (which are treated in the model as negative taxes) increase by between 5 percent and 10 percent of GDP for Germany, Italy, and Japan. By 2025, government spending in all three areas taken together increases by up to 10 percentage points of GDP; however, these increases differ markedly across countries. They are largest in Japan, Germany, and Italy, and smallest in the United States and Canada, as would be expected given the demographic trends discussed above.

3. Estimated Consumption Equation

This section describes the estimated consumption equation and compares the effect it attributes to the dependency ratio to effects

Table 2. Changes in Government Expenditures Due to Demographic Changes, 2000–25 (In Percent of GDP)

Country	Medical Expenditures (1)			Education (2)			Pension Expenditures (3)			Combined Effects of (1)–(3) (4)		
	2000	2010	2025	2000	2010	2025	2000	2010	2025	2000	2010	2025
United States	0.01	0.15	1.06	−0.92	−1.14	−1.29	−0.50	−0.60	0.60	−1.41	−1.59	0.37
Japan	0.67	1.25	1.63	−1.00	−0.50	−0.70	5.41	8.69	9.20	5.08	9.44	10.13
Germany, Fed. Rep. of	0.43	0.92	1.59	−0.63	−0.88	−0.81	3.80	5.30	7.20	3.60	5.34	7.98
France	0.34	0.40	0.80	−0.46	−0.54	−0.51	1.00	1.50	3.00	0.88	1.36	3.29
Italy	0.20	0.49	0.88	−0.80	−0.90	−1.00	2.50	4.60	8.60	1.90	4.19	8.48
United Kingdom	0.05	—	0.66	−1.00	−1.00	−1.10	0.85	1.42	2.56	−0.10	0.42	2.12
Canada	−0.06	0.18	1.45	−1.91	−2.15	−1.87	−0.40	−0.40	0.80	−2.37	−2.37	0.38

Note: Figures represent the difference between the share of spending projected for 2000–25 and its 1980 value (the latest year of historical data available from the Heller study). Medical expenditure figures were obtained directly from Peter Heller.

Source: Heller and others (1986, Table 14).

found in other studies. The starting point for the consumption equation is the intertemporal optimizing model of Blanchard (1985), as extended by Buiter (1988). This model makes consumption a function of financial and "human" wealth — that is, the expected value of lifetime earnings, discounted to the present. It is a useful tool for analyzing fiscal policy because it allows for an effect of the government stock of bonds on interest rates (provided the birthrate is nonzero); the model allows simple aggregation because of the assumption that the probability of death is the same for individuals of all ages. However, as noted by Blanchard (1985, p. 235), the model is not convenient for rigorously treating "saving for retirement" or for allowing for a path of labor income that abruptly drops to zero at a certain point. Moreover, it does not allow for constraints that individuals face on their borrowing. In our estimated model, we implement liquidity constraints in an error-correction framework, as in Davidson and others (1978) and Hendry and von Ungern-Sternberg (1981). We also add a dependency ratio to capture effects of differences in age structure on consumption and saving, admittedly in an ad hoc fashion. The data for human wealth used to estimate the consumption equation do not include adjustment for future demographic changes; rather, human wealth is the discounted value of future net disposable income from production, the latter variable extrapolated from historical data.

We implement the consumption model by allowing a lagged adjustment to the long-run wealth/consumption ratio. The specification, in logs, forces that ratio to be constant in the steady state. The dynamics are affected by the change in the log of disposable income and the level of the real interest rate. The latter variable serves two purposes: it captures intertemporal substitution, and it serves to pick up effects on the discounted present value of future income not captured in our measure of human wealth, which uses a constant discount rate. In addition, the path of consumption (and the long-run wealth/consumption ratio) is assumed to be influenced by the dependency ratio.

The equation was estimated using ordinary least squares with annual data from 1969 to 1987 pooled across the Group of Seven countries and the "smaller industrial country" block. The estimated equation, which is used in the simulations described below, is as follows:

$$\Delta \log C = \text{country constants} + \underset{(3.5)}{0.113 \log(W_{-1}/C_{-1})}$$

$$- \underset{(4.0)}{0.473 \, RLR} + \underset{(5.5)}{0.408 \, \Delta \log YD} + \underset{(1.5)}{0.124 \, DEM3}$$

$$+ \underset{(2.2)}{0.032 \, DEM3 * DUM80}$$

$$\overline{R}^2 = 0.641, \quad \text{SER} = 0.026,$$

where the numbers in parentheses are t-statistics ($\overline{R}^2$ is the coefficient of determination corrected for degrees of freedom and SER is the standard error), and where C is the real consumption expenditure, W is real wealth, RLR is the real long-term interest rate (expected inflation is proxied for estimation purposes by a centered ten-year moving average of actual inflation), YD is real, after-tax net domestic product, $DEM3$ is the overall dependency ratio (the ratio of dependents to the working age population),[8] and $DUM80$ is a dummy variable equal to 1.0 after 1980. This variable was included because visual inspection of our population data indicated a break in that year, perhaps because of imperfect splicing of census data with earlier estimates. It is important to note that wealth includes the discounted present value of future (non-interest) disposable income, WH.[9] Total wealth W is the sum of WH and the real value of financial wealth, held in the form of domestic outside money M, government bonds B, and net claims on foreigners NFA (in U.S. dollars; ER is the exchange rate):

$$W = WH + (M + B + NFA/ER)/P + 0.032 DEM3 * DUM80.$$

---

[8] Expressed as a decimal fraction, rather than in percent as in Table 1.

[9] As defined, therefore, WH includes the discounted present value of income to both labor and capital.

The disposable income variable YD is constrained by the error-correction specification to have only transitory effects, because liquidity constraints are assumed to operate only in the short to medium term.

The estimated equation attributes a positive effect on consumption of an increase in the overall dependency ratio — significant at the 5 percent level when the product of the dependency ratio and the dummy variable is considered. Including the youth and elderly dependency ratios separately did not significantly increase the explanatory power of the equation; hence, they were constrained to have the same coefficient. The data also could not reject the constraint of a common coefficient on the overall dependency ratio across countries. Some further estimation was done, after the above equation was incorporated into the model, in order to examine the robustness of the results. Using instrumental variables to estimate the equation[10] yielded a somewhat larger and more significant effect of the dependency ratio, as well as a higher coefficient on YD and a lower one on RLR (in absolute terms).[11] Adding the inflation rate (as in Bovenberg and Evans (1990; this issue)) in place of the post-1980 dummy variable, however, decreased the value of the coefficient on the remaining dependency ratio. Also, differences in sample periods or countries included could make a non-negligible difference to the results, and the sensitivity of our simulation results to this coefficient is discussed below. Nevertheless, there is some evidence from our results that increases in the dependency ratio may have been associated historically with increases in consumption relative to income and wealth, a conclusion that emerges more strongly from the quarterly estimation by Bovenberg and Evans (1990) using U.S. data of a specification similar to ours.[12]

---

[10]Instruments were the rate of money growth, the ratio of government spending to GDP, the lagged wealth/consumption ratio, the lagged change in disposable income, and the dependency ratio.

[11]Results from a similar specification are discussed in Masson, Symansky, and Meredith (1990).

[12]Their measure of wealth is household net worth, and they include separate population variables to capture dependents below age 20 and over age 65.

Macroeconomic Effects of Projected Population Aging   29

From our equation, a 1 percentage point increase in the dependency ratio is estimated to cause an increase in consumption in the post-1980 period of 0.16 percent in the short run and 1.4 percent in the long run (equal to 0.124 plus 0.032, divided by 0.113). It is of interest to compare these results to those found in other studies. Heller (1989) surveyed saving equations that included estimated effects of dependency ratios. Though the definitions of variables differ, as do sample periods, a rough comparison can be made with the equation estimated for MULTIMOD, after converting it to a saving equation. The private saving rate (s) can be defined as C above, divided by private national income (Y), and subtracted from unity: $s = 1 - C/Y$. Therefore, MULTIMOD's equation implies that the saving rate responds to the dependency ratio in the long run (for a given real interest rate and wealth/income ratio) as follows:

$$\frac{ds}{dDEM3} = -\frac{d(C/Y)}{dDEM3} = -\frac{d\log C}{dDEM3}C/Y = \frac{(0.124 + 0.032)}{0.113}C/Y.$$

Table 3 gives estimates for MULTIMOD as well as four other models.[13] It can be seen that MULTIMOD is near the center of the range of available estimates. Each estimate shows a powerful effect on saving of an increase in the elderly as a proportion of

Table 3. Long-Run Effects of an Increase in Elderly Dependency Ratio on Private Saving Rate in Various Models

Model	Estimate
Modigliani	−0.88
Modigliani and Sterling	−0.51
Feldstein	−1.21
Horioka	−1.61
Memorandum item:	
MULTIMOD	−1.10

Source: Heller (1989).

---

[13]The estimate for MULTIMOD assumes a consumption income ratio (C/Y) of 0.8.

the working-age population.[14] There thus appears to be considerable additional support for the hypothesis that the aging of the population projected for the next century is likely to increase consumption relative to income. However, it must be stressed that other studies (Aaron, Bosworth, and Burtless (1989), for instance, examining U.S. evidence), have failed to find a significant effect. The next section uses simulations of MULTIMOD to capture the implications of our estimated consumption equation for the effects of aging on macroeconomic variables, as well as effects through the other two channels mentioned above.

4. Simulation of the Effects of Population Aging

In order to study the macroeconomic effects of the demographic shifts discussed above, we use simulations of MULTIMOD, which is a macroeconometric model of the Group of Seven countries and the remaining industrial countries and of developing countries divided into capital exporters and capital importers (see Masson, Symansky, and Meredith (1990)). The simulations take place over a horizon from 1996 to 2025. The baseline simulation of the model is constructed by constraining growth rates of real variables to converge to current estimates of potential output growth, while private and government saving rates remain constant at their levels projected for 1995. With respect to the demographic variables, the dependency ratio and the labor force participation rate are assumed to remain constant in each country throughout the baseline. It should be emphasized that we are not attempting to construct an ex ante forecast for the Group of Seven countries through 2025 — we are only attempting to quantify the macroeconomic effects of aging over that horizon.

Demographic effects are captured in MULTIMOD using the dependency ratio defined above. This variable appears in the model in two equations for each industrial country: in the consumption

---

[14]These studies also estimate a separate effect of the proportion of the young in the population; in each case, this variable has the same sign but a smaller coefficient.

function, as described above, and in the production function, in which the total labor force is set equal to the working-age population times an exogenous participation rate. The working-age population is determined by the total population, which is exogenous, and the dependency ratio. The dependency ratio is also exogenous, but we simulate the model with an alternative path for this variable to quantify the effects of the projected aging of the population.

The alternative scenario we simulate with MULTIMOD allows the dependency ratio in each country to evolve along its projected path through 2025, rather than remaining constant as in the baseline scenario at its 1995 value. The labor force participation rate is, however, assumed to remain on its baseline path. As described more fully in Section 2 above, two different periods can be identified: in the first, through 2010, there is *differential* aging in the industrial countries, while the *average* dependency ratio remains roughly constant. In the second period, the populations in all industrial countries except Japan age steadily, and dependency ratios rise substantially. In Japan the dependency ratio remains approximately at the same level above baseline.

Finally, we include a simulation of the projected changes in government expenditures related to aging and a simulation of the combined effects.

4.1. *Effects of Aging on Consumption Expenditure*

As discussed in the Appendix, a shift in the dependency ratio affects the economy through several channels. The first channel is through the effect on consumption expenditure; as the ratio of dependents to the working-age population increases, consumption increases (for given values of income and wealth).

Table 4 presents the results of a simulation of the effects of a shift in dependency ratios over the period 1996–2025,[15] operating

---

[15]Because the model requires that terminal conditions be imposed on expectations variables, and in order to minimize the effects of those terminal conditions, the simulation period was extended to 2040. After 2025, the changes in dependency ratios were assumed to be gradually reversed.

32 Paul R. Masson and Ralph W. Tryon

Table 4. Demographic Shift: Consumption Effects (Deviations from Baseline)

Country	2000	2005	2010	2015	2020	2025
United States			*(in percent)*			
Real GNP	−1.0	−0.2	1.1	1.9	2.2	2.1
Real domestic demand	−2.8	−3.8	−3.7	−3.0	−2.2	−1.5
Real interest rate	0.6	−0.2	−0.5	−0.0	0.9	2.0
Real effective exchange rate	−6.2	−11.6	−12.8	−11.3	−8.4	−4.9
GDP per worker	−0.9	−0.6	0.0	0.4	0.4	0.1
Capital stock per worker	−0.5	−0.7	−0.4	0.0	−0.0	−0.8
			(as a percent of GNP)			
Current account balance	0.8	2.0	2.8	3.0	2.8	2.6
General government financial balance	−0.4	0.0	0.2	0.1	−0.0	−0.1
Private saving	1.3	1.4	2.3	2.6	2.3	1.6
Gross private investment	0.1	0.3	0.4	0.2	−0.3	−0.9
Net foreign assets	1.9	7.9	16.7	25.0	31.0	34.5
Government debt	1.3	1.7	0.7	−0.3	−0.7	−0.6
Japan			*(in percent)*			
Real GNP	2.1	0.7	−0.9	−2.8	−4.6	−6.1
Real domestic demand	7.1	9.6	9.9	8.2	5.1	1.8
Real interest rate	−2.3	−0.3	1.0	2.4	3.4	3.7
Real effective exchange rate	14.2	27.5	33.8	33.1	26.1	17.1
GDP per worker	2.5	2.1	1.2	0.0	−1.2	−2.2
Capital stock per worker	1.8	2.6	2.2	0.7	−1.4	−3.7
			(as a percent of GNP)			
Current account balance	−2.1	−3.5	−4.3	−4.5	−4.4	−4.2
General government financial balance	0.5	0.4	0.3	0.0	−0.3	−0.5
Private saving	−2.9	−4.8	−5.9	−6.2	−5.8	−5.2
Gross private investment	−0.2	−1.0	−1.4	−1.7	−1.7	−1.5
Net foreign assets	−11.3	−23.9	−35.7	−45.8	−53.6	−58.5
Government debt	−1.7	−3.2	−3.3	−2.5	−0.7	1.6
Germany, Fed. Rep. of			*(in percent)*			
Real GNP	0.7	0.0	−1.0	−1.5	−1.2	−0.5
Real domestic demand	1.1	2.4	2.6	1.8	1.0	1.2
Real interest rate	−0.3	−0.2	0.0	0.6	1.5	2.4
Real effective exchange rate	0.2	1.3	1.9	1.8	0.9	0.9
GDP per worker	0.5	0.5	0.1	−0.2	−0.2	0.0
Capital stock per worker	0.2	0.5	0.6	0.4	−0.2	−1.2

(Continued)

Table 4. (*Continued*)

Country	2000	2005	2010	2015	2020	2025
	(as a percent of GNP)					
Current account balance	−0.1	−1.3	−2.3	−2.2	−1.7	−1.2
General government financial balance	0.2	0.0	−0.1	−0.2	−0.2	−0.1
Private saving	−0.3	−1.3	−2.1	−2.0	−1.8	−2.1
Gross private investment	0.0	0.0	0.1	−0.0	−0.3	−0.9
Net foreign assets	−2.3	−6.6	−13.0	−18.2	−20.8	−21.4
Government debt	−0.4	−0.8	−0.4	0.3	0.9	1.0
Other industrial countries	*(in percent)*					
Real GNP	−0.2	0.1	0.2	0.7	0.3	−0.3
Real domestic demand	−0.3	−0.4	−0.6	−0.2	−0.4	−1.1
Real interest rate	−0.1	−0.1	−0.0	0.3	1.4	2.4
Real effective exchange rate	−0.8	−1.7	−2.5	−2.8	−2.4	−2.1
GDP per worker	−0.1	−0.0	−0.2	0.3	0.0	−0.4
Capital stock per worker	−0.1	−0.0	0.0	0.2	−0.2	−1.4
	(as a percent of GNP)					
Current account balance	0.2	0.6	0.7	0.6	0.4	0.2
General government financial balance	0.1	0.0	0.0	−0.1	−0.4	−0.4
Private saving	0.1	0.5	0.7	0.6	0.4	−0.2
Gross private investment	0.0	0.0	0.0	0.0	−0.4	−0.8
Net foreign assets	1.1	3.1	5.3	6.5	6.6	5.8
Government debt	0.5	0.3	0.1	−0.6	−0.0	1.7

only through the change in consumption behavior. In this simulation the labor force is held exogenous in each country, and no change is made to government expenditure. As shown in the table, the private saving rate in the United States is above its baseline level (which was assumed to be constant) throughout the simulation; it rises through 2015 (relative to the baseline, it is almost 3 percentage points higher then), and then drops back somewhat, as the dependency ratio first falls, and then rises. The rise in the saving rate is mirrored in the movement of domestic demand, which is below the baseline throughout the simulation, reaching its lowest level in 2005 before beginning to recover. The reduction in domestic demand is offset by an increase in demand for U.S. exports from abroad due both to lower saving rates abroad and to a real depreciation of the dollar.

As a result, real GNP in the United States is above the baseline after 2005.

The increase in the saving rate initially leads to a modest increase in investment, but this effect is offset later on by an increase in the real interest rate resulting from higher aggregate demand. The government balance is largely unchanged, as a share of GNP, so the increase in private saving is manifested primarily in the current account, which improves by up to 3 percent of GNP over the simulation range. As a result, the net foreign asset position of the United States improves steadily, and is higher by more than 30 percent of GNP at the end of the simulation.

In Japan, the private saving rate falls steadily through 2015 as a result of the aging of the population, leading to substantial increases in domestic demand. Real output is initially higher than in the baseline as a result of the increase in demand, but the real interest rate rises above the baseline, tending to crowd out domestic demand. The real exchange rate appreciates by about 30 percent at its peak, and the current account is substantially lower, as a share of GNP, throughout the simulation. As a result, Japan's net foreign asset position deteriorates substantially, by almost 60 percent of GNP, by 2025.

In the Federal Republic of Germany saving is also lower and domestic demand higher as a result of the demographic shift. The results for the external sector are, however, quite different: the real exchange rate appreciates very little, though the current account ratio falls substantially, by about 20 percent of GNP. The extent of the demographic shift is smaller in Germany than in Japan, which accounts for some of the difference. Also, imports of manufactures are a much larger share of GNP in Germany, so that a given change in the real exchange rate can achieve a larger demand shift in Germany than in Japan.[16]

---

[16] If relative price elasticities were the same, a unit change in the real exchange rate would bring about a larger change in imports as a share of GNP in Germany than in Japan as a result. In fact, the price elasticity of imports of manufactures is also higher in Germany; see Masson, Symansky, and Meredith (1990).

The effects of the demographic shift on all other industrial countries taken as a group are smaller in comparison. These countries include Canada, with demographic projections that resemble those for the United States, and European countries, with projections for aging that are closer to Germany's, but less severe. The saving rate, domestic demand, and real output for other industrial countries taken together are all roughly unchanged for most of the period, although by 2025 the real interest rate rises significantly and output declines.

In MULTIMOD, foreign and domestic assets are assumed to be perfect substitutes, so that real interest parity holds. Differences in real interest rates across countries therefore reflect expected future appreciation or depreciation of the real exchange rate, and the overall level of real interest rates reflects global saving and investment (or aggregate demand and supply). From 2015 onwards the demographic shift is toward more aging in all industrial countries, leading to global excess demand, and higher real interest rates in all countries. Before 2015, it is the composition of global demand that is shifting, leading to changes in real exchange rates, while the global real interest rate remains (approximately) unchanged.

4.2. *Effects of Aging on Production*

Demographic shifts also operate through a change in the labor force, which, assuming that the participation rate is constant, changes one-for-one with the decline in those aged 15–64. Aging of the population reduces the labor force and thereby reduces potential output, leading to excess demand for domestic output. As a result, real output would also be expected to fall, and the real exchange rate, to appreciate. The effect on real interest rates is ambiguous, since, on the one hand, a reduction in supply creates excess (global) demand for goods, which tends to raise the real interest rate, and, on the other hand, a fall in the labor force tends to lower the marginal product of capital and hence tends to lower the equilibrium real interest rate. In the long run, however, for a given saving rate a smaller labor force should lead to a proportionate contraction of the capital stock and output, leaving real interest rates unaffected.

36 *Paul R. Masson and Ralph W. Tryon*

Table 5 shows the results of a simulation in which the demographic shift affects only the total labor force in each country.[17] The results are consistent with the analysis given above — in both Germany and Japan real output falls steadily relative to the baseline, while the real exchange rate appreciates. In both countries the real interest rate is initially below the baseline, and then rises above it at the end of the simulation. In both countries also, the capital stock per worker is higher throughout, though investment as a share of GNP is below the baseline.

In the United States until 2010, the demographic shift leads to a larger labor force (and therefore to higher output), a depreciation of the real exchange rate, and a lower real interest rate. After 2010 the dependency ratio begins to rise, and these effects are in large part reversed.

In the other industrial countries, there is no substantial effect until 2020, when real output drops off significantly and real interest rates rise. There is only a negligible effect on the current account position of these countries. In sum, for all countries the net foreign asset implications of aging are simulated to be considerably less important through their effects on production reported here than those operating through consumption.

4.3.   *Effects of Aging on Government Expenditures*

An increase in the elderly dependency ratio would be expected to increase government expenditures on medical care, while a decline in the youth dependency ratio would lead to lower education expenditures. Furthermore, an increase in the number of retirees would increase payment of government pension benefits. Heller and others (1986) report projections for these components of government spending in individual Group of Seven countries for the years 2000, 2010, and 2025 (see Table 2); we interpolated these estimates to

---

[17]That is, the direct effects on consumption discussed above are ignored. However, changes in output do induce changes in human wealth and, hence, in consumption.

Table 5. Demographic Shift: Production Effects (Deviations from Baseline)

Country	2000	2005	2010	2015	2020	2025
United States			*(in percent)*			
Real GNP	1.0	2.9	3.7	2.4	−0.2	−2.9
Real domestic demand	0.8	2.2	2.9	1.8	−0.2	−2.5
Real interest rate	−0.3	−0.7	−0.8	−0.3	0.3	0.9
Real effective exchange rate	−1.0	−2.6	−3.1	−2.7	−2.2	−1.3
GDP per worker	−1.0	−1.2	−0.4	0.6	1.5	1.9
Capital stock per worker	−1.6	−2.6	−1.6	0.9	3.4	4.9
			(as a percent of GNP)			
Current account balance	0.0	0.2	0.2	−0.0	−0.3	−0.5
General government financial balance	0.2	0.4	0.2	−0.2	−0.5	−0.6
Private saving	0.0	−0.9	−0.5	−0.1	0.0	−0.1
Gross private investment	0.0	0.1	0.2	0.2	0.1	0.0
Net foreign assets	−0.1	0.3	1.0	1.1	0.2	−1.4
Government debt	−0.3	−1.5	−2.3	−1.6	0.3	2.7
Japan			*(in percent)*			
Real GNP	−1.8	−3.7	−5.7	−6.8	−7.0	−6.7
Real domestic demand	−1.4	−2.6	−4.2	−5.5	−6.2	−6.3
Real interest rate	−1.1	−1.0	−0.3	0.3	0.9	1.2
Real effective exchange rate	1.5	3.9	5.9	6.0	5.1	4.1
GDP per worker	1.5	3.2	3.6	3.4	2.5	1.7
Capital stock per worker	3.1	6.4	7.9	7.5	5.7	3.3
			(as a percent of GNP)			
Current account balance	−0.1	−0.3	−0.3	0.1	0.6	1.0
General government financial balance	−0.2	−0.3	−0.4	−0.3	−0.2	−0.0
Private saving	0.7	0.7	0.7	0.7	0.6	0.4
Gross private investment	0.5	0.7	0.6	0.3	−0.2	−0.6
Net foreign assets	−0.1	−1.1	−1.8	−1.2	0.7	3.6
Government debt	0.6	1.6	2.8	3.5	3.5	3.0
Germany, Fed. Rep. of			*(in percent)*			
Real GNP	−1.0	−2.1	−2.4	−2.2	−2.9	−4.7
Real domestic demand	−1.2	−1.8	−2.2	−2.5	−3.4	−5.1
Real interest rate	−0.6	−0.7	−0.6	−0.2	0.3	1.2
Real effective exchange rate	0.1	0.8	0.8	0.2	0.6	1.9
GDP per worker	0.3	0.9	0.4	0.4	1.4	2.5
Capital stock per worker	1.0	2.5	2.2	2.1	3.7	5.5

(*Continued*)

Table 5. (*Continued*)

Country	2000	2005	2010	2015	2020	2025
	(as a percent of GNP)					
Current account balance	0.2	−0.0	−0.0	0.3	0.5	0.9
General government financial balance	−0.1	−0.2	−0.1	−0.1	−0.2	−0.4
Private saving	0.5	0.4	0.4	0.6	0.7	0.7
Gross private investment	0.2	0.3	0.3	0.2	−0.1	−0.6
Net foreign assets	1.1	1.7	1.9	1.9	1.8	3.6
Government debt	0.5	1.0	1.3	1.3	1.6	2.5
Other Industrial Countries	*(in percent)*					
Real GNP	−0.0	0.4	0.5	−0.4	−2.4	−3.7
Real domestic demand	−0.0	0.3	0.4	−0.4	−2.4	−3.7
Real interest rate	−0.5	−0.6	−0.7	−0.2	0.6	0.9
Real effective exchange rate	−0.1	−0.3	−0.6	−0.5	−0.6	−1.0
GDP per worker	−0.0	0.1	0.2	1.0	1.0	1.8
Capital stock per worker	0.1	0.3	0.7	2.3	3.2	3.9
	(as a percent of GNP)					
Current account balance	−0.0	0.1	0.0	−0.1	−0.2	−0.3
General government financial balance	0.0	0.1	0.1	−0.2	−0.5	−0.4
Private saving	0.1	0.2	0.2	0.2	0.2	−0.0
Gross private investment	0.1	0.2	0.2	0.1	−0.1	−0.1
Net foreign assets	−0.1	0.0	−0.0	−0.2	−0.6	−1.5
Government debt	0.1	−0.4	−0.9	−0.6	1.8	3.6

obtain annual series.[18] Education and health care are components of government expenditure on goods and services, and so they directly increase aggregate demand. Pension benefits take the form of a transfer, which we treat in MULTIMOD as if it were a negative, non-distortionary tax. We do not examine the impact of funding social security expenditures, including pensions, and taxation is assumed not to be linked to those benefits.

Table 6 reports the results of a simulation of these changes in government expenditure. In the United States, government expenditure is reduced throughout the simulation, relative to the baseline,

---

[18]We used a simple average of the increases in the Group of Seven countries for the aggregate of smaller industrial countries.

Macroeconomic Effects of Projected Population Aging

Table 6. Demographic Shift: Government Expenditure Effects (Deviations from Baseline)

Country	2000	2005	2010	2015	2020	2025
United States			*(in percent)*			
Real GNP	−0.0	0.5	0.2	0.3	0.2	0.2
Real domestic demand	−0.6	−0.0	−0.3	−0.1	−0.2	−0.2
Real interest rate	−0.3	−0.1	−0.0	0.1	0.1	0.1
Real effective exchange rate	−1.7	−1.3	−1.2	−1.0	−1.0	−1.1
GDP per worker	−0.1	0.3	0.0	0.1	0.0	0.0
Capital stock per worker	0.0	0.2	0.2	0.2	0.1	0.0
			(as a percent of GNP)			
Current account balance	0.3	0.3	0.3	0.3	0.3	0.3
General government financial balance	0.9	0.5	0.3	−0.2	−0.5	−0.6
Private saving	−0.4	−0.2	0.0	0.5	0.8	0.8
Gross private investment	0.2	0.0	0.0	−0.0	−0.0	−0.1
Net foreign assets	0.6	1.9	2.6	3.2	3.6	4.0
Government debt	−2.4	−4.7	−4.8	−3.3	−0.6	2.0
Japan			*(in percent)*			
Real GNP	0.0	−0.4	−0.3	−0.5	−0.4	−0.5
Real domestic demand	1.2	0.9	0.9	0.5	0.6	0.6
Real interest rate	−0.0	0.0	0.1	0.0	0.1	0.1
Real effective exchange rate	2.8	3.0	2.9	2.4	2.4	2.5
GDP per worker	0.2	−0.0	0.0	−0.1	−0.1	−0.1
Capital stock per worker	0.1	0.1	0.0	−0.1	−0.1	−0.2
			(as a percent of GNP)			
Current account balance	−0.5	−0.6	−0.5	−0.4	−0.5	−0.5
General government financial balance	−3.1	−3.0	−2.9	−1.8	−1.3	−1.1
Private saving	2.3	2.3	2.3	1.3	0.8	0.5
Gross private investment	−0.2	−0.1	−0.2	−0.1	−0.1	−0.1
Net foreign assets	−2.7	−4.1	−5.2	−5.5	−6.1	−6.5
Government debt	9.0	19.7	27.0	29.3	27.6	24.9
Germany, Fed. Rep. of			*(in percent)*			
Real GNP	−0.0	−0.4	−0.2	−0.3	−0.3	−0.4
Real domestic demand	0.9	0.4	0.4	0.5	0.4	0.5
Real interest rate	−0.1	−0.0	−0.0	0.1	0.1	0.1
Real effective exchange rate	0.7	0.6	0.3	0.5	0.5	0.5
GDP per worker	0.2	−0.1	0.1	0.1	0.0	0.0
Capital stock per worker	0.1	0.1	0.1	0.1	0.1	−0.0

(Continued)

Table 6. (*Continued*)

Country	2000	2005	2010	2015	2020	2025
	(as a percent of GNP)					
Current account balance	−0.6	−0.5	−0.5	−0.5	−0.6	−0.6
General government financial balance	−2.0	−1.5	−1.2	−1.2	−1.2	−1.2
Private saving	1.5	1.0	0.7	0.7	0.6	0.6
Gross private investment	0.0	0.0	0.1	0.0	0.0	0.0
Net foreign assets	−2.2	−3.5	−4.6	−5.6	−6.5	−7.3
Government debt	6.1	11.6	14.0	15.3	16.2	16.9
Other Industrial Countries	*(in percent)*					
Real GNP	0.0	0.3	−0.0	0.1	0.0	0.0
Real domestic demand	−0.1	0.1	−0.1	−0.0	−0.1	−0.1
Real interest rate	−0.2	−0.1	0.0	0.1	0.1	0.1
Real effective exchange rate	−0.2	−0.3	−0.2	−0.3	−0.3	−0.3
GDP per worker	−0.0	0.2	−0.0	0.1	0.0	−0.0
Capital stock per worker	0.0	0.2	0.1	0.1	0.0	−0.1
	(as a percent of GNP)					
Current account balance	0.1	0.1	0.1	0.1	0.1	0.1
General government financial balance	−0.4	−0.5	−0.6	−0.7	−0.9	−0.9
Private saving	0.5	0.6	0.6	0.8	0.9	0.9
Gross private investment	0.2	0.0	0.0	0.0	0.0	−0.1
Net foreign assets	0.3	0.6	0.8	0.9	1.0	1.0
Government debt	1.4	2.5	4.2	6.0	7.9	9.7

leading to a reduction in domestic demand of only 1/4 of 1 percent in 2025. The reduction in Japanese net exports is enough to lead to a slight reduction in output, despite the increase in government expenditure resulting from an increased dependency ratio in that country. In Germany real output rises slightly as a result of higher government expenditure; in other industrial countries output is lower. In sum, although government debt rises substantially in Germany and Japan, effects on output and net foreign assets are relatively modest.

4.4. *Combined Effects*

The combined effects of the demographic shifts are shown in Table 7 (including results for France, Italy, the United Kingdom, Canada,

Macroeconomic Effects of Projected Population Aging

Table 7. Demographic Shift: Combined Effects (Deviations from Baseline)

Country	2000	2005	2010	2015	2020	2025
United States			*(in percent)*			
Real GNP	−0.1	3.2	4.9	4.7	2.5	−0.1
Real domestic demand	−2.7	−1.7	−1.0	−1.0	−2.2	−3.8
Real interest rate	0.1	−1.1	−1.4	−0.5	1.1	2.9
Real effective exchange rate	−9.1	−15.5	−16.6	−14.0	−9.9	−5.3
GDP per worker	−2.0	−1.4	−0.4	1.1	2.0	2.2
Capital stock per worker	−2.2	−3.1	−1.7	1.2	3.7	4.3
			(as a percent of GNP)			
Current account balance	1.1	2.5	3.1	3.0	2.8	2.7
General government financial balance	0.8	0.9	0.7	−0.3	−1.0	−1.3
Private saving	0.7	2.1	3.0	3.6	3.6	3.0
Gross private investment	0.3	0.5	0.6	0.3	−0.2	−1.0
Net foreign assets	2.7	10.4	19.9	27.9	33.1	36.2
Government debt	−1.5	−4.7	−6.5	−5.3	−1.3	3.5
Japan			*(in percent)*			
Real GNP	0.4	−3.1	−6.4	−9.5	−11.8	−13.2
Real domestic demand	6.8	7.2	5.8	2.4	−1.3	−4.7
Real interest rate	−3.3	−1.2	0.6	2.5	4.1	4.8
Real effective exchange rate	18.8	35.0	43.0	41.4	32.7	21.5
GDP per worker	4.4	5.1	4.8	3.2	1.2	−0.5
Capital stock per worker	5.1	9.1	10.2	8.3	4.3	−0.5
			(as a percent of GNP)			
Current account balance	−2.5	−3.8	−4.4	−4.5	−4.4	−4.0
General government financial balance	−2.5	−2.6	−2.8	−2.1	−1.9	−1.6
Private saving	0.1	−1.7	−2.7	−3.8	−4.2	−4.3
Gross private investment	0.0	−0.5	−1.1	−1.5	−1.7	−1.8
Net foreign assets	−13.4	−26.7	−38.5	−48.0	−55.0	−59.0
Government debt	7.5	16.3	23.0	26.1	26.9	27.3
Germany, Fed. Rep. of			*(in percent)*			
Real GNP	−0.2	−2.3	−3.6	−4.0	−4.6	−5.8
Real domestic demand	0.8	1.0	0.8	−0.4	−2.1	−3.9
Real interest rate	−1.1	−1.0	−0.7	0.3	1.7	3.6
Real effective exchange rate	1.0	2.7	3.0	2.3	1.9	3.2
GDP per worker	1.0	1.3	0.5	0.1	1.2	2.6
Capital stock per worker	1.3	3.2	3.0	2.7	3.6	4.2

(Continued)

Table 7. (*Continued*)

Country	2000	2005	2010	2015	2020	2025
	(as a percent of GNP)					
Current account balance	−0.5	−1.8	−2.7	−2.5	−1.8	−0.9
General government financial balance	−1.9	−1.5	−1.5	−1.5	−1.6	−1.5
Private saving	1.7	0.1	−0.8	−0.7	−0.5	−0.9
Gross private investment	0.3	0.4	0.4	0.2	−0.3	−1.5
Net foreign assets	−3.3	−8.1	−15.0	−20.9	−24.0	−23.5
Government debt	6.1	11.4	14.6	16.6	18.1	19.0
France	*(in percent)*					
Real GNP	−0.4	1.1	1.5	1.0	−0.3	−1.6
Real domestic demand	−0.9	−0.1	−0.1	−0.9	−2.2	−3.7
Real interest rate	−0.3	−1.0	−1.0	0.0	1.5	3.0
Real effective exchange rate	−1.2	−4.1	−5.4	−5.5	−4.8	−3.3
GDP per worker	−0.8	−0.2	−0.3	0.7	1.6	2.1
Capital stock per worker	−0.7	−0.7	−0.1	1.9	3.4	3.2
	(as a percent of GNP)					
Current account balance	0.5	0.7	0.8	0.8	0.9	1.3
General government financial balance	−0.3	−0.2	−0.4	−0.8	−1.1	−1.2
Private saving	0.9	1.2	1.6	1.9	1.8	1.6
Gross private investment	0.0	0.4	0.5	0.2	−0.2	−0.9
Net foreign assets	2.1	4.3	6.5	8.5	9.8	11.8
Government debt	2.2	2.9	2.9	4.1	6.6	9.0
Italy	*(in percent)*					
Real GNP	0.8	−0.2	−2.0	−1.6	−4.4	−3.3
Real domestic demand	2.1	1.1	−1.4	−1.9	−6.0	−5.2
Real interest rate	−1.4	−0.1	−0.0	0.3	2.8	2.0
Real effective exchange rate	1.8	4.1	1.3	−2.3	−3.7	−7.6
GDP per worker	1.7	1.6	−0.9	0.3	−1.5	1.8
Capital stock per worker	1.8	3.0	1.3	1.8	0.5	0.7
	(as a percent of GNP)					
Current account balance	−0.4	0.4	0.7	0.5	1.2	0.2
General government financial balance	−0.7	−1.2	−0.9	−1.7	−2.8	−2.5
Private saving	0.6	1.1	1.4	2.1	3.2	2.6
Gross private investment	0.3	−0.4	−0.1	−0.1	−0.7	−0.1
Net foreign assets	−0.6	0.1	1.9	2.7	5.6	7.4
Government debt	0.3	2.2	12.0	15.6	22.9	29.0

(Continued)

Table 7. (*Continued*)

Country	2000	2005	2010	2015	2020	2025
United Kingdom			*(in percent)*			
Real GNP	0.0	0.8	1.2	0.6	−1.4	−2.3
Real domestic demand	−0.8	−0.8	−1.1	−1.9	−4.3	−5.8
Real interest rate	−0.7	−0.9	−0.9	0.3	2.0	2.9
Real effective exchange rate	−2.0	−3.3	−4.9	−5.1	−5.9	−7.0
GDP per worker	−0.1	−0.4	−0.5	0.4	−0.1	1.0
Capital stock per worker	−0.1	−0.3	0.0	1.6	1.7	1.3
			(as a percent of GNP)			
Current account balance	0.4	1.1	1.0	0.9	0.3	−0.1
General government financial balance	0.0	−0.1	−0.3	−0.6	−1.1	−1.1
Private saving	0.7	1.4	1.8	1.8	1.4	0.7
Gross private investment	0.3	0.2	0.5	0.2	−0.0	−0.2
Net foreign assets	0.9	4.8	7.7	9.4	8.9	6.3
Government debt	0.2	0.2	1.0	2.7	6.1	9.5
Canada			*(in percent)*			
Real GNP	0.2	2.8	3.5	2.4	−0.2	−3.3
Real domestic demand	−1.1	1.2	1.7	1.0	−0.7	−2.9
Real interest rate	−0.5	−1.4	−1.5	−0.4	1.1	3.3
Real effective exchange rate	−5.5	−7.7	−7.1	−4.9	−1.8	2.4
GDP per worker	−0.3	−0.0	0.5	1.8	2.5	3.0
Capital stock per worker	−0.3	−0.5	1.1	3.7	5.5	5.8
			(as a percent of GNP)			
Current account balance	1.3	2.4	3.0	2.8	2.1	1.5
General government financial balance	1.6	1.3	0.8	−0.4	−1.3	−1.9
Private saving	0.0	1.3	2.2	2.5	1.8	0.4
Gross private investment	0.3	0.2	−0.0	−0.7	−1.6	−2.9
Net foreign assets	4.1	12.2	21.3	28.1	31.0	30.2
Government debt	−4.0	−9.2	−10.8	−8.0	−2.0	4.8
Smaller Industrial Countries			*(in percent)*			
Real GNP	−0.2	0.8	0.3	−0.7	−3.1	−3.3
Real domestic demand	−0.1	0.8	0.5	−0.3	−2.3	−4.2
Real interest rate	−0.8	−1.1	−0.7	0.3	1.9	3.3
Real effective exchange rate	−0.2	−1.0	−1.0	−1.3	−1.2	−1.1
GDP per worker	−0.2	0.6	0.4	1.1	1.4	1.7
Capital stock per worker	0.1	0.9	1.7	3.1	3.7	3.0

(Continued)

Table 7. (*Continued*)

Country	2000	2005	2010	2015	2020	2025
	(as a percent of GNP)					
Current account balance	−0.0	0.2	0.0	−0.3	−0.8	−1.1
General government financial balance	−0.5	−0.5	−0.8	−1.1	−1.5	−1.6
Private saving	0.7	1.0	1.1	0.8	0.3	−0.6
Gross private investment	0.3	0.3	0.3	0.0	−0.4	−1.1
Net foreign assets	1.1	1.6	1.2	−0.7	−3.4	−6.8
Government debt	2.1	3.3	5.0	7.4	10.8	14.5

and the remaining smaller industrial countries). The interpretation of the results is straightforward, since they are approximately a simple sum of the results for the three partial simulations just discussed. What is of interest is the magnitudes — the simulation shows that demographic shifts can be expected to have very substantial effects on the global pattern of external balances over the next 35 years. In the United States the net foreign asset position improves by over 35 percent of GNP in 2025, compared, for instance, with an assumed net debtor position in 1995 of about 23 percent of GNP.[19] In Japan and Germany the net foreign asset positions in 2025 are lower by about 60 and 25 percent, respectively, as compared with assumed net creditor positions in 1995 of 26 and 38 percent of GNP. It is clear that the aging of the population in the industrial countries has the potential to generate large swings in foreign indebtedness over time, and that a simple extrapolation of present current account positions is likely to be well off the mark.

The projected aging of the population also has significant implications for real GNP. In the simulation, the contraction in the labor force in the industrial countries after 2015 reduces real

---

[19] An alternative comparison would be what the net foreign asset position would be in 2025 *without* the shift in dependency ratios. In our baseline projection, which extrapolates medium-term trends but which is not intended to be a forecast, the net asset share in 2025 is − 39 percent for the United States, 37 percent for Japan, and 85 percent for Germany.

GNP in 2025 by 13 percent in Japan, by 6 percent in Germany, and by a somewhat smaller amount in the other industrial countries outside the United States. However, it should be noted that output per worker is higher in several countries, as is the capital stock per worker. In the United States aggregate output is roughly unchanged in 2025, and it is in fact higher for most of the simulation, as a result of the increase in the working-age population in the early part of the next century.

Fiscal deficits do not evolve as dramatically as external positions in these simulations, in large part because of endogenous tax increases. The real cost to the world economy shows up in the effect on production through a smaller labor force and a lower capital stock. Government financial positions do nonetheless weaken toward the end of the simulation period, as tax revenues fall and pension expenditures increase substantially in all industrial countries. In particular, government debt rises significantly in Japan and Germany.

Given the magnitude of the effects on net creditor and debtor positions, it is of interest to see how sensitive they are to estimated parameters and projections of key exogenous variables. Two such experiments are reported in Table 8. The first reduces the coefficients

Table 8. Effect of Aging on Net Foreign Assets in 2025 Under Three Alternative Assumptions (Deviations from Baseline as a Percent of GNP)

Country	Standard Model[a]	Consumption Coefficient[b]	Participation Rate[c]
United States	36	23	36
Japan	−59	−34	−59
Germany, Fed. Rep. of	−24	−16	−23
France	12	4	13
Italy	7	3	7
United Kingdom	6	−2	9
Canada	30	25	25

Notes: [a]From Table 7.
[b]The consumption coefficient of $DEM3$ is assumed to be halved.
[c]The participation rate is assumed to rise by one half of the proportionate decline in those aged 15–64.

on the dependency ratio (which were not very well determined statistically) by a factor of 2. The second supposes that aging of the population induces an increase in participation rates (for instance, because of delayed retirement or increased labor supply of those who must support aged relatives). In particular, participation rates are assumed to offset half of the effect on the labor force of the rise in dependency ratios.

The first change makes a substantial difference for net foreign asset positions, as can be seen in Table 8. The second assumption, in contrast, has only minor effects — as might be expected from the discussion of production effects above. Taken together, these simulations suggest that the numerical results discussed above should at best be considered rough orders of magnitude, and that they are especially sensitive to assumed effects of aging on saving rates.

5. Concluding Remarks

The paper has isolated some of the implications of the aging of the population that is projected for the next three and a half decades. Using MULTIMOD to simulate the net effect of aging through three channels — reduced saving rates, a lower labor force, and higher government expenditure — suggests that macroeconomic effects may be substantial by 2025. Moreover, though some of the effects are common to all countries — higher real interest rates and lower output in the later years of our simulation period — some of the effects differ substantially because of differences in the extent and speed of aging across countries. As a result, there are substantial long-run changes in current account and net foreign asset positions, in a direction that reverses recent tendencies among the three largest industrial economies.

A number of policy issues arise in the context of population aging; they are not, however, the subject of this paper. Governments can influence capital formation by their expenditure and tax policies; a key question is whether the capital stock will be adequate to support a higher consumption ratio and greater demands for government medical services in the future. Questions of intergenerational equity are at the heart of the debate over whether anticipated increases in government expenditure should be financed through government saving today, or through taxes on the working population in the next century (see Halter and Hemming (1987) and Aaron, Bosworth, and Burtless (1989)). Another important question relates to the prospects for capital accumulation and sustained growth in developing countries when industrial countries are saving less.

It is important to stress once again the limitations and uncertainties associated with our analysis. The prospect of substantial migration within Europe and North America makes any demographic projections 35 years into the future extremely tentative. Moreover, our model of household behavior is rudimentary, and the effects on consumption estimated over a historical period with a much younger population may not provide a good guide to the future. Other effects, which we have not considered, include an endogenous response of participation rates — for instance, because of a rise in two wage-earner households or an increase in the average retirement age — and effects of the age composition of the working population on productivity levels. We have also not analyzed the effects of a continued slowdown of population growth — which, in itself, might be expected to lower real interest rates and increase the capital stock per worker (see Appendix). Clearly, more research into these various questions is in order.

Appendix

Steady-State Effects of Demographic Changes

In this Appendix we work out analytically the long-run effects of having an older population. In MULTIMOD the effects of aging operate through three channels. (1) The consumption equation has an estimated positive coefficient on the dependency ratio, which is consistent with greater consumption during one's retirement years relative to income and wealth. (2) Potential output depends on the labor force, which is reduced when a larger fraction of the population is retired. (3) An older population is associated with higher government spending (based on estimates in Heller and others

(1986)). We also consider a decrease in the birthrate β, which for an unchanged mortality rate implies slower population growth, although these effects are not discussed in the text, given difficulties in simulating MULTIMOD with different population growth rates in different countries (implying the impossibility of ever reaching a steady state) and because of uncertainty concerning birthrate projections. The macroeconomic effects that one would expect to result through these linkages can be described in a simplified version of MULTIMOD, as laid out below.

If we ignore monetary factors and, as a result, can express all variables in real terms, we can represent MULTIMOD for the global economy as follows[20]:

$$C = (\rho + \lambda + \alpha\Delta)(B + H) \tag{1}$$

$$\dot{H} = (r + \beta)H - (Y - \delta K - T) \tag{2}$$

$$\dot{B} = rB + G - T \tag{3}$$

$$Y = F(K, L) \tag{4}$$

$$F_1(K, L) = r + \delta \tag{5}$$

$$Y = C + G + \delta K + \dot{K}. \tag{6}$$

Consumption C is modeled as in Blanchard (1985) and Buiter (1988), with the addition of a multiplicative term in the dependency ratio; liquidity constraints are ignored here. It is assumed that the birthrate β is exogenous; population (and all stock and flow variables in steady state) grows at rate $n = \beta - \lambda$, where λ is the mortality rate (constant, and independent of age), and ρ is the rate of time preference for any given individual. Productivity growth is assumed to be zero. As a result, consumption is proportional to wealth, with the constant of proportionality depending positively on the dependency ratio Δ (equation (1)). The only forms of wealth are government bonds B and human capital H; that is, discounted future after-tax income (including net income to capital K) (equation (2)).

---

[20]Implications for a single open economy are discussed below.

The government budget constraint makes bonds grow with the deficit (equation (3)), and bonds pay a real rate of interest r. Output is given by a production function that depends on capital K and the labor force L (equation (4)), and conditions for profit maximization imply that the marginal product of capital (F_1) equals the real rate of interest plus the rate of depreciation (equation (5)).[21] Finally, output produced has to equal demand on the part of households and the government (equation (6)), plus replacement investment.

In a steady state with growth at rate, $n = \beta - \lambda, \dot{H}, \dot{K}$ and $\dot{B}$ have to be equal to nH, nK, and nB, respectively. To consider steady-state effects, we therefore replace equations (2) and (3) with the following equations:

$$H = (Y - \delta K - T)/(r + \lambda) \tag{7}$$
$$B = (T - G)/(r - \beta + \lambda) \tag{8}$$
$$Y = C + G + (\beta - \lambda + \delta)K. \tag{9}$$

The effects of a greater proportion of the elderly show up in three exogenous variables: Δ, G, and L — the first two increase, and the third declines.[22] A decrease in birthrates produces a fall in β and therefore a fall in real growth n. We therefore differentiate the above system of equations (1), (7), (8), (4), (5), and (9) with respect to Δ, G, L, and β (noting that $dn = d\beta$). The results are as follows:

$$dC = (\rho + \lambda)(dB + dH) + \alpha d\,\Delta(B + H) \tag{10}$$
$$\begin{aligned}dH = {}&(dY - \delta dK - dT)/(r + \lambda)\\&- [(Y - \delta K - T)/(r + \lambda)^2]dr\end{aligned} \tag{11}$$
$$\begin{aligned}dB = {}&(dT - dG)/(r - \beta + \lambda)\\&- [(T - G)/(r - \beta + \lambda)^2](dr - d\beta)\end{aligned} \tag{12}$$
$$dY = F_1 dK + F_2 dL \tag{13}$$

---

[21] Corporate taxes are ignored; taxes are assumed to be lump-sum levies on households.

[22] For a given population P and participation rate R, Δ and L are related as follows: $L = \Delta RP$. In order to understand the mechanisms at work, we separate the labor force effects of a change in Δ from its effect on consumption.

$$F_{11}dK + F_{12}dL = dr \tag{14}$$

$$dY = dC + dG + (\beta - \lambda + \delta)dK + Kd\beta. \tag{15}$$

Equations (10)–(15) give six equations in seven endogenous variables — dC, dH, dB, dT, dY, dr, and dK. The underdetermination results from government variables; we take the steady-state bond stock to be exogenous (as is the case in MULTIMOD for the bond/GNP ratio). Moreover, to simplify the analysis, we consider the case where the primary deficit $(G - T)$ is zero; so from equation (12) $dT = dG$ (and also $B = 0$). In this case, lower birthrates have no effect on the long-run equilibrium real interest rate, except through the steady-state rate of investment, in (15).

It is straightforward to reduce the system of equations to three equations in three endogenous variables, dC, dK, and dr:

$$\begin{bmatrix} 1 & -\theta(F_1 - \delta) & \theta H \\ 0 & F_{11} & -1 \\ -1 & F_1 - \mu & 0 \end{bmatrix} \begin{bmatrix} dC \\ dK \\ dr \end{bmatrix} = \begin{bmatrix} \alpha H & \theta F_2 & -\theta & 0 \\ 0 & -F_{12} & 0 & 0 \\ 0 & -F_2 & 1 & K \end{bmatrix} \begin{bmatrix} d\Delta \\ dL \\ dG \\ d\beta \end{bmatrix}, \tag{16}$$

or

$$Ady = Bdx,$$

where $\theta = (\rho + \lambda)/(r + \lambda)$ and $\mu = \beta - \lambda + \delta$. It can be shown that $\rho \leq r < \rho + \lambda$ (provided bonds B are positive, but less than some upper limit), so $0 < \theta < 1$.

Now the determinant of the matrix A is equal to

$$\det(A) = F_1(1 - \theta) + F_{11}\theta H - (\mu - \delta\theta). \tag{17}$$

The marginal product of capital is positive, $F_1 > 0$, and by diminishing marginal returns, $F_{11} < 0$; $\det(A)$ can therefore not be signed a priori. However, stability of the dynamic system (not analyzed here) requires that at a point of equilibrium, an increase in the real interest rate should increase saving net of investment. This can be shown to imply that $\det(A) < 0$, as follows. The change in net savings dS is equal to

$$dS = dY - dC - \mu dK$$
$$= [(1-\theta)F_1 + \delta\theta]dK + \theta H dr - \mu dK$$
$$= (1-\theta)F_1 dr/F_{11} + \theta H dr - (\mu - \delta\theta)dr/F_{11}. \quad (18)$$

Multiplying by F_{11} (which is negative) shows from equation (17) that the condition that $dS/dr > 0$ is equivalent to $\det(A) > 0$.

Calculating $A^{-1}B$ and simplifying gives the following comparative static results:

$$
\begin{bmatrix} dC \\ dK \\ dr \end{bmatrix} = \frac{1}{\det(A)}
$$
$$
\cdot \begin{bmatrix}
\alpha H(F_1 - \mu) & D_1 & -\theta H F_{11} + n\theta & \theta K(F_1 - \delta - HF_{11}) \\
\alpha H & D_2 & (1-\theta) & K \\
\alpha H F_{11} & D_3 & F_{11}(1-\theta) & F_{11}K
\end{bmatrix}
$$
$$
\cdot \begin{bmatrix} d\Delta \\ dL \\ dG \\ d\beta \end{bmatrix}, \quad (19)
$$

where

$$D_1 = \theta H[F_{11}F_2 - (F_1 - \mu)F_{12}] - n\theta F_2$$
$$D_2 = (1-\theta)F_2 - \theta H F_{12}$$
$$D_3 = -(1-\theta)F_{11}F_{12} + F_1 F_{12}(1-\theta) - F_{12}(\mu - \delta\theta).$$

Noting that $F_{12} > 0, F_{11} < 0, F_1 - \mu = r - n > 0$, and $\mu - \delta\theta > 0$, and recalling that $\det(A) < 0$, the signs of the comparative statics results are as follows:

	$d\Delta$	dL	dG	$d\beta$
dC	−	+	−	−
dK	−	+	−	−
dr	+	0^{23}	+	+

---

[23] Assuming that G changes proportionately.

Let us consider in turn the changes in the exogenous variables. An increase in private consumption due to aging ($d\Delta > 0$) paradoxically *decreases* steady-state consumption. The reason is that it raises the real interest rate and lowers the capital stock, leading to lower output. Though there is short-run stimulus to consumption and to output demand, in the long-run steady state, aggregate supply effects dominate: an economy that saves less has a lower capital stock.[24] The effect of increased government spending $dG > 0$ is similar; it drains resources away from capital formation. A decrease in the labor force due to an increase in retirees ($dL < 0$) tends to *lower* aggregate consumption, capital, and output, but has no effects on per capita variables or the real interest rate, given the somewhat artificial assumption that the aggregate consumption/wealth ratio is unaffected and if one makes the further assumption that government spending per capita is unchanged. Such a change in L just corresponds to a scale change in the economy. A decline in population growth ($d\beta < 0$) should increase capital intensity and consumption and decrease the real interest rate.

Some intuition about long-run effects can be obtained with the help of a simple diagram, taken from the neoclassical growth literature (Fig. 1). All variables have been put in per capita terms; that is, divided by the labor force. A constant returns to scale production function (and the assumption that G grows with LF, discussed above) allows us to do this. In equilibrium, saving must equal investment. For the equilibrium to be a steady state, investment must be sufficient to maintain a constant capital/labor ratio k; that is, the capital stock must grow at the growth rate of the labor force n. Hence, saving per capita ($sf(k)$, where s is the saving rate) must equal investment per capita (nk).

Now a change in the level of the labor force would just scale up or down all macroeconomic flow and stock variables, but have no effect on such variables as capital intensity (plotted on the horizontal

---

[24]Provided it is below the golden-rule capital stock.

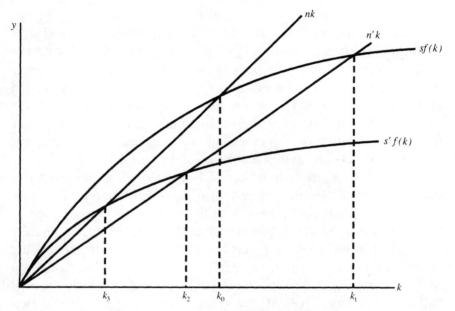

Figure 1. Steady-State Equilibrium with Different Saving Rates and Population Growth Rates

axis) or saving per capita (the curve $sf(k)$). The level of the real interest rate can be inferred from the value of the capital/labor ratio k; from the production function and the equilibrium condition that the marginal product of capital is equal to the real interest rate plus the depreciation rate, a higher value of k is associated with a lower real interest rate.

A permanent change in the age structure toward an older population, leaving population growth unaffected, would shift down the saving schedule because the aggregate saving rate would be lower. This would occur because the government would spend more in order to provide increased services and because the elderly save less. Lower saving for a given population growth would shift the $sf(k)$ curve down to $s'f(k)$ and lead it to intersect with investment at a lower capital labor ratio, k_3. In other words, capital intensity would be lower, and the real interest rate higher, with an older population.

A permanent decline in the population's growth rate, keeping age structure unchanged,[25] would have the opposite effect. It would shift down the investment line to $n'k$; with slower population growth, the economy can devote a lower proportion of its output to investment and yet maintain its standard of living. As a result, with unchanged saving behavior capital intensity rises to k_1, and the real interest rate falls. The net effect of slower population growth and an older population depends on the extent of the demographic changes and the size of effects on saving: k can either rise or fall.

In the case of an open economy facing the above demographic shifts, the results would be modified in several important ways. Suppose, first, that the country is small and that it alone experiences the demographic shifts. In the long run the home country's interest rate will equal the exogenous world rate. Therefore, instead of raising interest rates and lowering the capital stock, population aging will lead to a rundown of net claims on foreigners. Another channel will involve changes in the terms of trade. Increases in consumption demand and decreases in supply (through a shrinkage of the labor force) will each lead to an appreciation of the home country currency in real terms, which will also have the effect of pushing the current account position into deficit and leading to a decline in net foreign assets. Thus, in a small open economy model, crowding out of excess demand for the home good will occur through net exports and not through declines in investment and the capital stock, as in the closed economy model.

To the extent that the economy is large, there will be a combination of effects on real interest rates and on the foreign balance. Moreover, if the demographic shifts occur in a large number of countries, then the closed economy results will be approximated at the global level. If the shifts are of different magnitudes, however, the countries with the more pronounced aging will experience a decline in net exports, and a real appreciation, as described above.

---

[25]In practice, the two phenomena are interrelated: unless mortality rates change, permanently lower birthrates will yield an older population as well as slower population growth.

Acknowledgments

The authors are grateful to A. Lans Bovenberg, William Branson, Ernesto Hernández-Catá, Andrew Dean, Robert Hagemann, Richard Hemming, Robert Holzmann, Yusuke Horiguchi, and Mark Lutz for comments, and to Warwick McKibbin, Torsten Persson, and Lars Svensson for useful discussion.

References

Aaron, Henry Jacob, Barry Bosworth, and Gary Burtless, *Can America Afford to Grow Old? Paying for Social Security* (Washington: The Brookings Institution, 1989).

Auerbach, Alan, Lawrence Kotlikoff, Robert Hagemann, and Guiseppe Nicoletti, "The Economic Dynamics of an Ageing Population: the Case of Four OECD Economies," OECD Department of Economics and Statistics Working Paper 62 (Paris: Organization for Economic Cooperation and Development, January 1989).

Blanchard, Olivier, "Debt, Deficits, and Finite Horizons," *Journal of Political Economy*, Vol. 93 (April 1985), pp. 233–247.

Bös, Dieter, and Robert Weizsäcker, "Economic Consequences of an Aging Population," *European Economic Review*, Vol. 33 (March 1989), pp. 345–354.

Bovenberg, A. Lans, and Owen Evans, "National and Personal Saving in the United States: Measurement and Analysis of Recent Trends," *Staff Papers*, International Monetary Fund (Washington), Vol. 37 (September 1990), pp. 636–669.

Buiter, Willem H., "Death, Birth, Productivity Growth and Debt Neutrality," *Economic Journal*, Vol. 98 (June 1988), pp. 279–293.

Davidson, James E. H., and others, "Economic Modelling of the Aggregate Time-Series Relationship Between Consumers' Expenditure and Income in the United Kingdom," *Economic Journal*, Vol. 88 (December 1978), pp. 661–692.

Dean, Andrew, and others, "Saving Trends and Behaviour in OECD Countries," OECD Department of Economics and Statistics Working Paper 67 (Paris: Organization for Economic Cooperation and Development, June 1989).

Hagemann, Robert, and Giuseppe Nicoletti, "Ageing Populations: Economic Effects and Implications for Public Finance," OECD Department of Economics and Statistics Working Paper 61 (Paris: Organization for Economic Cooperation and Development, January 1989).

Halter, William A., and Richard Hemming, "The Impact of Demographic Changes on Social Security Financing," *Staff Papers*, International Monetary Fund (Washington), Vol. 34 (September 1987), pp. 471–502.

Heller, Peter, "Aging, Savings, and Pensions in the Group of Seven Countries: 1980–2025," *Journal of Public Policy*, Vol. 9 (April/June 1989), pp. 127–153.

Heller, Peter, and others, *Aging and Social Expenditure in the Major Industrial Countries, 1980–2025*, Occasional Paper 47 (Washington: International Monetary Fund, September 1986).

Hendry, David F., and Thomas von Ungern-Sternberg, "Liquidity and Inflation Effects on Consumers' Expenditure," in *Essays in the Theory and Measurement of Consumer Behaviour*, ed. by Angus Deaton (Cambridge: Cambridge University Press, 1981).

Herd, Richard, "The Impact of Increased Government Saving on the Economy," OECD Department of Economics and Statistics Working Paper 69 (Paris: Organization for Economic Cooperation and Development, June 1989).

Horne, Jocelyn, Jeroen Kremers, and Paul Masson, "Net Foreign Assets and International Adjustment in the United States, Japan, and the Federal Republic of Germany," IMF Working Paper WP/89/22 (Washington: International Monetary Fund, March 1989).

International Monetary Fund, *World Economic Outlook: A Survey by the Staff of the International Monetary Fund*, World Economic and Financial Surveys (Washington: International Monetary Fund, October 1989), pp. 28–34.

International Monetary Fund, *World Economic Outlook: A Survey by the Staff of the International Monetary Fund*, World Economic and Financial Surveys (Washington: International Monetary Fund, May 1990), pp. 100–113.

Lee, Ronald and Shelley Lapkoff, "International Flows of Time and Goods: Consequences of Slowing Population Growth," *Journal of Political Economy*, Vol. 96 (June 1988), pp. 618–651.

Masson, Paul, Steven Symansky, and Guy Meredith, *MULTIMOD Mark II: A Revised and Extended Model*, Occasional Paper 71 (Washington: International Monetary Fund, forthcoming 1990).

Ritzen, Jozef, and Hendrick P. van Dalen, "Taxation and Public Debt under a Demographic Transition," paper presented to the 45th Congress of the International Institute of Public Finance, Buenos Aires, August 28–31, 1989 (unpublished; Rotterdam: Erasmus University).

Chapter 3

Models of Inflation and the Costs of Disinflation*

**Bankim Chadha, Paul R. Masson
and Guy Meredith**

The focus of this analysis is on the output costs of disinflation. A model of inflation with both forward and backward elements seems to characterize reality. Such an inflation model is estimated using data for industrial countries, and the output costs of a disinflation path are calculated, first analytically in a simple theoretical model, then by a simulation of a global, multiregion empirical model. The credibility of a preannounced path for money consistent with the lowest output loss is considered. An alternative, more credible policy may be to announce an exchange rate peg to a low-inflation currency.

1. Introduction

It is now widely recognized that the primary objective of central banks is — or should be — the maintenance of price stability.[1] Recent initiatives in several countries have attempted to formalize this

---

*This chapter originally appeared in *Staff Papers* (International Monetary Fund) (1992), 39(2), 395–431. At time of writing, all three authors were staff members of the International Monetary Fund.

[1]The goal of price stability was the focus of the policy discussion in Chapter II of the May 1990 issue of the *World Economic Outlook* (International Monetary Fund (1990)), which presented an analysis based on a preliminary version of this paper.

objective: in the United States, a congressional resolution mandating a zero inflation target for the Federal Reserve has been proposed, while in Canada, the Bank of Canada has announced a near-term target for inflation and the ultimate goal of price stability.[2] In Europe the statutes for a European System of Central Banks, agreed at Maastricht in December 1991, state that price stability will be the primary objective.[3] In this respect, these statutes would echo the primary responsibility of the Deutsche Bundesbank, namely, to safeguard the stability of the currency.

Concern to reduce inflation has made disinflation a major macroeconomic issue of the past two decades.[4] Reducing the rate of inflation through contractionary aggregate demand policies has in all countries been associated with a decline in output and employment relative to potential; for the United States, estimates of the "sacrifice ratio" of percentage points of cumulative output loss that must be incurred in order to lower the rate of inflation by 1 percentage point range from 3 to 18 (Sachs (1985)). Yet the causes of these output losses are imperfectly understood. If nominal rigidity is due to the stickiness of the *levels* of wages (as in the models of Fischer (1977), Phelps (1978), Taylor (1979, 1980), or Calvo (1983a, 1983b)), then a path that leads to a lower rate of money growth (as opposed to a lower level of the money supply) need not cause output losses, as long as price expectations correctly anticipate the monetary deceleration. Such a disinflation path was calculated for a staggered wage contracts model by Taylor (1983).[5] In these circumstances, it is hard to understand why central banks could not convince the private sector that they were going to move to a money growth rate consistent

---

[2]See Selody (1990) and Lipsey (1990) for a discussion of the issues in a Canadian context.

[3]Commission of the European Communities (1990) discusses the goal of price stability in a European context.

[4]We will not consider the costs of inflation here; see, for instance, Fischer (1986, Chapters 1–4).

[5]A reasonably rapid credible disinflation could, in fact, cause a boom in output, not output losses, in a model with sticky wages and prices. See Rodriguez (1982), Fischer (1986, p. 252), and Ball (1991).

Models of Inflation and the Costs of Disinflation 59

with price stability, and when they did so, that wage increases would not decelerate smoothly, leaving employment unchanged. However, experience with disinflation suggests instead that there may be some fundamental stickiness in inflation rates that makes achievement of costless disinflation difficult, if not impossible.[6]

In this paper, we argue that modeling the process for inflation requires including both forward-looking and backward-looking elements. Inertia in inflation may be due to partially nonrational expectations; if expectations are adaptive, then the inflation process is purely backward looking, as in Ball (1990). In any case, a simple specification in which the two elements are present — in particular, expected future inflation and lagged inflation, with weights that sum to unity — rejects both restrictions of a unit coefficient or a zero coefficient on lagged inflation. Using this specification, we show that there is a critical value for the relative importance of the forward-looking part, above which a disinflation path with zero output losses is possible. Such a disinflation path, if it exists, implies a monotonic decline in inflation, which asymptotes to zero. The path for the money supply, however, is not monotonic.

The paper presents estimates of this inflation equation using pooled cross-section, time-series data for the industrial countries. Estimates of the forward-looking parameter are close to the threshold value mentioned above that permits costless disinflation. We then proceed to simulate various disinflation paths, using the estimated inflation equations in a global, multiregion model, MULTIMOD. These simulations imply sacrifice ratios that are positive, though below the range mentioned above. We explore the implications of changing the parameter on forward-looking behavior, by an amount suggested by the estimated standard error.

Another aspect of the disinflation problem is imperfect credibility of an announced deceleration of the money supply. Using model simulations, we illustrate how various degrees of credibility affect the output losses associated with a move to price stability. One

---

[6]Ball (1990) argued that output losses were the result of adaptive expectations.

particular feature of disinflation is that lower inflation is associated with *higher* money demand if money demand has a negative interest elasticity. To avoid a decline in the price level (that is, a period of negative inflation), the money supply has to be increased at some point through an *acceleration* of money growth. Such a path for the money supply may strain credibility, adding to output losses. An alternative available to some countries, for instance those in the European Monetary System (EMS), may be to use an exchange rate peg to a low-inflation currency as a focus for the disinflation policy, letting the path of the money supply be endogenous. We explore the implications of such a policy, compared to an imperfectly credible announced path for the money supply, accompanied by exchange rate flexibility.

A final section advances some conclusions on the basis of our results and sketches areas for further research.

2. Price Dynamics and the Phillips Curve

Many modern macroeconomic models, and most large macroeconometric models, embody some form of the expectations-augmented Phillips curve as the basic building block describing the adjustment over time of prices (wages) to movements in aggregate demand around potential, or capacity, output (the natural rate of unemployment). The specific form of the Phillips curve implemented can play a key role in determining the short-run response to changes in policy or exogenous shocks.[7]

The dynamics of price adjustment in Keynesian models has always been a subject of considerable debate. Much of the early literature on price adjustment in these models relied, either explicitly or implicitly, on mistaken expectations on the part of agents in goods

---

[7] For a comparison of alternative macroeconometric models see Bryant and others (1988). Obstfeld and Rogoff (1984) show how frequently used alternative price adjustment rules can alter even the qualitative response of the economy to the same shock.

or labor markets or on the ad hoc existence of asymmetrical rigidities between wages and prices. Since then, various attempts have been made to develop models of disequilibrium dynamics that do not rely on expectational errors.[8] An important and influential development has been the staggered contracts models of Phelps (1978), Taylor (1979, 1980), and Calvo (1983a, 1983b). (See also Blanchard (1983) and Mussa (1981a, 1981b).) These models emphasize that wages tend to be set in nominal terms for a discrete period of time and are set by different agents at different points in time — that is, they are asynchronous — and, therefore, contracts overlap. Agents are assumed to contract a wage in accordance with their anticipations of future price and output levels for the expected duration of the contract. These models typically assume that prices are a constant markup over wages and focus on the persistence induced in the aggregate price (average wage) level due to the asynchronous and overlapping nature of wage contracts.[9]

The staggered contracts model is consistent with various traditional reasons put forward for the existence of nominal rigidities or the incomplete adjustment of nominal prices to their equilibrium levels. Much of the literature on optimal price (wage) adjustment and contracting assumes a fixed, lump-sum real cost of adjustment or negotiation.[10] This assumption has been adopted by, among others, Barro (1972), Gray (1978), and Sheshinski and Weiss (1983). Given fixed, lump-sum costs of price adjustment, it will be optimal for

---

[8]This is not to imply that expectational errors cannot occur in these models, in that there are unanticipated shocks to the economy. The point is rather that agents do not systematically and continuously make mistakes in the same direction, as would occur, for example, in a model with adaptive expectations when the rate of inflation permanently increases.

[9]There is no presumption in this approach that formal contracts are written; only that nominal prices (wages) are preset for some period of time.

[10]Again, we do not distinguish between wages and prices, since this literature typically assumes that prices are a constant markup over wage costs.

firms in the presence of trend inflation, for example, to adjust their prices at discrete intervals of time.[11] (Romer (1990) examined the microeconomic foundations for the staggered contracts model.)

This section explores the implications of alternative hypotheses about the wage-setting process and alternative assumptions on expectations formation, with a view to determining the restrictions implied for the form of the Phillips curve, in particular the dependence of current inflation on past and future expected inflation. The implications of two extreme benchmark cases are considered. First, a model in the tradition of Phelps and Friedman with adaptive expectations is shown to imply a weight of unity on past inflation in determining current inflation — that is, there is complete "inflation stickiness" — and a weight of zero on future expected inflation. Second, the Calvo (1983a, 1983b) model is shown to place a weight of unity on future expected inflation, and actual inflation is independent of the past rate of inflation — so that there is no inflation stickiness. An intermediate, alternative model and its implications for the form of the Phillips curve are then discussed: it is shown that current inflation is determined as a weighted average of past and future expected inflation.

The traditional expectations-augmented Phillips curve usually posits that the rate of inflation, ΔP_t, equals the expected rate of inflation, π_t^e, plus a term representing excess demand[12]:

$$\Delta P_t = \pi_t^e + \beta y_t, \tag{1}$$

---

[11]For the price quotation or "contract" to be binding, it is necessary to make additional assumptions, since in a stochastic environment such contracts will typically be time inconsistent. An alternative approach was adopted by Barro (1972) and Sheshinski and Weiss (1983), who allowed the contract to be renegotiated when the benefits of such a renegotiation outweighed the costs. The optimal policy is an (S, s) policy; that is, the price is changed when it deviates by more than a critical magnitude from the optimal or equilibrium flexible price. Parkin (1986) examined the optimality of alternative wage-staggering rules.

[12]And perhaps, also, a term representing the change in excess demand, due to a variable markup of prices over unit costs.

Models of Inflation and the Costs of Disinflation 63

where expected inflation is computed as a weighted average of lagged inflation rates. Assuming a geometric lag distribution

$$\pi_t^e = (1 - \alpha) \sum_{i=0}^{\infty} \alpha^i \Delta P_{t-1-i}, \quad 0 < \alpha < 1, \tag{2}$$

which can be rewritten as

$$\pi_t^e = \alpha \pi_{t-1}^e + (1 - \alpha) \Delta P_{t-1}. \tag{3}$$

Then, substituting equation (3) into (1) and with some manipulation, current inflation is given by

$$\Delta P_t = \Delta P_{t-1} + \beta (1 - \alpha) y_t + \alpha \beta (y_t - y_{t-1}), \tag{4}$$

so that actual inflation equals last period's inflation, plus a function of current excess demand and the acceleration in excess demand. An important implication is that current inflation can be affected only by factors that alter current excess demand. In particular, disinflation must involve output losses.

We now turn to a version of the rational staggered contracts model in discrete time[13]: V_t is defined as the log of the wage embodied in contracts or wage quotations initiated at time t by a representative agent, and is fixed during the length of the quotation. The quotation expiration date is assumed to be stochastic and to follow a geometric distribution. It is posited that the level of the new negotiated wage is determined as a weighted average of all future price levels, P, and excess demand, y, so that

$$V_t = (1 - b) \sum_{s=t}^{\infty} E_t \left[P_s + \beta y_s \right] b^{s-t}, \tag{5}$$

or

$$V_t = b E_t V_{t+1} + (1 - b) P_t + (1 - b) \beta y_t, \tag{6}$$

where each period in equation (5) is weighted by the probability that the contract currently being negotiated will survive to that period;

---

[13]For a previous discrete-time version of the Calvo staggered contracts model, see Chadha (1989).

E_t denotes the expectations operator conditional on information available at time t. The (log of the) average price level (which equals the log of the average wage level), P, is then defined as a weighted average of all contract wages in existence:

$$P_t = (1 - b) \sum_{s=-\infty}^{t} b^{t-s} V_s, \tag{7}$$

where $(1 - b) b^{t-s}$ is the proportion of wages that were negotiated s periods ago. The general price level can be rewritten as a weighted average of last period's price level and the new contract wage; that is

$$P_t = bP_{t-1} + (1 - b) V_t. \tag{8}$$

The one-period-ahead expected rate of inflation (using all information available at t) can then be written alternatively as

$$E_t \Delta P_{t+1} = b\Delta P_t + (1 - b) [E_t V_{t+1} - V_t], \tag{9}$$

or

$$E_t \Delta P_{t+1} = (1 - b) [E_t V_{t+1} - P_t]. \tag{10}$$

Then, with substitution and rearrangement, the current rate of inflation can be written as

$$\Delta P_t = E_t \Delta P_{t+1} + \frac{(1 - b)^2}{b} \beta y_t. \tag{11}$$

Although equation (11) resembles the traditional expectations-augmented Phillips curve posited in equation (1), with the mathematical expectation today of the rate of inflation expected to prevail tomorrow, $E_t \Delta P_{t+1}$, replacing a distributed lag over past inflation, π_t^e, it is worth emphasizing that the difference has strong implications and will fundamentally alter the response of the economy to certain types of shocks. Note that equation (11) implies that regardless of the degree of price stickiness, as measured by the value of the parameter b, there is no stickiness in the rate of inflation. The rate of inflation is independent of the past rate of inflation and is free to jump to any value dictated by future expected inflation. The rate of inflation today will respond, therefore, to anticipated shocks that affect the

Models of Inflation and the Costs of Disinflation 65

rate of inflation tomorrow.[14] This is in sharp contrast to the previous model where current inflation was tied to past inflation and could be influenced today only by contemporaneous movements in excess demand.

The two approaches represent extremes, with the traditional model of adaptive expectations implying complete inflation stickiness, and the rational staggered prices model implying no inflation stickiness. Whether or not inflation has backward- and/or forward-looking elements is an empirical question that can only be settled by the data. Empirical testing is reported in Section 4 below. To allow for both backward- and forward-looking elements in the determination of inflation, we nest the two extremes in a more general model that includes both as special cases:

$$\Delta P_t = \delta E_t \Delta P_{t+1} \left(1 - \delta\right) \Delta P_{t-1} + \alpha y_t + \beta \Delta y_t. \tag{12}$$

Such a generalization could be given a heuristic justification by assuming the existence of both backward- and forward-looking agents. Alternatively, and somewhat more formally, there are wage-setting characteristics that would lead to some inflation stickiness — and in particular, to current inflation being a weighted average of both past inflation and future expected inflation.

These characteristics may be classified as "incomplete forward looking." The traditional adaptive expectations model discussed is, of course, an extreme example. We now present an example to illustrate the point more generally. Suppose that wage setters set contract wages according to the rule

$$V_t = V_{t-1} + E_t \Delta P_{t+1} + \beta y_t, \tag{13}$$

so that those negotiating wages today set theirs to emulate the level of wages contracted last period, adjusted to compensate for inflation expected next period, and also as a function of prevailing excess demand. Wage setters are, therefore, partly backward looking and

---

[14]As Végh (1991) points out, in the rational staggered prices framework, the rate of inflation is a purely forward-looking variable.

partly forward looking, but myopically so, in that they do not look at expected inflation or excess demand for the full duration of the contract. Then, again assuming that contract expiration dates are geometrically distributed, and substituting equation (13) into the first difference of equation (8) yields

$$\Delta P_t = b\Delta P_{t-1} + (1 - b) E_t \Delta P_{t+1} + (1 - b) \beta y_t, \tag{14}$$

so that current inflation is a weighted average of past and expected future inflation.

3. The Dynamics of Disinflation

This section considers the dynamics of disinflation along a path with zero output losses. An inflation equation with backward- and forward-looking elements,[15] as described above in equation (12), is embedded in a simple closed economy macromodel containing equations for aggregate demand and money demand. If perfect foresight prevails, then equation (12) can be written in terms of the acceleration of inflation η_t:

$$\eta_{t+1} = [(1 - \delta)/\delta] \eta_t - (\alpha/\delta) y_t - (\beta/\delta) \Delta y_t, \tag{15}$$

where $\eta_t \equiv \Delta P_t - \Delta P_{t-1}$. The root of this equation is equal to $\lambda = (1 - \delta)/\delta$, which is less than unity if and only if $\delta > 0.5$.

We combine the inflation equation with a simple aggregate demand relationship that relates the output gap, y_t, to the real interest rate (where $\theta < 0$):

$$y_t = \theta (i_t - \Delta P_{t+1}) \tag{16}$$

and with a money demand equation

$$M_t - P_t = \rho y_t - \gamma i_t + \phi(M_{t-1} - P_{t-1}), \tag{17}$$

---

[15]That is, with weights that sum to unity on lagged and led inflation. However, the term "backward-looking" is not intended to imply "nonrational" or myopic expectations.

Models of Inflation and the Costs of Disinflation 67

where i_t is the nominal interest rate, and M_t is the log of the nominal money stock.[16] In this model let us consider what the dynamics of disinflation must be in order to avoid output losses completely. We will call this the "costless disinflation path." From equation (15), setting $y_t = 0$ for all $t \geq 0$ gives a path for the inflation rate. This yields

$$\eta_{t+1} = \lambda \eta_t, \tag{18}$$

so the rate of inflation in any future period ($t \geq 1$) is given by

$$\Delta P_t = \Delta P_0 + \eta_1 \sum_{i=0}^{t-1} \lambda^i = \Delta P_0 + \eta_1 \left[\frac{1 - \lambda^t}{1 - \lambda} \right]. \tag{19}$$

Equation (19) expresses the path of inflation in terms of the initial *deceleration* of inflation, $\eta_1 < 0$, and the subsequent inflation dynamics, which depend on the weight given to future inflation in wage/price determination. It is clear from equation (19) that a necessary condition for convergence to zero inflation accompanied by zero output losses ($y_t = 0$) is $\lambda < 1$, which will hold if and only if $\delta > 0.5$.

Costless disinflation is thus possible only if δ is above 0.5, and provided the announced policy is credible.[17] The intuition for this result is as follows: if inflation is expected to fall next period, it pulls down this period's inflation, ΔP_t. The key to costless disinflation is to decelerate money growth at a rate such that the fall in inflation today (relative to last period's) is just offset by the further fall expected in the following period. The new steady-state rate of inflation is approached asymptotically — there is always an extra

---

[16]This model extends the model of the previous section because it makes money demand explicit and models the transmission of monetary policy through the channel of interest rates. For simplicity, we ignore the effect of trend growth in capacity output on money demand, and assume that equilibrium real interest rates are zero. These simplifications could be relaxed without changing the analysis.

[17]Phelps (1978) and Taylor (1983) also examined disinflation paths with zero output loss.

downward drag on today's inflation rate from a further expected decline. However, provided that the forward term more than offsets the past (that is, $\delta > 0.5$), and there is the expectation that inflation will decline in the future (that is, the policy is credible), then the whole process of deceleration from a positive inflation rate can be set in motion with a path of decelerating money growth, without incurring output losses.[18]

Assuming that costless disinflation is possible, we can calculate from equation (19) the initial deceleration of inflation that is needed to achieve price stability asymptotically, starting from an initial inflation rate, ΔP_0. If

$$\lim_{t \to \infty} \Delta P_t = \Delta P_0 + \eta_1 / (1 - \lambda) = 0, \tag{20}$$

then

$$\eta_1 = -\Delta P_0 (1 - \lambda). \tag{21}$$

The closer λ is to 1 — that is, the closer δ is to 0.5 — the more gradual is the initial deceleration of inflation, η_1, and also the slower is its subsequent decline, along a path with zero output losses. Of course, for estimates of δ slightly below 0.5, costs of disinflation, though positive, will be small; output losses will increase as δ declines further.

What does the path for the money supply look like along the costless disinflation path? Suppose we start from a position in which output is at potential, so $y_0 = 0$, and $\Delta P_0 = \Delta M_0$. Along the costless disinflation path, $y_t = \Delta y_t = 0$, and from equation (16), therefore, $i_t = \Delta P_{t+1}$ (for $t \geq 1$). If we take the first difference for the demand for money and substitute for Δy_t and Δi_t

$$\Delta M_t - \Delta P_t = -\gamma (\Delta P_{t+1} - \Delta P_t) + \phi (\Delta M_{t-1} - \Delta P_{t-1}). \tag{22}$$

---

[18]If $\delta < 0.5$, then zero output losses would require ever-accelerating declines in inflation, which, however, must eventually come to a halt to prevent ΔP_t from becoming unbounded in a downward direction. At this point (if not before), output losses would be incurred.

Models of Inflation and the Costs of Disinflation

Or, in terms of real balances, $(m_t \equiv M_t - P_t)$, since $\Delta P_t = \Delta P_0 \lambda^t$ on the costless disinflation path

$$\Delta m_t = \gamma (1 - \lambda) \Delta P_0 \lambda^t + \phi \Delta m_{t-1}. \tag{23}$$

In period 1

$$\Delta m_1 = \lambda \gamma (1 - \lambda) \Delta P_0 > 0, \tag{24}$$

so real balances increase, as do nominal balances (since $\Delta P_0 > 0$). It is clear from equation (23) that in subsequent periods, $(t > 1)$, real balances also increase.

It is also of interest to consider whether nominal balances accelerate or decelerate along the costless disinflation path; this depends on both the interest elasticity of money demand and the speed of adjustment of inflation. Since

$$\Delta M_1 = \Delta P_1 + \Delta m_1 = \lambda \Delta P_0 + \lambda \gamma (1 - \lambda) \Delta P_0$$
$$= \lambda \Delta P_0 [1 + \gamma (1 - \lambda)] \tag{25}$$
$$\Delta M_1 - \Delta M_0 = \lambda \Delta P_0 [1 + \gamma (1 - \lambda)] - \Delta P_0$$
$$= \Delta P_0 (1 - \lambda) [\lambda \gamma - 1]. \tag{26}$$

In the first period, nominal balances accelerate if $\lambda \gamma > 1$. Thus, the Cagan (1963) condition emerges here, though in a modified form: the rate of growth of the nominal money supply increases upon implementation of a disinflation policy, if the product of the interest semi-elasticity and 1 minus the speed of adjustment of inflation (that is, λ) exceeds unity. The parallel with the Cagan analysis of hyperinflation using adaptive expectations becomes clear when the path of inflation is written as a first-order equation, as follows:

$$\Delta P_t - \Delta P_{t-1} = (1 - \lambda) \left(\overline{\Delta P} - \Delta P_{t-1} \right),$$

where $\overline{\Delta P} = 0$, the long-run rate of inflation. If $\lambda \gamma > 1$, a small fall in inflation and, hence, interest rates, produces a large increase in the demand for real balances in period 1, which dominates the effect of a lower price level on nominal balances. In this case, the credibility of a costless disinflation path would be doubtful, since it involves an *acceleration* of money growth initially.

What about the subsequent paths for real and nominal balances? From equation (23), the solution for the change in real balances can be written

$$\Delta m_t = \lambda^t \gamma \, (1 - \lambda) \, \Delta P_0 \sum_{i=0}^{t-1} (\phi/\lambda)^i, \tag{27}$$

and the *acceleration* in real balances is

$$\Delta m_t - \Delta m_{t-1}$$

$$= \lambda^{t-1} \gamma \, (1 - \lambda) \, \Delta P_o \left\{ (\lambda - 1) \sum_{i=0}^{t-1} (\phi/\lambda)^i + (\phi/\lambda)^{t-1} \right\}. \tag{28}$$

Whether the acceleration of real balances is positive or negative depends on the sign of the term within the braces, $\{\}$. So, $\Delta m_t - \Delta m_{t-1} \gtrless 0$, if

$$(1 - \lambda) \sum_{i=0}^{t-2} (\phi/\lambda)^i \lessgtr \lambda \, (\phi/\lambda)^{t-1}. \tag{29}$$

It is not in general possible to sign this expression; for some parameter values, money balances may accelerate for a time, and then decelerate. To calculate the implied path for the money supply requires parameter estimates; we now turn to estimation of the inflation equation.

4. Estimation Results

Reflecting the discussion in Section 2, we now present estimates of a general form of the inflation equation where inflation is a function of both past and future expected inflation and the degree of capacity utilization. Variants of the equation are estimated that incorporate a nonlinear relationship between capacity utilization and inflation and country-specific parameters. Although little support for a nonlinear capacity utilization effect is found, there is some evidence

Models of Inflation and the Costs of Disinflation

of differences across countries in the degree of inflation stickiness. The polar cases of weights of unity on either lagged or led inflation are both strongly rejected.

4.1. *Equation to Be Estimated*

In addition to the lagged and led inflation terms, an absorption price term is included in estimation to allow for the potential desire of wage earners to be compensated for changes in the real *consumption* wage. The form of the equation that we estimate is the following:

$$\Delta P_t = \delta E_t \Delta P_{t+1} + (1 - \delta) \Delta P_{t-1} + \alpha (\Delta P A_t - \Delta P_t)$$
$$+ \gamma (P A_t - P_t) + \beta f (C U_t), \qquad (30)$$

where P_t is the logarithm of the non-oil gross national product (GNP) deflator in period t; PA_t is the log of the absorption deflator; CU_t is the capacity utilization rate defined to equal 100 when output is at its capacity level; and α, β, γ, and δ are parameters to be estimated. The function $f(CU)$ is a (possibly nonlinear) function of the contemporaneous capacity utilization rate.[19] The inclusion of either the level or the growth rate of the absorption price can be motivated by different theoretical models. The Calvo model, which specifies a fixed *level* for the wage over the life of a contract, implies that the relevant variable is the relative level of the absorption price. In other models, where contract wages grow over time, it is the growth rate that is relevant. Both terms have been included in equation (30) to nest these two possibilities in the initial specification.

The presence of ΔP_t and P_t on the right-hand side of equation (30) is likely to generate a negative correlation between the relative price terms and the structural disturbance: to reduce this problem, the equations were reparameterized by adding $(\alpha + \gamma)\Delta P_t$ to each side.[20] Dividing by $(1 + \alpha + \gamma)$ then yielded the following

---

[19]The first difference of capacity utilization did not enter significantly, and is ignored in what follows.

[20]Instrumental variables were used in estimation to control for the endogeneity of the other regressors, as is discussed below.

equation to be estimated:

$$\Delta P_t = (1 - \widetilde{\alpha} - \widetilde{\gamma}) \left[\delta E_t \Delta P_{t+1} + (1 - \delta) \Delta P_{t-1} \right]$$
$$+ \widetilde{\alpha} \Delta P A_t + \widetilde{\gamma} (P A_t - P_{t-1}) + \widetilde{\beta} f(CU_t), \qquad (31)$$

where

$$\widetilde{\alpha} = \alpha / (1 + \alpha + \gamma),$$

$$\widetilde{\gamma} = \gamma / (1 + \alpha + \gamma),$$

and

$$\widetilde{\beta} = \beta / (1 + \alpha + \gamma).$$

4.2. *Initial Parameter Estimates*

The initial stage of estimation involved testing equation (31) with expected inflation replaced by led inflation and alternatives that had constraints imposed on the coefficients on future and lagged inflation and on the relative price terms.[21] The limiting case of a zero weight on future inflation is consistent with the traditional Phelps-Friedman model with backward-looking expectations. At the other extreme, a weight of unity yields the Calvo model with fully forward-looking behavior and no inflation stickiness. A linear specification was initially used for the capacity utilization term, $f(CU) = CU/100 - 1$. This implies that capacity utilization exerts no pressure on inflation at a "normal" level of 100, consistent with the construction of the capacity utilization series as 100 times the ratio of actual to trend output.[22] In the absence of a constant term in the price equation, the "natural" rate of capacity utilization then equals 100.

---

[21] In what follows, time subscripts are omitted on currently dated variables; X_{t-1} is written X_{-1}; and X_{t+1} is written X_{+1}.

[22] The capacity utilization rate was constructed using a time-series filter to derive a capacity output series for each Group of Seven country from observed quarterly GNP data. The filter is the variant of the one developed by Hodrick and Prescott (1980), which has been used extensively to detrend economic data for the analysis of real business cycles (see, for example, Backus and others, (1989)).

To control for the endogeneity of the right-hand-side variables dated period t and $t + 1$, they were first regressed on a set of country-specific instruments consisting of the lagged level of capacity utilization; the lagged ratio of government spending to capacity output; lagged growth in the non-oil GNP deflator; and lagged growth in real money balances. A Zellner-efficient systems estimator was then used to jointly estimate equation (31) for the Group of Seven industrial countries over 1966–88, with common parameter values imposed across those countries. Because preliminary results revealed large outliers in the residuals for the United Kingdom, it was excluded from the pooled sample.[23]

The unconstrained parameter estimates obtained from estimation of equation (31) are shown in Line 1 of Table 1.[24] The weight on future inflation is estimated to be slightly less than one half; both of the terms in the absorption deflator have the expected (positive) sign; and the capacity utilization rate enters with the expected sign and its coefficient is statistically significant. Lines 2 and 3 present estimates with the parameter on future inflation constrained to zero and unity, respectively. The modified likelihood-ratio test suggested by Gallant and Jorgenson (1979) indicates either of these limiting values for $a1$ is strongly rejected by the data.[25] This suggests that the inflation process is characterized by a degree of inertia intermediate

---

[23]The problem with the U.K. data is associated with the surge in inflation from 7 percent in 1973 to over 27 percent in 1975, and the sharp decline thereafter. This surge of inflation was not related to strong economic activity — 1975 was a recession year in the United Kingdom — but rather seems to reflect a wage-price spiral caused by attempts to recover real wage losses following the first oil price shock.

[24]The (country-specific) constant terms were all small and insignificant in preliminary estimation: they have been constrained to zero. Estimation was also performed allowing for first-order autoregressive and moving average processes for the residuals: these coefficients were insignificant as a group and had little effect on the other parameter values and were thus excluded in further estimation. It should be noted that the estimate of the asymptotic variance-covariance matrix of the parameters used to construct the t-ratios may not be consistent for the reasons discussed in Cumby and others (1983).

[25]The test statistic is asymptotically distributed $\chi^2(n)$, where n is the number of linear constraints. It will not necessarily be positive in finite samples, because

74 Bankim Chadha, Paul R. Masson and Guy Meredith

Table 1. Estimation Results for the Non-Oil GNP Deflator, Common Parameters

$$\Delta P = (1 - a2 - a3)[a1\Delta P_{+1} + (1 - a1)\Delta P_{-1}] + a2\Delta PA + a3(PA - P_{-1}) + a4(CU/100 - 1))$$

Estimated Parameter	$a1$	$a2$	$a3$	$a4$	θ^a
1. Unconstrained	0.442	0.288	0.033	0.283	—
	(7.6)	(3.0)	(1.4)	(2.5)	
2. $a1$ constrained to 0	0.0	0.619	0.024	0.406	30.8
		(11.6)	(1.0)	(3.4)	
3. $a1$ constrained to 1	1.0	0.674	0.053	−0.043	33.1
		(12.0)	(1.9)	(0.5)	
4. $a2$ constrained to 0	0.458	0.0	0.043	0.353	9.1
	(8.8)		(1.5)	(3.0)	
5. $a3$ constrained to 0	0.423	0.306	0.0	0.285	0.1
	(7.3)	(3.2)		(2.5)	

Notes: The estimation period is 1966–88; the estimation technique is iterative Zellner-efficient with instrumental variables. Absolute values of asymptotic t-ratios in parentheses.
[a] Test of the null hypothesis that the constrained model is true; θ is asymptotically distributed $\chi^2(1)$: the critical value at the 2.5 percent significance level is 5.0.

between traditional backward-looking models, at one extreme, or the Calvo model, at the other extreme. Line 4 shows the results when the coefficient on growth in the absorption deflator is constrained to zero: a likelihood-ratio test indicates that this constraint is also strongly rejected by the data. In contrast, the constraint that the parameter on the *level* of the absorption deflator is zero cannot be rejected at conventional levels of significance, as shown in line 5. The latter estimates, then, represent the preferred price equation. They were used both as the starting point for the extended estimation results discussed below, and as the basis for the model simulations presented in the next section.

4.3. *Nonlinear Capacity Utilization Effects*

If there is an upper limit on the achievable level of output in the short run, then the output-inflation trade-off should become increasingly

---

the estimates of the variance-covariance matrix of the residuals in the restricted and unrestricted models are not identical.

Models of Inflation and the Costs of Disinflation　　　75

steep as this limit is approached. To test the empirical validity of this hypothesis, the equation was specified so that the degree of inflation pressure depends nonlinearly on the output gap. The functional form used was

$$f(CU) = a3 \left[\frac{a4^2}{a4 - (CU/100 - 1) - a4} \right]. \tag{32}$$

The expression is parameterized so that $a3$ has the same interpretation here as in the linear relationship when CU equals 100: specifically, inflation pressure is zero at this point, and the slope of the price-output trade-off is equal to $a3$. The trade-off becomes vertical as $CU/100 - 1$ approaches $a4$: the latter parameter thus determines the limiting rate of capacity utilization. As $a4$ becomes large, the curvature of the function decreases; when $a4$ approaches infinity the function becomes linear.[26] Because expression (32) is a nonlinear function of $a4$, a grid search was performed to identify the value that maximized the likelihood function.

Estimation results for this equation are shown in Table 2. The likelihood function reaches a maximum when $a4$ is about 0.08, implying that the short-run aggregate supply curve becomes vertical when output reaches 108 percent of long-run potential. The likelihood function, however, is quite flat for a range of values around this level. A test of the null hypothesis that the relationship is linear (that is, that $a4 = \infty$) yields a test statistic of 4.6, distributed asymptotically $\chi^2(1)$, thus the null hypothesis of a linear relationship cannot be rejected at the 2.5 percent level of significance (critical value 5.0), but it can at the 5 percent level (critical value 3.8). Although the historical data provide some evidence for a nonlinear trade-off between output and prices, it is not strong. For the purposes of further estimation and simulation, the null hypothesis of a linear trade-off was maintained.

---

[26]This can be seen by calculating $d^2 f(CU)/dCU^2 = (a4^2 - (CU/100 - 1))^3$. It is apparent that this expression — which indicates the change in the slope of the output-price trade-off as CU changes — goes to zero as $a4$ becomes large, regardless of the value of CU.

Table 2. Estimation Results for the Non-Oil GNP Deflator, Nonlinear Capacity Utilization Effect

$$(\Delta P = (1 - a2)[a1\Delta P_{+1} + (1 - a1)\Delta P_{-1}] + a2\Delta PA$$
$$+ a3[a4^2/(a4 - (CU/100 - 1)) - a4])$$

Imposed Value for $a4$	$a1$	$a2$	$a3$	Log-likelihood Function
0.05	0.450	0.326	0.203	517.94
0.07	0.442	0.320	0.232	520.30
0.08	0.440	0.318	0.240	520.40
0.09	0.438	0.317	0.246	520.39
0.10	0.436	0.316	0.251	520.32
0.15	0.432	0.312	0.265	519.90
0.20	0.429	0.311	0.271	519.57
∞^a	0.423	0.306	0.285	518.10

Note: [a]Linear specification.

4.4. Country-Specific Parameters

Finally, we tested for differences in parameters across countries. Because of a limited number of observations for each country, the six countries[27] were grouped into three geographic regions within which the same price behavior was assumed to prevail. The regions were Europe, consisting of Germany, France, and Italy; North America, consisting of the United States and Canada; and Japan. The results are shown in Table 3 for both the unconstrained equation and several parameter constraints. In the case where all three parameters ($a1$, $a2$, and $a3$) differ across regions (line 1), results for Japan were implausible, with a negative (but insignificant) weight on future inflation and a very large parameter on capacity utilization. In what follows, therefore, we have constrained $a1$ to be the same across regions. A likelihood-ratio test could not reject the hypothesis that they were all the same (line 2).

Tests were then performed to see if either $a2$ or $a3$, or both, differed significantly across regions when $a1$ was constrained to be

---

[27]As noted above, the United Kingdom was excluded.

Table 3. Estimation Results for the Non-Oil GNP Deflator, Region-Specific Parameters

$$\Delta P = (1 - a2)[a1\Delta P_{+1} + (1 - a1)\Delta P_{-1}]$$
$$+ a2\Delta PA + a3(CU/100 - 1))$$

Estimated parameters	$a1$	$a2$	$a3$	θ^a
1. Unconstrained $a1, a2, a3$				
North America	0.444	0.207	0.305	—
	(2.3)	(1.1)	(1.1)	
Europe	0.435	0.097	0.220	
	(7.3)	(0.6)	(1.4)	
Japan	−0.750	0.312	3.535	
	(0.6)	(0.4)	(0.6)	
2. Constrained $a1$				
North America	0.430	0.199	0.331	0.6
	(7.9)	(1.1)	(1.9)	
Europe	"	0.098	0.235	
		(0.7)	(1.7)	
Japan	"	0.675	0.240	
		(5.4)	(0.9)	
3. Constrained $a1$ and $a2$				
North America	0.390	0.282	0.324	1.7
	(6.3)	(2.5)	(2.0)	
Europe	"	"	0.196	
			(1.4)	
Japan	"	"	0.752	
			(1.8)	
4. Constrained $a1$ and $a3$				
North America	0.435	0.222	0.284	−0.1
	(8.1)	(1.4)	(2.5)	
Europe	"	0.095	"	
		(0.7)		
Japan	"	0.662	"	
		(6.0)		

Notes: Absolute values of asymptotic t-ratios in parentheses.
[a] θ is asymptotically distributed $\chi^2(2)$; the critical value at the 5 percent significance level is 6.0. Test of constrained model against the unconstrained model of line 1.

the same. When the parameter on absorption inflation ($a2$) varies across countries (lines 2 and 4), it is apparent that the coefficient is much larger for Japan than the other regions: however, the hypothesis that $a2$ is the same across regions cannot be rejected at conventional significance levels. The higher value for Japan may reflect two factors: a greater responsiveness of contract wages to consumption prices because, for instance, of bonus payments and indexation provisions in contracts; or a shorter average contract length than for the other regions.[28] The results shown in line 3 indicate that the parameter on capacity utilization, $a3$, is also higher for Japan than the other regions, though differences are again not significant. The higher parameter on capacity utilization may reflect either greater sensitivity of new-contract wages to market conditions, or, as for $a2$, a shorter average contract length, implying that a higher percentage of overall wages is affected by current conditions.

To summarize, these results support an inflation equation in which current inflation depends on a weighted average of past and future expected inflation. The restrictions implied by the pure forward-looking, level models of Calvo (1983a, 1983b) and by the pure backward-looking, traditional Phillips curve models are both convincingly rejected. The data do not strongly support the hypothesis of a nonlinear Phillips curve. The evidence in favor of differing parameters across countries in the price equation is inconclusive, largely because the individual parameters are not estimated precisely. The point estimates, however, suggest that the response of prices to current market conditions and to relative price movements may be greater in Japan than in the other industrial countries.

5. MULTIMOD Simulations of Disinflationary Policies

This section presents simulations of alternative disinflationary policies using MULTIMOD, a multiregion global macroeconomic model

---

[28]Other multicountry studies of price behavior also find a greater response in Japan to market conditions. See, for instance, Grubb and Jackman (1983) and Coe (1985).

developed at the Fund (see Masson, Symansky, and Meredith (1990)). The focus is on the transitional costs in terms of lower output of reducing the inflation rate: the long-run benefits of lower inflation, such as possible reductions in relative price variability, inflation uncertainty, and distortions in tax systems, are not captured by the macroeconomic simulations. The results indicate that the output costs are transitory, and vary according to factors such as the speed with which the disinflationary policy is phased in, the credibility of the authorities' commitment to reducing inflation, the degree of forward-looking behavior in price and wage setting, and the responsiveness of prices to demand conditions.[29] Sacrifice ratios are calculated that compare the cumulative output loss to the reduction in inflation: the implied costs of disinflation are lower than some others found in the literature. International aspects of disinflationary policies are also examined. In particular, we look at spillover effects on other countries of disinflationary policies in the United States, and also at the use of exchange rate versus money-supply targeting to reduce inflation.

5.1. Simulations of Disinflationary Policies in the United States

Alternative programs that reduce the target for U.S. money growth by 4 percentage points are described in Table 4a, and their cumulative effects on real output are shown in Table 4b.[30] Figure 1 gives year-by-year paths for output, inflation, the short-term interest rate, and the real exchange rate. The reduction in target money growth was chosen to represent roughly the difference between the existing trend U.S. inflation rate and price stability: since money demand is homogeneous of degree one in prices in MULTIMOD, a

---

[29]Subject to the usual caveats of the Lucas critique; in particular, the relative weights of forward- and backward-looking elements in the inflation process may themselves depend on monetary policy.

[30]Monetary policy is implemented in MULTIMOD in terms of an exogenous path for the target money supply. The actual money supply can differ in the short-run from the target, as the monetary authorities are assumed to smooth the interest rate changes that would be needed to keep money on target in each period.

Table 4a. Alternative Disinflation Programs

Program	Description
1	*Immediate disinflation.* Credible reduction in growth of U.S. money target of 4 percent a year starting in year 1.
1a	*Preannounced disinflation.* Program 1 starting in year 2.
2	*Phased-in disinflation.* Credible reduction in growth of U.S. money target of 1 percent a year starting in year 1 and reaching 4 percent by year 4.
2a	*Preannounced phased-in disinflation.* Program 2 starting in year 2 and reaching 4 percent by year 5.
3	*Noncredible phased-in disinflation.* Program 2, with lack of credibility; observed declines in money growth are expected to continue indefinitely.
4	*Very gradual phased-in disinflation.* Credible reduction in growth of U.S. money target of $1/2$ percent a year starting in year 2 and reaching 4 percent by year 9.

Table 4b. Cumulative U.S. GDP Losses for Alternative Disinflation Programs (Percent Deviation from Baseline)

Program	Sum: Five Years	Sum: Ten Years
1	-7.9	-7.4
1a	-6.0	-5.7
2	-5.2	-5.4
2a	-3.5	-4.3
3	-7.2	-7.0
4	-1.9	-3.2

permanent 4 percentage point decline in money growth leads over time to a 4 percentage point decline in the inflation rate. The price equation used for the simulations is shown in line 5 of Table 1 in the previous section, with common parameters across countries. The weight on future inflation is estimated to be 0.423. The simulations differ in terms of the speed with which the disinflationary policy is implemented, ranging from an immediate decline in money growth of 4 percentage points in 1990 (program 1), to a phase-in over an eight-year period starting in 1991 (program 4). In all cases except program 3, the policy is assumed to be fully credible, in the sense

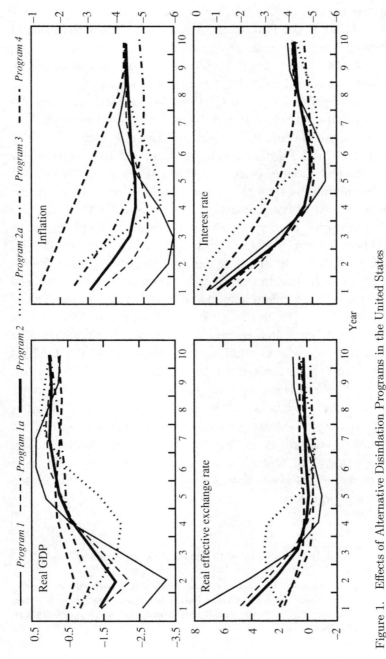

Figure 1. Effects of Alternative Disinflation Programs in the United States

Notes: The interest rate panel shows the percentage point deviation from baseline of the short-term nominal interest rate. The inflation panel shows the percentage point deviation from baseline of the rate of change of the absorption deflator. The other two panels show percent deviation from baseline. The programs are described in Table 4a.

that future reductions in money growth are anticipated at the time the policy is announced. For program 3, it is assumed that agents expect observed declines in money growth to continue indefinitely; as the program is phased in gradually, their expectations of future money growth are too high during the phase-in period.[31]

In the case of program 1, real GDP in the United States falls by 2.4 percent on impact and by a cumulative 7.9 percent over the first five years of the simulation. To understand the role played by price stickiness in the MULTIMOD results, it is useful to first consider those of a classical flexible price model where output is always at potential. In this model — which corresponds to having an infinite parameter on the capacity utilization rate in the MULTIMOD price equation — the price level jumps in each period to keep output at potential. There are two reasons why the price level changes: the first is to match the decline in nominal money balances associated with lower money growth; the second is to accommodate the increased demand for real money balances associated with a lower equilibrium nominal interest rate. The second effect — which is associated below with the "re-entry" problem — implies that the initial decline in the inflation rate exceeds its equilibrium decline. The MULTIMOD money demand function implies a total fall in the equilibrium price level in the first year of the simulation of about 14 percent: 4 percent to keep *real* money balances at their baseline level, and another 10 percent to accommodate the rise in real balances associated with a 4 percentage point decline in the nominal interest rate. Real interest rates are unchanged because both nominal interest rates and expected inflation beyond the initial period have fallen by 4 percentage points.[32]

---

[31]There are, of couse, other ways to model credibility. See, for instance, Calvo and Végh (1990).

[32]The real exchange rate would also be unchanged. The open interest parity condition implies that the real exchange rate depends on the differential between the domestic and foreign real interest rate; if real interest rates are unaffected, so is the real exchange rate.

The MULTIMOD results differ from those of the classical model because both the price level and the inflation rate are sticky. The inertia in the initial stages of a disinflationary process implies that current period inflation does not fall by the same amount as expected future inflation. As a result, the price level initially falls by less in MULTIMOD than in the long run. In the case of program 1, for instance, the GNP deflator drops by 3.9 percent on impact, compared to the 14 percent decline in the long run. This limits the decline in the short-term nominal interest rate to 60 basis points in the first year of the simulation, while expected inflation falls by about 5 percentage points. The resulting rise in real interest rates lowers domestic spending; in addition, the induced appreciation of the real exchange rate causes a deterioration in real net exports. It takes about five years for the negative effects on aggregate demand to wear off and for output to return to baseline.

The role of price stickiness in generating output losses can be reduced either by preannouncing the policy prior to reducing the money growth rate, or by phasing in the policy to achieve a more gradual reduction in inflation. Program 1a assumes a reduction in money growth that is (credibly) preannounced in year 1, but only implemented in year 2. The price level initially falls in anticipation of future declines in money growth; since actual money balances remain unchanged in year 1, the short-term interest rate drops by 160 basis points, as opposed to only 60 basis points under program 1 (Fig. 1). The appreciation of the real effective exchange rate is also reduced, from almost 8 percent in program 1 to 5 percent in program 1a. Both of these factors moderate the decline in demand and output: the total output loss over the first five years is 6.0 percent, as opposed to 7.9 percent.

Program 2 has reductions in money growth of 1 percentage point in the first year of the simulation, rising linearly to 4 percentage points in the fourth year. The steady decline in money growth rates is assumed to be fully anticipated when the policy is introduced. The output loss in this case is 5.2 percent over the first five years, about two thirds that observed in program 1.

Program 2a specifies the same phased reduction in money growth, but starting in the second year as opposed to the first year; this further reduces the five-year output loss to 3.5 percent. Finally, program 4 specifies an eight-year phase-in period for the reduction in money growth, lowering the output loss to only 1.9 percent. The sensitivity of the output loss to the disinflationary program is moderately reduced when a ten-year horizon is considered, as the gradual programs tend to postpone some of the cost to the later years.

These simulations, then, suggest that the output cost of disinflationary policies can be reduced by phasing in or preannouncing the policy, as long as the policy is fully credible. This may be implausible when the program is either not implemented immediately (program 1a), or is phased in over time (programs 2 and 2a). To evaluate the sensitivity of the results to incomplete policy credibility, program 3 assumes the same phased-in path of monetary deceleration as program 2. Expectations, however, adjust only to observed declines in the money growth rate, as opposed to announced future declines.

Specifically, the decline in expected future money growth is initially limited to the observed decline of 1 percentage point in year 1. In year 2 agents are surprised, as money growth falls 2 percentage points below baseline. By year 4, money growth has stabilized at 4 percentage points below baseline and expectations have become consistent with the actual stance of policy. The initial output loss is about one fourth that in program 1, in line with the reduction in the size of the expected money growth shock. While the initial output cost is smaller, so is the adjustment of the price level. The sequence of surprises implied by declining money growth rates beyond the first year, then, requires further price adjustment. In the event, the cumulative output loss over the first five years is 7.2 percent, almost as large as when the cut in money growth is implemented immediately. This suggests that the potential benefits from a phasing-in of disinflationary policies can be negated if the credibility of the policy suffers as a result.

The costs of disinflation also depend on how much inertia there is in the inflationary process, which is inversely related to δ, the parameter on led inflation. As discussed in Section 4, the historical

Models of Inflation and the Costs of Disinflation 85

evidence is consistent with a value of slightly under $1/2$. At the same time, it is interesting to examine the sensitivity of the results to different values for this parameter, both to verify the theoretical results presented in Section 3, and to examine the impact of more forward- or backward-looking behavior on output costs. Simulations were performed in which it varied from $1/4$ to 1, the latter representing the limiting case when there is no inflation stickiness.[33]

The results are shown in Table 5 for programs 1 and 2. For both programs, the cumulative output loss tends to fall as the parameter on future inflation rises. It is also apparent that the reduction in the loss is not uniform across disinflation programs: for program 1, raising the parameter from $1/2$ to 1 cuts the five-year loss in output from 7.1 percent to 5.8 percent, whereas for program 2 the loss falls from 4.0 percent to 0.4 percent. The reason for the different reductions in the output loss for the two programs involves the path followed by the inflation rate. When the weight on future inflation is 1, the inflation rate is not sticky and no output loss (or gain) is associated with "jumping" from an initial inflation rate to some arbitrary new rate, as long as it is expected to remain constant. When the decline in money growth is phased in gradually, inflation falls in the first year by 4.6 percentage points, close to the path consistent with a zero output loss when the parameter on future inflation is 1. When money growth is immediately reduced by 4 percentage points, the inflation rate overshoots its long-run level, falling by 6.9 percentage points in the first year of the simulation, then rising gradually back to its equilibrium level of 4 percentage points below baseline. This undershooting of the inflation rate reduces the benefits associated with having a higher weight on future inflation.

It is of interest to compare the output losses in these disinflation scenarios with estimates of what has occurred historically. A useful shorthand measure is the "sacrifice ratio" of percent output loss per

---

[33] Simulations were also run with a parameter of zero on future inflation, consistent with fully backward-looking models of price behavior. These results are not shown in Table 5, because, for some of the disinflation programs, the simulations exhibited potentially explosive cyclical behavior.

Table 5. U.S. GDP Losses for Alternative Disinflation Programs with Different Degrees of Inflation Stickiness (Percent Deviation from Baseline)

Program	Value of δ	Year								Sum: Five Years	Sum: Ten Years
		1	2	3	4	5	6	7	8		
1	0.25	-2.8	-4.1	-3.0	-1.4	-0.0	0.8	0.9	0.7	-11.3	-9.0
	0.50	-2.2	-2.9	-1.6	-0.5	0.2	0.3	0.2	-0.1	-7.1	-7.0
	0.75	-1.9	-2.2	-1.2	-0.4	-0.1	-0.0	-0.1	-0.2	-5.9	-6.6
	1.00	-1.7	-2.0	-1.2	-0.6	-0.3	-0.2	-0.3	-0.3	-5.8	-7.0
2	0.25	-1.6	-2.5	-2.1	-1.5	-0.8	-0.2	0.1	0.2	-8.5	-8.2
	0.50	-1.2	-1.5	-0.9	-0.4	-0.1	-0.0	-0.1	-0.1	-4.0	-4.3
	0.75	-0.8	-0.8	-0.2	0.1	0.1	0.0	-0.1	-0.1	-1.7	-2.0
	1.00	-0.6	-0.4	0.1	0.3	0.2	0.1	-0.1	-0.1	-0.4	-0.7

Models of Inflation and the Costs of Disinflation 87

percentage point reduction of inflation. Estimates of the sacrifice ratio for disinflations in the United States range from 3 to 18 (Sachs (1985)); for a typical estimate (a sacrifice ratio of 6), see Gordon and King (1982). In our scenarios, the fall in inflation is always 4 percentage points, so the cumulative output losses can be divided by 4 to obtain a sacrifice ratio. It can be seen from Table 4b that our estimates do not exceed 2 — at the bottom end of other estimates. However, it should be emphasized that our results imply that the sacrifice ratio is not a unique number; it depends also on the phase-in, on the extent of preannouncement, and on the credibility of the disinflation program. It could be that our estimate of output losses is low because the extent of inflation stickiness is underestimated: $\delta = 0.25$ would give a sacrifice ratio of 3 for program 1 (Table 5). A "cold turkey" disinflation without credibility (a combination of programs 1 and 3 in Table 4b) could generate even higher sacrifice ratios.[34]

U.S. disinflationary policies also affect the economies of other industrialized countries. Three channels are at work: the impact of the reduction in U.S. economic activity on the demand for their exports of trading partners; the *increased* demand for their exports arising from the real appreciation of the U.S. dollar; and the transmission abroad of the rise in U.S. real interest rates. It turns out that the effects of these factors on the real output of the other industrialized countries are roughly offsetting, as shown in Table 6. Their output declines slightly on impact, and is roughly unchanged in subsequent years. Even for a country as closely tied to the U.S. economy as Canada, the net effect is relatively small; the principal impact being a jump in the rate of change of the absorption deflator in the first year in response to the depreciation of the Canadian dollar.

Another question related to international spillovers is whether the output costs of a disinflationary policy depend on the policies

---

[34]Fischer (1986, Chapter 7), indicated sacrifice ratios of 1.9–3.7 (assuming perfect credibility) for a simple model with three-year contracts. He concluded that imperfect credibility is required to square the model with historical disinflation experience.

Table 6. MULTIMOD Simulation of the Effects on Other Industrial Countries of an Immediate Cut in U.S. Money Growth (Program 1) (Percent Deviation from Baseline)

Country	Year					Sum: Five Years
	1	2	3	4	5	
Other industrial countries — total Real GDP	−0.2	0.0	0.0	0.0	0.0	−0.2
Absorption inflation (percentage points)	0.6	−0.2	−0.3	−0.2	0.0	
Real effective exchange rate	−1.5	−0.7	−0.1	0.3	0.4	
Canada Real GDP	−0.2	−0.3	−0.1	0.1	0.2	−0.3
Absorption inflation (percentage points)	2.0	−0.7	−0.9	−0.6	−0.1	
Real effective exchange rate	−2.9	−1.7	−0.9	−0.4	−0.1	

pursued by other countries. For instance, are the costs of disinflating in Canada independent of whether the United States disinflates or not? The answer is suggested by the results in Table 6, which indicate that Canada is little affected by disinflation in the United States. This was confirmed by simulating disinflation programs in Canada with and without similar policies being pursued in the United States. The output loss for Canada of program 1 amounted to 8.1 percent over the first five years of the shock in the absence of a disinflation program in the United States; the loss was raised to 8.3 percent when both countries pursued program 1. The difference is similar to the change in Canadian output when the United States alone disinflates. The implication is that the output cost of disinflationary policies is not significantly affected by the disinflationary objectives of other countries. One caveat is that the credibility of the domestic policy is assumed to be unaffected by monetary policies pursued in other countries. In this context, pursuing disinflationary policies jointly with other countries would reduce the output cost if their credibility were enhanced as a result — as indicated by the results for the United States reported in Table 4b.

5.2. Effects of More Flexible Labor Markets: The Case of Japan

The evidence in Section 4 suggested that Japan may have more flexible labor markets than the other industrial countries, as reflected in larger coefficients on both capacity utilization and relative prices. Specifically, the pooled estimates give coefficients of 0.306 on the contemporaneous rate of change of the absorption price and 0.285 on the capacity utilization rate; when the Japanese coefficients are allowed to differ from those for the other regions, they are 0.675 and 0.240, respectively. After transforming capacity utilization coefficients to give estimates of β in equation (30) (by dividing by $1 - a2$), they equal 0.411 in the pooled case and 0.738 for Japan alone. One interpretation is that Japan has shorter contract lengths than the other countries, leading to a greater responsiveness of inflation to current economic conditions. This should reduce the output costs of a disinflationary policy by making Japan behave more like the purely classical economy discussed above. Indeed, as contracts become entirely contemporaneous, the parameter on capacity utilization becomes infinite.

The results of simulations for Japan using both the original and higher parameters are shown in Table 7. When programs 1 and 2 are simulated using the original equation, the output costs are slightly higher than those for the United States. Raising the parameters to their alternative values reduces the cumulative five-year output loss by about 30 percent for both programs 1 and 2. Greater price flexibility also leads to a sharper fall in inflation. Taking program 1 as an example, the rate of inflation initially drops by 5.8 percentage points with the higher parameters, as opposed to 4.6 with the lower parameters.

5.3. Exchange Rate Targeting Versus Monetary Targeting

The disinflation programs discussed above have all been implemented through lower targets for domestic money growth. Alternatively, the authorities could use an exchange rate target to reduce inflation.

Table 7. Japanese GDP Losses with Different Degrees of Price Flexibility (Percent Deviation from Baseline)

Program	Year							Sum: Five Years	Sum: Ten Years
	1	2	3	4	5	6	7		
1									
Equation (1)	−2.2	−3.0	−2.1	−1.1	−0.3	0.1	0.1	−8.7	−9.2
Equation (2)	−1.7	−2.1	−1.3	−0.7	−0.3	−0.2	−0.2	−6.0	−7.0
2									
Equation (1)	−1.2	−1.7	−1.3	−0.9	−0.6	−0.4	−0.3	−5.8	−7.0
Equation (2)	−0.9	−1.2	−0.9	−0.6	−0.5	−0.4	−0.3	−4.1	−5.5

Note: Equations: (1) $\Delta P = (1 - 0.306)(0.577\Delta P_{-1} + 0.423\Delta P_{+1}) + 0.306\Delta PA + 0.285(CU/100 - 1)$

(2) $\Delta P = (1 - 0.675)(0.570\Delta P_{-1} + 0.423\Delta P_{+1}) + 0.675\Delta PA + 0.240(CU/100 - 1)$.

Models of Inflation and the Costs of Disinflation 91

When the value of the domestic currency is fixed in terms of the currency of a trading partner with a lower inflation rate, the domestic rate of inflation will converge over time to that of the trading partner, absent an ongoing change in the real exchange rate. Under an exchange rate target, the domestic money supply would be endogenously adjusted to prevent the exchange rate from moving out of a target band.

There are three potential advantages to disinflating through exchange rate targeting as opposed to money targeting. The first involves the credibility of the policy. The private sector may view the institutional arrangements associated with pegging the exchange rate, such as the exchange rate mechanism (ERM) of the EMS, as being more binding on the monetary authorities than stated objectives for domestic money growth (Giavazzi and Pagano (1988) and Horn and Persson (1988)). The second advantage relates to the re-entry problem discussed above. The lower nominal interest rates associated with lower inflation raise the demand for real money balances (provided the demand for money depends negatively on the level of interest rates). With money targeting, this requires a once-and-for-all decline in the price level in addition to that associated with the reduction in money growth.[35] The additional downward effect on prices increases the output costs of the disinflationary policy. With a credible exchange rate target, in contrast, the nominal money supply shifts upward to accommodate higher money demand, reducing the downward pressure on prices and the associated output cost.[36]

The third advantage of the exchange rate is that it is directly observable, unlike the money supply which is typically published only once a month and with some delay, and hence an exchange rate target conveys more information (Bruno (1990)). The complicated

---

[35]Fischer (1986, Chapter 8) argued for the use of an exchange rate target in stabilization programs for this reason.

[36]It may also alter the timing of output losses. Calvo and Végh (1990) contrasted money-based stabilizations (recession now) with those based on exchange rates (recession later). Végh (1991) surveyed the experience of several Latin American countries and Israel, finding that the stabilizations based on exchange rates produced initial booms.

dynamics of money demand moreover may make interpretation of money targets difficult.

There are two *disadvantages* to exchange rate targeting. The first is the inability of the domestic monetary authorities to offset external shocks through changes in the nominal exchange rate as opposed to changes in domestic wages and prices.[37] This problem becomes less important the more highly integrated is the domestic economy with that of the country to whose currency the domestic currency is pegged — in particular, the greater is the extent of factor mobility and bilateral trade between them.[38] The second disadvantage, related to the first, is that for some countries, the trading partner with which they are most highly integrated may not have a lower inflation rate. For instance, the Canadian economy is strongly linked to the U.S. economy, but both countries have similar inflation rates; pegging the Canadian dollar to the U.S. dollar would not allow Canada to disinflate, unless the United States also chose to do so.

These considerations suggest that exchange rate targeting is more attractive when domestic inflation is initially higher than that in a major trading partner. This has been the case in the ERM. By establishing fixed parities versus the deutsche mark (or, more precisely, resisting downward realignments of those parities), non-German members, such as France, have successfully reduced their inflation rates to German levels. More recently, the entry of the United Kingdom into the ERM was designed to help achieve a reduction of high U.K. rates of inflation. The alternative for the United Kingdom would be to disinflate by tightening monetary conditions independently of the behavior of the exchange rate.

To examine the output costs of these alternative policies, simulations were run where a 4 percentage point reduction in the U.K. inflation rate was achieved by exchange rate versus money supply

---

[37] The conditions under which the exchange rate instrument can be abandoned without incurring much of a cost are discussed in the optimum currency area literature, pioneered by Mundell (1961). This issue is also considered in Fischer (1986, Chapter 8).

[38] For a survey of issues involved in currency unions, see Masson and Taylor (1991).

targeting (see also Bayoumi and Chadha (1991)). The exchange rate target was designed to be broadly consistent with a narrow-band ERM arrangement; a parity value for the pound sterling was established in terms of the deutsche mark that generated a 4 percent a year appreciation of the pound relative to its baseline path (which assumed a continual depreciation of the pound relative to the deutsche mark). Fluctuations in the exchange rate were restricted to a narrow range around this parity value.[39]

The results are shown in Table 8. For program 1, the output loss is cut almost in half under an exchange rate target compared to a money target.[40] The cycle in output is somewhat longer, however, with the cumulative loss over ten years rising from 4.7 to 4.8 percent, as opposed to falling from 8.3 to 7.2 percent under a money target. The reduction in the output loss is consistent with the paths of the inflation rate in the initial years of the simulation: the average inflation rate in years 1 and 2 falls by 5 percentage points (relative to baseline) with a money target, as opposed to 2.8 percentage points with an exchange rate target. As discussed above, the difference results from the price level adjustment needed to accommodate the higher demand for real money balances with a money target. The difference in output costs is even more evident when disinflation is phased in, as in program 2. This is because the costs associated with the re-entry phenomenon for a money target are similar for programs 1 and 2, whereas they are not relevant for an exchange rate target.

These simulations underline the importance of the re-entry problem in determining the costs of disinflation under a money target. To some extent, this is an artifact of the path specified for the money supply, which makes no allowance for the one-time

---

[39]The details of how the ERM is incorporated in MULTIMOD are discussed in Masson, Symansky, and Meredith (1990).

[40]In contrast to Calvo and Végh (1990), however, the exchange-rate-based disinflation is not associated with a boom in output. In their model, currency substitution between home and foreign money implies an expansion in output, but that effect is not present in MULTIMOD, which contains conventional money demand functions.

Table 8. U.K. GDP Losses with Exchange Rate Targeting Versus Monetary Targeting (Percent deviation from baseline)

Program				Year					Sum: Five Years	Sum: Ten Years
	1	2	3	4	5	6	7	8		
1										
Money target	−1.1	−2.8	−2.4	−1.5	−0.5	0.2	0.4	0.4	−8.3	−7.2
Exchange rate target	−0.3	−1.0	−1.2	−1.2	−1.0	−0.6	−0.2	0.1	−4.7	−4.8
2										
Money target	−0.6	−1.6	−1.4	−1.0	−0.6	−0.3	−0.0	0.0	−5.2	−5.4
Exchange rate target	−0.1	−0.2	−0.4	−0.6	−0.7	−0.7	−0.5	−0.3	−1.9	−3.6

increase in money demand resulting from lower interest rates. If the monetary authorities could accommodate the initial rise in money demand without jeopardizing the credibility of the policy, then the output losses associated with the two targeting regimes would be closer. Indeed, if the authorities could credibly commit policy to the same path for the money supply as is implied under an exchange rate target, the two simulations would give identical results. However, the fact that disinflation would be accompanied by periods of accelerating money growth might be very hard to justify in a context of intermediate targeting of the money supply.

6. Conclusions

This paper has examined the transitional output costs of disinflationary policies. These costs depend critically on the form of the Phillips curve. The well-known staggered contracts models of Taylor (1979, 1980) and Calvo (1983a, 1983b) emphasize the predetermination of individual nominal wages and prices, which are revised at discrete intervals of time in an asynchronous manner. Agents are assumed to be forward looking and to set a wage in accordance with expectations of future price and output developments for the duration of the interval between revisions. The overlapping nature of the wage-setting process results in an aggregate price level that is sticky. There is, however, no inherent inertia in the rate of change of the aggregate price level — the rate of inflation. Hence, these models typically imply a rapid convergence of inflation rates to their new levels, with little or no output losses for relatively rapid decelerations in monetary growth. At the other extreme, if wage setters were purely backward looking (that is, expectations were adaptive), there would be complete inflation stickiness.

A general form of the inflation equation, with inflation determined in part by the past rate of inflation and in part by expectations of future inflation, was estimated using pooled cross-section, time-series data for the major industrial countries. The hypotheses that inflation was determined only (1) by expectations of future inflation as implied by the rational staggered contracts models where only the aggregate price level is sticky, or (2) by past rates of inflation, as implied by the traditional Phillips curve models with adaptive expectations, were both convincingly rejected by the data. The estimates support, therefore, an inflation equation in which inflation is determined as a weighted average of past and future expected inflation.

The output costs of disinflation in a model with such a Phillips curve were examined analytically. It was shown that there is a critical value for the relative importance of the forward-looking component above which a disinflation path with zero output losses is possible. Such a disinflation path, if it exists, was shown to imply a monotonic decline in the rate of inflation. The path for the money supply, however, was shown not to be monotonic, because the money stock needs to rise initially in order to accommodate increased money demand accompanying the new lower rate of inflation and avoid the re-entry problem.

The effects of alternative disinflation policies were illustrated by simulations using MULTIMOD, the Fund's multiregion macroeconometric model. The results indicate that the output costs of a disinflationary policy are smaller (2) if the policy is announced in advance; (2) the more gradually the deceleration is phased in; (3) the more credible is the policy of disinflation; (4) (given credibility) the greater is the relative importance of expected future inflation in determining current inflation; and (5) the greater is the responsiveness of prices and wages to demand conditions. The international spillover effects of a unilateral disinflation in the United States were examined and were found to be largely offsetting and, on balance, small. Finally, the effects of disinflating with an exchange rate target rather than a money supply target were examined. It was shown that such a policy could avoid the re-entry problem, since the money supply would be endogenous at the targeted rate and any increase in money demand accompanying the lower inflation rate would be automatically accommodated without requiring a downward adjustment in the level of prices.

Acknowledgments

The authors are grateful to Ernesto Hernández-Catá for encouraging them to work in this area, to Joseph Gagnon and Ralph Tryon for discussions of the issues, and to Charles Adams, David Coe, Steven Symansky, and seminar participants at the Reserve Bank of Australia for their comments.

References

Backus, David K., Patrick J. Kehoe, and Finn E. Kydland, "International Borrowing and World Business Cycles," Working Paper 426R (Minneapolis, Minnesota: Federal Reserve Bank of Minneapolis, October 1989).

Ball, Laurence M., "Credible Disinflation with Staggered Price Setting," NBER Working Paper No. 3555 (Cambridge, Massachusetts: National Bureau of Economic Research, December 1990).

Ball, Laurence M., "The Genesis of Inflation and the Costs of Disinflation," NBER Working Paper No. 3621 (Cambridge, Massachusetts: National Bureau of Economic Research, February 1991).

Barro, Robert J., "A Theory of Monopolistic Price Adjustment," *Review of Economic Studies*, Vol. 39 (January 1972), pp. 17–26.

Bayoumi, Tamim, and Bankim Chadha, "The Transition Effects of Entry into the ERM" (unpublished; Washington: International Monetary Fund, May 1991).

Blanchard, Olivier, "Price Asynchronization and Price Level Inertia," in *Inflation, Debt and Indexation*, ed. by Rudiger Dornbusch and Mario Simonsen (Cambridge, Massachusetts: MIT Press, 1983).

Bruno, Michael, "High Inflation and the Nominal Anchors of an Open Economy," *NBER Working Paper No. 3518* (Cambridge, Massachusetts: National Bureau of Economic Research, November 1990).

Bryant, Ralph C., Dale W. Henderson, Gerald Holtham, Peter Hooper, and Steve Symansky, eds., *Empirical Macroeconomics for Interdependent Economies* (Washington: The Brookings Institution, 1988).

Cagan, Philip, "The Monetary Dynamics of Hyperinflation," in *Studies in the Quantity Theory of Money*, ed. by Milton Friedman (Chicago: University of Chicago Press, 1963).

Calvo, Guillermo Antonio, "Staggered Prices in a Utility-Maximizing Framework," *Journal of Monetary Economics*, Vol. 12 (September, 1983a), pp. 383–398.

Calvo, Guillermo Antonio, "Staggered Contracts and Exchange Rate Policy," in *Exchange Rates and International Macroeconomics*, ed. by Jacob A. Frenkel (Chicago: University of Chicago Press, 1983b).

Calvo, Guillermo Antonio and Carlos Végh, "Credibility and the Dynamics of Stabilization: A Basic Framework," *IMF Working Paper 90/110* (Washington: International Monetary Fund, November 1990).

Chadha, Bankim, "Is Increased Price Inflexibility Stabilizing?" *Journal of Money,Credit and Banking*, Vol. 21 (November 1989), pp. 481–497.

Coe, David (1985), "Nominal Wages, the NAIRU and Wage Flexibility," *OECD Economic Studies*, No. 5, pp. 87–126.

Commission of the European Communities, "One Market, One Money," *European Economy*, No. 44 (Brussels: October 1990).

Cumby, Robert, John Huizinga, and Maurice Obstfeld, "Two-Step Two-Stage Least Squares Estimation in Models With Rational Expectations," *Journal of Econometrics*, Vol. 21 (April 1983), pp. 333–355.

Fischer, Stanley, "Long-Term Contracts, Rational Expectations, and the Optimal Money Supply," *Journal of Political Economy*, Vol. 85 (February 1977), pp. 191–205.

Fischer, Stanley, *Indexing,Inflation,and Economic Policy* (Cambridge, Massachusetts: MIT Press, 1986).

Gallant, A. Ronald and Dale Jorgenson, "Statistical Inference for a System of Simultaneous, Non-Linear, Implicit Equations in the Context of Instrumental Variable Estimation," *Journal of Econometrics*, Vol. 11 (October/December 1979), pp. 275–302.

Giavazzi, Francesco, and Marco Pagano, "The Advantage of Tying One's Hands: EMS Discipline and Central Bank Credibility," *European Economic Review*, Vol. 32 (1988), pp. 1055–1075.

Gordon, Robert J., and Stephen R. King, "The Output Cost of Disinflation in Traditional and Vector Autoregressive Models," *Brookings Papers on Economic Activity: 1* (Washington: The Brookings Institution, 1982), pp. 205–242.

Gray, Jo-Anna, "On Indexation and Contract Length," *Journal of Political Economy*, Vol. 86 (February 1978), pp. 1–18.

Grubb, Dennis, Richard Jackman, and Richard Layard, "Wage Rigidity and Unemployment in OECD Countries," *European Economic Review*, Vol. 21 (March/April 1983), pp. 11–39.

Hodrick, Robert, and Edward C. Prescott, "Post-War U.S. Business Cycles: An Empirical Investigation," Carnegie-Mellon University Discussion Paper No. 451 (Pittsburgh: Carnegie-Mellon University, November 1980).

Horn, Henrik, and Torsten Persson, "Exchange Rate Policy, Wage Formation and Credibility," *European Economic Review*, Vol. 32 (October 1988), pp. 1621–1636.

International Monetary Fund, *World Economic Outlook*, World Economic and Financial Surveys (Washington: International Monetary Fund, May 1990).

Lipsey, Richard G., ed., *Zero Inflation: The Goal of Price Stability* (Ottawa: C.D. Howe Institute, 1990).

Masson, Paul R., Steven Symansky, and Guy Meredith, *MULTIMOD Mark II: A Revised and Extended Model*, IMF Occasional Paper No. 71 (Washington: International Monetary Fund, July 1990).

Models of Inflation and the Costs of Disinflation

Masson, Paul R., and Mark P. Taylor, "Common Currency Areas and Currency Unions: An Analysis of the Issues" (unpublished; Washington: International Monetary Fund, September 1991); forthcoming in *Journal of International and Comparative Economics*.

Mundell, Robert, "A Theory of Optimum Currency Areas," *American Economic Review*, Vol. 51 (September 1961), pp. 657–665.

Mussa, Michael (1981a), "Sticky Individual Prices and the Dynamics of the General Price Level," in *The Costs and Consequences of Inflation*, ed. by Karl Brunner and Allan H. Meltzer, Carnegie-Rochester Conference Series on Public Policy, Vol. 15, pp. 261–296.

Mussa, Michael (1981b), "Sticky Prices and Disequilibrium Adjustment in a Rational Model of the Inflationary Process," *American Economic Review*, Vol. 71 (December), pp. 1020–1027.

Obstfeld, Maurice, and Kenneth Rogoff, "Exchange Rate Dynamics with Sluggish Prices Under Alternative Price Adjustment Rules," *International Economic Review*, Vol. 25 (February 1984), pp. 159–174.

Parkin, Michael, "The Output-Inflation Trade-Off When Prices Are Costly to Change," *Journal of Political Economy*, Vol. 94 (February 1986), pp. 200–224.

Phelps, Edmund S., "Disinflation Without Recession: Adaptive Guideposts and Monetary Policy," *Weltwirtschaftliches Archiv*, Vol. 114, No. 4 (1978), pp. 783–809.

Rodriguez, Carlos A., "The Argentine Stabilization Plan of December 20," *World Development*, Vol. 10 (September 1982), pp. 801–811.

Romer, David, "Staggered Price Setting with Endogenous Frequency of Adjustment," NBER Working Paper No. 3134 (Cambridge, Massachusetts: National Bureau of Economic Research, 1990).

Sachs, Jeffrey, "The Dollar and the Policy Mix: 1985," *Brookings Papers on Economic Activity: 1* (Washington: The Brookings Institution, 1985), pp. 117–197.

Selody, Jack, "The Goal of Price Stability: A Review of the Issues," Technical Report No. 54 (Ottawa: Bank of Canada, May 1990).

Sheshinski, Eitan, and Yoram Weiss, "Optimum Pricing Policy Under Stochastic Inflation," *Review of Economic Studies*, Vol. 50 (July 1983), pp. 513–530.

Taylor, John B., "Staggered Wage Setting in a Macro Model," *American Economic Review, Papers and Proceedings*, Vol. 69 (May 1979), pp. 108–113.

Taylor, John B., "Aggregate Dynamics and Staggered Contracts," *Journal of Political Economy*, Vol. 88 (February 1980), pp. 1–23.

Taylor, John B., "Union Wage Settlements During a Disinflation," *American Economic Review*, Vol. 73 (December 1983), pp. 981–993.

Végh, Carlos, "Stopping High Inflation: An Analytical Overview," IMF Working Paper 91/107 (November 1991).

Chapter 4

German Unification: What Have We Learned from Multi-Country Models?[*][†]

Joseph E. Gagnon, Paul R. Masson and Warwick J. McKibbin

This study reviews early simulations of the effects of German unification using three different rational expectations multi-country models. Despite significant differences in their structures and in the implementations of the unification shock, the models delivered a number of common results that proved reasonably accurate guides to the direction and magnitude of the effects of unification on key macroeconomic variables. Unification was expected to give rise to an increase in German aggregate demand that would put upward pressure on output, inflation, and the exchange rate, and downward pressure on the current account balance. The model simulations also highlighted contractionary effects of high German interest rates on EMS countries.

---

[*]This chapter originally appeared in *Economic Modelling* (1996), 13(4), 467–497. At time of writing, authors' affiliations were the Board of Governors of the Federal Reserve System (Gagnon), the International Monetary Fund (Masson), and Australian National University and the Brookings Institution (McKibbin).
[†]This paper reflects the views of the authors and should not be interpreted as representing the views of the institutions with which the authors are affiliated.

1. Introduction

The unification of East and West Germany gave rise to one of the largest and most abrupt economic transformations of any major industrial country in the post-war era. Between November 1989 and January 1991, unification went from being almost inconceivable to an established fact. During these months economic and political observers around the world scrambled to assess the likely implications of unification for Germany and the rest of the world.

One approach to exploring the economic implications was through simulation of macroeconometric models. Unification posed a major challenge to modelers, however, because it promised a fundamental structural change to the German — and particularly the East German — economy. This fundamental change was of a nature not observed before. For the first time a socialist planned economy was being transformed into a capitalist market economy, and the transformation was occurring almost overnight.

Given the potential importance of unification for the world economy, from the first there were a number of simulation studies of its effects. However, traditional models with backward-looking expectations were not well suited to the task, because they did not allow for sharp anticipatory movements in asset prices. Already early in 1990 financial markets were trying to anticipate the future effects of unification, before any of its aspects (currency union, fiscal transfers, etc.) had occurred, and this produced a sharp rise in German interest rates.

In this paper, we report on simulation studies prepared early in 1990 using a new generation of forward-looking multi-country models with rational expectations and explicit attention to both stock and flow equilibrium. These models were the MULTIMOD model maintained by Paul Masson and colleagues at the International Monetary Fund; the MSG2 model maintained by Warwick McKibbin at the Brookings Institution; and the MX3 model maintained by Joseph Gagnon at the Board of Governors of the Federal Reserve System. These modeling groups investigated a variety of aspects of German unification with models having some basic similarities but using very different approaches to incorporating the shock of unification into their models.

The goal of this paper is to determine what lessons can be learned by comparing the early model simulations of unification with the macro data for Germany and the rest of the world in the 5 years since unification. The potential lesions can be divided into two categories. First, what aspects of unification were well captured by the models, and can the associated model properties be used to inform policymakers in the future? Second, what aspects of unification were not adequately described by the models, and can modelers improve their future performance? In particular, where the models did not perform well, was this due to government policies that were different from those assumed, or, instead, to structural deficiencies in the models?

2. An Overview of Developments Since Unification

This section provides a capsule summary of the evolution of the main macroeconomic variables since unification in July 1990. For some variables, unification has produced breaks in series, which make interpretation more difficult. Nevertheless, an overall picture emerges of a sharp fall in East German output, followed by a period of sustained growth that is faster than in the West. Investment is relatively strong in the East, but large fiscal transfers continue from West to East. West Germany faced an initial period of strong demand and inflationary pressures, countered by a restrictive monetary policy that raised interest rates in Germany and across Europe, and contributed to strains in the European Monetary System (EMS) and the crises of 1992–93. A European recession occurred in 1992–93, followed by a recovery of growth which nevertheless leaves unemployment high in a number of countries, including Germany.

2.1. *Output and Inflation*

Unification was accompanied by a continuation of the high output growth seen in Germany and in Europe generally in the late 1980s (Fig. 1). However, demand pressures in Germany began to put upward pressure on inflation in Germany, raising the rate of growth of the CPI to almost 6 percent by the end of 1991. The boom in output

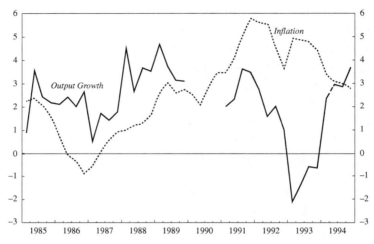

Figure 1. Unified Germany: Output Growth and Inflation, 1985–94, in Four-quarter Percentage Changes. Output Growth Excludes 1990 (Period of German Unification)

Source: IMF World Economic Outlook.

was followed by a short, sharp recession in 1993, with a resumption in growth in 1994.

In East Germany, there was an initial sharp fall in output, as the shift to the market economy made many products uneconomic. However, starting in 1991, annual output growth in the East has been in the 5–10 percent range, consistently higher than in the West (Fig. 2). Output in the East was sustained by strong investment growth (Table 1). Inflation rates in the East were high initially, accompanying major changes in relative prices of various goods and services, as well as large wage increases. By 1994, however, the rate of inflation was comparable to that in the West.

2.2. *Monetary and Exchange Rate Developments*

At the time it was announced in February 1990, the conversion rate of one Ostmark to one Deutschmark (DM) for assets[1] and wages

---

[1]The one-to-one conversion rate applied to a limited amount of monetary claims only — the average conversion rate for the banks' balance sheets was about 1.8 to 1.

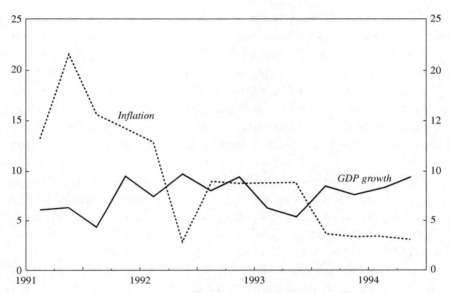

Figure 2. East Germany: Output Growth and Inflation, 1991Q3–1994Q4, in Four-quarter Percentage Changes
Sources: Deutsche Bundesbank, Monthly Report and Statistisches Bundesamt, Volkswirtschaftliche Gesamtrechnungen.

Table 1. East Germany: Composition of Real GDP, Annual Growth Rates, in Percent

	1992	1993	1994
Gross domestic product	7.8	5.8	9.2
Domestic demand	15.0	5.4	7.7
Private consumption	9.6	2.7	4.5
Government consumption	6.8	−1.2	1.8
Investment	27.8	14.1	16.5
Foreign trade balance[a]	−189.9	−199.2	−210.8
Exports	10.2	5.5	22.6
Imports	21.3	5.0	9.4

Note: [a] In DM billion, at 1991 prices.
Source: Statistisches Bundesamt.

generated concerns that this would create inflation as well as make East German salaries uncompetitive. These concerns were soon seen to be unfounded, as the size of the German money supply increase was commensurate with the size of the East German economy. Moreover, though East German salaries were not competitive at the conversion rate, they were made even less competitive by the subsequent actions of the trade unions, which aimed to equalize salaries across Germany and obtained large subsequent wage increases (see below).

Though the conversion of Ostmarks did not present an inflationary problem, the German money supply did grow strongly in the 1991–94 period, at times exceeding 10 percent on a 12-month basis (Fig. 3), as excess demand led to strong growth in nominal income; in addition, there were shifts out of other assets into M3, making the latter a less reliable indicator. Since German monetary targets involved keeping monetary growth for the year in the range of 3.5–5.5 (1992), 4.5–6.5 (1993), and 4–6 (1994), the Bundesbank raised short-term interest rates steadily over the 1990–92 period (Fig. 3, bottom panel).

Interest rates in other European countries also rose over this period, and in particular in countries that participated in the Exchange Rate Mechanism (ERM) of the EMS. These increases in interest rates were accompanied by increased tensions in the ERM, since the cyclical situation of countries outside Germany did not justify the same tight monetary policy pursued by the Bundesbank, leading to doubts about their commitment to their parties against the DM. The September 1992 ERM crisis led to the withdrawal of the U.K. pound and the Italian lira from the ERM and a series of subsequent devaluations of currencies that remained in the mechanism, in particular the Spanish peseta, the Portuguese escudo, and the Irish pound. Further tensions in the summer of 1993 led to the widening of ERM bands to 15 percent early in August, and several currencies depreciated beyond their previous lower margins. As a result, the DM appreciated strongly in 1992–93 in real effective terms, both against ERM currencies and more generally

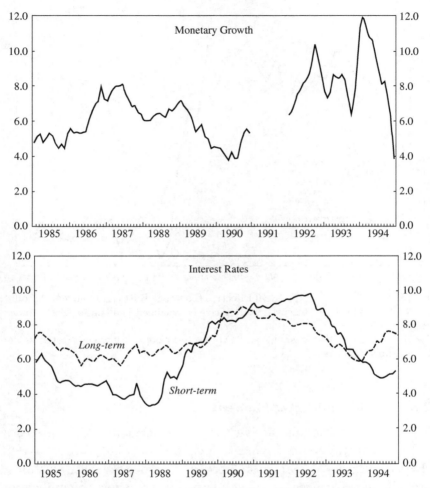

Figure 3. Unified Germany: Monetary Growth and Interest Rates, 1985–94. Monetary Growth Shows 12-month Rate of Change in M3: Excludes 1991 (Period of German Unification)

Source: IMF, Current Economic Indicators Database.

(Fig. 4). Already, strong demand pressures in Germany had led to a sharp decline in its current account position, from a surplus of over 4 percent of GDP in 1989 to a deficit of around 1 percent in the 1991–94 period (Fig. 4).

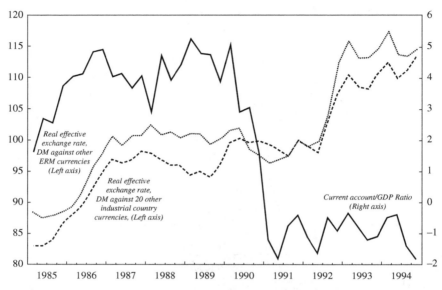

Figure 4. Unified Germany: Real Effective Exchange Rates and Current Account, 1985–94. The Former Measured by Relative Normalized Unit Labor Costs; Index, 1990 = 100
Sources: Deutsche Bundesbank and IMF; International Financial Statistics and Surveillance Database.

2.3. *Wages and Employment*

The boom in economic activity in West Germany led to a steady reduction of the unemployment rate, to about 5.5 percent in 1991 (Fig. 5). Excess demand for labor was associated with sustained growth in real wages. In East Germany, the shock of unification produced a large increase in unemployment, from the negligible levels that prevailed before unification. Despite unemployment rates that were persistently in the 10–20 percent range, real wages grew very strongly in East Germany (Fig. 6). From 1991Q1 to 1994Q4, the average annual increase in real wages was about 13 percent. Thus, initial disparities in unit labor costs were exacerbated by negotiated wage increases, and, as a result, there was no employment growth until 1994, even relative to the low levels of employment that prevailed soon after unification.

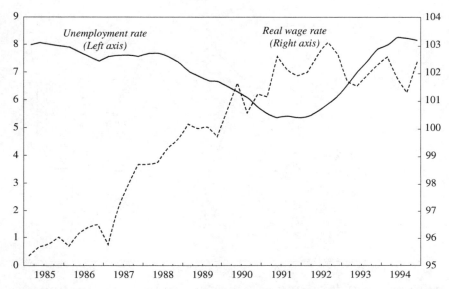

Figure 5. West Germany: Unemployment Rate and Real Wages, 1985–94. Real Wage Rate Shows Business Sector Wage Rate Divided by the GDP Deflator; Index, 1989 = 100

Source: OECD Analytical Database.

2.4. *Fiscal Policy*

It was clear from the start that unification would involve large government transfers from West to the East. However, their size and persistence were greater than most initial estimates. Total transfers, either gross or net of federal taxes paid in East Germany, grew steadily over the 1991–94 period, and by 1995, they constituted 5 percent of West German GDP and 41 percent of East German GDP (Table 2). About 60 percent of the transfers constituted support for consumption and social purposes, and 40 percent was support for public and private investment. The latter includes investment subsidies and grants, accelerated depreciation, and loans for investment purposes on subsidized terms.

Despite the enormous burden on the budget, Germany was relatively successful in limiting the increase in the overall budget deficit, through a combination of cuts in other spending (including low

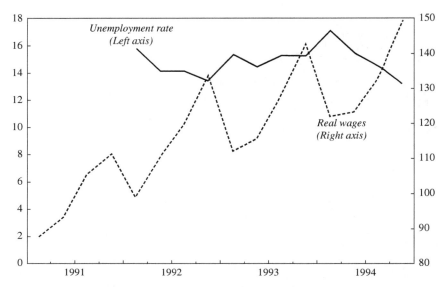

Figure 6. East Germany: Unemployment Rate and Real Wages, 1991–94. Real Wages Shows Hourly Wage Rate Index (1991 = 100) Deflated by Consumer Price Index (1991 = 100)

Source: Deutsche Bundesbank, Monthly Report.

public-sector wage increases), and, especially, through tax increases (Table 3). An important component of the latter was the 'solidarity' surcharge on income tax of 7.5 percent imposed in 1995. As a result, the general government deficit in that year is estimated at 3.6 percent of GDP, despite the inclusion for the first time of debt service costs of the Treuhand (which had been off budget before).

2.5. *Restructuring the East German Economy*

Despite major progress in integrating the East German economy, the tasks remaining are considerable. Clearly, a first priority was to reduce the extent of state ownership and to convert the economy to private ownership. This was the task of the Treuhand, which has restructured, sold, and, where necessary, closed existing state-owned enterprises. Despite initial problems due to the lack of transparency concerning property rights and the need to attempt restitution

German Unification

Table 2. Transfers to East Germany, in DM Billion

	1991	1992	1993	1994	1995
Gross transfers					
Federal government	75	88	114	128	151
Western laender	5	5	10	14	14
German unity fund	31	24	15	5	—
European Union	4	5	5	6	7
Federal labor office	24	25	15	14	14
Pension insurance	—	5	9	14	14
Total	139	152	168	181	200
Receipts					
Taxes and fees	33	37	39	42	45
Net transfers	106	115	129	139	155
Net transfers as a percentage of:					
West German GDP	4.0	4.1	4.5	4.7	5.0
East German GDP	51.4	43.8	42.3	40.5	40.6

Source: Deutsche Bundesbank, Monthly Report, July 1995.

Table 3. Germany: General Government Finances, in Percent of GDP

	1990	1991	1992	1993	1994	1995
Expenditure	42.3	48.9	49.6	50.5	50.1	50.6
Revenue	40.4	45.6	46.7	47.2	47.6	47.0
Fiscal balance	−1.9	−3.3	−2.9	−3.3	−2.5	−3.6

Source: IMF, *World Economic Outlook* Database.

of property expropriated by the former communist regime, it has achieved its mandate, having disposed over 13,000 businesses.

Moreover, new investment has been flowing into East Germany, and there are reports that new plants operating in the eastern part of Germany are as profitable as those in the West. However, average profitability levels clearly remain much below those in the West. Using data on potential output and potential man-hours-worked from the Bundesbank (*Monthly Report,* August 1995), output per man-hour at normal utilization rates amounted in 1994 to 64.4 DM (at 1991 prices) in the West, and only 21.5 DM in the East. Thus,

112   *Joseph E. Gagnon, Paul R. Masson and Warwick J. McKibbin*

East German labor productivity is only about one-third that in the West. Clearly, an extended period of investment is needed to raise the capital stock sufficiently to equalize productivity (and also, presumably, to provide training in areas not emphasized by the former regime). The transition process will also have to involve a reduction in government subsidies and income transfers to the East. Hence the challenges remain large.

3. The Models and Methods of Simulating the Impacts of Unification

In this section, we summarize the models used in the early studies of German unification and give an overview of the approach and results of each of the original studies. This overview is important because the studies were each undertaken independently in a period of great uncertainty about how the unification process was going to develop both politically and economically. The studies focused on important issues that would likely emerge such as the large worsening of the German current account, high interest rates in Germany and rising long-term real interest rates throughout the world, and significant pressure to be placed on countries within the ERM as they attempted to maintain parity while the DM appreciated significantly.

The three models discussed in this paper share a number of common features, which, in turn, generate a high degree of similarity in their simulations of unification. One of the key characteristics that differentiates these three models from many other empirical macroeconomic models is that each assumes that expectations are 'rational' in the sense that expected future variables are set equal to the model's prediction of these variables in the absence of shocks. The models focus on the main components of the national income accounts of individual countries or groups of countries aggregated together. Consumption is determined by expected permanent income and the real long-term interest rate. Investment is driven by the current and expected future marginal product of capital relative to the cost of capital, subject to adjustment costs. Government spending is exogenous, but a tax reaction function stabilizes the ratio of government debt to GDP. Goods produced in different industrial countries are assumed to be imperfect substitutes, so that trade flows respond to relative prices and aggregate demand in the importing country.

In the short-run, output may deviate from potential. In the long-run, prices adjust to return output to its sustainable level, which is a function of capital, labor, and technology. Price adjustment is primarily determined by an expectations-augmented Phillips curve or a forward-looking staggered-contracts model operating either on prices or indirectly through wages. Stocks of physical capital, government debt, and net foreign assets are cumulated from the relevant flow variables. Technology and labor supply are exogenous, at least in the long-run. The long-run equilibrium is essentially that of a Solow growth model. Long-term interest rates are determined by expected future short-term rates. Capital is assumed to be perfectly mobile between industrial countries so that exchange rates obey the open interest parity condition.

The primary areas of differences across the models are the country coverage, the data frequency, the adjustment dynamics, the estimated coefficients, and the specification of monetary policy.

3.1. *MULTIMOD*

MULTIMOD includes separate submodels for each of the Group of Seven countries, for the remaining industrial countries as a group, and for the developing countries (divided into capital exporting and capital importing countries).[2] The model uses annual data. In MULTIMOD, consumption behavior incorporates both a forward-looking permanent income component and a myopic component that responds to current disposable income. The sensitivity of consumption to current income permits fiscal policy to be expansionary, as in traditional Keynesian models, though to an extent that depends on the estimated coefficient of disposable income. In most

---

[2]See Masson, Symansky, and Meredith (1990) for a description of MULTIMOD Mark II.

114   *Joseph E. Gagnon, Paul R. Masson and Warwick J. McKibbin*

submodels, the monetary authority is assumed to move short-term interest rates in response to deviations of the main monetary aggregate from its targeted level. In the case of Germany, this aggregate is M3. In the case of other ERM countries (France, Italy, and the smaller industrial country group) the monetary authority moves the short-term interest rate to limit deviations in the exchange rate from its parity with the DM.

The approach used in simulating German unification in MULTIMOD was to treat the excess of spending over output in East Germany and the migration from the East to the West as the main 'shocks' to the global economy associated with unification.[3] It was assumed that, as of 1990, the scale of the transfers from West Germany to the East was correctly anticipated. No attempt was made to expand MULTIMOD to include East Germany; instead, exogenous inputs were used to quantify the increase in demand for West German goods (and those of other countries) that was expected to result from German unification.

Turning to the magnitude of the shocks, Table 4 presents two sets of assumptions of the fiscal transfers from the West and the increased net import demand in East Germany that were assumed to result from unification.[4] In the first one, which was termed the 'reference case', investment was assumed to proceed at a rapid enough rate to raise output per worker in East Germany to 80 percent of the level in the West by 2001. In the second — less optimistic — scenario, investment in the East was assumed to be lower but saving was also lower, and output per worker reached only 60 percent of West Germany's level in 2001. It was assumed that in the absence of unification, the current account position of East Germany would have been roughly in balance, so the figures in Table 4 constitute

---

[3]See Masson and Meredith (1990a,b). The two studies differ in the following ways: the earlier, unpublished version used preliminary estimates of the size of transfers from West to East Germany that were smaller than those in the published paper by about one-quarter, while the simulation of a 'European monetary policy' was removed from the published version.

[4]These assumptions were based on contemporaneous work by McDonald and Thumann (1990).

German Unification

Table 4. MULTIMOD Simulations of German Unification: Assumptions Concerning the Fiscal Cost and Increased Net Imports of East Germany, in Billions of 1990 DM, Percent of Trend West German GDP in Parentheses

| | Fiscal Transfers from West Germany | | Increased Net Imports of East Germany | |
	Reference Case (1)	Less Optimistic Scenario (2)	Reference Case (3)	Less Optimistic Scenario (4)
1990	95 (3.9)	95 (3.9)	116 (4.7)	116 (4.7)
1991	78 (3.1)	94 (3.7)	127 (5.0)	122 (4.8)
1992–94	42 (1.6)	71 (2.6)	101 (3.7)	103 (3.8)
1995–97	23 (0.8)	53 (1.8)	71 (2.5)	81 (2.8)
1998–2000	−3 (−0.1)	41 (1.3)	31 (1.0)	59 (1.9)
2001	−19 (−0.6)	33 (1.0)	5 (0.2)	43 (1.3)

Source: McDonald and Thumann (1990, Tables 3 and 6) and calculations based on *World Economic Outlook* Database.

additional demands on world saving. The baseline also assumed potential GDP growth of 2 percent in the East and 2.75 percent in the West. It should be noted, by comparison with Table 2, that both the magnitude and the persistence of the transfers to East Germany were greatly underestimated in the simulations.

Another significant aspect of unification was the re-establishment of free mobility between East and West Germany, resulting in substantial westward migration. The last few months of 1989 saw large population flows from the East, and substantial migration continued early in 1990. In the reference scenario, net migration from East to West Germany was assumed to be 280,000 in 1990, 100,000 in 1991, 70,000 in 1992, 40,000 in 1993, and 20,000 a year thereafter. In the less optimistic scenario with lower investment in the East, net migration was assumed to be the same in 1990–91, but to be considerably higher from 1992 onward: 270,000 in that year, 220,000 in 1993, and declining to 90,000 in the year 2001.

Migration was expected to lead to increases in both aggregate demand and supply in West Germany; the corresponding declines in the East were embodied in higher projected net imports. In MULTIMOD potential output is described by a production function that depends on capital and labor with constant returns to scale. For a given capital stock, migration would affect potential output through the induced increase in the labor force times the marginal product of labor; in the longer run, capital should increase with the labor force and potential output rise proportionately. The labor force increase was calculated as the population increase times the participation rate. In the reference case, potential output was projected to be 1.25 percent higher in West Germany by the year 2001 than it would have been in the absence of migration. In the less optimistic scenario, it was projected to be 4 percent higher, as a result of the larger migration.

The simulations highlighted three factors that were important in determining how much of an increase of demand from East Germany would show up in the form of increased output in West Germany, how much as lower combined German net exports, and how much as higher inflation: (1) the stance of monetary policy, (2) the influence of the level of capacity utilization on inflation, and (3) the interest elasticities of domestic components of demand.

It was recognized that the *conduct of monetary policy* could have been affected by currency union because (among other reasons) the income velocity of money might not be the same in the two parts of Germany. Rather than attempting to quantify those effects, it was assumed for the purposes of the simulations that targets would be appropriately adjusted to take into account velocity shifts and other factors that would otherwise affect the relationship between interest rates and economic activity.

Concerning the *effects of an increase in demand on inflation* and output, productive capacity is not an absolute constraint on output in MULTIMOD. Instead, the higher is the rate of capacity utilization, the greater are pressures on inflation. Moreover, the model implies a fairly flat (and linear) output–inflation tradeoff. Alternative simulations using a steeper, nonlinear tradeoff yielded slightly more inflation and slightly less output than the reference scenario, but the overall nature of the results was quite similar.

The effects of the unification shock depend importantly on the *interest elasticities of saving and investment.* The Mark II

German Unification 117

version of MULTIMOD had quite high elasticities. Some other evidence on Germany and other countries suggested that saving and investment might not be as sensitive to interest rates. The MULTIMOD simulations were performed using revised equations for consumption and investment (subsequently incorporated in the standard model) that embodied lower interest-rate effects than in the original Mark II model, making the results more consistent with this empirical evidence.

3.1.1. *The reference scenario (Table 5)*

The reference simulation of unification assumed that net imports into East Germany would increase by amounts given in column 3 of Table 4. This increase in demand was assumed to show up in the first instance in increased exports by West Germany (two-thirds of the amount) and by other countries (the remaining one-third, allocated on the basis of historical shares in imports of West Germany). The combined government deficit as reported here includes all unification-related government expenditures, as well as higher interest payments due both to a larger debt stock and to higher interest rates. In the reference case, tax *rates* are assumed to be the same as in the baseline, which assumes no unification. However, tax *revenues* are elastic, and increase roughly in proportion to GDP. The simulations also include the projections of migration from the East to the West described above, and the resulting increases of potential output in the West.

3.1.2. *A less optimistic scenario with slow growth in East Germany (Table 5)*

In an alternative, less optimistic scenario for unification, investment was assumed to be less buoyant. As a result, productivity growth converged less quickly, and by the year 2001, the productivity gap between East and West Germany would still be about 40 percent. Net imports by the East were not very different initially from those in the reference case (see Table 4), but the East's trade deficit would persist longer because output would not rise as much in the medium term. Correspondingly, income and saving are also lower there.

Table 5. MULTIMOD Simulations of German Unification

	United Germany			West Germany				Other ERM Countries	
	GDP[a]	Current Account Balance[b]	General Government Balance[b]	GDP[a]	Inflation[c]	Real Effective Exchange Rate[a]	Real Long-term Interest Rate[c]	GDP[a]	Inflation[c]
(1) Reference scenario									
1990	0.6	−1.3	−2.2	0.6	0.2	1.5	0.7	−0.2	−0.0
1991	2.4	−2.7	−4.4	1.9	0.7	1.8	0.8	−0.1	−0.0
1992–94	4.2	−2.3	−2.7	0.7	0.2	2.0	0.8	−0.4	−0.1
1995–97	8.3	−1.9	−2.1	0.6	−0.2	1.1	0.3	−0.2	0.0
2001	14.5	−0.9	−0.6	0.8	−0.2	−0.5	−0.1	0.2	0.3
(2) Less optimistic scenario									
1990	0.6	−1.3	−2.2	0.6	0.2	1.5	0.7	−0.2	−0.0
1991	1.6	−2.6	−4.8	2.0	0.8	1.8	0.8	−0.0	−0.0
1992–94	2.2	−2.6	−3.8	1.1	0.4	2.0	0.8	−0.3	−0.1
1995–97	4.4	−2.6	−3.7	1.4	−0.1	1.2	0.4	−0.2	0.0
2001	8.1	−2.3	−3.3	2.5	−0.1	−0.2	0.2	0.1	0.2

German Unification — 119

(3) ERM realignment with credibility loss

1990	0.6	−1.3	−2.2	0.6	0.2	1.5	0.7	−0.2	−0.1
1991	2.4	−2.6	−4.4	1.9	0.5	2.6	0.6	0.6	1.3
1992–94	4.2	−2.3	−2.6	0.7	0.3	1.8	0.7	−0.1	1.0
1995–97	8.2	−1.8	−2.2	0.5	−0.2	0.7	0.4	−0.4	0.0
2001	14.5	−0.6	−0.7	0.8	−0.2	−0.9	−0.2	0.2	0.4

Notes: [a] Percent deviation from baseline.
[b] Deviation in percent of baseline GDP. Government balance includes the deficit of the Unity Fund and the Trust Fund (Treuhand).
[c] Percentage point deviation from baseline.
Source: Masson and Meredith (1990b, Tables 4 and 5).

120 *Joseph E. Gagnon, Paul R. Masson and Warwick J. McKibbin*

In this scenario, real incomes are assumed to be lower in East Germany, and emigration higher than in the reference scenario: extra net emigration from the East to the West amounts to 200,000 in 1992, 180,000 in 1993, and gradually declining amounts thereafter (in addition to the projected migration in the reference scenario). Government expenditures in the West are assumed to be higher as a result of the increase in population relative to the reference scenario (due to increased expenditure on housing and social services, for instance). Unemployment benefit payments are also higher in the East, as a result of higher unemployment.

3.1.3. *An ERM realignment (Table 5)*

The reference scenario suggested that an appreciation of the DM of about 4 percent against the US dollar might result from unification. With fixed central parities with respect to other currencies participating in the ERM, real appreciation of the DM resulted from a combination of nominal appreciation against non-ERM currencies (principally the US dollar and the yen), increases in prices in Germany, and a tendency to deflation in other ERM countries. It was suggested in Masson and Meredith (1990b) that the tightening of monetary conditions in other ERM countries might be avoided by a realignment *vis-à-vis* the DM, also in principle permitting a smoother allocation of the increased demand from East Germany among European countries. The upward realignment of the DM would tend to remove some of the short-run pressure on existing capacity in Germany. These favorable effects, it was argued, would however have to be balanced against the negative effects of higher inflation in the short-run in other ERM countries, and consequently a possible loss of credibility of their commitments to price stability and to 'hard currency' policies. A realignment scenario was presented in which a depreciation of 4 percent of the other ERM currencies *vis-à-vis* the DM occurred in 1991, but had unfavorable effects on expectations of future exchange rate movements and inflation differentials. Specifically, the other ERM currencies were expected to depreciate by a further 1.5 percent a year against the DM in the years following the initial realignment, similar to the periodic realignments that were observed in the early years of the EMS.

3.2. *MSG2*

The version of the MSG2 model used in the original study included submodels of the United States, Japan, Germany, the rest of the EMS (REMS), the rest of the OECD, the non-oil developing countries, and the oil-exporting developing countries using annual data.[5] As in MULTIMOD, consumption in MSG2 depends on both permanent income and current disposable income. In most submodels, the monetary authority sets an exogenous path of the main monetary aggregate and the short-term interest rate is determined through the money demand equation. In the REMS submodel the monetary authority pegs the exchange rate to its parity with the DM.

The goal of the study reported in McKibbin (1990) and updated in McKibbin (1992) was to examine the impact on the global economy, in particular global asset markets, of the real transfer required to raise East German living standards toward those of West Germany. In particular the paper focused on the difference between financing the real transfers by fiscal versus monetary measures in Germany and the impact of the ERM on the adjustment of the world economy. The paper attempted to place some preliminary empirical magnitudes on possible alternative scenarios for German unification. The paper focused on the implications for aggregate demand and supply in a unified Germany and how these spill over into the rest of the world. It was not intended to be a precise forecast of the likely outcomes of unification but to focus on alternative scenarios. A further objective was to directly address the debate in the financial press about 'unexplainable' movements of real long-term interest rates and exchange rates from the end of 1989. The paper illustrated that the co-movements of asset prices within countries and between countries depend on the nature of actual and expected shocks.

---

[5] For a description of MSG2, see McKibbin and Sachs (1991).

122   *Joseph E. Gagnon, Paul R. Masson and Warwick J. McKibbin*

The basic hypothesis of the paper was that the policy response of making the East German currency convertible would do little to stem the tide of people moving from East to West. What was inevitable was going to be a transfer of physical capital from West Germany to East Germany in order to raise the marginal product of labor in East Germany. It was argued that this transfer could be accomplished in a variety of ways. Firstly, attracted by lower East German labor costs, private capital could flow into East Germany. Secondly, if wages in East Germany were raised artificially to West German levels, the West German government could effect the transfer of real resources from West to East via direct subsidies to employment in the East so that private capital would find it attractive to invest there despite the lower labor productivity. Under either scenario, there were going to be significant fiscal implications of granting East Germans West-German unemployment and social security benefits.

To understand the different implications for aggregate demand and supply, the paper examined a number of scenarios in turn.

3.2.1. *Fiscal expansion (Table 6)*

With elections looming in West Germany and promises of tax cuts, it was argued that these fiscal measures were likely to be financed through a larger German fiscal deficit. The first scenario considered the consequences of a substantial expected German fiscal expansion resulting from direct subsidies or unemployment compensation paid to East Germany. The fiscal expansion was assumed to equal 1.7 percent of baseline GDP in 1990 and 3.3 percent of baseline GDP from 1991 onwards. These scenarios focused on the implications of expansionary fiscal policy for the West German economy and they modeled the transfer as an increase in West German government consumption that was handed over to East Germans.

3.2.2. *Fiscal expansion with ERM realignment (Table 6)*

The second scenario was the same as scenario 1 except that the DM was allowed to appreciate against the US dollar and against the other

Table 6. MSG2 Model Simulations of Aspects of German Unification

	United Germany			West Germany				Other ERM Countries	
GDP[a]	Current Account Balance[b]	General Government Balance[b]	GDP[a]	Inflation[c]	Real Effective Exchange Rate[a]	Real Long-term Interest Rate[c]	GDP[a]	Inflation[c]
(1) German fiscal expansion (no ERM realignment)									
1990		−1.2	−1.7	−0.8	−1.2	2.2	0.9	−2.0	−1.8
1991		−2.2	−3.3	1.1	−0.3	4.0	1.3	−1.4	−1.5
1992–94		−2.3	−3.3	1.0	0.0	3.8	1.2	−0.6	−0.1
1995–97		−2.4	−3.4	0.9	0.1	3.4	1.2	−0.6	0.1
(2) German fiscal expansion (with ERM realignment)									
1990		−1.8	−1.7	−1.0	−1.5	6.2	0.7	0.0	0.4
1991		−2.8	−3.3	1.2	−0.3	7.0	1.1	−0.5	−0.5
1992–94		−2.9	−3.3	1.0	0.0	6.5	1.1	−0.2	0.1
1995–97		−3.1	−3.4	0.9	0.1	6.0	1.0	−0.3	0.2

(*Continued*)

Table 6. (Continued)

	United Germany			West Germany				Other ERM Countries	
	GDP[a]	Current Account Balance[b]	General Government Balance[b]	GDP[a]	Inflation[c]	Real Effective Exchange Rate[a]	Real Long-term Interest Rate[c]	GDP[a]	Inflation[c]
(3) German monetary expansion (2% increase in rate of growth)									
1990		0.2	0.3	0.9	0.7	−0.6	−0.1	0.9	0.8
1991		0.1	0.4	1.4	1.3	−0.9	−0.3	1.4	1.4
1992–94		0.1	0.6	1.8	1.8	−1.1	−0.4	1.7	1.8
1995–97		0.1	0.6	2.1	1.9	−1.2	−0.5	2.0	1.9
(4) Supply-side effects of full integration (ignoring fiscal and monetary)									
1990	0.8	−2.7	−1.0		−2.1	−11.0	1.2	2.5	1.8
1991	3.4	−2.8	−0.3		−1.6	−12.2	0.9	1.5	0.9
1992–94	5.5	−3.0	0.3		−0.6	−14.3	0.7	1.1	0.3
1995–97	7.2	−3.1	0.8		−0.3	−16.4	0.6	1.0	0.2

Notes: [a]Percent deviation from baseline.
[b]Deviation in percent of baseline GDP.
[c]Percentage point deviation from baseline.
Source: McKibbin (1990, Tables 1 through 4).

ERM currencies which remain approximately unchanged relative to the US dollar.

3.2.3. *Monetary expansion (Table 6)*

The third simulation was a relaxation of German monetary policy. This could be interpreted as the result of currency unification with an unrealistically strong exchange rate for East German prices and wages and no other direct measures for East Germany. In this case, it is likely that a severe slowdown would result in East Germany (still not explicitly part of the model) and that this would lead to pressure on the Bundesbank to ease policy. Abstracting from money demand changes originating in the East, scenario 3 considered an increase in the money growth rate of 2 percent per year.

3.2.4. *Supply-side effects (Table 6)*

The final scenario was intended to capture the possible macroeconomic consequences for the world economy of the supply-side effect of a completely unified Germany; both the East German capital stock and work force were incorporated into the West German economy. This simulation assumed no adjustment in fiscal and monetary policies in the new Germany in excess of the policies in place in West Germany before unification. In other words, the fiscal balance changes little and the money supply was raised by enough to keep German interest rates almost unchanged in the face of the increase in aggregate supply. It assumed that East German labor was integrated into West Germany at the West German wage rate despite a large productivity differential. The stickiness of wages initially led to severe unemployment, despite assuming full employment of existing East German physical capital. In the long-run, wages adjusted and physical capital was put in place to absorb the unemployed according to standard neoclassical growth theory. In the short-run, severe dislocation of resources resulted. This scenario showed the extent of the problem of attempting to integrate two economies with very different productivity levels, quickly and without restrictions. It was argued that the results

126   *Joseph E. Gagnon, Paul R. Masson and Warwick J. McKibbin*

showed clearly that attempting full integration in the way predicted would be potentially disruptive, but it would not automatically be ruled out due to political considerations. It was argued to be a useful benchmark for evaluating alternatives.

3.3. *MX3*

The MX3 model includes submodels of the United States, Germany, Japan, and the rest of the world (ROW) using quarterly data.[6] Unlike MULTIMOD and MSG2, MX3 does not include a component of consumption that is proportional to current disposable income. Instead, consumption in MX3 follows a lagged adjustment to its forward-looking permanent income level. This property makes output in MX3 much less sensitive to fiscal policy than in the other two models. In MX3, the monetary authorities are assumed to move short-term interest rates in response to deviations of a target variable from its targetted level. In the simulations of German unification, monetary policy was assumed to target the price level in most cases.

In MX3, German unification was modeled by augmenting the supply equations in the West German model to include East German factors of production. This modification required not only changing the structure of the supply side but also choosing the baseline levels of important variables and parameters. Choices regarding these magnitudes determine both the speed with which the East German economy converges with the West German economy and the strength of the spillover effects on other countries. The critical assumption was that East Germany brings relatively more labor than capital to the union, creating a substantial differential between the capital–labor ratios in the two regions. As a result, unification increased German aggregate demand — primarily through increased investment and consumption — more than it increased German aggregate supply.

Two studies of German unification were conducted with MX3. The results presented here are drawn from Adams, Alexander, and Gagnon (1993), which is the published version of *International*

---

[6]For a description of the MX3 model, see Gagnon (1991).

Finance Discussion Paper No. 421, January 1991. An earlier study, Alexander and Gagnon (1990), reached similar conclusions but did not consider the implications of unification for ERM countries.[7] One difficulty in examining the effect of unification on ERM countries is that MX3 consolidates the non-German ERM countries with all other countries in the ROW block. The approach taken was to obtain some boundaries on the ERM effect by running simulations in which ROW has a freely floating exchange rate and compare them with simulations in which ROW pegs its exchange rate to Germany's.

The most significant changes to the model involved adding separate expressions for East German capacity, fixed investment, and labor supply. Productive capacity in East Germany was modeled as a Cobb–Douglas function of East German technology, capital, and labor. The East German labor force was set at 30 percent of the West German labor force in 1990 and it was assumed to remain constant over time while the West German labor force was assumed to grow at 0.5 percent per year. East German labor productivity was assumed to be one-third that of West Germany. This lower productivity was modeled as due to both lower technology and a lower capital–labor ratio in East Germany. After unification, the East German technology factor was assumed to exogenously converge to the West German level over 5 years. Alternative simulations were conducted to examine the sensitivity of the results to different assumptions about the level and rate of convergence of East German technology. Investment in East Germany was modeled as a stock-adjustment process designed to gradually raise the East German capital stock until the marginal product of capital was equal to that of West Germany.

---

[7]Other significant differences between the two studies are that the later study assumed lower values for East German capital and technology and it allowed for persistent unemployment in East Germany as unions pressed to catch up to West German wage levels. These differences led to a modest quantitative — but no qualitative — change in the model simulations of key German macroeconomic variables.

In the West German sector of MX3, equilibrium labor supply is simply a constant fraction of the exogenous labor force. In order to model the initial increase in East German unemployment, an 'effective' East German labor supply was constructed that was a negative function of the excess of West German over East German wages. Labor demand in both parts of Germany was determined by aggregate demand in the short-run and by equalizing the marginal product of labor with the real wage in the long-run. Together, labor demand and labor supply implied that the non-accelerating inflation rate of unemployment (NAIRU) would be higher in East Germany as long as wages were lower than in West Germany. There was assumed to be no net migration between the two parts of Germany after 1990.[8]

The simulation results for unified Germany are expressed relative to a baseline in which the labor productivity of East Germany is fixed at one-third that of West Germany. The unification shock is implemented by augmenting the German supply sector as described above and by raising government spending exogenously. These shocks have an immediate effect on private aggregate demand. Consumption increases because the new expectation of a more productive future East Germany raises permanent income. Investment increases due to the higher marginal product of capital in East Germany.

3.3.1. The reference scenario (Table 7)

In the reference scenario, fiscal policy was modeled by setting government spending in unified Germany equal to that of baseline West Germany on a per-worker basis. This implied a large increase in government spending relative to the combined baselines of East and West Germany. Over time, the tax reaction function ensures that the ratio of government debt to GDP returns to its baseline level. In simulations, the tax reaction function eliminated the fiscal deficit more quickly than in the real world, since a large deficit still remains in 1996. Alternative simulations were conducted with

---

[8]An alternative simulation showed that the results for unified Germany were relatively insensitive to migration (1 million workers were assumed to migrate from East to West over a 5-year period).

Table 7. MX3 Simulations of German Unification

	United Germany			West Germany				Other ERM Countries	
	GDP[a]	Current Account Balance[b]	General Government Balance[b]	GDP[a]	Inflation[c]	Real Effective Exchange Rate[a]	Real Long-term Interest Rate[c]	GDP[a]	Inflation[c]
(1) Reference scenario (no ERM)									
1990	0.2	0.3	−3.0	0.1	5.1	0.4	0.0	0.0	
1991	1.1	−0.9	−4.9	0.2	9.7	0.8	0.0	0.0	
1992–94	5.4	−2.6	−1.0	0.0	8.3	0.7	0.0	0.0	
1995–97	12.8	−3.5	1.4	0.0	6.4	0.6	−0.1	0.0	
(2) ERM scenario (ROW pegged to DM)									
1990	0.2	0.0	−3.1	0.1	2.0	0.6	−1.3	−1.7	
1991	0.9	−1.6	−5.1	0.1	6.8	1.2	−3.9	−5.7	
1992–94	5.1	−1.6	−1.0	0.2	11.2	1.4	−3.0	−1.1	
1995–97	12.3	1.0	1.6	0.2	9.0	1.2	−1.1	2.1	
(3) ERM scenario with accommodative German monetary policy									
1990	0.4	0.1	−3.1	0.4	2.2	0.5	−0.9	−1.2	
1991	1.6	−1.3	−5.3	1.3	7.0	0.8	−3.0	−3.9	
1992–94	5.8	−1.8	−1.2	0.5	11.1	0.9	−1.8	−0.8	
1995–97	13.0	−0.5	1.4	−0.4	8.6	0.7	−0.6	0.8	

Notes: [a]Percent deviation from baseline.
[b]Deviation in percent of baseline GDP. Government balance includes the deficit of the Unity Fund and the Trust Fund (Treuhand).
[c]Percentage point deviation from baseline.
Source: Adams, Alexander and Gagnon (1993, Tables A1, A7 and A9).

a more persistent fiscal deficit, but the main conclusions were little affected because the forward-looking consumers in MX3 are only mildly sensitive to the time path of taxes, i.e. MX3 is close to Ricardian equivalence. In the reference scenario, exchange rates are freely floating between all countries.

3.3.2. *ERM scenario (Table 7)*

Scenario 2 augmented scenario 1 with an approximation of the ERM effect. In this scenario, the short-term interest rate in ROW was assumed to target the exchange rate with Germany.

3.3.3. *ERM scenario with accommodative monetary policy (Table 7)*

Scenario 3 combines scenarios 1 and 2 with accommodative German monetary policy. In this scenario the Bundesbank raises its price level target by one percentage point per year for 3 years.

4. Results from the Models and Key Issues Raised in the Early Studies

In Section 3, we outlined three studies, focusing on the characteristics of the models, the approach to modeling unification, and the issues that were addressed. In this section we present some key results from each model and draw out some overall lessons from the studies and their implications for model development and policy formulation. The results from each study depended on the model used as well as the assumptions about likely developments in Germany from 1990 forward. A surprising aspect of the results was that there was a great deal of consensus across these studies about some aspects of unification that subsequently emerged as important issues after the studies were completed. These aspects were ignored by many commentators at the time and are still ignored by some analysts who argue that no one could have foreseen the problems that emerged in unifying the two Germanies.

Tables 5 through 7 present results for a number of variables for each model from 1990 to 1997 or later. Detailed descriptions of each scenario can be found in Section 3. Table 5 contains standardized results for MULTIMOD, Table 6 contains standardized results for MSG2, and Table 7 contains standardized results for MX3. We have selected variables that each model can produce, although in some cases the selected variables were not presented in the original studies. In these cases, the selected variables were calculated using other variables that were included in the original studies. The variables presented are for: United Germany (GDP, current account, and fiscal balance), West Germany (GDP, inflation, real effective exchange rate, and real long-term interest rate), and other ERM countries (GDP and inflation).

Each variable is expressed either as a percent deviation from baseline (e.g. GDP), a percent-of-GDP deviation from baseline (e.g. current account, fiscal balance), or a percentage point deviation from baseline (e.g. inflation, interest rates). Each scenario produced by the models is given a scenario number based on the assumptions discussed in Section 3. The scenario ordering is based on the original studies and is not necessarily the same across models.

These tables can be compared by focusing either on the differences between results or on similarities. However, a true comparative analysis is difficult because each study undertook different simulations under different assumptions about policy responses. Nonetheless, we can draw out the major mechanisms from each model.

First, each study presumed that there would be a significant fiscal expansion in Germany although the size and persistence of the fiscal stimulus varied across models. This aspect of unification is illustrated for MULTIMOD and MX3 in each scenario, and in MSG2 in scenarios 1 and 2. In the MULTIMOD results for scenario 1 and 3 and all the MX3 results the fiscal deterioration lasts for up to 5 years, whereas in the MSG2 scenarios and MULTIMOD scenario 2, the fiscal stimulus is more permanent. Despite these differences in assumptions, the adjustment process is essentially similar across the models. The announcement of the fiscal stimulus in Germany raises long-term and short-term real and nominal interest rates in Germany.

In roughly comparable scenarios real long-term interest rates rise between 80 and 130 basis points in each model.

The rise in interest rates leads to a capital inflow that appreciates the DM in both real and nominal terms. The rise in the real effective exchange rate is somewhat more dispersed across models, ranging from a low of 2 percent for the MULTIMOD reference scenario to a high of 11 percent for the MX3 scenarios that peg the German–ROW exchange rate. The capital inflow and exchange rate adjustment are reflected in a deterioration in the German current account of between 2 and 3 percent of GDP across the models. The first clear message from the models was that the adjustment process of getting the required resources into Germany would be via a deterioration in the current account facilitated by an appreciation of the DM.

The fiscal aspect of unification would tend to raise GDP and inflation in Germany relative to what they otherwise would have been. In contrast to MULTIMOD and MX3, the results for MSG2 have output lower than otherwise and inflation lower in 1990 but if combined with some monetary stimulus this result for MSG2 disappears. The reason for this result in MSG2 from the purely fiscal shock is that the anticipated fiscal program crowds out private investment in 1990 before the full spending increase begins. In addition the appreciation of the DM lowers imported goods prices which reduces inflation initially.

The models also show that the extent of output, price, and exchange rate change depends importantly on the assumption of the response of German monetary policy. Both the MSG2 and MX3 models showed that more monetary accommodation in Germany after 1990 leads to a larger rise in GDP and inflation and less appreciation of the DM.

Another lesson that is common to all three studies is the implication of the unification process in Germany for the other countries in the ERM. With upward pressures on the DM, other ERM countries were forced to raise interest rates to maintain exchange rate parities. This tightening of monetary policy in the rest of Europe was contractionary for GDP and placed strain on the ERM. Comparisons of scenario 3 and 1 for MULTIMOD, scenarios 2 and 1 for MSG2 and scenarios 1 and 2 for MX3 clearly illustrate this point. The extent of output loss for the rest of the ERM differs across models from between 0.4 percent and 3.9 percent (at the peak) relative to a range of 0 percent–0.5 percent if an ERM realignment was implemented. Again, the size of results varies across the models because of model differences and different assumptions about the extent of fiscal adjustment in Germany. Nonetheless, this important lesson is amply demonstrated in these results. German unification was likely to be contractionary for the rest of Europe if ERM parities were maintained and there would be stress within the ERM as a result.

The unanimity of the model results with respect to the ERM countries reflects four common properties shared by the models and their implementation of unification. First, unification led to a positive aggregate demand shock in Germany. Second, aggregate demand in each country is biased toward domestic goods. Third, goods produced in different countries are imperfect substitutes. Fourth, German monetary policy was assumed to target domestic nominal variables without regard for the behavior of these variables in other countries.[9] Under these conditions, the ERM countries were forced to accept the same high interest rates and exchange rates as Germany without the benefit of the full aggregate demand shock that took place in Germany. The immediate conclusion is that the ERM countries faced a reduction in growth and inflation.

One interesting area of dissimilarity across these models is the long-run supply effect of unification on Germany's real effective exchange rate. In the standard trade equations used by most models, exports depend on foreign income and imports depend on domestic income. Since German unification implies a long-run increase in German income as technology transfer and capital accumulation raise East Germany's productivity toward the West German level,

---

[9] A scenario reported in Masson and Meredith (1990a) showed that targeting a European monetary aggregate produced smaller negative output effects for the other ERM countries.

unified Germany tends to experience an increase in imports relative to exports unless the exchange rate depreciates in real terms.[10]

A supply-induced depreciation shows up strongly in MSG2 scenario 4. Scenarios 1 and 2 demonstrate that the real depreciation may be offset by fiscal expansion, but the appreciation caused by fiscal expansion is reversed over time while the depreciation caused by higher supply continues to grow, so that the DM must depreciate in the long-run. The MULTIMOD scenarios incorporate aspects of both fiscal expansion and supply increase, and they exhibit a real depreciation of the DM, albeit a small one, in 2001. This property is absent from the MX3 simulations because the income elasticity of imports is a function of the cyclical position of income (i.e. relative to potential income). MX3 assumes that all trade flows grow in proportion to world capacity in the long-run.

5. Conclusions and Lessons for Policymakers and Modelers

Table 8 gives some data for the macroeconomic outcomes over the 5 years of unification, 1990–94, and for the previous year. A comparison of 1989 with the subsequent years gives some indication of the results of unification — though of course other shocks or dynamic adjustment could explain why 1990–94 differed from 1989.[11] There is some justification for doing so, nevertheless; 1989 was a normal year for Germany, and hence a good starting point — the

---

[10]Wyplosz (1991) made this argument in the context of a theoretical model. He also pointed out that a reduction in the German current account balance would lower net foreign assets in the long-run relative to their position in the absence of unification, and that this should lead to a further depreciation of the real exchange rate. This net foreign asset mechanism is incorporated into all three sets of model simulations described here.

[11]An alternative procedure to evaluate the simulations would be to recreate the baselines actually used in the simulations reported in Section 3. However, this has the disadvantage of requiring three different evaluations; moreover, since the models considered are, for most purposes, close to linear, the baseline used is irrelevant.

Table 8. Germany: Selected Macroeconomic Variables, 1989–94, in Percent

	United Germany			West Germany						Other EU Countries	
	GDP Growth	Output Gap[a]	Current Account Balance[b]	General Government Balance[b]	GDP Growth	Inflation	Real Effective Exchange Rate[c]	Real Long-term Interest Rate	Net Migration from East Germany[d]	GDP Growth	Inflation
1989	3.6	—	4.8	0.1	3.6	2.8	—	4.2	383.3	3.5	5.3
1990	5.7	2.0	3.0	−1.9	5.7	2.7	5.3	6.0	359.1	2.2	6.0
1991	2.8	3.2	−1.1	−3.3	5.0	3.5	4.2	5.0	169.5	0.7	5.5
1992	2.2	1.8	−1.1	−2.9	1.8	4.0	7.6	3.9	87.8	0.8	4.4
1993	−1.2	−2.2	−0.8	−3.3	−1.7	4.1	15.5	2.5	53.3	−0.3	3.5
1994	2.9	−2.2	−1.0	−2.5	2.3	3.0	17.9	3.9	27.3	2.8	3.1

Notes: [a]Actual/potential output deviation from 1989 value, in percentage points.
[b]Ratio to GDP.
[c]Percent deviation from 1989 value.
[d]In thousands of persons. *Source*: Statistisches Bundesamt, *Wirtschaft und Statisik* 12/95 and 1/95.
Sources: *World Economic Outlook* and *Current Economic Indicators* Databases.

136 *Joseph E. Gagnon, Paul R. Masson and Warwick J. McKibbin*

fiscal position was in balance, inflation was roughly consistent with the Bundesbank's long-run target, and growth was reasonably strong.

Table 8 suggests that output growth and inflation in Germany were stimulated by unification, that interest rates rose and the DM appreciated, and that as a result the fiscal position deteriorated sharply and the current account went from a surplus of almost 5 percent to a deficit of 1 percent of GDP. These are stylized facts that accord well with the model simulations reported above. As expected, these effects seem to die out over time, though in several respects the outcomes, when compared with 1989, differ from the model simulations of unification when compared with baseline. The sharpest difference is that output actually declined in 1993. None of the models predicted a recession in 1993, although MULTIMOD did predict a modest reduction in the growth rate of West Germany relative to baseline. Other differences are predominantly a matter of timing, including the fact that the real effective exchange rate of Germany continues to appreciate through 1994 and inflation in Germany peaks in 1992–93.

One potential explanation for these differences is that none of the simulations adequately captured the interaction of inflation and monetary policy in Germany. The year-over-year German inflation rate increased by over one percentage point between 1990 and 1992,[12] prompting a tightening of monetary policy that led to a recession in 1993 and the subsequent decline of inflation in 1994 and 1995. In contrast, many of the model simulations showed very little increase in inflation, and none of the simulations that did have higher inflation were able to match the timing of the realized data. It is not clear whether these discrepancies are due to errors in the price-adjustment sectors of the models or to misspecification of the behavior and credibility of the monetary authorities.

Another important question is the extent to which the recession in Europe can be attributed to German unification rather than to other causes. The model simulations highlighted the negative

---

[12]The 12-month inflation rate peaked considerably higher, as discussed above.

transmission effects on output in other European countries, and the actual outcomes indicate a slowdown in growth for the rest of the European Union which occurs much earlier than in Germany. Relative to 1989, the decline in output growth is 2.8 percent already in 1991. In this instance, the realized data appear quite favorable for the model predictions.

A related issue is whether the model simulations clearly anticipate the tensions in the ERM, which ultimately led to the crises of 1992–93. Though the directions of the effects — the increase in interest rates in Germany and the necessity for other ERM countries to raise rates in the face of downward pressures on output — are captured in these simulations, it must be recognized that the models cannot fully capture the induced effects on the credibility of these countries' commitments to their central parities, nor the reluctance of Germany to defend those rates. Therefore, the model simulations can be taken to be indicative of pressures, but they do not predict the response of policymakers to these pressures.

A further interesting question is whether the model results (or the exogenous assumptions) correctly captured the nature of the transformation process in East Germany. There are several aspects to this question. First, it seems that the size of the transfers that were needed from the West was larger than most commentators initially expected. Second, wage growth in the East much exceeded what was justified in terms of relative productivity levels. Third, and related to the second, output declines in East Germany were larger than anticipated.

The models differ in the extent to which they attempted to model developments in East Germany. The MULTIMOD simulations used the net imports generated from a separate real aggregate demand–supply model of East Germany as an estimate of the relevant shocks to the West Germany economy. MSG2 simulated different aspects of unification independently; one of these aspects was the supply-side effect of adding East German labor and capital to West Germany at West German wage rates. MX3 focused on the supply-side implications of unification with very little attention to the fiscal aspects.

Despite these differences, all the inputs to the model simulations embodied an overestimate of the output level in East Germany and an underestimate of the persistence of fiscal transfers to the East. These failures stem largely from an overly optimistic assumption about the effective value of the East German capital stock. This mistake was shared by most observers at the time.

None of the models correctly anticipated the size and persistence of excess unemployment in East Germany. MSG2 scenario 4 highlighted the importance of the unemployment problem, but overestimated the adjustment speed to equilibrium. The second MX3 study made some progress on the persistence of unemployment, but only by modifying the model structure in light of data from late 1990.

As for migration from East to West — an issue highlighted only in the MULTIMOD simulations — this ceased to be an important factor after 1992, as can be seen from Table 8. Thus, the assumption of the less optimistic scenario that there would be continuing large net migration was not borne out. However, the reference case in Table 5 underestimated migration in 1990–91 by about 75,000 each year.

Altogether, the model simulations provided a reasonably accurate guide to the direction and magnitude of the effects of unification on most key macroeconomic variables. However, the model simulations were frequently wrong on the timing of these effects. The models tended to predict the strongest effects within a year or so after unification, whereas the data show that many of these effects required 2 or 3 years to reach their peak. This discrepancy is most likely due to the implementation of rational expectations as perfect foresight, in which agents are assumed to fully understand and anticipate all aspects of unification at the beginning of the simulations. One lesson for rational expectations modelers may be to incorporate learning behavior into the model when analyzing the effect of large and unusual shocks such as German unification (for a discussion of how to do so, see Hall, (1993)).

It is always easier with hindsight to explain major economic events. In this paper we focused on a major economic event that is not only a fascinating study in economic adjustment in its own right, but that also produced data for evaluating a range of empirical issues. In particular, German unification provided us with the opportunity to evaluate the usefulness of a new generation of multi-country models that evolved during the 1980s. The experiment is interesting because the consequences of this major economic event were analyzed independently by three modeling groups using these new modeling tools and the results were made public in the very early stages of the unification process. The insights from these three models are still relevant in understanding the actual outcomes of German unification as well as a range of other issues currently facing the world economy. Despite the widespread distrust of large scale modeling (primarily because of the poor performance of an earlier generation of demand-side models in the face of the oil price shocks of the 1970s) this particular exercise illustrates that the new generation of these models has proven useful in gaining insights of importance for policymakers. Our study also shows that the widely argued proposition that no one could have foreseen the consequences of German unification is an exaggeration. Indeed, there was a great deal of predictive material available from these three studies, as well as other academic papers based on the same underlying theories.

References

Adams, G., L. Alexander, and J. Gagnon, 1993, German unification and the European monetary system: A quantitative analysis, *Journal of Policy Modeling* 15, 353–392.

Alexander, L.S., and J.E. Gagnon, 1990, The global economic implications of German unification, *International Finance Discussion Papers No. 379*, Board of Governors of the Federal Reserve System, April.

Gagnon, J.E., 1991, A forward-looking multicountry model for policy analysis: MX3, *Economic and Financial Computing 1*, 311–361.

Hall, S., 1993, Modelling structural change using the Kalman filter, *Economics of Planning* 16, 1–13.

Masson, P.R., and G. Meredith, 1990a, Domestic and international macroeconomic consequences of German unification, *IMF Working Paper WP/90/85*, September.

Masson, P.R., and G. Meredith, 1990b, Domestic and international macroeconomic consequences of German unification, in: L. Lipschitz and D. McDonald, eds., German unification: Economic issues, *IMF Occasional Paper No. 75*, December.

Masson, P.R., S. Symansky, and G. Meredith, 1990, MULTIMOD Mark II: A revised and extended model, *IMF Occasional Paper No. 71*, July.

McDonald, D., and G. Thumann, 1990, East Germany: The new Wirtschftswunder?, in: L. Lipschitz and D. McDonald, eds., German unification: Economic issues, *IMF Occasional Paper No. 75*, December.

McKibbin, W.J., 1990, Some global macroeconomic implications of German unification, *Brookings Discussion Paper in International Economics No. 81*, The Brookings Institution, May.

McKibbin, W.J., 1992, The new Europe and its economic implications for the world economy, *Economic and Financial Computing 2*, 123–149.

McKibbin, W.J., and J.D. Sachs, 1991, Global linkages: Macroeconomic interdependence and co-operation in the world economy, The Brookings Institution, Washington.

Wyplosz, C., 1991, On the real exchange rate effect of German unification, *Weltwirtschaftliches Archiv 127*, 1–17.

Part II

Exchange Rate Regimes and International Currencies

Chapter 5

Exchange Rate Regimes of Developing Countries: Global Context and Individual Choices*

Esteban Jadresic, Paul R. Masson and Paolo Mauro

This paper argues that, in analyzing the choice of exchange rate regimes in developing and transition countries in the present global economic context, it is essential to distinguish between those countries with substantial involvement in international financial markets and those where involvement is limited. For developing countries with important linkages to modern global capital markets, an important lesson of the recent crises in emerging market countries is that the requirements for sustaining pegged exchange rate regimes have become significantly more demanding. For many emerging market countries, therefore, regimes that allow substantial actual exchange rate flexibility are probably desirable. If supported by the requisite policy discipline and institutional structures, however, hard currency pegs may also be appropriate for some of these countries. Beyond the emerging markets countries, for many developing countries with less linkage to global capital markets, traditional exchange rate pegs and intermediate regimes are more viable and retain important advantages.

---

*This chapter originally appeared in *Journal of the Japanese and International Economies*, (2001), 15(1), 68–101. At time of writing, the authors were staff members of the International Monetary Fund.

1. Introduction

The exchange and payments crises of the 1990s, the general increase in capital mobility, and the boom–bust character of capital flows to developing countries have raised anew the issue of appropriate exchange rate arrangements. In response to these developments, an increasingly fashionable (and forcefully proposed) view has emerged, that countries should either let their exchange rates float freely or peg them firmly to a stable currency (Eichengreen, 1998; Obstfeld and Rogoff, 1995), with some authors advancing the proposition that in many developing countries only currency boards or dollarization would be sensible choices (Calvo, 1999; Hausman *et al.*, 1999). Yet another view is that on this issue not much has changed, i.e., that intermediate regimes between the extremes of pure floating and rigid fixity generally continue to be appropriate (Frankel, 1999).

This paper reviews the exchange rate regime choice of developing and transition countries in the context of the present economic and financial characteristics of these countries and of the world economy. The countries whose exchange arrangements are the subject of this paper cover a very broad range of economic development, from the very poorest to newly industrialized economies with relatively high per capita incomes. Correlated with the level of economic development, but not perfectly so, are both the degree of domestic financial sophistication and the extent of involvement with the global financial markets. The 30 or so countries that are most advanced in this last regard are what are commonly referred to as the *emerging markets.*

The paper argues that, in analyzing the choice of exchange rate regimes in developing and transition countries in the present global economic context, it is essential to distinguish between those countries with substantial involvement in international financial markets and those where involvement is limited. For developing countries with important linkages to modern global capital markets, an important lesson of the recent crises in emerging market countries is indeed that the requirements for sustaining pegged exchange rate regimes have become significantly more demanding. For many emerging market countries, therefore, regimes that allow substantial actual exchange rate flexibility are probably desirable. If supported by the requisite policy discipline and institutional structures, however, hard currency pegs may also be appropriate for some of these countries.

Beyond the emerging market countries, for many developing countries with less linkage to global capital markets, traditional exchange rate pegs and intermediate regimes are more viable and retain important advantages. Exchange rate pegs can provide a useful and credible nominal anchor for monetary policy and avoid many of the complexities and institutional requirements for establishing an alternative anchor (such as a credible inflation target backed by an operationally independent central bank). In addition, in the absence of sophisticated financial systems, many of these countries lack a deep and broad market for foreign exchange, which can provide reasonable exchange rate stability in the absence of official guidance. Exchange rate pegs can also be particularly attractive for countries with a dominant trading partner that maintains a stable monetary policy. Finally, the few developing countries that still confront the problem of stabilizing from very high inflation may also find virtue in exchange-rate-based stabilization plans, while giving due attention to timely implementation of an exit strategy. For them and many other countries, the exchange rate regime is not a once-and-for-all choice, but will depend on circumstances facing the country at a particular time. Thus, the intermediate regimes may not be as sustainable as the polar cases, but they are often not intended to be permanent. Indeed, history shows us that there have been frequent shifts between regimes, toward greater flexibility and back again. (See Masson, 2000, which rejects the hypothesis that intermediate regimes are tending to disappear).

The remainder of this paper is organized as follows. Section 2 considers key changes in the economic situations of developing and transition countries that have implications for exchange rate regime choice. Section 3 discusses the recent foreign exchange and financial crises that have affected many emerging market countries and seeks to draw lessons from these experiences for exchange rate policy. Section 4 considers the characteristics of countries for which some form of pegged exchange rate may be desirable and examines the relative virtues of alternative exchange rate regimes along the spectrum from hard pegs to free floats. The role of the exchange rate as a nominal anchor under various forms of pegged rate regimes and the need for an alternative nominal anchor under loosely managed or free floats are also discussed, along with the use of intervention and controls for countries that do not practice benign neglect toward their exchange rates. Section 5 concludes, summarizing the main implications for exchange regime choice by developing and transition countries in the present global economic environment.

2. The Economic Environment Facing Developing and Transition Countries

Adapting both to expanding opportunities from deeper involvement in an increasingly integrated global economy and to changes in their own economic situations, developing and transition countries have been shifting their exchange rate regimes toward greater flexibility, accompanied by a generalized move to current account convertibility and a somewhat less dramatic removal of capital account restrictions (Fig. 1).[1] This section considers key changes in the economic situations of developing and transition countries associated with these policy developments.

2.1. *Increased Capital Mobility*

Gross capital flows to developing countries have risen considerably as a share of GDP since the early 1980s (Fig. 2), reflecting greater capital account liberalization and capital market integration, especially of emerging market economies. Higher gross flows have created the potential for large and sudden reversals in net flows, particularly in the case of private flows. Net private flows to developing countries, after hovering around 0.5 percent of GDP throughout the 1970s and

---

[1]Since the concept of transition countries has only become relevant during the past decade or so, Figs. 1 through 7 concentrate on developing countries.

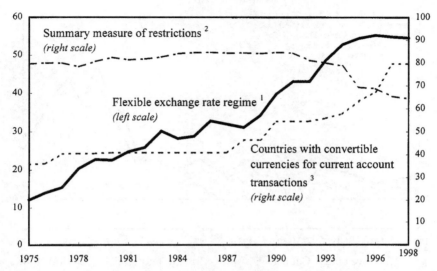

Figure 1. The Evolution of Exchange Rate Regimes and Exchange Restrictions, 1975–1998, in Developing Countries (in Percentages)

Notes: [1] In percentage of total number of developing countries. Flexible exchange rate regimes include arrangements in which the exchange rate has limited flexibility with respect to another currency, is adjusted according to a set of indicators, and follows a managed float or is independently floating. The number for 1998 is preliminary. [2] Cross-country average of an index reflecting restrictions on capital account transactions, multiple exchange rates, and surrender of export proceeds. The index ranges from 0 when no restrictions are present to 100 when all restrictions are present. To reflect a change in methodology in 1996 for restrictions on capital account transactions, the 1996 and 1997 capital account restrictions indicators are rescaled so that the value in 1996 is the same as that in 1995. It is likely, however, that capital account liberalization took place between 1995 and 1996. [3] Percentage of developing countries that have accepted Article VIII of the IMF's Articles of Agreement; countries are weighted by their 1990–1995 share of aggregate exports of all developing countries.

Source: International Monetary Fund, Annual Report on Exchange Arrangements and Exchange Restrictions.

1980s, rose sharply to 3 percent of GDP in the mid-1990s, only to drop back to 1.5 percent of GDP in 1998. Similar developments are also evident in the case of outstanding bank claims, which fell abruptly in Asia, Latin America, and Eastern Europe in the context of the recent emerging market crises (Fig. 3), discussed

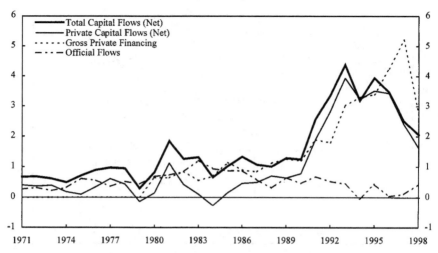

Figure 2. Developing Countries: Total, Private and Official Capital Flows, 1971–1998 (in Percentage of GDP)
Source: International Monetary Fund, World Economic Outlook Database and Developing Countries Bonds, Equities and Loans Database.

in the next section. As is well known, capital flow reversals have been associated with currency crises and these crises have had large real economic costs. However, this phenomenon of the boom–bust cycle in private capital flows and its attendant costs is relevant primarily for the emerging market economies, which have important involvement in modern global financial markets. It has not directly affected the wide range of developing countries with little or no such involvement.

2.2. *Exposure to Exchange Rate Risk*

As previously noted, residents of developing and transition countries generally find it difficult to borrow abroad in their own currencies, and nonresidents are generally reluctant to take net long positions in those currencies. In net terms, the foreign currency liabilities of residents of developing and transition countries usually exceed their assets in foreign currencies, implying that they are exposed to exchange rate risk on their balance sheets as well as through

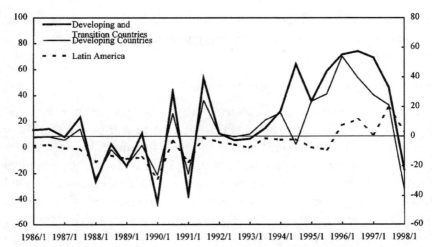

Figure 3. Developing Countries: Change in Bank Loans, 1986–1998 (in Billions of U.S. Dollars)
Source: Bank for International Settlements.

trade. Issues of both sovereign and corporate bonds on international markets are overwhelmingly in foreign currencies, even in the case of an advanced economy such as Korea or a country whose exchange rate is strongly pegged to the U.S. dollar, such as Argentina. While part of this exchange rate risk can be hedged, this can only be done (in the aggregate for a given developing country) to the limited extent that nonresidents are willing to hold local currency exposure.[2] Moreover, few of these countries have organized markets for currency futures and options, and those located in industrial countries deal mainly in the currencies of industrial countries (IMF, 1995a).[3] Also, while forward foreign exchange contracts are allowed in many

---

[2] Hedging can take many forms, including nonresidents holding local-currency-denominated equities. For example in 1996, the share of total market capitalization held by nonresidents in the stock markets of Argentina, Korea, Mexico, Thailand, and the Philippines ranged between 15 and 40 percent (The World Bank, 1997, p. 306).

[3] However, currency futures are available in the United States for the Brazilian real, the Mexican peso, and the Russian ruble.

emerging markets (IMF, 1995b, p. 22), there is no indication of significant net capacity to shift foreign exchange risks abroad at a reasonable price.

2.3. *Portfolio Diversification*

Another consequence of globalization has been a greater internationalization of balance sheets, with the private and public sectors of emerging market countries holding an increasing quantity and variety of foreign currency assets and liabilities. For instance, 28 percent of the international bonds issued by emerging market countries in 1996–1998 were denominated in a currency other than the U.S. dollar, with the recent launch of the euro contributing to further increase the share of the nondollar sector to 33 percent during the first half of 1999.[4] However, the international market for the local-currency-denominated liabilities of emerging market countries is, at best, very limited.

2.4. *Increased Openness to International Trade*

The developing economies' degree of openness to international trade has increased over the past few decades. The average developing country's share of external trade (measured by exports plus imports, divided by two) in GDP rose from about 30 percent in the late 1960s to about 40 percent in the late 1990s (Fig. 4). This trend has been more marked in the case of the East Asian countries — mirroring their export-led growth. As imports and exports have come to represent a larger share of developing countries' GDP, given changes in the exchange rate have a greater impact on output and prices.

2.5. *Shift of Exports Toward Manufactures*

At the same time, the composition of developing countries' trade by type of product has changed considerably, with a move away from commodity exports and toward manufactured exports (Fig. 5),

---

[4] *Source*: Capital Data Ltd.

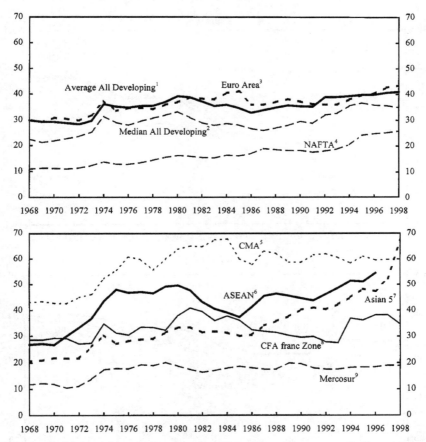

Figure 4. Advanced and Developing Countries: Measures of Openness of Economies, 1968–1998

Notes: [1] The unweighted average across countries of exports and imports (divided by two) in percent of GDP. [2] The median value of country's exports and imports (divided by two) in percent of GDP. [3] Euro Area: Austria, Belgium-Luxembourg, Finland, France, Germany, Ireland, Italy, Netherlands, Portugal and Spain. [4] NAFTA: Canada, Mexico and the United States. [5] CMA: Botswana, Lesotho, Namibia, South Africa and Switzerland. [6] ASEAN: Cambodia, Indonesia, Laos, Malaysia, Myanmar, Philippines, Singapore, Thailand and Viet Nam. (Brunei data not available). [7] Asian 5: Indonesia, Korea, Malaysia, Philippines and Thailand. [8] CFA franc Zone: Berlin, Burkina Faso, Cameroon, Central African Republic, Chad, Republic of Congo, Cote d'voire, Equatorial Guinea, Gabon, Guinea-Bissau, Mail, Niger, Senegal and Togo. The sharp increase in the openness measure in 1994 reflects the CFA franc's 50 percent devaluation. [9] Mercosur: Argentina, Brazil, Paraguay and Uruguay, as well as associated members Bolivia and Chile.

Source: International Monetary Fund, World Economic Outlook.

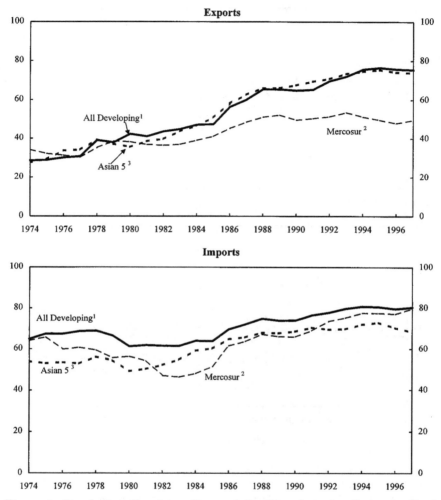

Figure 5. Developing Countries: Share of the Manufacturing Sector in Total Trade, 1974–1997

Notes: [1] The sum of the following SITC categories: (5) chemicals, (6) basic manufactures, (7) machines and transport equipment, (8) miscellaneous manufactures goods, and (9) goods not classified by kind, in percent of total trade. [2] Mercosur: Argentina, Brazil, Paraguay and Uruguay, as well as associate members Bolivia and Chile. [3] Asian 5: Indonesia, Korea, Malaysia, Philippines and Thailand.

Source: United Nations, Trade Analysis and Reporting System.

especially for the emerging market economies. This shift in composition has made developing countries' terms of trade more stable, but it has also made those countries with growing manufactured exports more sensitive to exchange rate fluctuations. Prices of most commodities are set in global markets, and supply and demand for individual exporters are largely independent of the exchange rate. In contrast, supply and demand for exports of manufactured products show significant sensitivity to exchange rates.

2.6. Trade Diversification

Consistent with the trend toward globalization, many developing and especially the emerging market economies now trade with a wide range of partner countries. With the notable exception of Mexico where four-fifths of trade is with the United States, a typical mid-sized developing country's share of trade with a single currency area is below one-half in the case of Africa, the Middle East, and Europe and below one-third in the case of Asia and Latin America. Trade shares are usually sizable with at least two of the major currency areas (the United States, the euro area, and Japan) implying that developing countries with single-currency pegs remain significantly exposed to the wide fluctuations among major currencies.

2.7. Greater Intraregional Trade

The importance of intraregional trade for developing countries, though still moderate compared with their trade with industrial countries, is increasing, especially for key regional groups of emerging market economies. Table 1 illustrates this by considering several regions, including Mercosur, the five East Asian countries most affected by the recent emerging market crises, ASEAN, the central and eastern European countries (CEEC) that initiated accession negotiations with the EU in March 1998, and the CFA franc zone. (For comparison purposes, data on the euro area and NAFTA are also presented.) As shown in Table 1, intraregional trade in each of these regions has increased substantially during the

Table 1. Regional Trade Patterns, 1980–1998 (Selected Years, in Percentage of Total Regional Trade)

	1980		1985		1990		1995		1998	
	Exports	Imports	Exports	Imports	Exports	Imports	Exports	Imports	Exports	Imports
Mercosur[a]										
Within Mercosur	15.8	11.3	8.2	13.8	11.6	17.5	22.6	20.2	26.8	22.7
With United States	14.7	20.3	22.8	19.1	20.4	19.3	15.0	20.6	15.1	21.6
With euro area	27.4	17.8	24.4	15.9	28.8	20.1	21.3	22.3	21.3	22.0
With other industrial countries	13.3	14.7	12.1	12.8	14.6	15.4	14.3	13.7	10.6	13.3
With other developing countries	27.1	35.2	30.0	36.5	23.2	26.6	26.0	22.1	25.0	19.5
Asian 5[b]										
Within Asian 5	4.9	6.0	6.4	7.8	6.7	6.6	8.4	8.1	10.2	12.5
With Japan	29.9	25.1	24.7	23.8	22.2	26.1	15.9	25.8	11.6	17.8
With the United States	20.8	18.3	26.1	18.4	23.9	18.2	19.5	17.3	20.2	14.4
With euro area	11.8	8.7	8.6	9.7	11.8	11.3	10.4	11.6	10.7	8.6
With other industrial countries	5.8	9.7	7.9	10.9	8.3	10.6	6.6	9.4	8.1	7.4
With other developing countries	25.6	31.0	24.7	26.2	25.0	24.1	36.9	26.1	36.5	36.6

ASEAN[c]										
Within ASEAN	17.4	14.6	18.6	17.2	19.0	15.2	24.6	18.0	22.1	24.1
With Japan	29.6	22.3	25.1	20.5	18.9	23.1	14.2	23.8	11.1	16.9
With the United States	16.3	15.3	19.5	15.2	19.4	14.4	18.6	13.8	20.6	13.8
With euro area	10.4	9.6	8.4	10.0	11.7	11.2	10.8	11.1	11.9	8.9
With other industrial countries	6.1	10.3	6.2	9.7	7.6	9.8	6.9	8.1	8.6	6.7
With other developing countries	20.2	28.6	21.5	26.7	23.1	25.2	24.3	24.3	25.2	28.5
CFA franc Zone[d]										
Within CFA franc zone	6.6	6.1	6.8	6.7	8.1	9.3	6.7	6.9	8.5	8.5
With euro area	56.7	57.6	53.2	53.9	50.9	52.0	46.1	45.8	40.7	45.6
With other industrial countries	18.1	14.7	22.8	18.1	20.9	14.3	22.5	14.7	21.1	12.5
With other developing countries	18.9	21.2	14.0	18.7	18.0	21.1	21.7	29.2	26.2	29.6

(*Continued*)

Table 1. (*Continued*)

	1980		1985		1990		1995		1998	
	Exports	Imports	Exports	Imports	Exports	Imports	Exports	Imports	Exports	Imports
CEEC 5[e]										
Within CEEC 5	—	—	—	—	—	—	5.9	4.7	6.5	4.7
With euro area	—	—	—	—	—	—	56.7	54.5	57.4	60.4
With other industrial countries	—	—	—	—	—	—	11.9	16.3	14.2	12.9
With other developing countries	—	—	—	—	—	—	23.7	23.9	21.7	21.6
Euro Area[f]										
Within euro area	50.6	44.2	47.1	46.1	54.1	52.8	51.2	50.7	48.7	48.5
With Japan	0.9	2.3	1.2	3.1	2.0	4.1	2.0	3.8	1.6	3.8
with the United States	4.7	7.8	8.9	7.2	6.1	6.7	5.9	6.8	7.6	7.8
With other industrial countries	18.5	15.6	20.2	17.2	19.5	16.7	18.3	16.8	18.9	16.6
With other developing countries	23.5	29.7	21.0	25.8	17.2	19.1	21.3	21.0	22.0	22.4

NAFTA[g]

Within NAFTA	33.6	32.8	43.9	34.4	41.4	33.9	46.2	38.4	51.0	40.4
With Japan	8.3	10.6	8.8	16.9	10.5	15.2	8.6	13.7	6.4	10.9
With euro area	17.4	10.3	13.5	13.7	15.6	13.2	11.7	11.6	11.3	12.4
With other industrial countries	10.1	7.9	8.4	7.9	9.4	7.8	7.2	6.2	7.6	6.2
With other developing countries	28.8	37.0	23.9	26.4	23.0	29.1	26.1	29.8	23.6	29.7

Source: International Monetary Fund, Direction of Trade Statistics.

[a]Mercosur: Argentina, Brazil, Paraguay, Uruguay, and associate members Bolivia, and Chile. [b]Asian 5: Indonesia, Korea, Malaysia, Philippines, and Thailand. [c]ASEAN: Cambodia, Indonesia, Laos, Malaysia, Myanmar, Philippines, Singapore, Thailand, and Viet Nam (Brunei data are not available). [d]CFA franc Zone: Benin, Burkina Faso, Cameroon, Central African Republic, Chad, Republic of Congo, Cote d'Ivoire, Equatorial Guinea, Gabon, Guinea Bissau, Mali, Niger, Senegal, and Togo. [e]CEEC 5: Czech Republic, Estonia, Hungary, Poland, and Slovenia — the countries that initiated accession negotiations with the EU in March 1998, a group chosen purely for illustration purposes. [f]Euro Area: Austria, Belgium, Finland, France, Germany, Ireland, Italy, Luxembourg, Netherlands, Portugal, and Spain. [g]NAFTA: Canada, Mexico, and the United States.

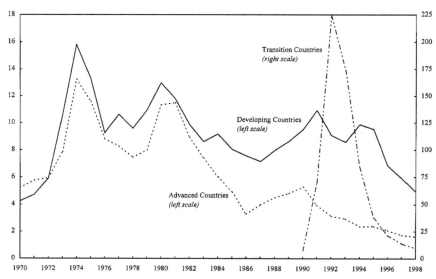

Figure 6. Advanced, Developing (Excluding Transition Economies) and Transition Countries: Median Inflation Rate, 1970–1998

Source: International Monetary Fund, World Economic Outlook.

past decade.[5] The growing importance of intraregional trade for key developing countries has increased the magnitude of the real effects of the fluctuations in the bilateral exchange rates between neighbor (or near-neighbor) developing countries.

2.8. *Reduced Inflation*

Another important development in recent years has been the fall in inflation in most developing countries. The median inflation rate fell to about 5 percent in the late 1990s from the 10 percent or more prevailing between the early 1970s and the early 1990s (Fig. 6). While the widespread decline of inflation in developing and transition countries has benefited from positive supply shocks (in particular

---

[5]Data for CEEC negotiating EU accession cover too short a period to draw any firm conclusions, and in any case, this set of countries has no particular significance as a regional trading group. More important is the strength of their trade linkages with the EU.

Exchange Rate Regimes of Developing Countries

lower petroleum prices) and the anti-inflationary environment in industrial countries, it also reveals the broad acceptance now among the public of these countries that the key objective of monetary policy should be to deliver low inflation and that fiscal policy should not rely on the inflation tax.

3. Lessons From Recent Emerging Market Crises

Recent crises involving emerging market economies, from the tequila crisis of 1995 through the Asian–Russian–Brazilian crises of 1997–1998, carry important lessons for exchange regimes of developing and transition countries. Indeed, these experiences have led qualified observers, such as Eichengreen (1998), to conclude that pegged exchange rate regimes are inherently crisis-prone for emerging market economies and that these countries should be encouraged, in their own interest and for the broader interests of the international community, to adopt floating rate regimes.

There is little doubt that, for those emerging market countries that were most severely affected by recent crises, their exchange rate regimes were clearly important factors in their vulnerability.[6] The most severely affected countries all had *de jure* or *de facto* exchange rate pegs or otherwise substantially limited the movement of their exchange rates. In contrast, emerging market economies that maintained greater flexibility in their exchange rate regimes generally fared much better. For example, Chile, Mexico, Peru, South Africa, and Turkey all seem to have benefited from the flexibility of their exchange rates during the recent international crisis.

Indeed, for the countries most adversely affected by recent crises there was an intrinsic perversity in the interactions between their exchange rate regimes and other problems in these economies, especially weaknesses in their financial sectors. When the exchange

---

[6]The countries most severely affected in recent crises were Argentina and Mexico in the tequila crisis; Indonesia, Korea, Malaysia, Thailand, and (to a lesser extent) Hong Kong SAR in the Asian crisis; Russia in the Russian crisis; and Brazil and Argentina in the Brazilian crisis.

rate is pegged or tightly managed and it is believed that this will continue, there is often little perceived risk for domestic firms or financial institutions to borrow in foreign currency. If domestic-currency interest rates rise above foreign-currency rates (because of efforts to contain domestic overheating by tighter monetary policy together with sterilized intervention to resist exchange rate appreciation), then there is a positive incentive to borrow foreign currency. As international credits are generally most cheaply and easily available for short maturities, foreign-currency borrowing tends to be short term.

If, because of adverse domestic or international developments, market sentiment turns and the exchange rate comes under downward pressure, the authorities are understandably reluctant to resist by raising domestic interest rates, as this will further undermine already weak banks and businesses. Adjustment of the exchange rate is also resisted — through sterilized official intervention — because a substantial depreciation would raise the burdens of foreign-currency denominated debts.[7] Once it becomes clear that the authorities are caught in a situation where they want to defend the exchange rate, but dare not raise domestic interest rates (credibly and substantially), and are running short of reserves, then speculative pressures against the exchange rate become overwhelming. If the peg is broken, depreciation is likely to be substantial as private agents rush to cover their remaining foreign exchange exposures and as foreign and domestic capital attempts to flee the developing crisis. The authorities, with limited remaining reserves, are in a poor position to help stabilize the rate, and the market, which is not used to operating without official support, tends to become illiquid and move erratically. Downward pressures build and are further

---

[7]Beyond normal intervention, the authorities may resort to the forward market (Thailand in 1997) or futures market (Brazil, 1997–1998), they may exchange domestic-currency debt for foreign-currency linked debt (Mexico, 1994 and Brazil, 1997–98), or they may loan official reserves to domestic institutions experiencing financing difficulties (Korea, 1997). These strategies may help to forestall a crisis, but if the crisis breaks they can also make it much more damaging.

reinforced by the recognition of the adverse consequences of financial disruption associated with massive depreciation. Thus, pegged or quasi-pegged exchange rates (or heavily managed floats) do tend to contribute to other problems that make them prone to damaging financial crises. The likelihood of prolonged speculative attack and indeed of a downturn in sentiment is reduced to the extent that the credibility of the peg is high; this is most obvious in the case of a currency board.

A genuine floating exchange rate, by contrast, allows greater flexibility for monetary policy at times of exchange rate pressures and economic difficulty. Also, provided that the exchange rate really does move up and down in response to market forces, businesses and financial institutions are forced to recognize the risks inherent in foreign-currency borrowing and other exposures to foreign exchange risk. Floating does not preclude the use of official intervention and adjustments of monetary policy to influence the exchange rate. However, efforts to manage tightly the exchange rate primarily through (sterilized) official intervention tend to recreate the risks and problems of a pegged exchange rate. If the exchange rate is managed, interest rates should be a primary tool so that private sector behavior will be appropriately attuned to situations where aggressive interest rate adjustments may occasionally be required to support the exchange rate objective. For countries that are substantially involved in modern global financial markets, policy regimes that seek to provide a high degree of stability of both exchange rates and interest rates, and that induce private risk taking on the presumption that both are simultaneously possible, are an invitation to trouble.

However, a reasoned judgment on the desirable exchange rate regime needs to be based not only on how it performs in a crisis, but how it performs on average over time. For instance, Argentina, with its currency board, had strong growth in the 1990s, despite the negative effects of the tequila and Russia crises. That said, it must be emphasized that the costs of recent crises to the most affected countries have been very large, and especially so for those countries whose pegged or quasi-pegged exchange regimes broke down in the crisis. There is an undeniable lesson here about the difficulties and dangers of running pegged or quasi-pegged exchange rate regimes for emerging market economies with substantial involvement in global capital markets, as evidenced by the fact that only the emerging market countries with the hardest pegs were able to maintain their exchange rates.

In considering this conclusion, it is also important to stress a critical caveat: while recent crises have directly and adversely affected many emerging market economies with important links to modern global financial markets, these crises have only indirectly affected (through movements in world commodity prices and trade flows) the majority of developing and transition countries. Accordingly, lessons for exchange rate regimes from these crises relate primarily to emerging market countries (and to countries that may soon join this group) and not necessarily more broadly.

4. Exchange Regime Choice: Emerging Markets and Beyond

The preceding discussion strongly suggests that for emerging market countries with substantial involvement in modern global financial markets, floating exchange rate regimes should be an increasingly relevant choice. Looking beyond the emerging market economies to the large number of developing and transition countries that do not yet have important involvement with modern global financial markets, the rigors of maintaining a pegged exchange rate regime are less demanding. For such countries, and especially those without a well-developed financial infrastructure including sophisticated financial institutions and broad and deep markets for foreign exchange, pegs can provide a simple and credible anchor for monetary policy. While the precise requirements for a successful float are not the subject of this paper, it can safely be said that many developing and transition economies do not satisfy them. Indeed, while an increasing number of these countries (together with the emerging market countries) officially describe their exchange rate regimes as *managed floating* or *independent floating* (see Fig. 1), the fact is that most of these countries do maintain some form of *de jure* or *de facto* exchange rate peg or otherwise narrowly limit fluctuations of the exchange rate. The economic criteria usually thought to influence the appropriateness of adopting a fixed, as opposed to a flexible, exchange rate regime provide at least a partial explanation of this phenomenon. Specifically, the following conditions are likely to influence whether some form of pegged exchange rate regime is judged to be appropriate[8,9]:

- The degree of involvement with international capital markets is low;
- The share of trade with the country to which it is pegged is high;
- The shocks it faces are similar to those facing the country to which it pegs;
- It is willing to give up monetary independence for its partner's monetary credibility;
- Its economy and financial system already extensively rely on its partner's currency;
- Because of high inherited inflation, exchange-rate-based stabilization is attractive;
- Its fiscal policy is flexible and sustainable;
- Its labor markets are flexible;
- It has high international reserves.

---

[8]For reviews of the literature on the choice of exchange rate regime, see among others Wickham (1985), Aghevli *et al.* (1991), Isard (1995), Obstfeld (1995), and Obstfeld and Rogoff (1995).

[9]Since available empirical studies on the effects of alternative regimes on economic performance (e.g., Ghosh *et al.,* 1995, and Hausman *et al.,* 1999) do not control for these conditions, they are not very illuminating for the discussion in this paper. Other problems of these studies are difficulties in classifying the regimes, a lack of robustness of results across samples and periods, and the small number of developing countries that have had floating exchange rates for a significant number of years. For a discussion of some of these issues, see Edwards and Savastano (1998).

4.1. Countries with Pegged Exchange Rate Regimes

If these criteria are applied, one group of countries for which pegged exchange rates would seem to remain sensible are small economies with a dominant trading partner that maintains a reasonably stable monetary policy. For such countries, there is generally little point in incurring the costs of attempting to run an independent monetary policy. As shown in Table 2, a clear majority of countries with annual GDPs of less than $5 billion have pegged exchange rate regimes. For most of these countries, not only is it clear that they should peg, but it is also clear what they should peg to. Small Caribbean Island economies, some small Central American countries, and some Pacific Island economies peg to the U.S. dollar. The CFA franc zone countries peg to the French franc (and now to the euro). Lesotho, Namibia, and Swaziland peg to the South African rand. Bhutan and Nepal (which has an annual GDP slightly above $5 billion) peg to the Indian rupee. Other small countries, generally with more diversified trade patterns, peg to currency baskets. Table 3 provides detailed information on all countries with annual GDPs of less than $5 billion. The proportion of countries with pegged exchange rate regimes is slightly lower for countries with GDPs between $5 billion and $20 billion (Table 2 — the full detail on these countries is in Table 4). Indeed, Table 2 suggests that the larger a country is, the more likely it is to choose flexible exchange rate regimes.[10]

On the basis of the above criteria, another group of countries for which pegged exchange rate regimes would appear relevant, for the future if not necessarily for the near term, are the more advanced transition economies of central and eastern Europe that aspire to membership in the European Union and to eventual participation in EMU. The criteria of dominant trading partner (and the benefits of closer economic integration with that partner) as

---

[10]That general pattern is partially masked by the notable exception of those advanced European economies that opted for successive cooperative arrangements culminating in the creation of the euro. Table 2 also suggests that more open economies are more likely to peg their exchange rates; by contrast, there is no obvious relationship between GDP per capita and exchange rate regimes.

Table 2. Exchange Rate Regimes and Size, Development, and Openness, 1998 (in Percentage of Total Number of Countries in the Group[b])

	Number of Countries in the Group[a]	Currency Pegged to					Flexibility Limited in Terms of a Single Currency or Group of Currencies		More Flexible	
		U.S. Dollar	French Franc	Other Single Currency	SDR	Other Basket	Single Currency	Cooperative Arrange-ments	Managed Floating	Independently Floating
Size of economy (GDP in billions of U.S. dollars)										
Below 5	72	16.7	18.1	11.1	0.0	9.7	0.0	0.0	20.8	23.6
Between 5 and 20	42	9.5	4.8	4.8	4.8	7.1	4.8	2.4	38.1	23.8
Between 20 and 100	30	3.3	0.0	0.0	3.3	10.0	3.3	3.3	63.3	13.3
Above 100	32	3.1	0.0	0.0	3.1	0.0	3.1	31.3	21.9	37.5
Trade openness (Average of exports and imports, in percent of GDP)										
Below 20 percent	21	4.8	0.0	0.0	4.8	9.5	0.0	9.5	33.3	38.1
Between 20 and 40 percent	68	2.9	16.2	2.9	1.5	2.9	2.9	8.8	35.3	26.5
Between 40 and 60 percent	59	11.9	3.4	6.8	3.4	11.9	1.7	3.4	30.5	27.1

(*Continued*)

Table 2. (*Continued*)

	Number of Countries in the Group[a]	Currency Pegged to					Flexibility Limited in Terms of a Single Currency or Group of Currencies		More Flexible	
		U.S. Dollar	French Franc	Other Single Currency	SDR	Other Basket	Single Currency	Cooperative Arrangements	Managed Floating	Independently Floating
Above 60 percent	26	23.1	7.7	15.4	0.0	7.7	3.8	7.7	30.8	3.8
GDP per capita[c] (in U.S. dollars)										
Below 1000	20	0.0	35.0	0.0	0.0	5.0	0.0	0.0	20.0	40.0
Between 1000 and 2000	28	0.0	21.4	14.3	0.0	3.6	0.0	0.0	32.1	28.6
Between 2000 and 10,000	75	13.3	1.3	6.7	2.7	8.0	0.0	0.0	46.7	21.3
Above 10,000	39	7.7	0.0	2.6	0.0	10.3	7.7	30.8	17.9	23.1

Source: *World Development Indicators*, the World Bank; *World Economic Outlook, International Financial Statistics* and *Exchange Arrangements and Exchange Restrictions*, International Monetary Fund.
Note: All data refer to 1998.
[a]The total number of countries for which data are available differs depending on whether the countries are sorted by total GDP, trade openness, or GDP per capita. [b]The total of each row sums to 100. [c]Purchasing-power-parity adjusted.

Exchange Rate Regimes of Developing Countries

Table 3. Economies with GDPs below \$5 billion[a] — Exchange Rate Arrangements and Selected Indicators (1998 unless otherwise indicated)

	Size of Economy (Billions of U.S. Dollars)	Trade as Share of GDP[b]	Largest Export		Tourism Receipts in Percentage of Exports[e]	Controls on Current Account[e]
			Share[c]	Partner[d]		
Pegged arrangements: Pegged to a single currency						
Pegged to the U.S. dollar						
Antigua and Barbuda	0.61	87.0	18.8	Spain	—	1
Bahamas, The	4.12	52.0	22.7	United States	80.0	1
Barbados	2.33	58.4	14.3	United Kingdom	—	1
Belize	0.67	53.0	28.9	United States	27.8	1
Djibouti	0.53	51.4	38.3	Somalia	1.7	0
Dominica	0.25	56.8	22.5	United Kingdom	31.4	1
Grenada	2.30	10.3	30.0	United States	—	1
Liberia[f]	3.07	30.4	27.4	Singapore	—	0
Maldives[f]	0.40	117.0	32.4	United States	68.7	0
Marshall Islands	0.10	—	—	—	—	0
Micronesia, Fed. States of	0.21	—	—	—	0.0	0
Netherlands Antilles	2.51	66.5	17.5	United States	—	1
St. Kitts and Nevis	0.29	60.9	60.3	United States	50.7	1
St. Lucia	0.68	70.1	51.9	United Kingdom	—	1
St. Vincent and the Grenadines	0.30	57.9	31.3	United Kingdom	—	1
Suriname[f]	0.82	83.7	16.2	United States	—	1
Pegged to the French franc						
Benin	2.32	27.8	23.4	Brazil	5.5	1
Burkina Faso	2.54	38.4	67.2	Cote d'Ivoire	7.8	1

(*Continued*)

Esteban Jadresic, Paul R. Masson and Paolo Mauro

Table 3. (*Continued*)

	Size of Economy (Billions of U.S. Dollars)	Trade as Share of GDP[b]	Largest Export		Tourism Receipts in Percentage of Exports[e]	Controls on Current Account[e]
			Share[c]	Partner[d]		
Central African Rep.	1.06	27.2	42.5	Belgium	2.3	1
Chad	1.67	25.8	24.4	Germany	3.3	1
Comoros	0.19	28.6	62.1	France	46.0	1
Congo, Rep. of	1.99	96.2	86.7	United States	0.2	1
Equatorial Guinea	0.46	88.7	87.6	United States	0.5	1
Gabon	4.57	70.6	75.0	United States	0.2	1
Guinea-Bissau	0.20	62.5	85.0	India	—	1
Mali	2.65	28.7	21.8	Italy	3.3	1
Niger	2.01	18.9	68.3	France	6.0	1
Senegal	4.86	34.5	21.5	France	10.8	1
Togo	1.51	37.1	11.3	Canada	2.1	1
Pegged to Other Currency						
Bhutan[g]	0.36	53.7	—	—	4.9	1
Brunei Darussalam[h]	4.86	50.2	51.4	Japan	—	1
Cape Verde[i]	0.50	46.7	89.3	Portugal	11.4	1
Kiribati[j]	0.06	72.6	21.3	Japan	15.4	0
Lesotho[k]	0.83	116.1	—	—	10.9	0
Namibia[k]	2.99	60.0	—	—	11.1	1
San Marino[l]	—	—	—	—	—	0
Swaziland[k]	1.18	99.8	12.8	South Africa	3.4	1
Pegged arrangements: Pegged to a currency basket						
Botswana	5.11	40.3	—	—	—	0
Burundi	0.98	10.2	34.9	Germany	1.0	1
Fiji	2.33	58.5	32.1	Australia	25.6	1
Malta	3.99	96.3	18.0	United Kingdom	23.2	1
Samoa	0.21	43.0	51.1	Australia	50.3	1
Seychelles	0.56	69.5	22.1	United Kingdom	34.2	0

(*Continued*)

Exchange Rate Regimes of Developing Countries

Table 3. (Continued)

	Size of Economy (Billions of U.S. Dollars)	Trade as Share of GDP[b]	Largest Export		Tourism Receipts in Percentage of Exports[e]	Controls on Current Account[e]
			Share[c]	Partner[d]		
Tonga	0.17	49.4	50.3	India	28.6	1
Vanuatu	0.25	53.6	30.5	Japan	39.5	0
Flexible arrangements: Other managed float						
Azerbaijan	4.10	42.5	23.7	Iran	13.8	1
Kyrgyz Rep.	1.87	48.8	25.0	Germany	0.6	0
Lao PDR	1.11	51.5	13.0	Thailand	12.9	0
Macedonia FYR	3.25	52.0	20.5	Germany	—	1
Malawi	1.69	40.2	14.4	South Africa	1.1	1
Mauritania	0.90	71.9	18.2	Japan	2.4	1
Mauritius	4.03	62.4	30.5	United Kingdom	18.0	0
Nicaragua	2.07	30.2	54.5	United States	9.3	0
Solomon Islands	0.32	82.4	36.0	Japan	5.4	1
Tajikistan	0.98	83.8	46.4	Uzbekistan	—	1
Turkmenistan	1.64	201.2	22.0	Iran	0.9	1
Flexible arrangements: Independent float						
Albania	3.94	20.1	59.4	Italy	4.5	0
Armenia	1.86	37.1	23.2	Belgium	3.6	0
Eritrea	0.65	34.1	—	—	37.2	1
Gambia, The	0.41	54.5	72.8	Belgium	9.6	0
Guinea	3.83	21.5	14.9	United States	0.7	1
Guyana	0.74	103.4	25.2	Canada	—	0
Haiti	3.89	15.3	86.3	United States	36.6	0
Madagascar	3.75	25.0	45.7	France	8.7	0
Moldova	2.25	55.6	50.5	Russia	3.3	1
Mongolia	1.06	52.2	49.5	China, PR Mainlar	4.4	0
Mozambique	3.89	28.7	17.1	Spain	—	0
Papua New Guinea	3.70	63.7	18.7	Australia	2.9	1

(Continued)

Table 3. (*Continued*)

	Size of Economy (Billions of U.S. Dollars)	Trade as Share of GDP[b]	Largest Export		Tourism Receipts in Percentage of Exports[e]	Controls on Current Account[e]
			Share[c]	Partner[d]		
Rwanda	2.08	13.8	32.9	Belgium	0.7	1
Sao Tome and Principe	0.04	66.6	85.9	Netherlands	32.3	1
Sierra Leone	0.65	26.7	33.5	Belgium	10.9	1
Somalia	2.16	16.4	59.8	Saudi Arabia	—	1
Zambia	3.35	33.8	10.3	Saudi Arabia	5.1	0
Memorandum item: Fraction of countries with controls						
Small economies	0.67					
Industrial countries	0.00					
Other Developing countries	0.59					
Other Transition countries	0.44					

Notes: [a]Countries with estimated nominal GDP less than 5 billion U.S. dollars in 1998 (subject to availability of data from the WEO). [b]Average of exports and imports in percent of GDP. [c]Country's exports to most important trading partner as a share of total exports. [d]Partner country for largest exports. [e]As of 1997. [f]Country officially reports a managed or independent float. [g]Pegged to the Indian rupee. [h]Pegged to the Singapore dollar. [i]Pegged to the Portuguese escudo. [j]Pegged to the Australian dollar. [k]Pegged to the South African rand. [l]Pegged to the Italian lira.
Source: International Monetary Fund, World Economic Outlook, Direction of Trade Statistics and Annual Report on Exchange Arrangements and Exchange Restrictions and country desks; World Bank, World Development Indicators.

well as willingness to give up monetary independence are clearly relevant, indeed controlling, in the longer term. For the near to medium term, however, various considerations argue against hard pegs and in favor of more flexible exchange arrangements. Time is needed to strengthen fiscal policies and to address weaknesses in financial sectors and thereby better prepare for full capital market

Exchange Rate Regimes of Developing Countries

Table 4. Economies with GDPs between \$5 billion and \$20 billion[a] — Exchange Rate Arrangements and Selected Indicators (1998 unless otherwise indicated)

	Size of Economy (Billions of U.S. Dollars)	Trade as Share of GDP[b]	Largest Export		Tourism Receipts in Exports[e]	Controls on Current Account[e]
			Share[c]	Partner[d]		
Pegged arrangements: Pegged to a single currency						
Pegged to the U.S. dollar						
Panama	9.22	37.1	42.2	United States	4.5	0
Bahrain[f]	5.35	88.5	17.2	India	—	0
El Salvador[g]	12.13	28.9	56.0	United States	2.5	0
Lebanon	17.07	33.0	12.1	Saudi Arabia	64.2	0
Lithuania	10.69	62.2	16.5	Russia	6.9	0
Oman	14.96	50.2	21.2	Thailand	1.4	1
Qatar[f]	11.70	48.9	47.5	Japan	—	0
Syrian Arab Republic	15.37	33.5	14.5	Germany	22.1	1
Pegged to the French franc						
Cameroon	8.70	25.6	20.7	Italy	1.6	1
Cote d'Ivoire	11.10	41.0	—	—	1.8	1
Pegged to Other Currency						
Bulgaria[h]	12.06	49.5	13.1	Italy	6.3	1
Estonia[h]	5.11	82.0	18.9	Sweden	13.2	0
Nepal[i]	5.71	31.2	32.8	India	16.2	1
Luxembourg[j]	16.59	40.3	29.5	Germany	—	0
Pegged arrangements: Pegged to a currency basket						
Jordan	7.45	63.0	15.0	Saudi Arabia	19.5	0
Latvia	6.19	56.2	15.6	Germany	6.4	0
Cyprus	8.88	26.7	17.6	United Kingdom	—	1
Iceland	8.30	36.6	18.9	United Kingdom	5.8	0

(Continued)

Table 4. (*Continued*)

	Size of Economy (Billions of U.S. Dollars)	Trade as Share of GDP[b]	Largest Export		Tourism Receipts in Exports[e]	Controls on Current Account[e]
			Share[c]	Partner[d]		
Flexible arrangements: Other managed float						
Angola	6.65	52.6	59.1	United States	0.2	1
Belarus	14.28	69.2	60.9	Russia	0.6	1
Bolivia	8.68	20.4	19.4	Spain	13.2	1
Cambodia	13.80	1.3	37.3	United States	16.2	1
Costa Rica	10.42	47.7	51.7	United States	16.8	0
Dominican Republic	16.04	35.0	9.3	United States	32.8	1
Ecuador	19.30	28.6	35.5	United States	4.8	0
Ethiopia	6.38	21.6	26.0	Germany	3.5	1
Georgia	5.47	15.8	19.8	Russia	—	1
Honduras	5.37	42.3	73.2	United States	5.5	0
Kenya	10.37	30.9	14.0	United Kingdom	13.4	0
Paraguay	10.93	26.0	27.2	Brazil	17.5	1
Slovenia	19.99	56.1	28.4	Germany	12.2	0
Sri Lanka	15.70	41.4	37.6	United States	3.8	1
Sudan	10.11	13.3	22.2	Saudi Arabia	1.3	1
Flexible arrangements: Independent float						
Congo, Dem. Rep. of	6.16	21.2	52.1	Belgium	0.1	1
Ghana	7.17	29.9	11.8	United Kingdom	16.1	1
Guatemala	19.43	21.8	51.5	United States	10.2	0

(*Continued*)

Exchange Rate Regimes of Developing Countries

Table 4. (*Continued*)

	Size of Economy (Billions of U.S. Dollars)	Trade as Share of GDP[b]	Largest Export		Tourism Receipts in Exports[e]	Controls on Current Account[e]
			Share[c]	Partner[d]		
Jamaica	7.06	50.9	38.7	United States	35.6	0
Tanzania	8.09	22.2	8.5	India	30.0	1
Trinidad and Tobago	6.13	44.0	38.4	United States	7.6	0
Uganda	6.06	20.5	14.3	Spain	12.5	0
Yemen, Rep. of	5.33	53.8	30.6	China, PR Mainland	2.7	0
Zimbabwe	5.66	47.3	13.7	South Africa	8.2	1

Notes: [a]Countries with estimated nominal GDP greater than 5 and less than 20 billion U.S. dollars in 1998 (subject to availability of data from the WEO). [b]Average of exports and imports in percent of GDP. [c]Country's exports to most important trading partner as a share of total exports. [d]Partner country for largest exports. [e]As of 1997. [f]Country officially reports a regime of limited flexibility in terms of a single currency. [g]Country officially reports a regime of managed floating. [h]Pegged to the deutsche mark. [i]Pegged to the Indian rupee. [j]Pegged to the Belgian franc (adopted the Euro since January 1999).
Sources: International Monetary Fund, World Economic Outlook, Direction of Trade Statistics and Annual Report on Exchange Arrangements and Exchange Restrictions and country desks; World Bank, World Development Indicators.

opening. It is also important to allow for a possible conflict between exchange rate stability and price stability that may arise because of substantial differences in productivity growth as the transition countries continue to catch up with their more mature partners (Masson, 1999). Nevertheless, with a view toward their ultimate objective, these countries will want to lay the firm foundations that are demanded for successful exchange rate pegs by countries substantially open to global financial markets.

Yet a third group for which exchange rate pegs are relevant is that of developing countries that face the difficult problem of stabilizing from a situation of high inflation. Exchange-rate-based stabilizations have been used quite successfully by a number of countries in this situation (see IMF, 2000). The key to success in many cases, however, has been in knowing when and how to exit from an exchange rate peg that has done its job in helping to achieve (often dramatic) disinflation with comparatively little economic cost, but which is not sustainable in the longer term.

Beyond these specific groups (which together account for a substantial number of countries), there are a significant number of large, mid-sized, and smaller developing and transition countries for which some form of pegged exchange rate, tight band, crawling band, or heavily managed float is the relevant exchange rate regime. One important example is the largest developing country, China.

China's official exchange rate policy is a managed float, but within that policy, the exchange rate of the yuan has been tightly linked to the U.S. dollar since mid-1995. With a substantial (but recently declining) current account surplus, with large foreign exchange reserves, and with controls that sharply limit short-term capital inflows and outflows, China has maintained its *de facto* exchange rate peg through all of the turmoil of recent emerging market crises, thereby making an important contribution to the restoration of financial stability in the region. The financial infrastructure for a broad, deep, and resilient foreign exchange market for the Chinese currency does not now exist and would take time to develop. A gradual move to more flexibility in the future, combined with development of the financial infrastructure, would be consistent with other desirable reforms in the Chinese economy.

Other developing countries (of varying economic size) are in situations not too different from that of China, at least with respect to their exchange rate regimes. Without significant involvement in global financial markets, especially for short-term flows, these countries are generally less vulnerable than most emerging market economies to a rapid and massive build-up of speculative pressures against a pegged exchange rate. Often lacking the relevant infrastructure for a viable foreign exchange market that would operate with reasonable stability in the absence of guidance from the authorities, these countries typically have either pegged or heavily managed exchange rates.

Many of these exchange rate regimes can, and do, function reasonably successfully provided that some key conditions are met. The most important ones concern the nexus between exchange rate policy and monetary policy — the subject of the next section. While monetary policy may have some limited flexibility to pursue other objectives, it is essential that the expansion of domestic money and credit not undermine the exchange rate regime. If significant disequilibria begin to develop between the actual exchange rate and its economically appropriate level, it is important that decisions to adjust the exchange rate be taken before the necessary adjustment becomes seriously destabilizing. To contain the potential damage from exchange rate adjustments when they are needed, it is also important to ensure that domestic businesses and financial institutions do not take on substantial net foreign-currency liabilities under the incentives created by the quasi-insurance suggested by a pegged exchange rate — a task that is presumably easier in countries with only limited access to modern global financial markets.

4.2. *Exchange Rate Pegs as Nominal Anchors*

It is important to recognize that for centuries up until the 1970s, the values of all national monies, except for occasional periods of war or other substantial disruption, were fundamentally defined by linking their values to some external asset. Gold and silver were the key external assets through the early part of this century. After World War II, under the Bretton Woods system, nations pledged to maintain the values of their currencies within narrow bands of central parities defined against the U.S. dollar, and the dollar was pegged (somewhat tenuously) to gold. Only since 1973 have we had an international monetary system in which exchange rates of the national currencies of the three largest industrial countries and some of the mid-sized industrial countries float in response to market pressures without much official guidance. Indeed, most of the mid-sized industrial countries in Europe have not liked free floating, have instead fastened their exchange rates increasingly tightly to the deutsche mark, and have now moved on to monetary union.

For many developing countries, particularly those with less sophisticated financial systems, it may simply be unreasonable to think that there can be a credible anchor for expectations about monetary policy and for the exchange rate if the authorities do not establish some guide for the value of the money that they create in terms of some readily available alternative asset of stable value. Pegging the exchange rate, or tightly managing its range of variability, is a simple, transparent, and time-honored way of providing such an anchor, and for many developing countries there may be no readily available alternative.

4.3. *Pegs, Baskets, Bands, and Crawls*

The general characteristic of pegged exchange rate regimes is that the policy authorities undertake an explicit or understood commitment to limit fluctuation of the exchange rate to a degree that provides a meaningful nominal anchor for private expectations about the behavior of the exchange rate and the requisite supporting behavior of monetary policy. There is a broad range of regimes with this general characteristic, in terms of the degree of permissible exchange rate flexibility, from very hard, single-currency pegs, to basket pegs, to bands, to adjustable pegs and bands, to crawling pegs and bands, and to managed floats.

Aside from outright adoption of another country's currency, the hardest form of a pegged exchange rate regime is a currency board.[11] Under a currency board, monetary policy is entirely subordinated to the exchange rate regime; and expansions and contractions in the supply of base money (and, therefore, movements in domestic interest rates) are determined by foreign exchange inflows and

---

[11] Currency boards have been in operation in several countries, including Djibouti (since 1949), Brunei Darussalam (since 1967), Hong Kong China (since 1983), Argentina (since 1991), Estonia (since 1992), Lithuania (since 1994), Bulgaria (since 1997), and Bosnia and Herzegovina (since 1997). For further discussion of currency board arrangements, see Baliño and Enoch (1997).

outflows. These arrangements leave no room for adjustments in the real exchange rate through changes in the nominal exchange rate. Accordingly, adjustments to changing economic conditions affecting the equilibrium real exchange rate, including temporary shocks, must be made by other means, including changes in the levels of domestic prices and costs and (usually short-run) changes in the levels of economic activity and employment. Thus, among the criteria that make a pegged exchange rate regime economically sensible, countries with currency boards need to be particularly mindful of the desirability of flexibility in their economies and in their economic policies (other than exchange rate and monetary policy). The key conditions for the successful operation of a currency board, in addition to the usual conditions deemed desirable for a fixed exchange rate regime, are a sound banking system, because the monetary authorities cannot extend credit to banks experiencing difficulties, and a prudent fiscal policy, owing to the prohibition of central bank lending to the government.

Even for countries that adopt currency boards, as well as for less stringent forms of pegged exchange rate regimes, one way to retain the main anchor properties of an exchange rate peg while gaining some adaptability to one potentially important source of external disturbances — fluctuations among the exchange rates of the major international currencies — is to peg to a currency basket. The weights of the various currencies in the basket could reflect, for example, the geographical composition of the country's trade pattern or the currency weights of the SDR. Relative to a single-currency peg, this alternative has the advantage of reducing the volatility of the effective exchange rate, especially for countries with diversified trade patterns vis-à-vis the major currency areas. Basket pegs, however, may reduce the microeconomic and informational benefits of maintaining constant at least one, typically the most important, bilateral exchange rate relevant for price comparisons and economic transactions. Also, basket pegs may be less transparent than single-currency pegs. This may be particularly the case in countries where there is widespread use of a foreign currency and pegging to that currency has immediate popular understanding. In

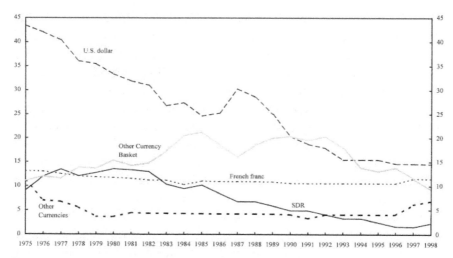

Figure 7. Developing Countries: Evolution of Pegged Exchange Rate Regimes, based on Officially Reported Exchange Rate Arrangements as of year-end, 1975–1998 (in percentage of Total Number of Developing Countries)
Source: IMF's Annual Report on Exchange Arrangements and Exchange Restrictions.

practice, basket pegs are not used as often as single-currency pegs, and their popularity, which peaked in the first half of the 1980s, declined during the 1990s (Fig. 7). This decline probably is related to the fact that basket pegs share many of the characteristics of single-currency pegs, which have also been in decline in the officially reported exchange rate regimes.

Most countries with pegged exchange rate regimes do not fix the rate absolutely, but rather undertake an official commitment to keep the exchange rate from fluctuating beyond some permissible band.[12] This commitment can take the form of a public announcement of a band of admissible values for the exchange rate which the authorities will defend by buying or selling in the market, or there could be a

---

[12] The distinction between a peg and a band is somewhat arbitrary, but a peg is usually understood as a band in which the margins on either side of its central parity are less than or equal to 1%. In addition, note that a peg or a band can be fixed or can be reset periodically in a series of mini devaluations. In the latter case, it is customary to label the peg or band as a crawling or a sliding peg or band.

de facto band where the public learns of the government's policy through its actions in the market.[13]

When the inflation rate in a country is substantially above that in the major industrial countries (and an immediate effort to reduce inflation to very low rates is not feasible or desirable), a crawling peg or crawling band becomes a relevant exchange regime option. A passive crawling peg or crawling band where the parity is adjusted for past inflation has the virtue that it avoids a tendency for the real exchange rate to appreciate out of line with economic fundamentals, and the rate of crawl can be adjusted to deal with changes in fundamentals. The disadvantage of such a regime, however, is that while it may help stabilize the behavior of the exchange rate in the relatively short run, it provides no medium-term nominal anchor. The tendency is to have not a crawling, but rather a galloping peg or band that keeps inflation running at a high rate. A strategy that has been used to deal with this problem and to help bring about a gradual disinflation (for example, in Israel since the late 1980s and 1990s and in Poland since the mid 1990s) is to use an active crawling peg or band where the rate of crawl is preannounced for up to a year in advance, with the objective of influencing expectations and price setting behavior.

For an active band or crawling band to be useful in stabilizing expectations, however, it is necessary that the authorities be perceived to have a serious commitment to the arrangement. This, in turn, requires that the authorities face significant costs from abandoning their commitment — costs that are well illustrated by some initially successful exchange-rate-based stabilizations that subsequently broke down.

---

[13]In the words of Frankel (1999, p. 6), when a central bank "announces a band around a crawling basket peg, it takes a surprisingly large number of daily observations for a market participant to solve the statistical problem, either explicitly or implicitly, of estimating the parameters (the weights in the basket, the rate of the crawl, and the width of the band) and thus testing the hypothesis that the central bank is abiding by its announced regime. This is particularly true if the central bank does not announce the weights in the basket (as is usually the case) or other parameters. By contrast, market participants can instantly verify the announcement of a simple dollar peg."

Indeed, the principal difficulty of band arrangements, including crawling bands, is that when the exchange rate is driven to the limits of the band (particularly the most depreciated limit), these arrangements work pretty much as standard exchange rate pegs, and thus can face the same type of problems. The currencies of Mexico before December 1994, Indonesia before August 1997, and Russia before August 1998 were all in crawling band arrangements. In fact, an exchange rate band may be less credible than a peg, especially a hard peg such as a currency board, which typically conveys the impression of stronger commitment of monetary policy to the exchange rate regime. Bands typically function best as regimes of policy compromise when there is the readiness to adjust the central parity (or rate of crawl) in a timely manner in response to changing economic fundamentals.

Somewhere along the spectrum of regimes of increasing exchange rate flexibility lie regimes of *managed floating*. Unfortunately this has a sufficiently ambiguous meaning that it seems to cover a range from *de facto* pegging to something close to a free float. For those managed floats that lie close to the pegging end of the spectrum, the comments that have already been made about various forms of pegged exchange rate regimes continue to apply. There can be some flexibility in the exchange rate, but there must also be a meaningful commitment to defend what the public understands to be the authorities' commitments regarding the exchange rate and related policies. Tightly managed floats provide a nominal anchor and help to stabilize exchange rates and expectations concerning exchange rates, inflation, and monetary policy, but they are subject to market pressures, potential crises, and costly breakdowns. Monetary policy arrangements with floating exchange rates under a loosely managed float allow market forces substantial latitude to influence the exchange rate in the short term and in the longer term. Through official intervention and adjustments of monetary policy, the authorities may seek to limit exchange rate fluctuations in the near term, but there is no policy commitment, explicit or implied, to keep the exchange rate within some range or crawling band. The exchange rate in this case is not a nominal anchor. In these critical respects, loosely managed floats are in the same basic category of exchange rate regimes as free floats. Under the evolving conditions described in Section 2, especially the increasing involvement in global capital markets, a number of developing countries have moved to exchange rate regimes in this category.[14]

It is important to emphasize that, for floating rate regimes to function effectively, exchange rates should actually be allowed to move — in both directions — in response to market forces, sometimes by significant amounts in short periods. Only such movement can persuade private economic agents to recognize and to manage prudently the foreign exchange risks that are inescapable for countries open to global financial markets. This does not imply a policy of benign neglect toward the exchange rate. For emerging market countries that are generally quite open to international trade as well as to global finance, movements in exchange rates have important economic consequences, and it is often appropriate for economic policies, including monetary policies and official exchange market intervention, to take account of and react to exchange rate developments. However, tight management of the exchange rate that provides the convenience of limited exchange rate volatility in normal times also tends to foster dangerous complacency about foreign exchange risks that can suddenly become quite large, as was dramatically illustrated in the Asian crisis. Thus, for emerging market countries that cannot or choose not to undertake the very strict regimen necessary to sustain pegged exchange rate regimes in an environment of international capital mobility, it is essential that floating exchange rates really do float.

As the exchange rate does not fulfill the role of nominal anchor in these floating rate regimes, a key issue is how to establish a credible alternative nominal anchor. Institutional arrangements are important in this regard. In particular, central bank independence is important to help to mitigate fears that the lack of exchange

---

[14]For analyses of the float of the Mexican peso, see Edwards and Savastano (1998) and Carstens and Werner (1999).

rate anchor could let loose the money-printing demon.[15] The central bank need not have goal independence, but it should have substantial operational independence (and tenure protection) to pursue an appropriate nominal target that is independent from the financing needs of the public sector and from short-sighted considerations associated with the political cycle. The fact that most developing countries have brought inflation down suggests that there may be a growing political consensus in these countries on the need to liberate monetary policy from these inflationary pressures.

The successful adoption of floating exchange rate arrangements also requires definition of the objective that is to guide the conduct of monetary policy and, accordingly, provide the foundation for private sector expectations. For this purpose, inflation targeting frameworks such as those adopted in several industrial countries since the early 1990s are likely to receive increasing attention. Under these frameworks, monetary policy is characterized by the announcement of targets for the rate of inflation at some low level or range, the periodic assessment of expected inflation over a medium-term horizon, and the systematic adjustment of the monetary policy instrument in order to maintain the relevant inflation measure in line with the target. In addition, inflation targeting frameworks have often been characterized by increased transparency and accountability of monetary policy, though these features are in principle independent of them and desirable in themselves.

An inflation targeting framework allows a degree of discretion and flexibility in the conduct of monetary policy. On the one hand, in practical inflation targeting frameworks, monetary policy decisions are made on a day-to-day basis with no precise rules for the setting of the level of the monetary policy instrument. Also, the inflation targets only are set for a medium-term horizon and, in some cases, the central bank reserves the right to make *ad hoc* adjustments to the

---

[15]Many developing countries have already increased the degree of independence of their central banks. See Cottarelli and Giannini (1997).

inflation measure being targeted. On the other hand, the emphasis on inflation as the overriding objective of the central bank, and the increased transparency and accountability of monetary policy that often have accompanied the adoption of inflation targeting frameworks, can help to put some checks or limits on the degree to which the discretionary powers of the central bank may be used in practice.

The fact that actual inflation targeting frameworks do not tie tightly the hands of the monetary authority, however, implies that the adoption of such a framework could deliver the costs of discretion rather than the benefits of flexibility. For this reason, the importance of the institutional preconditions mentioned above, particularly central bank independence, cannot be exaggerated. Technical expertise is also of key importance for the successful implementation of an inflation targeting framework.[16] In particular, since there are considerable lags in the effect of monetary policy on inflation, it is important to have an effective forecasting procedure which will signal when changes in the monetary stance are needed to avoid deviations from the target. In addition, many developing countries suffer from large supply shocks and have a substantial number of administered prices. Since on occasion it may be difficult to disentangle the effects on inflation of those shocks from those implied by monetary policy mistakes, the accountability of monetary policymakers under inflation targeting may thus be lower in these countries than in the advanced countries. Notwithstanding these difficulties, several advanced developing and transition countries are putting in place inflation targeting frameworks as part of a move away from the use of the exchange rate as nominal anchor. These countries include Brazil, Chile, the Czech Republic, Israel, Mexico, and Poland.

An alternative to an inflation target as a nominal anchor under a floating exchange rate regime is to announce targets for the growth

---

[16]The preconditions for the successful adoption of an inflation targeting framework are discussed in Masson *et al.* (1998).

184   *Esteban Jadresic, Paul R. Masson and Paolo Mauro*

rate of some monetary aggregate (or group of aggregates). Such arrangements would presumably be attractive in countries where the relation between monetary growth and inflation is reasonably reliable and where the monetary authorities have relatively good control of the targeted aggregate. However, these conditions seem rarely to be met in developing countries. Nevertheless, money growth targets may still be useful if they are an effective means of communicating the intentions of the monetary authorities, with the understanding that the authorities have a responsibility to explain deviations from their announced targets as an essential part of their public accountability. Thought of in this way, money growth targets can be used as a supplement to, rather than a replacement for, inflation targets.[17]

4.4. *Benign Neglect, Intervention, and Controls*

Under all exchange regimes other than absolute free floating, ancillary policies to affect the foreign exchange market through official intervention and controls merit attention. Here, the key point to recognize is that, even for those developing and transition countries for which it is reasonable and appropriate to move toward the floating rate end of the spectrum of exchange arrangements, benign neglect of the exchange rate is unlikely to be a desirable policy. If the foreign exchange market is thin and dominated by a relatively small number of agents, it is likely that the exchange rate will be volatile unless the authorities provide some guidance and support. This problem is compounded if, as is often the case, there is no long track record of stable macroeconomic policies that can firmly anchor market expectations about the future monetary and exchange rate policy. Also, underdeveloped and incomplete financial markets imply that hedging against exchange rate risk is usually costly

---

[17] A recent survey of the use of explicit targets for monetary policy conducted by the Bank of England (see Sterne, 1999) reports that countries that had both inflation and money targets (and sometimes exchange rate targets as well) substantially exceeded the number of countries that had either only an inflation target or only a money target.

and sometimes impossible.[18] As a result, the costs of exchange rate volatility can be substantial for individual agents and for the economy as a whole. In particular, economies with weak financial sector regulation and supervision, and where banks and corporations have a large exposure to foreign currency borrowing, can be highly vulnerable to unexpected fluctuations in the exchange rate.

Indeed, the facts reveal that developing countries with relatively flexible exchange rate regimes generally do not practice benign neglect of the exchange rate. Compared to the G-3 countries, these developing countries tend to put much more of the weight of the adjustment to macroeconomic shocks on variations in interest rates and in international reserves than on variations in the exchange rate. This is illustrated in Table 5, which reports the volatility of the monthly exchange rates, interest rates, and international reserves in selected developing and developed countries between January 1995 and December 1998. The typical developing country in this category showed a similar degree of exchange rate volatility to that observed in industrial countries with floating regimes. However, the volatility of interest rates in developing countries with flexible exchange rate regimes was substantially larger than in the G-3 and typically larger than in other industrial countries. Also, the volatility of international reserves of the developing countries with flexible regimes tended to be higher than in the G-3. Thus, facing generally larger macroeconomic shocks than the industrial countries, developing countries with flexible exchange rate regimes placed substantially greater importance on the stability of their exchange rates than did the G-3 or other industrial countries with floating rates. That developing countries care more about exchange rate fluctuations is also reflected in the fact that, when measured relative to imports, GDP, and especially broad money, their demand for international reserves tends to be much larger than for industrial country floaters.

---

[18]Pegged rates may also in the past have discouraged the development of hedging instruments by underplaying the risk of exchange rate fluctuations.

Table 5. Selected Countries with Flexible Exchange Rate Arrangements: Volatility of Exchange Rate, Interest Rate and International Reserves, January 1995–December 1998

	Volatility[a] of			Ratio of Exchange Rate Volatility to		International Reserves		
	Exchange Rate[b]	Interest Rate	International Reserves	Interest Rate Volatility	International Reserve Volatility	In Months of Imports	In Percentage of GDP	In Percentage of Broad Money
Developing countries								
Boliviac[c]	0.3	1.2	6.7	0.3	0.0	5.2	10.9	25.1
Chile[c]	1.6	3.6	3.0	0.4	0.5	8.9	22.2	55.5
Colombia[c]	2.5	6.5	3.0	0.4	0.8	6.0	9.9	49.1
Gambia[d]	0.8	0.1	3.7	6.6	0.2	5.7	25.7	103.1
Ghana[d]	1.8	1.5	11.0	1.2	0.2	2.9	9.5	57.7
India[d]	1.8	0.4	3.9	4.2	0.5	6.8	5.5	12.5
Mauritius[c]	1.8	0.6	4.4	3.2	0.4	3.6	18.7	25.4
Mexico[d]	4.6	9.1	19.7	0.5	0.2	2.5	6.1	23.5
Peru[d]	1.0	4.2	3.4	0.2	0.3	14.2	15.8	73.5
Singapore[c]	2.4	1.0	2.6	2.4	0.9	7.1	81.3	95.2
South Africa[d]	3.2	0.9	20.2	3.6	0.2	1.1	2.4	3.9
Sri Lanka[c]	0.5	13.6	4.7	0.0	0.1	4.3	14.4	45.6
Tanzania[d]	2.4	5.2	19.9	0.5	0.1	3.3	5.5	29.4

Turkey[c]	2.0	9.1	8.1	0.2	0.3	4.7	9.3	36.8
Uruguay[c]	0.7	9.7	6.2	0.1	0.1	3.7	7.1	18.0
Zambia[d]	4.0	2.7	113.1	1.5	0.0	1.9	6.8	42.8
Zimbabwe[d]	5.2	3.9	28.9	1.3	0.2	1.7	5.7	23.6
G-3 countries								
Germany[d]	2.6	0.1	2.3	22.4	1.1	2.1	3.6	6.3
Japan[d]	4.3	0.1	3.0	35.9	1.4	7.5	4.7	4.2
United States[d]	1.5	0.1	3.6	11.2	0.4	0.9	0.8	1.5
Other industrial countries								
Australia[d]	2.5	0.2	6.8	15.9	0.4	2.5	3.7	5.8
Canada[d]	1.4	0.4	7.2	3.3	0.2	1.2	3.1	5.2
Israel[c]	2.2	0.6	5.5	3.5	0.4	2.8	15.9	19.2
New Zealand[d]	2.7	0.7	6.5	4.0	0.4	3.9	7.7	9.2
United Kingdom[d]	1.9	0.3	3.5	5.5	0.5	1.5	3.0	3.0

Notes: [a]Volatility is defined as the standard deviation of the monthly growth rate of the series for the exchange rate and for international reserves and as the standard deviation of the difference for the interest rate.

[b]Bilateral versus the U.S. dollar for all countries except the United States; nominal effective exchange rate for the United States.

[c]Managed floaters.

[d]Independent floaters.

Source: International Monetary Fund, International Financial Statistics, World Economic Outlook.

In the absence of a policy of benign neglect of the exchange rate, an important issue is the extent to which sterilized interventions may help to deal with temporary perturbations in the foreign exchange market. In general, this type of intervention is likely to be more effective in countries with limited access to international capital markets and, therefore, where the authorities have relatively greater capacity to influence conditions in the foreign exchange market by directly buying or selling foreign exchange. For emerging market economies characterized by high international capital mobility, the effectiveness of sterilized interventions is likely to be more limited or larger interventions will be required to achieve a given effect. The willingness of the central bank and the treasury to defend the exchange rate using their own resources, however, may help to modify the expectations of other market participants, thus affecting also the level of supply and demand in the market. On the other hand, if private agents come to the conclusion that official efforts to control an exchange rate through intervention — especially intervention unsupported by monetary policy — are unsustainable, large resources to carry out intervention may be viewed as a profit opportunity.

Another important issue concerns the usefulness of controls as an element of exchange rate policy by countries that do have significant links to global capital markets. Here, it is relevant to distinguish between controls on capital outflows, which are put on to resist downward pressures on the exchange rate, and controls on capital inflows, which are intended to discourage particular forms of inflows. In the case of the former, success has been limited in the face of substantial and sustained pressures.[19] Concerning controls on inflows, for countries that maintain substantial openness to global financial markets (despite such controls), it is unclear

---

[19]Malaysia imposed outflow controls on September 1, 1998. In this case, the controls were never really tested in the sense that the exchange rate of the ringgit (like that of the other Asian crisis countries that did not impose controls) was not under significant downward pressure at the time the controls were imposed, since it came after the period of large depreciation.

whether they can have much effect in relieving upward pressures on the exchange rate. They may, however, be able to influence the composition of capital inflows — for good or ill. Controls that discourage foreign direct investment or longer-term credit inflows may indirectly encourage short-term credit inflows. Controls that sought to discourage short-term credit inflows (which are usually denominated in foreign currency) would tend to shift the composition of inflows in the reverse direction. Short-term credit inflows pose particular risks of financial crises and of possible systemic defaults, so that measures to shift the composition of international capital flows away from these inflows can help to diminish risks of crisis. In addition, to the extent that these measures raise the cost of short-term external indebtedness, they might also facilitate the defense of the exchange rate from the upward pressure stemming from the temporary inflows, while maintaining a degree of independence in the conduct of monetary policy.

5. Summary and Conclusions

For the broad range of developing and transition countries, exchange rates are typically very important macroeconomic variables and increasingly so because of the trends toward greater involvement of these countries in the global economic system. Reflecting wide differences in levels of economic and financial development and in other aspects of their economic situations, no single exchange rate regime is most appropriate for all of these countries, and the regime that is appropriate for a particular country may change over time.[20] Despite the diversity of possible arrangements, however, the following general conclusions can be stated.

First, for most emerging market countries, primarily in Asia and Latin America (but also some in Eastern Europe and South Africa), floating exchange rate regimes appear to be the increasingly relevant choice. For these emerging market countries, the tequila crisis of

---

[20]This is consistent with Frankel (1999): "...no single currency regime is right for all countries at all times."

1995 and the Asian–Russian–Brazilian crises of 1997–1998 forcefully illustrated what was demonstrated for the industrial countries in the ERM crises of 1992–1993 — that the policy requirements for maintaining a pegged exchange rate can be very demanding in circumstances of high international capital mobility. In this situation, several emerging market countries (including Mexico, Peru, and South Africa) successfully maintained floating exchange rate regimes. This provides evidence that floating rates are often the most workable regimes for many emerging market countries.

Second, for certain emerging market countries, pegged exchange rate regimes and their required supporting policies and institutions can be workable, despite substantial involvement with global financial markets. Notable in this category are countries that have already put in place the policies and institutions needed to support a pegged exchange rate, have established the credibility of those policies and institutions, and have induced appropriate behavior of the economic and financial system to the characteristics of the regime. For such countries, in general, the harder and more credible the peg, the better. In contrast, a pegged exchange rate regime that is adopted (*de jure* or *de facto*) when conditions are favorable, but without adequate policy commitment and institutional foundations, can become an invitation to costly crisis when conditions turn less favorable. An environment of capital mobility allows massive pressures to be exerted against a pegged exchange that, for whatever reasons, has become suspect in the market. To defend the peg, monetary policy must be able to respond forcefully, and the economy and financial system must be able to withstand the strain if the regime is to be credible. And, even for countries with strong foundations, maintenance of pegged exchange rates in a crisis environment can be a demanding endeavor.

Third, beyond the 30 or so emerging market economies, the majority of developing and transition economies do not have highly sophisticated domestic financial systems, are not deeply integrated into world capital markets, and (in many cases) maintain fairly extensive controls on capital account (and current account) transactions. These countries presently include a number of the larger

Exchange Rate Regimes of Developing Countries 191

and mid-sized developing countries. If inflation in these countries is high because of needs for monetary finance of the fiscal deficit or for other reasons, then exchange rate pegs cannot be sustained for long periods. However, if monetary policy can maintain reasonable discipline, then pegged exchange rate regimes (or bands, crawling pegs, or crawling bands) can on the contrary be viable and, if adjustments are undertaken in a timely manner, they need not be associated with costly crises. Nevertheless, as they become more developed, more financially sophisticated, and more integrated into global financial markets, these countries also will need to consider regimes of greater exchange rate flexibility.

Also in the group of peggers are many smaller countries that account for only a modest share of world output but are a substantial fraction of the countries in the world. Even for the most advanced of these small countries that want to maintain pegged exchange rates, moderate constraint on the development of financial instruments and practices that might facilitate speculation against the peg can probably help, along with disciplined monetary policy, to sustain the exchange rate regime. Moreover, for the many small countries that do maintain pegged exchange rates, the currencies to which they peg generally have a sensible and clearly understandable rationale.

Finally, another group of countries for which pegged exchange rates offer important attractions are countries that need to stabilize from situations of high inflation. The main challenge in these endeavors is to recognize that while an exchange rate peg may initially be very useful in the stabilization effort, the exchange rate peg (or crawling peg or band) may not be sustainable in the longer term. Thus, it is very important to know when, and under what circumstances, it may be appropriate to move away from a peg to forestall risks of a major future crisis. This is the issue of exit from an exchange rate peg that was discussed intensively in Eichengreen *et al.* (1998).

Acknowledgments

This paper is derived from a larger study that also considers the exchange rate regimes of industrial countries. The authors are grateful to a number of their colleagues, in particular to Andy Berg, Michael Mussa, and Alexander Swoboda, who participated in the larger study, and to participants in the ADBI/CEPII/KIEP conference on "Exchange Rate Regimes for Emerging Market Economies," held in Tokyo on December 17–18, 1999. Research assistance by Freyan Panthaki and Haiyan Shi is gratefully acknowledged. The views expressed are those of the authors and do not necessarily represent those of the IMF or other official institutions.

References

Aghevli, B. B., Khan, M. S., and Montiel, P. (1991). "Exchange Rate Policy in Developing Countries: Some Analytical Issues," IMF Occasional Paper 78, International Monetary Fund, Washington, DC.

Baliño, T., Enoch, C., and others (1997). "Currency Board Arrangements: Issues and Experiences," IMF Occasional Paper 151, International Monetary Fund, Washington, DC.

Calvo, G. (1999). "Capital Markets and the Exchange Rate, with Special Reference to the Dollarization Debate in Latin America," mimeograph, University of Maryland, October.

Calvo, G. and Végh, C. A. (1999). "Inflation Stabilization and BOP Crises in Developing Countries," NBER Working Paper 6925, February.

Carstens, A. G. and Werner, A. M. (1999, May). "Mexico's Monetary Policy Framework Under a Floating Exchange Rate Regime," Serie Documentos de Investigación 9905, Bank of Mexico.

Cottarelli, C. and Giannini, C. (1997). "Credibility without Rules? Monetary Frameworks in the Post-Bretton Woods Era," IMF Occasional Paper 154, International Monetary Fund, Washington, DC.

Edwards, S. and Savastano, M. (1999). "Exchange Rates in Emerging Economies: What Do We Know? What Do We Need to Know?" NBER Working Paper 7228, July.

Edwards, S. and Savastano, M. (1998). "The Morning After: The Mexican Peso in the Aftermath of the 1994 Currency Crisis," NBER Working Paper 6516, April.

Eichengreen, B. (1998). The only game in town, The World Today, December.

Eichengreen, B., Masson, P., Bredenkamp, H., Johnston, B., Hamann, J., Jadresic, E., and Ötker, I. (1998). "Exit Strategies: Policy Options for Countries Seeking Greater Exchange Rate Flexibility," IMF Occasional Paper 168, International Monetary Fund, Washington, DC.

Frankel, J. A. (1999, August). No single currency regime is right for all countries or at all times, in "Essays in International Finance," No. 215, Princeton University, Princeton, NJ.

Exchange Rate Regimes of Developing Countries

Ghosh, A. R., Gulde, A.-M., Ostry, J. D., and Wolf, H. C. (1995). "Does the Nominal Exchange Rate Regime Matter?," IMF Working Paper 95/121, International Monetary Fund, Washington, DC.

Hausman, R., Gavin, M., Pages-Serra, C., and Stein, E. (1999). "Financial Turmoil and the Choice of Exchange Rate Regime," mimeograph, Inter-American Development Bank.

IMF (1995a, August). "International Capital Markets Report," International Monetary Fund, Washington, DC.

IMF (1995b, April). "Issues in International Exchange and Payment Systems," International Monetary Fund, Washington, DC.

IMF (2000). "Exchange Rate Regimes in an Increasingly Integrated World Economy," IMF Occasional Paper 193, International Monetary Fund, Washington, DC.

Isard, P. (1995). "Exchange Rate Economics," Cambridge University Press, Cambridge, UK.

Masson, P.R. (1999). "Monetary and Exchange Rate Policy of Transition Economies of Central and Eastern Europe After the Launch of EMU," IMF Policy Discussion Paper 99/5, International Monetary Fund, Washington, DC.

Masson, P.R. (2000). Exchange rate regime transitions, *J. Devel. Econ.*, in press. [Also IMF Working Paper 00/134.]

Masson, P., Savastano, M., and Sharma, S. (1997). "The Scope for Inflation Targeting in Developing Countries," IMF Working Paper 97/130, International Monetary Fund, Washington, DC.

Obstfeld, M. (1995a). International currency experience: New lessons and lessons relearned, *Brookings Pap. Econ. Activity* **I**, 119–195.

Obstfeld, M. and Rogoff, K. (1995b). The mirage of fixed exchange rates, *J. Econ. Persp.* **9**, 73–96.

Sterne, G. (1999). The use of explicit targets for monetary policy: Practical experiences of 91 economies in the 1990s, *Bank of England Quart. Bull.*, August.

The World Bank (1997). "Private Capital Flows to Developing Countries," Oxford University Press, Oxford.

Wickham, P. (1985). The choice of exchange rate regime in developing countries, *Staff Papers* **32**, 248–288.

Chapter 6

Should African Monetary Unions Be Expanded? An Empirical Investigation of the Scope for Monetary Integration in Sub-Saharan Africa[*,†]

Xavier Debrun, Paul R. Masson and Catherine Pattillo

This paper develops a cost–benefit analysis of monetary integration and applies it to the currency unions being actively pursued in Africa. While many related studies have highlighted the problems associated with shock asymmetries, very few analyses have attempted to weigh these against potential benefits. In our model, the benefits of monetary union come from a more credible monetary policy and a correspondingly lower inflationary bias, while the costs derive from both output shock asymmetries (which are identified with different terms of trade movements) and fiscal disparities. Using African data, we estimate key equilibrium relationships of the model. These capture quite well the cross-country variation in inflation and fiscal revenues, allowing us to calibrate the

---

[*]This chapter originally appeared in *Journal of African Economies*, (2011), 20 (Suppl. 2), 104–150. At time of writing, Debrun and Pattillo were International Monetary Fund staff members, and Masson was Adjunct Professor at the University of Toronto.

[†]Revised version of the paper presented at the AERC Plenary Session on "Central Banking in a Changing African Environment", 29 November 2009, Nairobi, Kenya.

195

196   *Xavier Debrun, Paul R. Masson and Catherine Pattillo*

full model. The model simulations indicate that the proposed East African Community, Economic Community of West African States and Southern Africa Development Community monetary unions bring about net benefits to some potential members, but that many other prospective members record relatively modest net gains and sometimes net losses. The paper also discusses how strengthening domestic monetary and fiscal institutions is an alternative that can provide some of the same benefits of monetary unions and therefore reduce their relative attractiveness.

1. Introduction

Africa is the continent with the largest number of countries and, despite the existence of currency (or monetary) unions that share the CFA franc,[1] also with the largest number of currencies. Since many of the countries are small, both in population and economic terms, it is natural to ask whether greater regional integration — including monetary integration — is in Africa's interest. Over the decades since independence, various regional groupings have been involved in free trade arrangements, in some cases continuing or reviving those that existed under the colonial regimes. The CFA franc zones and the Common Monetary Area (CMA) in Southern Africa are the only monetary integration arrangements that are still in place. However, several regional currency union projects are actively being planned at present, and a common currency for Africa remains a long-term goal of the African Union.

This paper discusses the conditions for monetary integration to be beneficial, and attempts to give a quantitative assessment of the costs and benefits of the currency unions currently pursued in Africa. There have already been many studies of monetary union proposals for Africa, most of them illustrating the potential costs of a one-size-fits-all monetary policy for the members of those prospective unions. Regardless of the methodology, these studies mainly conclude that African economies are too different on too many counts to allow for sustainable monetary unions. Problematic asymmetries range

---

[1]Actually two separate currencies, the CFA francs issued by the West African and Central African central banks (BCEAO and BEAC, respectively). A survey of the monetary regimes in Africa is provided in Masson and Pattillo (2005).

from production structures (and hence different shocks to the terms of trade (TOT) and output) to institutional effectiveness — such as democratic accountability, control of corruption and government efficiency — all contributing to major disparities in economic performance, including public finances, inflation and growth.

This paper updates and extends our earlier work (Debrun *et al.*, 2005, 2008; Masson and Pattillo, 2005). Our contribution is to integrate traditional arguments against monetary unions — i.e., the costs of a one-size-fits-all monetary policy in a heterogeneous region deprived of fiscal federalism — with potential benefits in terms of enhanced policy credibility. These benefits were extensively debated in the European context. While they are in our view even more relevant in Africa, they have been consistently ignored by the literature on African integration. The novel elements of this paper include a more coherent calibration of the theoretical model based on more robust and updated empirical estimates and an explicit modelling of the substitutability between monetary integration and domestic institutional reforms. Our approach goes beyond traditional illustrations of disparities in output and price behaviors and establishes the relevance of asymmetries in institutional quality and credibility of national commitments to macroeconomic stability.

Although the simulation results are slightly more favourable to monetary union projects than in our earlier work, net gains still appear uncomfortably small or even negative for a number of potential members in all envisaged groupings. These results reflect the slow convergence in fiscal policy performance and the persistently low degree of regional trade integration. We also show that improved monetary policy credibility and effectiveness — the key source of gross benefits from monetary union — could be obtained by strengthening domestic fiscal frameworks and enacting greater central bank independence without incurring any of the costs of monetary unification.

The rest of the paper is structured as follows. Section 2 reviews the existing literature on African currency unions, concluding that it is generally biased towards an analysis of the costs and that it often lacks sound theoretical foundations. The model and its analytical solutions are discussed in Section 3. Section 4 reviews progress with respect to three major monetary union projects — namely those for the East African Community (EAC), the Southern Africa Development Community (SADC) and the Economic Community of West African States (ECOWAS). In Section 5, we calibrate the theoretical model to assess the viability of the above projects in terms of their net economic benefits. Although none of them is found to be severely detrimental to its potential members, net gains only appear significant for a minority of countries. Section 6 discusses the potential for domestic institutional reforms and the substitutability with country-specific incentives to pursue regional integration. Finally, Section 7 draws policy implications and identifies topics for further research.

2. The Desirability of African Monetary Unions: A Survey

There is an extensive literature assessing the advantages and disadvantages of monetary unions — actual and proposed — in Sub-Saharan Africa (SSA).[2] Broadly speaking, this literature has developed three main empirical approaches for considering the desirability of monetary unions: (i) attempts to measure the asymmetry of shocks, inspired by optimum currency area (OCA) theory pioneered by Mundell (1961); (ii) studies comparing macroeconomic performance of existing monetary unions with that of non-members; and (iii) measures of the convergence of various macroeconomic indicators among countries of the region, viewed as criteria for membership. These three traditional approaches all have their drawbacks. They do not provide any way of assessing whether benefits exceed costs, or whether joining monetary union would be better than strengthening domestic institutions. Moreover, they do not properly capture the dynamic nature of economic performance. A few recent papers deal

---

[2]This literature is too large to be exhaustively surveyed here. A comprehensive survey of the literature for Southern Africa is Tavlas (2009).

with some of these issues in the African context and are surveyed in the last sub-section.

2.1. *Studies of Exogenous Shock Asymmetry*

Focusing on the problems that asymmetric shocks among participants create for a monetary union, this approach requires identifying the relevant shocks. Many studies have used vector autoregressions (VARs) to explain the systematic fluctuations in output, the residuals being the shocks that may or may not be correlated across countries. Following Blanchard and Quah (1989), the VAR approach allows for an identification of demand and supply shocks. The latter pose greater problems for a monetary union because demand shocks can be expected to become more similar with a common monetary policy, while supply shocks cannot.

Bayoumi and Ostry (1997) also use a VAR to calculate the correlation of shocks to GDP growth affecting countries in the two CFA franc zones, ECOWAS, COMESA and SADC. Taking the correlations among the three largest industrial countries (Germany, Japan and the USA) as a benchmark, they conclude that the lower correlations observed among African countries weakens the case for monetary unions in Africa.

Horváth and Grabowski (1997) find that supply shocks — which pose the greatest problem for a currency union — are highly asymmetric. In a more detailed analysis of the CFA franc zones, Fielding and Shields (2001) find that price shocks are quite positively correlated, while for output shocks, in contrast, there are pairs of countries with negative correlations, which could be a potential problem for the existing CFA franc zones.

More recent studies have echoed the broad conclusion that real shocks hitting African economies, including those in the same region, are highly asymmetric, due in part to very different mixes of commodity production. Buigut and Valev (2006) confirm this conclusion for Eastern and Southern Africa, though they do find a few sub-regional clusters that may benefit from a currency union. Houssa (2008) relies on the more parsimonious dynamic structural factor analysis to identify demand and supply shocks, supporting the conclusion that countries would find forming a monetary union challenging.

Debrun *et al.* (2005) simply assume that supply shocks originate in the TOT. A small open economy faces exogenous TOT, so that the endogeneity of output fluctuations does not need to be filtered out. They found that TOT correlations were low, and sometimes negative, for pairs of ECOWAS countries, while Masson and Pattillo (2005) found a similar result for other regions. Wang *et al.* (2007) found that even the CMA countries, with tight trade links and long-standing exchange rate union, do not exhibit consistently positive TOT correlations.

2.2. *Comparison of Macroeconomic Performance and Fiscal Discipline in Currency Unions with Other SSA Countries*

The desirability of monetary unions can be assessed by comparing economic performance in existing unions to that of countries that have retained national monetary autonomy. While some of these studies are purely empirical, others attempt to understand the complex interaction between monetary and fiscal policies in monetary unions, and whether membership enhances fiscal and monetary discipline.

Early literature concluded that the two CFA zones provided better real economic performance than the rest of SSA (Guillaumont and Guillaumont, 1984; Devarajan and de Melo, 1987), but the over-valuation of the currency deteriorated economic growth, requiring a large devaluation in 1994. However, it remains that inflation rates have been unambiguously lower over the past 5 decades than in the rest of SSA (Masson and Pattillo, 2005, Chapter 4).

The reasons why a monetary union in SSA might provide better economic performance are discussed in a series of articles. Collier (1991) suggests that it provides an 'agency of restraint' for fiscal policies, and in particular, the French treasury enforced that discipline for the CFA franc zone, via the exchange rate peg to the franc and statutory limits on lending associated with the treasury's guarantee of the peg. Guillaume and Stasavage (2000), however, conclude that the two CFA central banks did not in fact discipline fiscal policies because they evaded the statutory limits, and that these lapses contributed to the problems that CFA countries faced in the late 1980s and early 1990s. Masson and Pattillo (2002) argue that a monetary union in ECOWAS would be insufficient in itself to exert fiscal discipline and would have to be supported by effective institutions of regional surveillance over fiscal policies.

Even if the regional central bank does not necessarily discipline fiscal policy, it does have a different status relative to national finance ministries than does a national central bank. In essence, the power of each country's fiscal policy to extract financing from the central bank is weakened in a regional context. The model used in Debrun *et al.* (2005) and Masson and Pattillo (2005) incorporates that feature, while also including the asymmetry of shocks (highlighted by the OCA literature) in the welfare calculus. Despite this, those two studies were relatively pessimistic that extending monetary unions beyond the CFA to ECOWAS, or the creation of new African monetary unions, would enhance welfare.

2.3. *Regional Convergence as a Precondition to Membership*

Prospective monetary unions have also been evaluated on the basis of largely *ad hoc* convergence criteria.[3] Drawing on the EU experience, these studies have concentrated on convergence of inflation to a low value, and the reduction of public deficits and debt ratios below some critical values. In addition, since the range of levels of development is much greater than in Europe, some proxy for them, such as per capita income, has sometimes been applied. Generally, these studies highlight the challenges of achieving regional convergence: there are

---

[3]While structural and fiscal variables can give a good sense of an economy's resilience to shocks, purely nominal variables (interest rates, inflation, exchange rate fluctuations) are less informative on the fitness to join a given union because much of these nominal discrepancies are precisely due to the absence of such a union in the first place (Wyplosz, 1997).

large initial differences, and partial success in narrowing them is often reversed subsequently.

Jenkins and Thomas (1996), for instance, concluded that the SADC had not reached sufficient convergence to plan for a monetary union, a conclusion echoed by Masson and Pattillo (2005) almost a decade later. Agbeyegbe (2008) estimates a model with time varying parameters and concludes that there is lack of convergence of nominal exchange rates and consumer prices among SADC countries. However, Burgess (2009) found that the SADC countries, except for Zimbabwe, had made solid progress in macroeconomic convergence, so that prospects for proceeding to monetary union were more favourable.

In West Africa, data using the convergence criteria adopted by WAEMU showed that a period of convergence towards fiscal discipline in the aftermath of the 1994 devaluation was followed by a relaxation of efforts and divergence in these countries (Doré and Masson, 2002). As for the non-CFA countries in the region that are preparing for a monetary union — the West African Monetary Zone (WAMZ) — the most recent convergence report (WAMZ, 2008) concluded that 'the pace of progress has been slow' in achieving the convergence criteria that were to have led to a monetary union in 2009, now postponed until 2015. More formal analyses of cross-country dispersion examine convergence of macroeconomic variables. A recent study for the EAC found some evidence of convergence of monetary policy variables, no evidence for fiscal and mixed results on other macroeconomic indicators (Opolot and Luvanda, 2009).

2.4. Alternatives to the Traditional Approaches

The shortcomings of the traditional approaches — OCA theory, comparison of macroeconomic performance, convergence criteria — have generated a search for more comprehensive alternatives. First, none of the traditional approaches gives a precise criterion to judge why joining a monetary union would be preferable to retaining one's own currency. Instead, they typically evaluate similarity with reference to other countries already in a monetary union. However, as Mundell emphasises, the problem is multidimensional since labour mobility and other structural factors can compensate for shock asymmetry. Second, the criteria are not sufficiently dynamic. As Rose (2000) argued, membership in a monetary union may increase trade and hence synchronicity of business cycles. Finally, institutional features of monetary unions need to be given more attention, including whether there is an anchor able to provide the credibility for monetary policy, like the Bundesbank in the EU. Tavlas (2009) devotes considerable attention to the endogeneity of OCA criteria and also the possibility of importing monetary policy credibility, in a survey of the literature on possible monetary unions in Southern Africa.

In order to address the multidimensional nature of the problem, several studies have used cluster analysis to group countries together into potential monetary unions. Bénassy-Quéré and Coupet (2005) and Tsangarides and Qureshi (2008) apply clustering analysis to ECOWAS, using variables suggested by convergence criteria and OCA literature, finding that the CFA countries do not all belong to the same cluster and throwing doubt on the ECOWAS monetary union.

A substantial literature has mushroomed around the seminal work of Andrew Rose, developing the idea that the extent of intra-regional trade is not a good measure of the potential benefits of monetary union, since joining a monetary union is likely to increase trade and also reduce the asymmetry of shocks. Tsangarides *et al.* (2006) estimate that a monetary union increases intra-union trade by a factor of 1.7 in Africa, controlling for the effect of a free trade agreement. Tapsoba (2009) finds that monetary integration increases trade intensity and business cycle synchronisation, but less so in Africa than among industrial countries. While these studies suggest that static criteria are biased against accepting countries into monetary unions, they fail to provide any way to evaluate whether trade intensity and synchronisation will increase enough to make monetary union worthwhile — especially given the very low initial level of African trade. Masson (2008) shows that even a doubling of intra-regional trade would not be sufficient to make most African monetary unions desirable.

Yehoue (2005) also applies a dynamic approach to the formation of monetary unions, based on the endogeneity of the trade externality and a threshold on the amount of trade needed to make a country join a monetary union. He finds that the size and configuration of an existing union affects its attractiveness for new members: the integration path matters. He finds nevertheless that this analysis does not suggest ultimate convergence to a single African currency.

Several studies have attempted to assess benefits and compare them to costs. Khamfula and Tesfayohannes (2004) discuss in an informal way the various factors affecting costs and benefits of monetary union in Southern Africa. Karras (2007) takes the main benefit to be enhanced price stability, while the main cost is higher business cycle volatility due to shock asymmetry. Though he does not have a metric for comparing the two, he finds that the costs and benefits are sometimes positively correlated: those countries that have a lot to gain from a monetary union (Uganda, Ghana and Guinea) also have a lot to lose from it, since they face asymmetric shocks. Conversely, those which would have little benefit would also not find joining very costly (Morocco, Côte d'Ivoire and Gabon).

A full welfare analysis with a general equilibrium model provides a comprehensive approach to costs and benefits. This requires, of course, numerical values for parameters including those for preferences. Debrun et al. (2005) and Masson and Pattillo (2005) provide such a calibrated model whose costs reflect the OCA and fiscal asymmetries, while the benefits derive from reduced temptation in a monetary union to use monetary policy to achieve 'beggar-thy-neighbour' output stimulation. The model is described further below, and a new, more comprehensive and consistent calibration of parameters is provided. A more dynamic general equilibrium model is developed in Batte et al. (2009) and applied to Nigeria and WAEMU; preliminary results suggest that the optimal policy regime differs between the two, with Nigeria preferring a flexible exchange rate.

3. A Comprehensive Framework for Evaluating Monetary Unions

The formation of a mutually beneficial currency area ultimately depends on the capacity of the common monetary policy to provide adequate macroeconomic stability both in terms of cushioning national economies against shocks and of securing appropriately low inflation. While the OCA literature emphasises the first dimension, pointing to the need for economies to be sufficiently similar or integrated, institutional changes accompanying monetary unification have received considerable attention since the EMU debate. In particular, it was shown that countries with different records of macroeconomic stability and policy credibility could agree on a set of common institutions that would make a monetary union among them desirable. The possibility that a group of heterogeneous countries failing most OCA tests could nevertheless form a sustainable currency union is particularly relevant in the African context.

3.1. Modelling Strategy: Combining Credibility and Stabilization Issues

The main objective of our model is to incorporate in a tractable analytical framework the impact of monetary integration on strategic interactions between monetary and fiscal authorities. These interactions are essential in establishing credibility and in shaping the policy response to shocks. Attention to credibility dominated the debate on European monetary unification (Beetsma and Giuliodori, 2010), and those arguments are likely to apply with even greater strength in the African context (Debrun et al., 2005).[4]

Despite considerable improvement in recent years, macroeconomic policies in many African countries remain vulnerable to

---

[4]Admittedly, policymakers' incentives to form (or to stay in) a currency union often go beyond macroeconomic stability and include factors such as history — e.g., the legacy of colonial monetary arrangements — and regional integration objectives of a largely political nature; but we will not consider these motivations here, focusing instead on strictly economic arguments.

institutional weaknesses that undermine the credibility of commitments to low inflation and sustainable public finances. Although institutional reform is often high on policymakers' agendas, effective implementation can suffer from capacity and political-economy constraints. One important source of risk to credibility is related to the combination of weak tax mobilisation (Keen and Mansour, 2009) and strong expenditure pressure, leading to excessive deficits (Debrun and Kumar, 2007) and undue reliance on the inflation tax (Catão and Terrones, 2005).

Combining the traditional OCA dimension with credibility and institutional issues involves difficult modelling choices. On the one hand, full-fledged dynamic stochastic general-equilibrium models lack the flexibility needed for a simple treatment of strategic interactions between monetary and fiscal authorities subject to time inconsistency. It is also difficult to calibrate these models to analyse policy interactions among a large group of heterogeneous, low-income countries.[5] On the other hand, models focusing on credibility and institutions — in the Barro and Gordon (1983) and Rogoff (1985) tradition — fail to properly capture economic dynamics, complicating efforts to identify realistic parameter values, but they allow for a simple and intuitive analysis of strategic interactions under a variety of institutional arrangements. Given the importance of these aspects in recent and current discussions about monetary integration in various parts of the world, we opted for such a model.

In the spirit of Beetsma and Bovenberg (1998, 1999) and Martin (1995), our model — a variant of Debrun *et al.* (2005), hereafter DMP—incorporates (i) the role of macroeconomic institutions in cementing the credibility of a commitment to low inflation, (ii) the implications of financing beneficial public expenditure through the inflation tax versus other distortive taxes, and (iii) the role of monetary policy in stabilising output (as in the OCA literature).

---

[5]Note, however, that Bayesian estimation has been applied to overcome data scarcity and find plausible calibrations of these models for individual low-income countries (Peiris and Saxegaard, 2007).

3.2. Structure of the model and equilibrium policies under autonomy

3.2.1. The model

DMP depicts a static, n-good, n-country region assumed to be small *vis-à-vis* the rest of the world so that strategic interactions with governments outside the region can be ignored (Table 1).[6] Economic activity responds to macroeconomic policies through an open-economy new-classical Phillips curve equation (1). Unexpected inflation thus raises output, while distortive taxation reduces it. Spillovers from monetary policies elsewhere in the region are negative and measured by $\theta_{i,k}$,[7] in line with the presumption that depreciations boost competitiveness at the expense of trade partners (Debrun *et al.*, 2005).There is a proportional value-added tax at rate τ_i. Direct fiscal policy spillovers are ignored.

In addition to their joint impact on output, monetary and fiscal policies are linked through an instantaneous budget constraint forcing government expenditure to match revenue [equation (2)].[8] Introducing public debt would significantly complicate the strategic analysis without qualitatively affecting our conclusions. equation (2) also introduces two important elements affecting the conduct of fiscal policy. First, each government is assumed to have a certain propensity to spend public resources on socially wasteful projects, creating a wedge δ_i between actual spending and the socially beneficial items entering g_i. Second, the budget constraint accounts for the possibility that the government extracts a rent $\bar{\rho}_i$ from natural resource endowments. To preserve tractable analytical solutions, we ignore any 'Dutch-disease' type of distortion possibly related to resource wealth so that $\bar{\rho}_i$ is equivalent to a lump-sum tax instrument.

---

[6]See also Debrun *et al.* (2008).
[7]Complete derivations are available from the authors upon request. Loungani *et al.* (2002) derive a new-Keynesian, open-economy Phillips curve which includes foreign output and consumption as well as surprises in the real exchange rate.
[8]See Alesina and Tabellini (1987).

Table 1. The DMP Model

National policymaking

    Open-economy Phillips curve

$$y_i = y_N + c\left(\pi_i - \pi_i^e - \tau_i\right) - \sum_{k \neq i, k=1}^{n} \theta_{i,k} c\left(\pi_k - \pi_k^e\right) + \varepsilon_i, \quad i = 1, \ldots, n \quad (1)$$

    Government budget constraint (no debt)

$$g_i = \overline{\rho}_i + \mu\pi i + \tau_i - \delta_i \quad (2)$$

    Government's utility function

$$U_i^G = \tfrac{1}{2}\left\{-a\left(\pi_i - \widetilde{\pi}_i\right)^2 - b\tau_i^2 - \gamma\left(g_i - \widetilde{g}_i\right)^2\right\} + y_i \quad (3)$$

    Trade-off between output and inflation variability

$$\widetilde{\pi}_i = -\eta\varepsilon_i \text{ with } \eta > 0 \quad (4)$$

Supranational monetary policy

    The Phillips curve faced by the CCB

$$y_i = y_N + c\left(1 - \theta_i^M\right)\left(\pi_M - \pi_M^e\right) - c\tau_i - \sum_{k \notin M} \theta_{i,k} c\left(\pi_k - \pi_k^e\right) + \varepsilon_i,$$

    for each member of M

$$\forall i \in M, \text{ with } \theta_i^M = \sum_{k \in M} \theta_{i,k} \quad (1')$$

Key variables and parameters

π_i	Inflation rate in country i. A superscript e designates a rationally expected value
y_i	Logarithm of output in country i
y_N	Logarithm of the natural level of output at zero taxation. Without loss of generality, we assume $y_N = 0$
τ_i	Corporate income tax rate (also tax revenues in percent of output)
$\theta_{i,k}$	Marginal effect of monetary policy in country k on output in country i
ε_i	TOT shock (zero-mean, transitory and with finite variance)
g_i	Socially beneficial government expenditure in percent of output
μ	Inflation tax base in percent of output
$\overline{\rho}_i$	Permanent non-tax revenue from natural resource endowment in percent of output
δ_i	Funds diverted from socially beneficial government expenditure in percent of output
η	Relative preference for output stability against inflation stability

Under monetary autonomy, the authorities of each country i (government and a politically dependent central bank) set policy instruments so as to maximise an explicit utility function [equation (3)]. The authorities dislike deviations of public expenditure and inflation from specific targets ($\widetilde{g}_i$ and $\widetilde{\pi}_i$, respectively), as well as the variability in distortive tax rates — over and above the induced output loss. Output enters linearly — as in Barro and Gordon (1983) — which greatly simplifies the notation of equilibrium policies and amounts to assume that macroeconomic instruments are used to stimulate activity beyond the natural level y^N, the key assumption underlying the expansive bias of time-consistent policies. To introduce the usual trade-off between the *variability* of inflation and that of output without adding a quadratic output term, we use equation (4). Indeed, offsetting supply shocks with macroeconomic policies requires that higher inflation be tolerated in the face of an adverse shock, and lower inflation be targeted in case of a positive shock.

Under monetary union with membership M, a common central bank (CCB) chooses monetary policy to maximise a GDP-weighted sum of individual members' utilities. The CCB faces steeper *national* Phillips curves [equation (1′)] than a national central bank by a factor $1 - \sum_{k \in M} \theta_{i,k}$ in each country i because unlike national monetary policy, the common monetary policy cannot operate through bilateral exchange rates *vis-à-vis* other members of the union. As π is effectively the monetary instrument — we do not model the money market — this means that a given monetary impulse will affect output by less if it is decided by a CCB, than if it is implemented by a national central bank in isolation.

3.2.2. *Equilibrium policies under monetary autonomy*

Our benchmark institutional setting assumes that fiscal and monetary policies are decided by national governments. Equilibrium (time-consistent) policies differ from the social optimum, the key feature being an inflation bias described in equation (7) (Table 2).[9] That bias reflects policymakers' preference for pushing output beyond its potential ('natural') level (Barro and Gordon, 1983) and the impact of public sector inefficiencies δ_i on the financing need (FN) at any given level of valuable expenditure. The classic Barro–Gordon bias is magnified by the fact that for given expenditure, inflation substitutes for the costly turnover tax, and that for given tax revenues, it allows higher spending (Alesina and Tabellini, 1987). Also, greater inefficiencies lead to higher inflation and tax rates, and lower productive expenditure, *ceteris paribus*. Excessive inflation is an equilibrium because rational agents fully understand policymakers' motivations, allowing them to anticipate the rate of inflation from which the latter have no incentive to deviate. Any *ex ante* promise to keep inflation below that level is not credible.

The inflationary bias distorts the level and financing structure of expenditure, as higher inflation boosts seigniorage revenues. In comparison to the social optimum, the government can thus spend more and tax less, with some beneficial repercussions on potential output. However, these second-order gains are more than offset by the first-order impact of excessive inflation on welfare.

In sum, equilibrium policies are shaped by two key elements: the level of tax and seigniorage revenues required to deliver the socially optimal productive expenditure (i.e., $\tilde{g}_i + \delta_i - \overline{\rho}_i$, or FN), and the stabilising response of monetary policy to shocks. Correspondingly, the country-specific costs of a common monetary policy will be related to the imperfect correlation of shocks between the country and the rest of the union — the OCA dimension — and divergences in FNs. We now turn to an explicit cost–benefit analysis of monetary unification in the model.

---

[9]See Debrun *et al.* (2005, 2008) for more extensive discussions. The socially optimal solution (first best) assumes that policymakers can make credible precommitments on any policy and enact structural fiscal reforms ensuring that public resources are spent only on socially beneficial items [equation (6)]. Unless the natural resource rent (or revenues from lump sum taxes) is very large, first-best inflation is positive on average, reflecting the optimal inflation tax.

Should African Monetary Unions Be Expanded?

Table 2. Inflation Rates under Alternative Monetary Regimes

Monetary Regime	Equilibrium Inflation (Country i)

Autonomy

The equilibrium (time-consistent) inflation is ...

$$\pi_i^* = \pi_i^{**} + \frac{\gamma\mu b}{\Lambda}\delta_i + \frac{(b+\gamma)}{\Lambda}c \quad (5)$$

... while the socially optimal rate is ...

$$\pi_i^{**} = \underbrace{\frac{\gamma\mu b}{\Lambda}}_{\substack{\text{Size of financing} \\ \text{requirement}}} [\widetilde{g}_i - \overline{\rho}_i] + \underbrace{\frac{\gamma\mu}{\Lambda}c}_{\substack{\text{Output cost} \\ \text{of taxation}}} - \underbrace{\frac{a(b+\gamma)\eta}{\Lambda}\varepsilon_i}_{\text{Output stabilization}},$$

$$\text{with } \Lambda = a(b+\gamma) + \gamma\mu^2 b > 0 \quad (6)$$

... so that the inflation bias is ...

$$\pi_i^* - \pi_i^{**} = \underbrace{\frac{(b+\gamma)}{\Lambda}c}_{\substack{\text{'Augmented'} \\ \text{Barro--Gordon} \\ \text{inflation bias}}} + \underbrace{\frac{\gamma\mu b}{\Lambda}\delta_i}_{\substack{\text{Public sector} \\ \text{inefficiency}}} \quad (7)$$

Monetary union M(utilitarian CCB)

$$\pi_i^{M*} = \frac{\gamma\mu b}{\Lambda}(\text{FN}_A^M) + \frac{(1-\theta_A^M)(b+\gamma)+\gamma\mu}{\Lambda}c$$

$$- \frac{a(b+\gamma)\eta}{\Lambda}\varepsilon_A^M, \quad \text{for all } i\epsilon M, \text{ with } x_A^M = \sum_{i\in M}\omega_i^M x_i,$$

for $x \in \{\text{FN}, \theta, \varepsilon\}$ (cross-country, output-weighted averages within M), and $\text{FN}_i = \widetilde{g}_i + \delta_i - \overline{\rho}_i$. Hence

$$\pi_A^{M*} = \underbrace{\pi_A^*}_{\substack{\text{Average inflation} \\ \text{under national} \\ \text{policies}}} - \underbrace{\frac{\theta_A^M(b+\gamma)}{\Lambda}c}_{\substack{\text{Average reduction in the} \\ \text{Barro--Gordon bias}}} \quad (8)$$

Legally independent national central banks

$\pi_i^* = \pi_i^{**} + \frac{\lambda_i(b+\gamma)}{\Lambda}c + \frac{\gamma\mu(b-(1-\lambda_i)\gamma)}{\Lambda}\delta_i$, with $0 \leq \lambda_i \leq 1$, the extent of political interference. If $\lambda_i = 0$, the government has no influence on central bank's decisions; and if $\lambda_i = 1$, the government effectively sets monetary policy [see equation (5)] (9)

Note: Complete solutions are available from the authors upon request.

3.3. Institutional Change and the Gains from Monetary Unions

Institutions can reduce policy bias to the extent that (i) they effectively modify policymakers' incentives in a durable way (ii) and that they are more difficult to change than policies themselves (Jensen, 1997). Participation in a currency union arguably satisfies these two conditions. First, a regional central bank inevitably has different motivations than national monetary authorities, which in turn affects the strategic interplay between monetary and fiscal decisionmakers. Second, any decision to exit is likely to entail significant political and reputational costs (kept implicit here).

As excessive inflation is rooted in short-term incentives of elected policymakers, the proposed reforms of macroeconomic institutions generally aim at a strict separation of tasks between the government and the central bank. While the latter is often mandated to set monetary policy in line with specific *ex ante* objectives for inflation,[10] rules-based fiscal frameworks seek to discourage the former from abusing fiscal discretion by establishing clear numerical benchmarks and enhancing democratic accountability and transparency.

In the remainder of this section, we first discuss the impact of monetary unification on equilibrium inflation, assuming that political interference remains. Second, we explore the possibility for governments to set up legal guarantees against such interference at the regional and national levels.

3.3.1. *Monetary unification as a substitute for national reform*

Participation in a currency union necessarily implies a separation of monetary and fiscal powers, as monetary policy is centralised while fiscal policy is not. In DMP, the CCB maximizes the GDP-weighted sum of national governments' utilities so that regional and national objectives can only coincide if all member governments have identical preferences and FNs. Hence, in contrast to a purely national monetary reform, this setup does not presume formal independence from politics. Specifically, regional monetary authorities remain

---

[10]See Svensson (1997). Rogoff (1985) is the first to show that the Barro–Gordon inflationary bias can be reduced if monetary policy is *delegated* to a non-politicized agency that is not subject to the same motivations as policymakers themselves. The inflation bias can also be reduced through reputational mechanisms if policymakers face penalties for undue monetary expansions. Based on repeated games, that approach exhibits multiple equilibria. We prefer the analytically simpler route of a 'one-shot' interaction in alternative institutional setups.

subject to the influence of member governments proportionally to their respective economic size.

The constraints facing the CCB also differ in comparison to national monetary policies, as the CCB perceives a steeper Phillips curve than a national central bank. The steepening of the Phillips curves is measured by θ_A^M. Since the CCB's marginal utility from a given monetary stimulus is lower than that of a national central bank, equilibrium inflation in the union is lower than the average equilibrium inflation rate under national currencies. The higher is θ_A^M (reflecting extended membership or more intense trade linkages among member states), the greater is the induced reduction in the average Barro–Gordon bias. As the average gain in terms of lower credible inflation arises only from steeper Phillips curves, the public finance motives to generate inflation remain, including the trade-off between distortive taxation and seigniorage $(\gamma\mu\Lambda^{-1}c)$. However, the level of the inflation tax in each country will now reflect the average FN in the Union (FN_A^M, including the average of political distortions), instead of the strictly national FN_i under monetary autonomy.

In this setup, heterogeneity in FNs has an ambiguous effect on the desirability of monetary unification for individual members of a given group. On the one hand, different FNs may hinder the formation of the union because the regional inflation rate will only by chance coincide with a country's desired composition of government revenues. On the other hand, differences in FNs may also be a source of gains for governments with relatively high FN, as low-FN partners exert a restraining influence on the CCB. The sustainability/feasibility of a fiscally heterogeneous union could be at risk if low-FN countries were better off keeping national currencies. This will be the case if θ_A^M is too small to offset the destabilizing influence of high-FN members.

The possibility for the CCB to pursue specific objectives independently of political interference raises two questions. First, if guarantees of central bank independence are at least somewhat credible at the national level, to what extent could this affect the size and number of sustainable currency unions in the region? Second,

3.3.2. *Independent central banks: Regional or national?*

As the separation of monetary and fiscal powers allows the central bank to maximise its own utility function under constraints that may also differ from the government's, one has to wonder what maximisation problem would deliver a time-consistent inflation rate as close as possible (or identical) to the socially optimal rate? Here, we consider the two dimensions of the inflation bias. First, to remove the Barro–Gordon bias, the central bank would have to refrain from trying to push output beyond its potential level and focus only on its stabilization. That would require the maximisation of a utility function U_i^C (where C stands for 'commitment') defined as: $U_i^C \equiv U_i^G - y_i$. The second dimension concerns fiscal policy: an independent central bank would have to ignore the government's desire to finance useless projects, therefore internalising a *non-distorted* government's budget constraint: $g_i = \bar{\rho}_i + \mu\pi_i + \tau_i$.

In practice, however, even legally independent central banks remain under pressure to accommodate society's desire to maximise output, especially when institutional weaknesses prevent or complicate an effective separation of powers. To account for that possibility, we define the central bank's utility function as $U^{CB} \equiv \lambda_i U^G + (1 - \lambda_i) U^C = U^C + \lambda_i y_i$, while the government budget constraint perceived by the bank is $g_i = \bar{\rho}_i + \mu\pi_i + \tau_i - \lambda_i \delta_i$. Clearly, if the central bank is under complete political control ($\lambda_i = 1$), then the optimal control problem and the corresponding solutions are the same as in Section 3.2. On the contrary, a completely independent central bank ($\lambda_i = 0$) would manage to credibly eliminate the Barro–Gordon bias, but it would still have to partly account for the government's desire to finance wasteful spending.[11]

---

[11]This is because the bank values public finance objectives. Should it ignore them ($b = \gamma = 0$), or should it be indifferent to the fact that higher spending is financed with higher distortive taxes ($b = \gamma$), it would not respond to δ_i and deliver the socially optimal inflation rate.

Equation (9) characterizes equilibrium inflation for all intermediate levels of political interference. Comparing that result with equation (8) formally establishes that participation in a currency union M has the same effect on the Barro–Gordon bias as making the national central bank formally independent under a level of political interference: $\lambda_i = 1 - \theta_A^M$. One additional effect of independence is that the political inflation bias is also reduced as λ_i decreases below 1.

Our model thus shows that the country-specific incentives to form a monetary union among a given set of countries are affected by the capacity of individual governments to build credible monetary institutions at home. As this capacity increases, the relative attractiveness of monetary integration becomes increasingly dominated by shock-stabilization/OCA arguments rather than credibility gains. That said, supranational institutions are arguably more credible than national efforts: international treaties are more difficult to reverse than national law, and supranational institutions are more difficult to influence because that requires *ex ante* coordination efforts. We could, for instance, develop a scenario where a formally independent CCB would, by definition, face a lower λ_A^M than the individual λ_i's achievable with purely national reforms. This would then shift the balance back to credibility considerations in the cost–benefit analysis of a monetary union among the members of M. We leave a formal analysis of these aspects for future research, as it requires a detailed assessment of individual countries' capacity to enact credible reforms.

4. Status of Monetary Union Projects in Africa

The 1991 Abuja Treaty establishing the African Economic Community (which became effective in May 1994 after the required number of signatures) outlines six stages for achieving an integrated economic and monetary zone for Africa that were set to be completed by approximately 2028. The strategy for African integration is based on progressive integration of the activities of the regional economic communities, which are regarded as building blocks for Africa.

We will briefly sketch out the status of monetary union projects for the regions that are actively making preparations for monetary integration. The timetables appear overly ambitious, particularly as the history of the EU demonstrates the very long time that was needed to reach the final stage of a common currency. We will not consider here the ultimate goal of a single currency for Africa.[12]

4.1. *East African Community*

The 1999 treaty establishing the EAC (founding members Kenya, Tanzania and Uganda), formally launched in 2001, provides for the formation of a customs union, to be followed by a common market, monetary union and ultimately a political federation. While monetary union was seen in the early years of the EAC as a rather distant goal, a number of successful steps in the economic integration process have put monetary union plans higher on the agenda. The customs union was successfully launched in 2005, and the protocol for establishment of the planned 2012 common market, including free movement of goods, services, labour and capital, was signed by the heads of state at a November 2009 summit.[13] In August 2007, the heads of state decided to fast-track implementation of the monetary union, advancing the targeted launch date from 2015 to 2012. However, similar to plans in other SSA regions, the current timetable appears overly ambitious.

So far, the customs union does not appear to have contributed to a significant increase in intra-regional trade, which has remained in the same range, registering 17.5% of total exports, and 7% of imports in 2007 (Burundi and Rwanda source 20% of their imports from other EAC countries, and over 20% of Kenya's and Uganda's exports go to EAC partners). Understanding and application of the rules of

---

[12]See Masson and Pattillo (2005, Chapter 9).

[13]On a range of contentious issues, relating to aspects of labour mobility, trading of services and acquisition of land, the countries seem to have agreed to disagree and not include these in the protocol. See 'East Africa economy: in your own time', Economist Intelligence Unit, 29 May 2009.

origin have been problematic issues, compounded by the problem of overlapping memberships in other regional economic communities.[14]

4.2. Southern African Development Community

The SADC, the largest regional economic community in SSA, adopted a Regional Indicative Strategic Development Plan (RISDP) in 2003. The plan sets out a timetable for deepening regional integration, calling for the creation of a free trade area (FTA) by 2008, a customs union by 2010, a monetary union by 2016 and a single currency by 2018. While the FTA was launched in August 2008, only part of the 85% reduction of internal trade barriers that was specified to occur in the previous 8 years has taken place to date, given members' concerns about risks and differentiated schedules (Braude and Sekolokwane, 2008).

The way forward on economic integration in the region appears quite murky, with calls for different directions from a number of quarters. The Southern Africa Customs Union (SACU) has been called the anchor and potential driver of deeper integration in the SADC, and weak production structures identified as the constraint to more balanced trade in a wider SADC FTA. However, SACU is currently experiencing serious strains due to the global crisis, consequent sharp declines in output and the revenue pool, and reportedly South Africa may propose another change in the revenue-sharing formula.[15] There are concerns that the 2010 target date for an SADC customs union is not feasible, while the floated idea of an SADC-COMESA-EAC FTA has also sparked some interest. Finally, some tensions have arisen over the EU Economic Partnership Agreement. Botswana, Lesotho, Namibia and Swaziland have signed interim agreements on trade in goods, but South Africa argues

---

[14]Tanzania is a member of SADC, while Kenya, Tanzania, Burundi and Rwanda are members of COMESA. While in October 2008 ministers from the EAC, COMESA and SADC announced their intention to merge the blocs into a large FTA, no specific plans for this merger have been developed yet.

[15]'Trade-So Africa: Effort Afoot to Save Rickety Customs Union', Inter Press Service, 5 October 2009.

218   *Xavier Debrun, Paul R. Masson and Catherine Pattillo*

that the agreements will complicate regional integration by creating market-opening obligations to the EU before the region builds its own rules in new areas such as services and investment.[16]

There are wide disparities in per capita incomes and economic structures across SADC's 15 economies. They can be grouped into middle countries — SACU countries Botswana, Namibia, Swaziland and South Africa, plus Mauritius, and Seychelles, which just rejoined the SADC in 2008; low-income countries — Lesotho (SACU), Madagascar, Malawi, Mozambique, Tanzania and Zambia; fragile countries — Democratic Republic of Congo and Zimbabwe; and an oil exporter — Angola.

Intra-regional trade flows account for about 20 percent of total trade, but only 5 percent if South Africa is excluded (Burgess, 2009). These trade flows vary significantly across countries, with South Africa a major source of imports for most countries, particularly SACU neighbours, and a market for exports for some countries, including Namibia, Swaziland, Zambia and Zimbabwe. FDI from South Africa accounts for around 6 percent of the total FDI stock in the SADC (Burgess, 2009). The average of the correlations of TOT changes among member countries is quite low.

4.3. *Economic Community of West African States/ West African Monetary Zone*

The plan for monetary union in West Africa is a proposed common currency among the members of ECOWAS that are not presently part of the West African Economic and Monetary Union, or WAEMU.[17] The non-WAEMU countries,[18] in particular Nigeria, Ghana, the Gambia, Guinea and Sierra Leone, intend to create a

---

[16]'South Africa Wants Proper Integrated, Competitive Regional Market', by Rob Davies, South African Minister of Trade and Industry, Business Report, 17 July 2009.

[17]Benin, Burkina Faso, Côte d'Ivoire, Guinea-Bissau, Mali, Niger, Senegal and Togo. Guinea-Bissau joined WAEMU in 1997. Data availability for that country is poor, and hence we do not analyse its impact on proposed monetary unions.

[18]Liberia has declined to participate, while the remaining member of ECOWAS, Cape Verde, is pegged to the euro.

common currency area (WAMZ) and eventually to merge it with the WAEMU to form a single-currency area for the whole of ECOWAS. The launch date for the WAMZ's common currency, initially set for 2003, has already been postponed several times, and in June 2009 the WAMZ heads of state agreed to further postpone the start date for the WAMZ common currency until 2015 (and the ECOWAS currency to 2020), citing the global financial crisis. The decision also appears compelled by lack of sufficient macroeconomic convergence, and the reality that completing all the legal and institutional steps for a CCB is still a long way off.

Trade among WAMZ countries, at around 2% of their total trade in 2007, is much lower than trade among WAEMU countries, even though GDP of the former group is higher. Though this trade may be endogenous, ECOWAS countries also face asymmetric TOT shocks, particularly since Nigeria is the only oil exporter. TOT shock correlations are higher among WAEMU countries (see below), while on average the correlations among WAMZ countries have become even more negative in recent periods.

Of the three monetary union expansion/revival projects, the WAMZ is the most advanced in terms of institutional, legal and regulatory preparation, although some observers have noted that the political commitment has been limited. An important question is whether three postponements of the common currency start date will cause the project to lose momentum, or instead now establish a more realistic timetable, recognizing, as the director of WAMI noted, that the journey towards a monetary union is a marathon not a sprint race.[19]

5. Creation or Expansion of Monetary Unions: A Model-based Approach

We now turn to a full-fledged analysis of the costs and benefits of monetary unification in the sub-regions studied in Section 4, using

---

[19]'West African Monetary Zone (WAMZ) — The Journey towards a Monetary Union Is a Marathon ...', Business Day, 4 June 2009.

the DMP model presented in Section 3. As described above, the model combines an emphasis on the role of fiscal discipline to provide an underpinning for low inflation with the traditional OCA criteria of symmetry of shocks to evaluate possible gains and losses from monetary unions. Welfare comparisons can be made of the decision of a country to retain its own currency against the alternative of adopting the currency of another country or joining a currency union with others. Welfare is measured in percent of GDP equivalents, so is scaled by the size of the country. It is assumed to depend positively on output growth, and negatively on deviations from targets for inflation, tax revenues and government spending (the latter two as ratios to GDP). The calibration of the model's parameters is described fully in Debrun et $al.$ (2010). In most cases, parameters have been chosen to fit cross-country fiscal and institutional data over 1994–2005[20] and the variance–covariance matrix of TOT and output over 1990–2008.

As defined above, the FN consists of two components: society's target for government spending $\widetilde{g}$, and a diversion wedge δ due to inefficient tax collection and wasteful spending that adds to the amount that needs to be financed, without increasing welfare. We regress aggregate government spending and revenues on governance indicators to gauge directly what amounts of excess spending and tax losses are due to poor governance. We then set the governance indicators to their 'ideal' levels: the resulting figures for ideal government spending give the estimate for $\widetilde{g}$, and the difference between the ideal and actual figures for the deficit provide the estimate for δ.

---

[20]Data up to 2005 were used because some of the data series (for example, the World Bank governance indicators) were not available for some countries after 2005, and to exclude the one-off impact of the 2006 multilateral debt relief. Contrary to expectations, terms-of-trade correlations were not higher using more recent data, i.e., extending the period until 2008. Clearly, however, the pattern of trade shocks may not be stationary; for example, the correlations between Nigeria and other West African countries may rise as more countries (Ghana, Niger) develop oil resources.

The effects of poor governance were captured using ICRG indicators for the 29 SSA countries for which they and the other explanatory variables were available. Other factors were also included to explain the systematic variation in revenues across countries. In particular, revenues depend systematically on the level of per capita income, the share of oil production in GDP and the ratio of grants to GDP. Since we used a 12-year average (1994–2005), those variables were assumed to be at long-run, sustainable levels. Since grants are endogenous (depending on both governance indicators and per capita income), as are expenditures, three-stage least squares were used to estimate a system of three equations — for revenues excluding grants, grants and government expenditure. The system of equations does a good job in explaining the cross-country variation in non-grant revenues, grants and expenditures (Debrun *et al.*, 2010, Appendix 1).

We use this system of equations to estimate the 'ideal' revenues, which determines the FN, as follows. We first put all the countries on the same footing by adjusting revenues, expenditures and grants to what they would be if all countries had the same per capita income and the same share of oil revenues in their GDP (the mean for SSA). Using the normalized values, a second adjustment sets the governance indicators to ideal values. The resulting figures for FNs were used in cross-country regressions and in our welfare calculations for forming monetary unions.

It is worth noting that estimated equilibrium relationships derived from the model provide a reasonably good explanation of inflation and fiscal variables across SSA countries, including those in monetary unions. As detailed in Section 3, the model implies that inflation (π_i) should depend on a country's FN (FN_i), or, if it is a member of a monetary union, on the average FN of the union's members, which we denote by FNA. We let FNA be a cross-sectional variable that combines those two possibilities, if the country has its own currency or is in a monetary union. Moreover, the model implies that the level for inflation (i.e., the bias towards too expansionary monetary policy) will be reduced in a monetary union by the amount of intra-union trade, which we capture in the variable $\theta_{A,i}$. Further, the model explains tax revenues as ratios to GDP (rev) by FNs (with positive impact), and also on the difference between a member of a monetary union's FNs relative to the average (since seigniorage revenues depend only on the average). In a monetary union, tax revenues will also have to be higher to compensate for the lower inflation bias. We estimated these two equations using a cross-section of 45 SSA countries, with data for each country averaged over 1994–2005, yielding the following results (standard errors in brackets):

$$\pi_i = \underset{(9.717)}{-2.812} + \underset{(0.218)}{0.399} \, \text{FNA}_i - \underset{(0.319)}{0.577} \theta_{\text{A},i}$$
$$R^2 = 0.207 \quad p\text{-value} = 0.0028$$

and

$$rev_i = \underset{(4.969)}{-1.173} + \underset{(0.111)}{0.547} \, \text{FN}_i + \underset{(0.185)}{0.137} (\text{FN}_i - \text{FNA}_i) + \underset{(0.162)}{0.109} \, \theta_{\text{A},i}$$
$$R^2 = 0.473 \quad p\text{-value} = 0.0000.$$

It can be seen that despite including countries with a wide range of inflation outcomes (for instance, Angola and Zimbabwe at the high end and the CFA franc zone countries at the low end), the model has decent explanatory power. FN has the expected positive effect, and membership in a monetary union the expected negative effect. Government tax revenues are well explained by FNs and the additional effects of monetary union membership mentioned above.

These estimates, together with estimates of the trade internalized in a monetary union, are used to calibrate the model's utility-function parameters a, b, and γ, while the average money-income ratio provides the estimate for μ, as described in detail in Debrun et al. (2010). Variances of TOT shocks and of output and inflation are used to calibrate two other key parameters that capture the stabilization role of monetary policy (η) and the effect of the latter on output (c).

The estimated parameter values and their standard errors are as follows:

Parameter	Estimate	Standard error
c	0.63735	0.16294
μ	0.37657	—
a	1.20359	1.7006
b	2.33295	3.2573
γ	2.35337	4.8626
η	4.32130	1.6642

It is worth noting that the estimate for c indicates that monetary policy is relatively ineffective: a 1 percent inflation surprise is associated with a 0.6 percent rise in output.

To account for the significant under-recording of intra-regional trade flows, recorded trade is scaled up by 25 percent to produce the estimates of internalized trade.

Rather than examining all possible combinations of countries as candidates for monetary unions, we consider a more focused question, namely whether several proposed regional groupings of countries into monetary unions discussed in the previous section seem to increase welfare for the countries involved. In particular, we consider the creation of a monetary union among EAC countries and the formation of an SADC monetary union, and monetary union among all ECOWAS countries, or a selective expansion of the existing WAEMU, which uses the CFA franc.

5.1. *East African Community*

As shown in Table 3, there are major differences among the EAC countries. Aside from the correlations between TOT shocks of Burundi and Uganda, and Tanzania and Uganda, other shock correlations are generally not very high (though higher typically than within ECOWAS or the CMA).

Table 3. EAC: Selected Indicators, 1994–2005 (in Percent)

Correlations of Changes in TOT with:						Standard Deviation of TOT Shocks	Openness[a]: 0.5(X + M)/GDP	Adjusted Standard Deviation
	Burundi	Kenya	Rwanda	Tanzania	Uganda			
Burundi	1.00	−0.27	0.07	0.12	0.54	8.66	15.82	1.37
Kenya	−0.27	1.00	0.01	0.10	−0.02	3.68	26.67	0.98
Rwanda	0.07	0.01	1.00	0.13	−0.17	7.89	39.38	3.11
Tanzania	0.12	0.10	0.13	1.00	0.53	5.64	20.32	1.15
Uganda	0.54	−0.02	−0.17	0.53	1.00	8.61	17.27	1.49

Note: [a] Average, 2000–2006, as percent of GDP.
Source: Authors' estimates.

Model simulations suggest that a monetary union among all five countries would significantly improve welfare for Burundi and Kenya, but leave Rwanda and Uganda with modest gains (less than one percent of GDP) and Tanzania with a small net loss (Table 4). The latter is related to Tanzania's better record of macroeconomic stability, and in particular, a lower FN. Rwanda's losses, reflecting low or negative shock correlations, would be more than offset by greater imported monetary stability.

5.2. *Southern Africa Development Community*

The SADC is composed of a large and diverse set of countries.[21] A subset of SADC countries comprise an exchange rate union centred around South Africa's rand, the CMA. Given the size of South Africa's economy, that country would likely dominate any SADC monetary union. Indeed, within the CMA, it sets monetary policy. Thus, Table 5 highlights correlations between other countries' and South Africa's TOT shocks. Several countries, including an existing CMA member (Namibia), have negative correlations. As documented earlier, fiscal and institutional convergence is low among SADC countries so that FNs vary considerably. Tanzania and all CMA members except Lesotho have low FNs, whereas Angola, Lesotho and Zimbabwe have high FNs. Angola also has a considerably higher standard deviation of TOT shocks than other SADC countries, reflecting the large weight of oil in the country's exports.

Consistent with this assessment, welfare calculations of an SADC monetary union including all these countries are mixed, suggesting sizeable net gains only in those more profligate countries that would benefit from greater union-wide discipline. Net losses are obtained for Angola and Mauritius, reflecting considerable shock asymmetry in the former case, and a likely loss of credibility in the latter case (Table 6). As for Tanzania, it would have a small net gain from membership in this monetary union, unlike the EAC's, because an

---

[21] The Seychelles are omitted from our calculations because its high per capita income gives implausible figures for its FN variable.

Table 4. EAC Monetary Union: Welfare Gains or Losses

	Welfare Gain[a]	Due to (in percent):			GDP Share (in percent)	Shock Correlation	FNA/FN
		Monetary Externality	Fiscal Asymmetry	Shock Asymmetry			
Burundi	2.90	0.81	2.36	−0.20	1.87	0.17	0.75
Kenya	1.40	0.81	0.67	−0.07	41.67	0.58	0.92
Rwanda	0.64	0.81	0.76	−0.91	5.26	0.22	0.91
Tanzania	−0.30	0.81	−1.09	−0.05	31.69	0.78	1.17
Uganda	0.52	0.81	−0.16	−0.14	19.51	0.62	1.02

Note: [a]Welfare is expressed in percentage points of GDP.
Source: Authors' estimates.

Should African Monetary Unions Be Expanded? 227

Table 5. SADC Countries: Selected Indicators, 1994–2005

	TOT Correlations with South Africa	FN	Standard Deviation of TOT Shocks	Openness[a]: $0.5(X+M)/$ GDP	Adjusted Standard Deviation of TOT
Angola	0.13	57.79	10.82	71.96	7.79
Botswana	0.35	42.17	3.83	44.09	1.69
Democratic Republic of Congo	0.28	37.56	3.04	25.15	0.77
Lesotho	0.45	66.55	1.46	74.14	1.08
Malawi	0.14	46.71	5.91	32.57	1.92
Mauritius	0.32	27.58	1.34	59.66	0.80
Mozambique	−0.16	42.58	2.09	28.35	0.59
Namibia	−0.07	41.55	4.25	46.07	1.96
South Africa	1.00	33.34	1.81	25.64	0.46
Swaziland	0.23	44.43	1.78	79.87	1.42
Tanzania	0.05	31.06	5.64	20.32	1.15
Zambia	−0.08	46.58	5.08	35.78	1.82
Zimbabwe	−0.39	52.14	2.49	33.20	0.83

Note: [a]Average, 2000–2006, as percent of GDP.
Source: Authors' estimate.

SADC monetary union would be largely anchored by a country, South Africa, with a reasonable degree of fiscal discipline. These calculations assume that the SADC central bank would reflect the FNA of all member countries.

The other countries including the largest, South Africa, would record only modest net gains (of less than half a percent of GDP) from such a monetary union. Thus, expansion of the CMA would not seem to be economically harmful for many potential participants, despite limited macroeconomic convergence and trade integration, but not particularly beneficial. The results hold irrespective of whether the simulations assume that South Africa's Reserve Bank retained sole responsibility for monetary policy or not. A selective expansion of the CMA (not reported) is generally mutually beneficial

Table 6. SADC Monetary Union: Welfare Gains or Losses

	Welfare Gain (percent of GDP)[a]	Due to (in percent):			GDP Share (in percent)	Shock Correlation	FNA/FN
		Monetary Externality	Fiscal Asymmetry	Shock Asymmetry			
Angola	−0.12	1.35	4.03	−5.30	5.07	0.80	0.63
Botswana	2.20	1.35	1.12	−0.22	2.99	0.49	0.87
Democratic Republic of Congo	1.45	1.35	0.19	−0.08	2.68	0.09	0.97
Lesotho	0.24	0.89	−0.44	−0.02	0.43	0.27	0.55
Malawi	2.88	1.35	2.00	−0.38	0.97	0.09	0.78
Mauritius	−0.61	1.35	−1.91	−0.13	0.62	−0.39	1.33
Mozambique	2.45	1.35	1.20	−0.05	1.95	0.30	0.86
Namibia	0.34	0.89	−0.54	0.01	1.96	0.16	0.88
South Africa	0.34	0.89	−0.57	−0.02	71.61	0.68	1.10
Swaziland	0.38	0.89	−0.53	0.05	0.79	0.62	0.82
Tanzania	0.10	1.35	−1.16	−0.14	4.54	0.16	1.18
Zambia	2.86	1.35	1.97	−0.37	1.88	−0.07	0.79
Zimbabwe	4.09	1.35	3.02	−0.13	4.52	−0.36	0.70

Notes: Welfare is expressed in percentages points of GDP.

[a]Relative to the CMA for Lesotho, Namibia, South Africa and Swaziland; relative to independent currencies for the remaining countries.

Source: Authors' estimates.

Should African Monetary Unions Be Expanded?   229

for the country concerned (except for Angola and Mauritius) and for existing CMA members.

5.3. *Economic Community of West African States*

ECOWAS is composed of two groups of countries: those in WAEMU[22] and those in WAMZ.[23] Table 7 summarizes some key features of the two groups of countries. While WAEMU countries have relatively more similar production structures, with reasonably

Table 7. ECOWAS Countries: Selected Indicators (Averages, 1994–2005)

	TOT Correlations with			Standard Deviation of TOT Shocks	Openness[a]: $0.5(X+M)/$ GDP	Adjusted Standard Deviations of TOT
	Other WAEMU	Other WAMZ	FN			
WAEMU						
Benin	0.22	0.00	35.65	7.45	20.93	1.56
Burkina Faso	0.26	0.06	39.47	7.68	17.57	1.35
Côte d'Ivoire	0.03	0.07	37.91	7.75	38.87	3.01
Mali	0.18	−0.10	42.36	4.73	28.73	1.36
Niger	0.05	0.12	39.59	4.62	22.53	1.04
Senegal	−0.01	−0.06	37.22	1.55	32.84	0.51
Togo	0.20	−0.14	38.37	9.35	35.78	3.34
WAMZ						
Gambia	−0.05	−0.06	40.49	10.16	51.80	5.26
Ghana	0.36	−0.05	45.81	5.33	43.98	2.34
Guinea	0.07	−0.05	33.38	4.52	25.08	1.13
Nigeria	−0.37	−0.27	31.48	9.37	39.38	3.69
Sierra Leone	−0.04	0.03	43.00	4.27	25.08	1.07

Note: [a]Average, 2000–2006, as percent of GDP.
Source: Authors' estimates.

---

[22]We do not include Guinea-Bissau in our tables, since it is a member of WAEMU only since 1997.
[23]We do not include Liberia or Cape Verde in our set of countries, which have not participated in WAMZ.

high correlations of their TOT, the WAMZ countries have much lower correlations among themselves (and with WAEMU).

Nigeria, in particular, faces very different TOT shocks when compared to its neighbours, reflecting the particular importance of oil exports (though Côte d'Ivoire produces a modest amount of oil). Nigeria's TOT shocks are negatively correlated with all the other ECOWAS countries (with an unweighted average correlation of -0.37 with WAEMU countries and -0.27 *vis-à-vis* other WAMZ countries). In contrast, all the WAEMU countries except Senegal have positive correlations against the average of other WAEMU countries, and each of them has stronger correlations against the average of WAEMU countries than against that of WAMZ countries. Ghana is the one exception among WAMZ countries, since it is strongly correlated with WAEMU, its TOT shocks exhibiting correlations of 0.58, 0.70 and 0.74 with those of Benin, Burkina Faso and Cote d'Ivoire, respectively.

The FNA does not differ markedly between WAEMU and WAMZ, unlike in our previous work which applied to an earlier period when fiscal discipline was markedly lower in WAMZ. In fact, due to the deterioration in the finances in some WAEMU countries, in particular Côte d'Ivoire, and the marked improvement in Nigeria's fiscal position, WAEMU's FNA (weighted by GDP) is 38.5 percent of GDP, compared to 33.4 for WAMZ. Nevertheless, among the WAMZ countries, there is wide variation, with Nigeria having a figure of 31.5 and Ghana 45.8.

Table 8 reports the welfare gains or losses from a full ECOWAS monetary union, with the WAEMU members' welfare compared to the status quo of their current membership in WAEMU, and the WAMZ countries compared to their retention of independent currencies. As in other sub-regions, gains in terms of greater credibility usually more than offset losses that would arise from asymmetric shocks, so that only the Gambia is found to be a net loser. Two of the WAMZ countries would reap net gains in excess of 2 percent of GDP, while gains for WAEMU countries would be roughly 1 percent, or less.

Table 8. Full ECOWAS Monetary Union: Welfare Gains or Losses

Country	Welfare Gain (percent of GDP)[a]	Due to (in percent):			GDP share (in percent)	Shock Correlation	FNA/FN
		Monetary Externality	Fiscal Asymmetry	Shock Asymmetry			
Benin	0.73	0.62	0.69	-0.56	2.92	-0.56	0.98
Burkina	0.69	0.62	0.67	-0.56	3.42	-0.70	0.89
Côte d'Ivoire	0.06	0.62	0.68	-1.20	12.99	-0.39	0.92
Mali	1.08	0.62	0.66	-0.14	3.58	-0.04	0.83
Niger	1.06	0.62	0.67	-0.19	2.24	-0.39	0.88
Senegal	1.18	0.62	0.68	-0.09	5.95	-0.30	0.94
Togo	0.73	0.62	0.68	-0.53	1.64	0.00	0.91
Gambia	-0.31	1.75	1.10	-3.09	0.43	-0.07	0.87
Ghana	2.44	1.75	2.13	-1.30	7.48	-0.69	0.77
Guinea	0.96	1.75	-0.34	-0.48	3.64	-0.28	1.05
Nigeria	0.59	1.75	-0.73	-0.46	54.77	0.97	1.11
Sierra Leone	2.81	1.75	1.59	-0.43	0.93	-0.19	0.81

Notes: Welfare is expressed in percentage points of GDP.
[a]Welfare gain calculated relative to WAEMU for WAEMU members, relative to independent currencies for WAMZ countries.
Source: Authors' estimates.

Decompositions of the net gains[24] suggest that shock asymmetries are an important part of the story for several countries, helping to explain the loss for the Gambia, and also the very modest gain for Côte d'Ivoire. The latter country would go from a monetary union in which it was the largest country, and hence had the most influence on monetary policy, to one in which the union's policy would be more strongly influenced by others with different TOT shocks. Nigeria, on the other hand, would dominate the monetary union as its largest member and hence would have TOT shocks similar to the average. Despite the fact that the ECOWAS average FN was higher than its own, our model indicates that Nigeria would gain enough from the monetary externality to more than offset the impact of shock asymmetry and extract a small net gain.

To illustrate further the key drivers of the welfare effects associated with monetary unification in DMP, we look at the addition of a single country to the existing WAEMU. Such a scenario reduces both the credibility effect stemming from the internalization of the monetary externality and the increased asymmetry of shocks coming from a full ECOWAS union.

These calculations, reported in Table 9, suggest that no WAMZ country would both increase its welfare by joining and also increase the welfare of all existing WAEMU members. It should also be noted that the current composition of WAEMU is calculated to be an improvement over the hypothetical case of independent currencies for all members (first column), while WAMZ is calculated to be worse than retention of independent currencies by the Gambia and Guinea (last column). This latter result calls into question the strategy of first creating a WAMZ monetary union, since on its own it would produce little benefit, and even with the advent of a WAMZ common

---

[24]The three components are the reduced temptation for inflationary policies of a (larger) monetary union due to internalizing the monetary externality (this is the same for all the WAEMU countries, and for all of the WAMZ countries), a gain or loss due to fiscal asymmetries (recalling that a country would like the monetary union's fiscal discipline to be somewhat better than its own) and finally loss of welfare due to the asymmetry of shocks to output.

Table 9. Welfare Gains or Losses from Adding Single Countries to WAEMU (in Percent)[a]

| | Existing WAEMU | Country Added | | | | | Creating WAMZ |
		Gambia	Ghana	Guinea	Nigeria	Sierra Leone	
Benin	0.38	0.03	−0.03	0.07	0.21	−0.04	
Burkina	1.17	0.03	−0.02	0.09	0.18	−0.04	
Côte d'Ivoire	0.71	0.01	−0.01	0.02	−0.51	−0.05	
Mali	1.60	0.02	−0.07	0.10	0.65	−0.04	
Niger	1.06	0.03	−0.04	0.11	0.60	−0.03	
Senegal	0.66	0.03	−0.06	0.11	0.73	−0.04	
Togo	0.30	0.01	−0.07	0.04	0.27	−0.06	
Gambia		−1.46					−1.52
Ghana			2.39				0.72
Guinea				−0.08			−0.37
Nigeria					0.44		0.18
Sierra Leone						1.79	1.49

Notes: [a]Relative to independent currencies for new members, relative to WAEMU for existing members, except for first column in which the welfare from membership in WAEMU is evaluated. Welfare is expressed in percentage points of GDP.
Source: Authors' estimates.

currency the path towards a full ECOWAS monetary union would remain uncertain.

5.4. Sensitivity to Parameter Values

The parameterization is subject to considerable uncertainty. To gauge how the results would be affected by changes to the parameters, we therefore mechanically halve or double in turn the key parameters a, b, γ, c, η and investigate what doing so would imply for the gainers and losers from two monetary unions: the actual WAEMU and the proposed full ECOWAS monetary union — both of which are discussed above. While these changes are arbitrary, they span a considerable range of values.

Table 10 shows that the net gain or loss of welfare is more sensitive to some of the changes than to others. In particular, halving any parameter, except c, produces welfare gains that are qualitatively

Table 10. Sensitivity Analysis: Effect of Halving/Doubling Parameters on Countries Gaining/Losing from WAEMU/ ECOWAS Monetary Unions

Number of Countries Gaining/Total	WAEMU[a]	ECOWAS[b]
Base case	7/7	11/12
Parameter halved		
a	7/7	12/12
b	7/7	10/12
c	3/7	5/12
γ	7/7	10/12
η	7/7	12/12
Parameter doubled		
a	3/7	4/12
b	7/7	12/12
c	7/7	12/12
γ	7/7	12/12
η	3/7	4/12

Notes: [a]Gain or loss relative to independent currencies.
[b]Gain or loss relative to WAEMU for WAEMU countries, relative to independent currencies for others.
Source: Authors' estimates.

similar to those for the base case, where both WAEMU and ECOWAS are deemed welfare-improving for (almost) all members. Similarly, doubling each of the parameters except a and η also has little effect. The remaining cases are related to each other, since increasing a and η increases the value to keeping inflation at its target, on the one hand, and makes the target more sensitive to the TOT (output) shocks, on the other. Conversely, lowering c (while keeping other parameters unchanged) makes monetary policy less effective in affecting output, requiring more active use of monetary policy and more variation in inflation. All of these considerations make the retention of an independent currency and an independent monetary policy more valuable, for a given level of shock asymmetries. In contrast, the two parameters that quantify the welfare effects of fiscal policy, b and γ, have less impact on the welfare comparisons for these two monetary unions.

6. The Attractiveness of Monetary Unions: Beyond the Model

Model simulations discussed above exhibit two shortcomings that warrant a broader discussion of the plausible dynamics of monetary integration in Africa. The first is that simulations can give only a static picture of monetary unions likely to be sustainable given the current state of macroeconomic and institutional convergence. The second is that for obvious tractability reasons — and in particular the need to use objective benchmarks for welfare comparisons — we ignored the possibility for countries to enact credible institutional reforms aimed at containing policy biases and enhancing macroeconomic stability. Such reforms include the adoption of medium-term fiscal frameworks that impose binding numerical constraints on budgetary aggregates, and the formal delegation of monetary policy responsibilities to an independent central bank, including an explicit mandate to deliver monetary stability and strong guarantees against political interference.

As indicated earlier, the extent to which national central banks can be formally insulated from policy bias matters for the relative attractiveness of monetary union membership. In fact, data suggest that central banks in SSA received greater legal independence since the end of the 1980s, very much in line with the trend observed elsewhere.[25] It also appears that SSA central banks for which data are available enjoy levels of legal independence comparable to the rest of the sample. If legal independence as measured by the index effectively goes along with lesser government influence on monetary policy decisions (i.e., λ_i goes down in terms of our model), then the relative attractiveness of a regional currency as a way to establish monetary credibility could be reduced. The reason is that the marginal welfare gain from lower inflation would decrease. Although it is difficult to quantify the contribution of improved monetary institutions to the global disinflation of the last 15 years, it is noticeable that Africa was no exception to these trends, suggesting that domestic reforms can deliver appreciable benefits in terms of monetary stability in a wide variety of countries. In the presence of 'domestic substitutes' to credible regional institutions, it is unclear whether many of the countries envisaged in our analysis would still experience net welfare gains from monetary integration.

One could argue, however, that domestic institutions are only imperfect substitutes for regional ones because (i) regional institutions enjoy economies of scale from pooling scarce human and financial resources, and (ii) guarantees against interference are inherently more credible for regional bodies. While it is difficult to assess the importance of economies of scale, it is worth noting that central bank independence indices for the existing regional banks (BEAC and BCEAO) are comparable to other central banks in the SSA sample. So the strength of the argument relies solely on the greater difficulty for a single government to influence a supranational decisionmaker. One important reason may be that it would take costly coordination efforts among member governments either to influence the CCB or to repeal these guarantees. Moreover, countries aware that they could not credibly implement legal guarantees protecting domestic

---

[25]Data are from Crowe and Meade (2007), who calculated the Cukierman–Webb–Neyapti Index for 142 countries, including 27 SSA countries and the two regional banks of the Zone Franc (BCEAO and BEAC).

Should African Monetary Unions Be Expanded? 237

institutions may find it in their best interest to endorse a CCB with institutional guarantees close or equivalent to the most independent national central bank among potential members.[26]

That said, supranational constraints are not necessarily difficult to lift if a critical mass of member states find it in their interest to do so. This was demonstrated by the suspension and subsequent watering down of EU's rules-based fiscal framework (the Stability and Growth Pact) in November 2003. As for the advantages of pooling resources and the economies of scale involved in creating regional institutions, they may not result if new monetary unions supplement national central banks with a supranational one, rather than replacing them.

Following on the points above, there are, of course, a number of wider considerations related to the desirability and feasibility of particular monetary unions. For a potential ECOWAS monetary union, the likelihood that the French Treasury's guarantee of convertibility of the CFA franc to the euro at a fixed parity would be extended to the wider union has been questioned. Moreover, since the model simulation results question the net benefits of WAMZ for some members, this raises doubts about the charted path to an ECOWAS union. Finally, though the simulations do not indicate that the presence of Nigeria with its asymmetric TOT shocks would necessarily make an ECOWAS union infeasible, Nigeria's short track record with fiscal reforms could fuel reluctance of other countries to partner with it in a monetary union.

7. Conclusions

Monetary integration remains an important policy issue in Africa, justifying further efforts to provide a comprehensive analysis of its costs and benefits. In this paper, we selectively surveyed the existing

---

[26]Debrun (2001) establishes that argument in a game-theoretical setting where countries bargain over the type of central bank they would agree to establish at the regional level. The model is consistent with the fact EMU countries with weak macroeconomic institutions and performance embraced participation in a monetary union, with a central bank looking very much like the German Bundesbank.

literature and expanded our own contribution to it. We have done so with a model that integrates the traditional OCA criteria with the FNs of governments, since fiscal discipline is a prerequisite for price stability. Disparities in fiscal discipline constitute a challenge to the construction of monetary unions, because they make it unattractive to admit countries whose large FNs would put pressure on a CCB. We also discussed institutional reforms that would make central banks more independent of government FNs and that would help improve government capacity to mobilize revenues and decrease unproductive spending.

Despite the large asymmetries of shocks and of FNs, the model gives a somewhat more agnostic assessment than in previous, mostly critical, work (including our own) of the prospects for sustainable monetary unions in the three regions where they are being actively pursued: the EAC, ECOWAS and SADC. With a few exceptions, the model suggests that the gains stemming from enhanced monetary stability tend to offset — albeit often by a very narrow margin — the costs arising from the impossibility to stabilize idiosyncratic shocks with national monetary policy. However, the net gains tend to be quite small, suggesting that while the welfare impact may not be harmful, it may not be particularly beneficial either. In addition, these results depend critically on a proper assessment of (i) policy preferences with regard to inflation and output stabilization and (ii) the effectiveness of monetary policy.

Our analysis points to the need for further research in a number of areas. The first is the importance of developing similar cost – benefit assessments in models with richer economic dynamics. Ideally, we would like to estimate the model using panel data, to capture time series as well as cross-sectional dimensions. To do so successfully, we would need to expand the model with a view to incorporate adequate leads and lags in the inflation process. The second task would be to account for the dynamic nature of the gains themselves, specifically the fact that economic structures and performance adjust to the new regime, making monetary unions (more) desirable only *ex post*. The third is to develop a better understanding of non-observable or hard-to-observe variables — such as policymakers' preferences and institutional quality — for which basic data are still limited for many African countries (e.g., the effectiveness of budgetary institutions in planning and implementing fiscal policy). Related to this is the important issue of how best to construct new, more effective institutions. In particular, there is only little formal analysis as to why regional institutions would be inherently more credible than national ones. So far, economists have mostly assumed that supranational bodies enjoy stronger political independence and economies of scale stemming from pooling scarce human and financial resources. Should such gains be substantial, one should study ways to marshal the political will to support the development of these regional institutions.

Acknowledgments

Without implication, we would like to thank colleagues in the IMF African Department for insightful comments. The views expressed are those of the authors and do not necessarily represent those of the International Monetary Fund or International Monetary Fund policy.

References

Agbeyegbe, T. (2008) 'On the Feasibility of a Monetary Union in the Southern Africa Development Community', *International Journal of Finance and Economics*, 13: 150–57.

Alesina, A. and G. Tabellini (1987) 'Rules and Discretion with Noncoordinated Monetary and Fiscal Policies', *Economic Inquiry*, 25: 619–30.

Barro, R. and D. Gordon (1983) 'A Positive Theory of Monetary Policy in a Natural Rate Model', *Journal of Political Economy*, 91: 589–610.

Batte, L., A.B. Quéré, B. Carton and G. Dufrénot (2009) Terms of Trade Shocks in a Monetary Union: An Application to West Africa. CEPII Working Paper 2009–07. Paris: Centre d'Etudes Prospectives et d'Informations Internationales.

Bayoumi, T. and J. Ostry (1997) 'Macroeconomic Shocks and Trade Flows within Sub-Saharan Africa: Implications for Optimum Currency Arrangements', *Journal of African Economies*, 6(3): 412–44.

Beetsma, R.M.W.J. and A.L. Bovenberg (1998) 'Monetary Union without Fiscal Coordination May Discipline Policymakers', *Journal of International Economics*, 45: 239–58.

Beetsma, R.M.W.J. and A.L. Bovenberg (1999) 'Does Monetary Unification Lead to Excessive Debt Accumulation?' *Journal of Public Economics*, 74: 299–325.

Beetsma, R. and M. Giuliodori (2010) 'The Macroeconomic Costs and Benefits of the EMU and Other Monetary Union: An Overview of Recent Research', *Journal of Economic Literature*, 48(3): 603–41.

Bénassy Quéré, A. and M. Coupet (2005) 'On the Adequacy of Monetary Arrangements in Sub-Saharan Africa', *World Economy*, 28(3): 349–73.

Blanchard, O.-J. and D. Quah (1989) 'The Dynamic Effects of Aggregate Demand and Supply Disturbances', *American Economic Review*, 79(4): 655–73.

Braude, W. and K. Sekolokwane (2008) *The Missing Piece in the Southern African Customs Union's Regional Trading Arrangements*. Winnepeg, Canada: International Institute for Sustainable Development.

Buigut, S. and N. Valev (2006) 'Eastern and Southern Africa Monetary Integration: A Structural Vector Autoregression Analysis', *Review of Development Economics*, 10(4): 586–603.

Burgess, R. (2009) The Southern African Development Community's Macroeconomic Convergence Program: Initial Performance, IMF Staff Position Note (SPN/09/14). Washington, DC: International Monetary Fund.

Catão, L. and M. Terrones (2005) 'Fiscal Deficits and Inflation', *Journal of Monetary Economic*, 52: 529–54.

Collier, P. (1991) 'Africa's External Economic Relations, 1960–90', *African Affairs*, 90: 339–56.

Crowe, C. and E. Meade (2007) 'Evolution of Central Bank Governance around the World', *Journal of Economic Perspectives*, 21: 69–90.

Debrun, X. (2001) 'Bargaining over EMU vs. EMS: Why Might the ECB be the Twin-Sister of the Bundesbank?' *The Economic Journal*, 111: 566–90.

Debrun, X. and M. Kumar (2007) The Discipline-enhancing Role of Fiscal Institutions: Theory and Empirical Evidence, IMF Working Paper 07/171. Washington, DC: International Monetary Fund.

Debrun, X., P. Masson and C. Pattillo (2005) 'Monetary Union in West Africa: Who Might Gain, Who Might Lose and Why?' *The Canadian Journal of Economics*, 38 (May): 454–81.

Debrun, X., P. Masson and C. Pattillo (2008) 'Modeling policy options for Nigeria: fiscal responsibility, monetary credibility, and regional integration', in P. Collier, C. Pattillo and C. Soludo (eds), *Economic Policy Options for a Prosperous Nigeria*, chapter 4. Basingstoke: Palgrave-Macmillan, pp. 93–120.

Debrun, X., P. Masson and C. Pattillo (2010) Should African Monetary Unions Be Expanded? An Empirical Investigation of the Scope for Monetary Integration in Sub-Saharan Africa. IMF Working Paper WP10/157. Washington, DC: International Monetary Fund.

Devarajan, S. and J. de Melo (1987) 'Evaluating Participation in African Monetary Unions: A Statistical Analysis of the CFA Zones', *World Development*, 15(4): 483–96.

Should African Monetary Unions Be Expanded? 241

Doré, O. and P. Masson (2002) Experience with Budgetary Convergence in the WAEMU. IMF Working Paper 02/108. Washington, DC: International Monetary Fund.

Fielding, D. and K. Shields (2001) 'Modelling Macroeconomic Shocks in the CFA Franc Zone', *Journal of Development Economics*, 66: 199–223.

Guillaume, D.M. and D. Stasavage (2000) 'Improving Policy Credibility: Is There a Case for African Monetary Unions', *World Development*, 28(8): 1391–407.

Guillaumont, P. and S. Guillaumont (1984) *Zone franc et développement Africain.* Paris: Economica.

Horváth, J. and R. Grabowski (1997) 'Prospects of African Integration in the Light of the Theory of Optimum Currency Areas', *Journal of Economic Integration*, 12(1): 1–25.

Houssa, R. (2008) 'Monetary Union in West Africa and Asymmetric Shocks: A Dynamic Structural Factor Model Approach', *Journal of Development Economics*, 85(1–2): 319–47.

Jenkins, C. and L. Thomas (1996) 'Is Southern Africa ready for regional monetary integration?', in L. Petersson (ed.) (1998), *Post-Apartheid Southern Africa: Economic Challenges and Policies for the Future.* London/New York: Routledge, pp. 145–70.

Jensen, H. (1997) 'Credibility of Optimal Monetary Delegation', *American Economic Review*, 87: 911–20.

Karras, G. (2007) 'Is Africa an Optimum Currency Area? A Comparison of Macroeconomic Costs and Benefits', *Journal of African Economies*, 16(2): 234–58.

Keen, M. and M. Mansour (2009) Revenue Mobilization in Sub-Saharan Africa: Challenges from Globalization. IMF Working Paper 09/157. Washington, DC: International Monetary Fund.

Khamfula, Y. and M. Tesfayohannes (2004) 'South Africa and Southern African Monetary Union: A Critical Review of Sources of Costs and Benefits', *South African Journal of Economics*, 72(1): 37–49.

Loungani, P., A. Razin and C.-W. Yuen (2002) The Open Economy Phillips Curve: 'New Keynesian' Theory and Evidence. *CEPR Discussion Papers No. 3582*, London: Center for Economic Policy Research.

Martin, P. (1995) 'Free-riding, Convergence and Two-speed Monetary Unification in Europe', *European Economic Review*, 39: 1345–64.

Masson, P.R. (2008) 'Currency Unions in Africa: Is the Trade Effect Substantial Enough to Justify Their Formation?' *The World Economy*, 31(4): 533–47.

Masson, P.R. and C. Pattillo (2002) 'Monetary Union in West Africa: An Agency of Restraint for Fiscal Policies?' *Journal of African Economies*, 11(3): 387–412.

Masson, P.R. and C. Pattillo (2005) *The Monetary Geography of Africa*, Washington, DC: Brookings Institution.

Mundell, R. (1961) 'A Theory of Optimum Currency Areas', *American Economic Review*, 51(4): 657–65.

Opolot, J. and E. Luvanda (2009) Macroeconomic Convergence in the East African Community: Progress and Implications for the Proposed Monetary Union. Bank of Uganda Staff Papers, Vol. 3, No. 1, Bank of Uganda, Mimeo, pp. 53–79.

Peiris, S. and M. Saxegaard (2007) An Estimated DSGE Model for Monetary Policy Analysis in Low-income Countries. *IMF Working Paper 07/282*. Washington, DC: International Monetary Fund.

Rogoff, K. (1985) 'The Optimal Degree of Commitment to an Intermediate Monetary Target', *Quarterly Journal of Economics*, 100: 1169–90.

Rose, A. (2000) 'One Money, One Market: Estimating the Effect of Common Currencies on Trade', *Economic Policy*, 30: 9–45.

Svensson, L. (1997) 'Optimal Inflation Targets, "Conservative" Central Bankers, and Linear Inflation Contracts', *American Economic Review*, 87: 98–114.

Tapsoba, S.J.-A. (2009) 'Trade Intensity and Business Cycle Synchronicity in Africa', *Journal of African Economies*, 18(2): 287–318.

Tavlas, G. (2009) 'The Benefits and Costs of Monetary Union in Southern Africa: A Critical Survey of the Literature', *Journal of Economic Surveys*, 23(1): 1–43.

Tsangarides, C. and M. Qureshi (2008) 'Monetary Union Membership in West Africa: A Cluster Analysis', *World Development*, 36(7): 1261–79.

Tsangarides, C., P Ewenczyk and M. Hulej (2006) Stylized Facts on Bilateral Trade and Currency Unions: Implications for Africa. IMF Working Paper 06/31. Washington, DC: International Monetary Fund.

WAMZ (2008) Final Report of the 23rd Meeting of the Convergence Council of the Ministers and Governors of Central Banks of the West African Monetary Zone (WAMZ). Banjul, The Gambia, November 7, 2008.

Wang, J.-Y., I. Masha, K. Shirono and L. Harris (2007) The Common Monetary Area in Southern Africa: Shocks, Adjustment, and Policy Challenges. IMF Working Paper 07/158. Washington, DC: International Monetary Fund.

Wyplosz, C. (1997) 'EMU: Why and How It Might Happen?' *Journal of Economic Perspectives*, 11(4): 3–21.

Yehoue, E. (2005) On the Pattern of Currency Blocs in Africa. *IMF Working Paper 05/45*. Washington, DC: International Monetary Fund.

Chapter 7

Currency Unions in Africa: Is the Trade Effect Substantial Enough to Justify Their Formation?*

Paul R. Masson

1. Introduction

Interest in the adoption of a common currency within Africa is particularly high at the moment, stimulated by the generally small size of individual economies — leading to a desire to promote regional integration as a means of forming more significant units — and by the successful launch of the euro, which is viewed by some as a model for the creation of currency unions in other regions. Monetary (or exchange rate) unions[1] have a rich history in Africa,

---

*This chapter originally appeared in *The World Economy*, (2008), 31(4), 553–547. At time of writing, the author was Adjunct Professor at the University of Toronto.

[1] A currency union can take the form of a multilateral monetary union (countries sharing the same central bank and currency) or dollarisation (the unilateral adoption of another country's currency). Examples in Africa of the former are the CFA franc zones (in Western and Central Africa), and of the latter, Liberia's adoption (at various times in the past) of the US dollar. A weaker form of monetary integration is an exchange rate union: a permanent arrangement linking the currencies of member countries at fixed parities (as is the case in the Common Monetary Area, or CMA, in Southern Africa). See Masson and Pattillo (2005, Box 1–1).

243

also making it natural that they should be under consideration in various parts of the continent. Indeed, several regional groupings, including ECOWAS, COMESA and SADC, are considering, or have agreed, timetables for the creation of currency unions among their member countries.[2] In addition, one of the goals of the African Union (AU) is to build on regional currency unions and eventually bring into being a single currency for Africa.

There has been considerable discussion of whether Africa trades less than economic theory and a comparison with other continents would imply. The main tool for examining that question is the gravity model, which has both solid theoretical underpinnings (see Anderson, 1979; and Baldwin, 2006) and empirical success in explaining the strength of trade linkages. That model posits, and empirical evidence supports, the following variables for explaining the importance of trade for any pair of countries: the level of each country's GDP and GDP per capita, with higher values of both in either country tending to increase trade; the distance between them, which will tend to decrease their trade; and other variables that affect transactions, communication and transportation costs, all of which reduce trade. Africa's trade with the rest of the world, in particular with the euro area, is much larger than intra-African trade, and this is explained in the gravity model by the much higher level of Europe's GDP, which exerts a 'gravitational force' on African countries' trade. But even that trade is not particularly significant from a global perspective, and Africa's share of world trade is under 2 percent.

Given the low level of African trade — whether it is fully explained by the gravity model or not — and the benefits from the increased efficiency and stimulus to output that expanded trade is expected to bring, a crucial issue for Africa remains whether there are measures that can be taken to stimulate trade. In this context, a provocative article by Andrew Rose (Rose, 2000) suggests that a solution to this problem may be at hand: two countries sharing a common currency trade, on average, three times more than countries

---

[2]See Table 1 for the membership of regional economic communities.

with similar characteristics that have different currencies. While later work by Rose and his collaborators reduces the size of the effect somewhat (Rose and van Wincoop, 2001; and Glick and Rose, 2002), it remains substantial — roughly a doubling of trade.

If one restricts the sample to the African countries alone, the estimates of the effect of currency unions using the same methodology are very close to Rose's estimates (Masson and Pattillo, 2005; and Tsangarides *et al.*, 2006). Despite refinements, the methodology remains subject to numerous criticisms and there is still widespread belief among economists that the size of the Rose effect is implausibly large.[3] Baldwin (2006) concludes that reasonable estimates for Europe should be in the range of a 5 to 15 percent increase. Estimates for Africa are strongly affected by the treatment of zero observations for bilateral trade (which are widespread, even between pairs of countries sharing a common currency), and their omission probably biases upward the currency effect.[4] However, leaving aside the debate between Rose and his critics, which are not the subject of this paper, and assuming that a reasonable upper bound of the effect of a common currency is a doubling of bilateral trade, the paper considers whether such trade effects provide a strong case for proceeding with African currency unions.[5]

In earlier work — Debrun *et al.* (2005) and Masson and Pattillo (2005) — using a model calibrated to African data, we found that proposed African common currency areas would not be welfare improving for all (or even most) of their potential members. The

---

[3]Nitsch (2002) shows that seemingly innocuous changes in specification and data corrections reduce the estimated effect. See Baldwin (2006) for an extensive and very readable survey of econometric problems.

[4]These zero observations are routinely dropped when the usual log form of the gravity model is estimated.

[5]Some estimates of the currency union effect suggest that a common currency might also increase trade with third countries. While this is plausible for the adoption of the US dollar or the euro, which are international currencies and whose use would facilitate trade with all countries, it makes much less sense for a monetary union with a currency that would not have widespread international use, as is likely to be the case for new African currencies.

model is based on an open-economy Barro-Gordon supply equation, a government budget constraint, and a welfare function valuing government spending and output, but penalizing higher inflation and taxes. A higher share of internal trade removes incentives on the part of the central bank to stimulate output by causing surprise depreciation relative to neighboring countries. So a larger monetary union (in the sense of greater internal trade) is a better one, *ceteris paribus,* because it tends to offset the bias toward higher inflation; conversely, the more heterogeneous it is, the less likely the common monetary policy will suit a member country's needs. These two features imply a tradeoff that determines the net welfare effects of membership. However, our earlier work ignored the possible trade-creation effects of a common currency. The current paper examines the robustness of those results to an endogenous increase in trade.

The organization of the paper is as follows. Section 2 quantifies the potential increase in trade for the African regional economic communities and for Africa as a whole. Section 3 reassesses the potential welfare gains from African regional monetary unions or a single African currency in the light of these potential trade increases. Section 4 concludes.

2. Quantifying the Trade Expansion of Proposed African Currency Unions

The creation of a common African currency has long been a pillar of African unity, and a timetable for it was established in the 1991 Abuja Treaty that set up the African Economic Community. A single African currency is to be created in stages, and to use regional economic communities (RECs) as building blocks. Within the RECs, free trade areas would first be created, then they would be merged into a common African customs union, leading by 2028 to a single African currency to be issued by an African central bank. Subsequent declarations have suggested that an earlier achievement of an African currency should be the objective. In addition, the RECs themselves (or other groupings of countries) have established their own projects

Currency Unions in Africa 247

for currency unions, which presumably would be subsumed into the pan-African currency union at a later stage.[6]

The regions that are designated as building blocks for African integration are listed in Table 1, with their present membership. It can be noted that there is overlapping membership; the Democratic Republic of the Congo (Zaïre) belongs to three RECs, and several other countries belong to two of them. COMESA, the largest geographical grouping, includes countries from north, central and southern Africa, with vastly different characteristics and no strong leading country, since Egypt, which has by far the largest GDP in the group, takes only a passing interest in its activities (see Appendix Table A.1 for data on all African countries in our sample).[7] SADC, in contrast, is more geographically cohesive and benefits from the active participation of the Republic of South Africa, the largest economy in Sub-Saharan Africa. ECOWAS has achieved some of its integration objectives, including the effective deployment of a peace-keeping force largely staffed from Nigeria. ECCAS has not been active, given wars within and between several of its member countries, while AMU has had little impact.

Among the RECs, at least three have explicit projects for creating their own monetary unions: COMESA, ECOWAS and SADC. Of these, ECOWAS is the most advanced. However, a complication that affects prospects for a single currency in West Africa is that there is an existing currency union, the West African Economic and Monetary Union (WAEMU), grouping roughly half of the ECOWAS countries. While expanding that monetary union by admitting the remaining countries might make sense, this is politically unacceptable to the other, mainly Anglophone, countries, who view the CFA franc zone as a relic of France's colonial past. So instead, a subset of ECOWAS countries (the Gambia, Ghana, Guinea, Nigeria and Sierra Leone) have agreed in principle to create a second monetary union, the West African Monetary Zone (WAMZ) and eventually to

---

[6]See details in Masson and Pattillo (2005).

[7]Missing are Eritrea, Libya and Somalia. In addition, trade data are not available for some of the other countries.

248 *Paul R. Masson*

Table 1. Composition of Regional Economic Communities and African Union and Status of Monetary Union Projects

Grouping	Countries	Monetary Union Status
Arab Maghreb Union (AMU)	Algeria, Libya, Mauritania, Morocco, Tunisia	No project
Common Market for Eastern and Southern Africa (COMESA)	Angola, Burundi, Comoros, D.R. Congo, Djibouti, Egypt, Eritrea, Ethiopia, Kenya, Libya, Madagascar, Malawi, Mauritius, Rwanda, Seychelles, Sudan, Swaziland, Uganda, Zambia, Zimbabwe	Target date: 2025
Economic Community of Central African States (ECCAS)	CEMAC (Cameroon, C. Afr. Rep., Chad, Equatorial Guinea, Gabon, Rep. Congo) plus Burundi, D.R. Congo, Rwanda, S. Tomé and Prince	CEMAC countries are members of CFA franc zone; no project for ECCAS as a whole
Economic Community of West African States (ECOWAS)	WAEMU (Benin, Burkina Faso, Côte d'Ivoire, Guinea-Bissau, Mali, Niger, Senegal, Togo) plus Cape Verde, the Gambia, Ghana, Guinea, Liberia, Nigeria, Sierra Leone	WAEMU countries are members of the CFA franc zone; the non-WAEMU countries aim to form a monetary union in 2009; ECOWAS to achieve a full monetary union at some future date
Southern African Development Community (SADC)	CMA (Lesotho, Namibia, South Africa, Swaziland) plus Angola, Botswana, D.R. Congo, Malawi, Mauritius, Mozambique, Tanzania, Zambia, Zimbabwe	CMA constitutes an exchange rate union; SADC aims to achieve full monetary union by 2016
African Union	All the above members of regional economic communities	Single African currency by 2028

Source: Official websites, April 2006.

merge it with WAEMU (on terms to be decided). However, deadlines for creating WAMZ have been missed twice, and the target date, now 2009, may also be ignored given decreasing enthusiasm among potential member countries.

COMESA has an ambitious list of monetary harmonization objectives, leading eventually to a common currency. However, other aspects of regional integration, in particular implementation of the preferential trading arrangement, have not been achieved as planned. Given the diversity of countries, a comprehensive monetary union may be difficult to achieve.

Leaders of SADC countries, meeting in Maseru, Lesotho, in August 2006, agreed to aim for a regional monetary union by 2016. This would be the culmination of other steps fostering regional integration, including creation of a common market by 2015.

Table 2 first indicates the extent of trade within the main African regional economic communities. It can be seen that, with a few exceptions, intra-regional trade is relatively unimportant as a proportion of each region's total exports. The exceptions are ECOWAS and SADC, where exports to other countries within the region are about 10 percent of exports. This figure is still very low when compared to intra-European Union trade, for instance, which amounts to over 50 percent of EU exports. Trade *between* African RECs is even lower.

Table 2. Exports of Regional Economic Communities (Sum of Member Countries' Bilateral Trade) Averages 1995–2000 (In Percent of Each REC's Total Exports)

| REC | Destination of Exports | | | | | | |
	AMU	COMESA	ECCAS	ECOWAS	SADC	European Union	Rest of World
AMU	2.74	0.67	0.11	0.45	0.06	71.78	24.19
COMESA	0.77	5.47	0.74	0.19	5.94	41.25	45.64
ECCAS	0.61	0.67	1.89	0.68	0.95	43.76	51.45
ECOWAS	1.01	0.56	1.61	9.08	1.25	37.15	49.34
SADC	0.19	8.28	0.83	0.79	10.28	36.87	42.76

Source: Masson and Pattillo (2005, Table 9-1).

250   *Paul R. Masson*

Table 3. Regional Economic Communities: Intra-regional Trade and Trade with Euro Zone (In Percent of GDP)

	Share of AU GDP	Openness (Trade/GDP)	Trade with Euro Zone/GDP	Intra-regional Trade/GDP
AMU	20.35	66.95	43.29	1.50
COMESA	29.40	60.86	22.96	1.52
ECCAS	5.72	65.77	38.36	1.36
ECOWAS	14.54	47.82	25.06	5.57
SADC	34.01	58.91	18.70	7.53
AU (Aggregated from RECs)	104.01	62.26	27.75	4.53

Source: Frankel and Rose (2002, Table V) (augmented version from Rose's website), World Bank African Development Indicators for 2001, Masson and Pattillo (2005, Table 9-1), and author's calculations. Trade is the sum of imports and exports.

The off-diagonal elements are rarely much over 1 percent of a region's exports, the one exception being trade between SADC and COMESA (and this is partly due to overlap in their membership).

In contrast, the European Union is a very important destination for African exports, the proportion being highest for the North African countries of the AMU. The AU as a whole sends about 50 percent of its exports to the European Union. As discussed above, this is consistent with the gravity model's predictions, given the size of EU GDP.

Using existing trade patterns, the importance of intra-regional trade as a proportion of GDP can be quantified, and this is presented in Table 3 for each of the RECs.[8] Using a doubling of trade by currency union membership as an upper bound, the figures in Table 3 also represent the potential gains from increased trade that would result from either the creation of a hypothetical regional currency or adoption of the euro by each region (the last two columns). The gains from intra-regional trade expansion are dwarfed by potential

---

[8]Note that the sum of the RECs' GDP exceeds 100 percent as the result of country overlap.

trade increases from adopting the euro.[9] Using the euro would also save on the resource costs of operating a central bank, and the euro would likely be a more stable currency with better attributes of means of payment and store of value than a new African currency. However, adopting the euro would mean transferring seigniorage to the European central bank, loss of monetary sovereignty and abandoning a symbol of African unity. For these reasons, it is unlikely to occur to any great extent — though it may be envisaged by a few African countries.

3. Welfare Implications of Creating African Currency Unions

In Debrun *et al.* (2005) and Masson and Pattillo (2005), we presented a model of the welfare implications of creating a currency union, based on the assumption that the new central bank could not be guaranteed its independence by statute, but rather would reflect the objectives of the member countries' governments (weighted by their size). Thus, the composition of a monetary union is crucial to the properties of the currency: a monetary union with countries having large financing needs, because of excessive government spending, corruption or inefficient tax collection, would put pressures on the central bank to generate seigniorage for financing those governments. Given costs of inflation, membership in such a currency union for a country benefiting from fiscal discipline could be welfare inferior to maintaining its own currency.

The model assumes that central banks have an incentive to stimulate output through unexpected inflation, leading in an open economy to beggar-thy-neighbor depreciation of the currency. That incentive is, however, decreased in a monetary union, because the latter internalizes more trade. Thus, the stimulative effect through currency depreciation is smaller, and the central bank will, other things being equal, produce lower inflation. Thus, the net welfare gains of a monetary union depend on the size of trade within the union, balanced by

---

[9]Linking African countries to the euro has been advocated by Honohan and Lane (2001).

the effects of fiscal heterogeneity (and also the asymmetry of shocks, as in the standard optimum currency area analysis).

The model can be summarized by three equations — the authorities' objective function, a supply equation and the government's budget constraint. Aggregate supply (y) is affected positively by monetary surprises, but negatively by monetary stimulus abroad. Thus there is the possibility of a beggar-thy-neighbor monetary policy, which could be explained by competitive devaluation or by regional congestion effects. A monetary union would eliminate the possibility of each country providing selective stimulus and thus eliminate the temptation to exploit this externality, since all countries would share the same inflation rate. In equation (1), the externality is captured by parameters $\theta_{i,k}$ representing the marginal effect of a monetary policy action in country k on output in country i, and proxied by the extent of their bilateral trade as a ratio of GDP. Output is also subject to a country-specific shock related to the terms of trade, ε_i:

$$y_i = c\left(\pi_i - \pi_i^e - \tau_i\right) - \sum_{k \neq i, k=1}^{n} \theta_{i,k} c\left(\pi_k - \pi_k^e\right) + \varepsilon_i, \quad i = 1, \ldots, n.$$

(1)

The one-period budget constraint (there is no borrowing) is given by:

$$g_i = \mu \pi_i + \tau_i - \delta_i, \quad i = 1, \ldots, n,$$

(2)

where g_i and τ_i are the ratios of socially beneficial government spending and fiscal revenues to GDP, respectively, and μ is the inflation tax base. The fixed parameter δ_i accounts for country-specific inefficiencies affecting fiscal policy, such as tax collection costs, the appropriation of tax revenues by corrupt officials and socially wasteful spending.

We assume that policymakers maximize utility functions:

$$U_i^G = \frac{1}{2}\{-a\left(\pi_i - \tilde{\pi}\left(\varepsilon_i\right)\right)^2 - b\tau_i^2 - \gamma\left(g_i - \tilde{g}_i\right)^2\} + y_i, \quad i = 1, \ldots, n.$$

(3)

The target inflation rate is contingent on supply shocks: $\tilde{\pi}(\varepsilon_i) = -\eta\varepsilon_i$ with $\eta > 0$. A negative (positive) output shock thus incites the policymaker to tolerate positive (negative) inflation.

With autonomous monetary policies, policymakers independently choose effective tax rates τ_i and inflation rates π_i maximizing (3). Policy choices are made simultaneously by all governments, taking the neighbors' policies as given (Nash conjecture). The optimal, time-consistent policy mix is derived under standard assumptions; that is, complete information, rational expectations and the following sequence of events: (i) binding nominal wage contracts are signed, (ii) shocks are realized and perfectly observed by all, and (iii) monetary and fiscal policies are decided. Under monetary autonomy, the time-consistent inflation rate (denoted by a star superscript) for any country i will be:

$$\pi_i^* = \frac{\gamma\mu b}{\Lambda}F_i + \frac{(b+\gamma)+\gamma\mu}{\Lambda}c - \frac{a(b+\gamma)\eta}{\Lambda}\varepsilon_i, \quad i=1,\ldots,n, \quad (4)$$

where $F_i = \tilde{g}_i + \delta_i$ and $\Lambda = a(b+\gamma) + \gamma\mu^2 b > 0$.

In a monetary union, it is assumed that monetary policy is decided by a common central bank, which maximizes a GDP-weighted average of national utility functions, and thus is subject to the same type of political pressures as a national central bank would be. The only difference is that, in a monetary union, individual pressures are diluted according to the relative weight of the country in the joint decision process.

Letting the subscript A designate cross-country, output-weighted averages, and θ_A the amount of trade (as a ratio to GDP) internal to the monetary union, the equilibrium rate of inflation will be given by:

$$\pi_{MU}^* = \frac{\gamma\mu b}{\Lambda}F_A + \frac{(1-\theta_A)(b+\gamma)+\gamma\mu}{\Lambda}c - \frac{a(b+\gamma)\eta}{\Lambda}\varepsilon_A. \quad (5)$$

The properties of the equilibrium policy mix reflect the fact that the gains from monetary unification essentially depend on the ability of the new regime to address the excessive inflation problem. However, this also has implications for fiscal policies (the equations

254   *Paul R. Masson*

for which are not reported here): with the common central bank now determining seigniorage revenues according to union-wide objectives, policymakers also need to adjust national tax and expenditure choices. The welfare consequences of monetary union thus reflect three separate effects: (1) lower inflation bias, (2) effects of asymmetries in fiscal policies and (3) lack of flexibility to respond to asymmetric shocks (the traditional optimum currency area criterion).

We calibrated the model to available data from all African countries (see Masson and Pattillo, 2005, Appendix A.1), and that calibration is used in the assessment below of the welfare effects of creating monetary unions for each of the RECs and for the AU as a whole. Simulations in Masson and Pattillo (2005) suggested that each of the regional currency unions would be problematic if they included all countries, because there were large differences in the degree of fiscal discipline and large asymmetries in terms-of-trade shocks. Thus, admitting all countries would lead to the creation of currencies that exhibited high inflation and responded to an average terms-of-trade shock that was not well correlated with that in each member country. This would lead to a fall in welfare for some potential members.[10]

However, neither the analysis of regional currency unions nor of an African currency took into account the potential increase in trade from the creation of a monetary union. In what follows, we assess the welfare effect of African currency unions using the trade-creation effects estimated in Table 3. Tables 4–6 report results for COMESA, ECOWAS and SADC, respectively, comparing the calculations without any induced increase in trade as a result of the currency union with those from a doubling of trade.[11] Not all

---

[10]Debrun *et al.* (2005) presented a sensitivity analysis for ECOWAS, showing that the signs of the welfare results were robust to reasonable variations in the parameters. Optimal policies depend only on the ratios a/c, b/c, γ/c and η. However, the level of welfare is proportional to c.

[11]Trade includes an estimate for informal trade equal to 25 percent of reported trade; this amount is, however, not doubled, since a currency union might well decrease informal trade in some cases. For instance, trade between Niger and Nigeria has in the past been stimulated by the desire of Nigerians to obtain a

Currency Unions in Africa

Table 4. COMESA: Net Welfare Gains from Regional Currency (Log GDP Equivalents)

| | | Welfare Gain/Loss | | |
	GDP Share	With No Trade Expansion	With Trade Doubling	Memo: Increase in Exports/GDP (Percent)
Angola	0.0465	0.1893	0.1973	0.1
D.R. Congo	0.0382	0.1303	0.1443	0.5
Egypt	0.5273	0.0038	0.0236	0.9
Ethiopia	0.0418	0.0980	0.1136	3.5
Kenya	0.0681	−0.0086	0.0117	26.9
Madagascar	0.0245	−0.0313	−0.0102	6.7
Malawi	0.0129	0.0581	0.0756	6.5
Mauritius	0.0279	−0.2191	−0.1920	3.4
Namibia	0.0234	−0.1084	−0.0846	3.0
Seychelles	0.0039	0.2572	0.2578	0.7
Sudan	0.0644	0.0494	0.0673	4.4
Swaziland	0.0090	−0.1259	−0.1015	6.0
Uganda	0.0416	−0.0505	−0.0287	1.1
Zambia	0.0222	0.0326	0.0511	10.3
Zimbabwe	0.0485	0.0665	0.0837	9.4

Source: Author's calculations.

countries are included in the monetary unions because of a lack of data.

Estimates for COMESA show significant welfare losses[12] for a number of countries from a common currency, as a result principally of shock asymmetries and because the countries with the losses have more disciplined fiscal policies than the average for the union. Doubling of trade reduces those losses (and increases the gains for the other countries), but, except for Kenya (which has substantial exports to neighboring countries), does not change the signs of the

---

convertible currency, the CFA franc (see Azam, 1999). Results differ slightly from Masson and Pattillo (2005) because of data changes.

[12] The units are log GDP equivalents, so that 0.01 indicates the welfare equivalent of a one percent increase in GDP.

256 *Paul R. Masson*

Table 5. ECOWAS: Net Welfare Gains from Regional Currency (Log GDP Equivalents)

| | | Welfare Gain/Loss | | Memo: Increase in Exports/GDP (Percent) |
	GDP Share	With No Trade Expansion	With Trade Doubling	
WAEMU Members		**Relative to CFA Franc**		
Benin	0.0340	−0.0873	−0.0594	0.4
Burkina Faso	0.0406	−0.0734	−0.0497	1.3
Côte d'Ivoire	0.1706	−0.0853	−0.0580	7.9
Mali	0.0407	−0.0780	−0.0527	0.3
Niger	0.0301	−0.0890	−0.0603	4.1
Senegal	0.0749	−0.0855	−0.0580	2.8
Togo	0.0215	−0.0839	−0.0566	8.7
Non-WAEMU Countries		**Relative to Independent Currencies**		
Gambia	0.0061	−0.0210	0.0038	0.0
Ghana	0.1078	0.0497	0.0711	5.4
Guinea	0.0597	−0.1153	−0.0862	0.4
Nigeria	0.4037	0.1145	0.1322	5.4
Sierra Leone	0.0104	−0.0397	−0.0139	0.0

Source: Author's calculations.

net welfare gains.[13] Thus, it does not seem likely that all COMESA countries would find it in their interest to join in creating a single currency for the region. If a regional currency were nevertheless created, it would be subject to pressures to provide government financing and would therefore not yield monetary stability.

Turning to ECOWAS, the comparison is made between the welfare derived by existing WAEMU members from their use of the CFA franc, with that from a new common regional currency; for the other countries, their welfare gain is compared to the existing situation of independent currencies (ignoring the potential creation

---

[13]It needs to be noted that since the union's inflation rate reflects the total amount of trade internalized within it, the increase of trade for each country individually is not the main determinant of its welfare gain or loss.

Table 6. SADC: Net Welfare Gains from Regional Currency (Log GDP Equivalents)

| | | Welfare Gain/Loss | | Memo: |
	GDP Share	With No Trade Expansion	With Trade Doubling	Change in Exports/GDP (Percent)
CMA	**Relative to Existing Exchange Rate Union**			
Lesotho	0.0049	−0.0175	−0.0075	13.4
Namibia	0.0184	−0.0338	−0.0147	8.6
South Africa	0.7285	−0.0360	−0.0158	3.8
Swaziland	0.0070	−0.0339	−0.0148	18.8
Non-CMA	**Relative to Independent Currencies**			
Angola	0.0365	0.2320	0.2360	0.3
Botswana	0.0264	0.0874	0.1030	1.7
Congo, D.R.	0.0300	0.2247	0.2316	0.6
Malawi	0.0102	0.1360	0.1490	4.7
Mauritius	0.0219	−0.0907	−0.0684	1.4
Mozambique	0.0177	0.1412	0.1541	2.2
Seychelles	0.0030	0.2539	0.2507	0.4
Tanzania	0.0398	0.0454	0.0628	0.5
Zambia	0.0175	0.1152	0.1292	4.7
Zimbabwe	0.0382	0.1448	0.1575	7.8

Source: Author's calculations.

of the WAMZ in the meantime). Here, the WAEMU countries are all welfare losers from the creation of an ECOWAS currency, while the same is true of some of the non-WAEMU countries. The principal gainer is Nigeria, which would have the greatest weight in setting monetary policy because of its size. The very different evolution of its terms of trade from its partners (it is an oil exporter, unlike the others) and its undisciplined fiscal policies would produce a currency whose higher inflation and greater variability would make it unattractive to WAEMU members, as well as to the Gambia and Guinea, when compared to their existing currencies.

Finally, a monetary union for SADC also implies a number of losers as well as gainers. In particular, the countries of the existing CMA would lose by the replacement of their exchange rate union, whose monetary policy is set by South Africa, with a monetary union whose monetary stance would be set to reflect the average conditions of all countries in the region. A doubling of trade would not overturn that result.

In Table 7, a single currency for Africa is evaluated relative to the hypothetical creation of regional currencies in all of the RECs. Here it is assumed that, despite drawbacks highlighted above, regional currencies have been created; and the welfare effects of merging those regional currencies into an AU-wide currency are assessed. Again, asymmetries in fiscal discipline and terms-of-trade shocks come into play, making the single African currency welfare-improving only for COMESA and ECOWAS. These are also the regions having on average the greatest problems with fiscal discipline, so that a currency that included them would be more inflationary than would be desired by the remaining regions. Doubling the trade effects is not unambiguously welfare-improving, because by reducing inflation it also reduces seigniorage available to finance government spending. In any case, the trade-inducing effects, as ratios to each region's GDP, are very small (note that the increase in exports alone is reported here, while in Table 3 it is the sum of intra-regional exports and imports). Only the sign of AMU's net gain changes to a small positive value with a doubling of trade, thus suggesting that a single African currency would likely run into resistance, even if the regional building blocks were created. Thus, accounting for the potential trade-creation

Table 7. A Single African Currency: Average Net Welfare Gain Relative to Hypothetical Regional Currencies (Log GDP Equivalents)

REC	No Trade Expansion	With Trade Doubling	Memo: Increase in Exports/GDP (Percent)
AMU	−0.0011	0.0104	0.2
COMESA	0.0395	0.0484	0.2
ECCAS	−0.0128	−0.0012	0.7
ECOWAS	0.1125	0.1062	1.0
SADC	−0.0739	−0.0778	0.8

Source: Author's calculations.

effects of forming a monetary union does not overturn the conclusion that monetary unions in Africa are not likely to be welfare-improving if they included all countries.

4. Conclusions

The striking empirical results of Rose and others that membership in a currency union might increase trade by a factor of two or more have been used to promote the creation of new currency unions, following the example of the euro zone. Given the small size of Africa's trade, the formation of currency unions seems a logical way to boost trade and to improve monetary policy.

This paper and previous work give several reasons, however, for doubting that currency unions provide a panacea for Africa's problems — or even a partial solution. Favorable effects from forming a currency union depend very much on the membership of that union. A currency union that internalizes a high level of trade will be expected to produce more benefits than one where the natural level of trade (e.g., as predicted by the gravity model) is low. In addition, absent institutional guarantees of the central bank's independence (and a clear objective given to the central bank) the properties of the currency will depend on the priorities of the national governments, in particular their financing needs.

A model that incorporates those features was used to analyze the possible currency unions in Africa. Despite potential doubling of trade, the conclusion emerges clearly that asymmetries across countries would make even regional currencies, much less a single African currency, undesirable for some countries. Rather than an all-encompassing project of a continent-wide currency, selective expansion of existing monetary integration projects (principally the CFA franc zone and the CMA, or rand zone), could be envisaged.

Leaving currency issues aside, it is clear that African countries can do much to increase trade. This includes improving infrastructure, reducing political tensions, and reducing tariff and non-tariff barriers to trade. There is much evidence that transportation costs are higher in Africa than elsewhere and are affected by poor

260 *Paul R. Masson*

infrastructure and civil unrest (Yeats *et al.*, 1996; and Longo and Sekkat, 2004). Efforts should be made to reduce these costs by building better roads and ports, strengthening air links, and making the unloading and processing of merchandise more efficient.

Acknowledgments

A preliminary version of this paper was presented at the 9th Annual GTAP Global Economic Analysis Conference, UNECA, Addis Ababa, 15–17 June, 2006. The author is grateful to David Coe, Patrick Osakwe and Charalambos Tsangarides for comments.

Appendix: Country Data Availability

Table A.1. GDP, Openness and Trade with Euro Zone

Country Name	Euro Zone Share of Trade (Percent)	Openness Trade/GDP (Percent)	Euro Zone Trade/GDP (Percent)	GDP, 1999 (US$, Millions)	Share of Africa GDP (Percent)
Algeria	62	59	36.58	47,872	9.30
Angola	34	110	37.40	8,545	1.66
Benin	45	63	28.35	2,414	0.47
Botswana	n.a.	n.a.	n.a.	5,996	1.16
Burkina Faso	71	41	29.11	2,580	0.50
Burundi	75	33	24.75	714	0.14
Cameroon	69	46	31.74	9,187	1.78
CAR	72	49	35.28	1,053	0.20
Chad	75	76	57.00	1,530	0.30
Comoros	70	64	44.80	193	0.04
Congo, Dem. Rep.	57	59	33.63	7,752	1.51
Congo, Rep.	77	128	98.56	2,217	0.43
Côte d'Ivoire	73	77	56.21	11,206	2.18
Djibouti	38	99	37.62	519	0.10
Egypt, Arab Rep.	38	53	20.14	89,148	17.31
Equit. Guinea	45	154	69.30	696	0.14
Ethiopia	53	38	20.14	6,439	1.25
Gabon	33	93	30.69	4,352	0.85

(*Continued*)

Currency Unions in Africa

Table A.1. (*Continued*)

Country Name	Euro Zone Share of Trade (Percent)	Openness Trade/GDP (Percent)	Euro Zone Trade/GDP (Percent)	GDP, 1999 (US$, Millions)	Share of Africa GDP (Percent)
Gambia, The	51	132	67.32	393	0.08
Ghana	40	60	24.00	7,774	1.51
Guinea	56	48	26.88	3,733	0.72
Guinea-Bissau	73	47	34.31	218	0.04
Kenya	35	73	25.55	10,638	2.07
Lesotho	n.a.	n.a.	n.a.	874	0.17
Madagascar	55	55	30.25	3,721	0.72
Malawi	26	73	18.98	1,810	0.35
Mali	51	60	30.60	2,608	0.51
Mauritania	60	112	67.20	960	0.19
Mauritius	36	122	43.92	4,244	0.82
Morocco	59	61	35.99	34,998	6.80
Mozambique	22	88	19.36	4,142	0.80
Namibia	n.a.	n.a.	n.a.	3,075	0.60
Niger	71	40	28.40	2,018	0.39
Nigeria	34	30	10.20	35,045	6.81
Rwanda	50	36	18.00	1,956	0.38
Senegal	69	69	47.61	4,801	0.93
Seychelles	16	104	16.64	545	0.11
Sierra Leone	54	39	21.06	669	0.13
South Africa	29	50	14.50	131,127	25.46
Sudan	n.a.	n.a.	n.a.	9,718	1.89
Swaziland	n.a.	n.a.	n.a.	1,223	0.24
Tanzania	61	63	38.43	8,760	1.70
Togo	42	75	31.50	1,405	0.27
Tunisia	75	93	69.75	20,944	4.07
Uganda	58	32	18.56	6,411	1.24
Zambia	17	91	15.47	3,150	0.61
Zimbabwe	21	91	19.11	5,608	1.09

Source: Euro zone trade and openness from Frankel and Rose (2002); GDP data from World Bank African Development Indicators.

References

Anderson, J. (1979), 'The Theoretical Foundations of the Gravity Equation', *American Economic Review*, **69** (March), 106–116.

Azam, J.-P. (1999), 'Dollars for Sale: Exchange Rate Policy and Inflation in Africa', *World Development*, **27** (October), 1843–1859.

Baldwin, R. (2006), 'The Euro's Trade Effects. With Comments by Jeffrey Frankel and Jacques Mélitz', ECB Working Paper No. 594 (Frankfurt: European Central Bank, March).

Debrun, X., P. R. Masson and C. Pattillo (2005), 'Monetary Union in West Africa: Who Might Gain, Who Might Lose, and Why?' *Canadian Journal of Economics*, **38** (May), 454–481.

Frankel, J. and A. Rose (2002), 'An Estimate of the Effect of Common Currencies on Trade and Income', *Quarterly Journal of Economics*, **117**, 2, 437–466.

Glick, R. and A. Rose (2002), 'Does a Currency Union Affect Trade? The Time Series Evidence', *European Economic Review*, **46** (June), 1125–1151.

Honohan, P. and P. R. Lane (2001), 'Will the Euro Trigger More Monetary Unions in Africa?' in C. Wyplosz (ed.), *The Impact of EMU on Europe and the Developing Countries* (Oxford: Oxford University Press), Chapter 12.

Longo, R. and K. Sekkat (2004), 'Economic Obstacles to Expanding Intra-African Trade', *World Development*, **32**, 8, 1309–1321.

Masson, P. and C. Pattillo (2005), *The Monetary Geography of Africa* (Washington, DC: Brookings Institution Press).

Nitsch, V. (2002), 'Honey, I Just Shrunk the Currency Union Effect on Trade', *The World Economy*, **25**, 4, 457–474.

Rose, A. (2000), 'One Money, One Market: Estimating the Effect of Common Currencies on Trade', *Economic Policy*, Issue 30, 9–45.

Rose, A. K. and E. van Wincoop (2001), 'National Money as a Barrier to International Trade: The Real Case for Currency Union', *American Economic Review*, **91** (May), 386–390.

Tsangarides, C., P. Ewenczyk and M. Hulej (2006), 'Stylized Facts on Bilateral Trade and Currency Unions: Implications for Africa', IMF Working Paper WP/06/31 (Washington, DC: International Monetary Fund, January).

Yeats, A., A. Amjadi, U. Reincke and F. Ng (1996), 'What Caused Sub-Saharan Africa's Marginalization in World Trade?' *Finance and Development* (Washington, DC: IMF and World Bank, June).

Chapter 8

Fiscal Asymmetries and the Survival of the Euro Zone*

Paul R. Masson

A model of a dependent central bank that internalizes the government's budget constraint is used to examine the optimal composition of the euro zone. The model embodies the desire to stimulate output and to provide monetary financing to governments. Unable to pre-commit to first-best policies, the central bank produces excess inflation — a tendency partially reduced in a monetary union. On the basis of this framework, calibrated to euro zone data, the current membership is shown not to be optimal: other members would benefit from the expulsion of several countries, notably Greece, Italy, and France. A narrow monetary union centered around Germany might be able to guarantee central bank independence, but simulation results suggest that such a narrow monetary union would not be in Germany's interest relative to a return to the deutsche mark.

1. Introduction

The current crisis in the euro zone has highlighted once again the strains put on a monetary union by the lack of fiscal discipline. While the interaction of fiscal and monetary policies is complex,

---

*This chapter originally appeared in *International Economics* (2012), 129, 5–29. At time of writing, the author was Adjunct Professor at the University of Toronto.

supporters of monetary union have long argued that statutory central bank independence and credible restraints on fiscal policies would provide an adequate framework for the European Central Bank to deliver the benefits of low inflation and monetary integration.[1] The failure of the Stability and Growth Pact to enforce fiscal discipline has, according to some economists,[2] led the ECB to violate the spirit, if not the letter, of the prohibition of bailouts in the Maastricht Treaty.

European public finances are in dire straits, and the rudimentary EU structural funds and the newly created European Financial Stability Fund (EFSF) and European Stability Mechanism (ESM) are inadequate to bail out all the governments with severe debt sustainability problems. Fears of default and shrinking liquidity have led to sharp increases in the interest rates prevailing on several governments' marketable debt. As a result, the ECB has purchased in secondary markets[3] large amounts of the government debt of some highly indebted euro zone countries — including Greece, Ireland, Italy, Portugal, and Spain. By lowering their borrowing costs, it hopes to make their debt more sustainable and avoid a default. Default would endanger the solvency of commercial banks in the euro zone, which hold large amounts of the debts of these countries, and the fiscal authorities of all the euro zone countries would then face further large expenditures required to recapitalize their banks. While Greece has imposed a haircut on holders of its debt, the impact on euro zone banks is manageable, given Greece's relatively

---

[1] For a retrospective look at the debates on the design of the ECB and the euro zone, see Wyplosz (2006).

[2] Notably, Axel Weber, then President of the Bundesbank, called for an early end to the ECB's bond purchases ("ECB's Trichet rejects Weber's call to end bond purchase program", Bloomberg, October 17, 2010.

[3] Thus getting around the prohibition in Article 21 of the ECB's Statutes against purchasing debt directly from government entities. However, the distinction here is nearly meaningless, since purchasing debt in secondary markets also influences the cost of debt issuance in primary markets — which seems to be the real purpose of the ECB's actions.

modest size; default by Spain or Italy would have much more severe consequences.

The extraordinary measures taken by the ECB to purchase debt of the crisis countries have raised concerns that monetary policy may be influenced by the financing needs of highly-indebted countries.[4] While the ECB has made clear that it intends to cease the extraordinary measures it has undertaken,[5] and the EFSF and ESM have been set up to take its place, there is doubt about the effectiveness of those institutions, given their limited resources. Others have pointed to imbalances in payments between the ECB and national central banks as a hidden bailout, since the ECB has accumulated large claims on banks in the weaker members of the Eurozone.[6] The size of the ECB's exposure increased considerably with the introduction of Long-Term Refinancing Operation (LTRO) three-year, low-interest-rate credits to banks.

Pressures to provide direct or indirect monetary financing to governments may undermine ECB independence in the future, especially since the banks themselves are heavily exposed to euro-zone sovereign debt. ECB executive board member Juergen Stark is reported to have resigned as a protest against the ECB's program of bond purchases of government debt, stating in an interview that "the political pressure on the ECB is enormous at the moment".[7] He went on to say "There is an open discussion about extending our mission. This not only affects our independence, it threatens it".[8]

---

[4]See, for instance, Kenneth Rogoff, "A gravity test for the euro", Project Syndicate, November 2, 2011, which suggests that inflation may be needed to recapitalize the ECB if it suffers losses on its sovereign debt portfolio (http://www.project-syndicate.org/commentary/a-gravity-test-for-the-euro).

[5]See, for instance, "Trichet rejects ECB role as lender of last resort", *Financial Times*, October 4, 2011.

[6]Hans-Werner Sinn, "The ECB's stealth bailout", VoxEU, June 1, 2011, http://www.voxeu.org/index.php?q=node/6599.

[7]"ECB independence threatened by government pressure", Reuters, November 26, 2011.

[8]Interview with the *Frankfurter Allgemeine Zeitung*, cited in http://www.cre itwritedowns.com/2011/11/juergen-stark-on-ecb-inflation-monetisation.html.

Central bank independence requires political support to be effective, and the euro zone suffers from the lack of other aspects of integration that would provide that support-strong regional political institutions or fiscal federalism. As mentioned above, the ECB was to be insulated from financing governments by statute, and the pressures on it were in addition to be minimized by effective controls on fiscal policies, but the latter have failed.[9] As the only EU institution with the power to act swiftly and with substantial financial resources, the ECB was necessarily at the center of policy responses to recent financial turmoil. Moreover, Paul De Grauwe has argued that the very architecture of the euro zone requires the ECB to become a lender of last resort to governments (and not just banks): because countries are borrowing in "foreign" currencies (that is, they no longer can rely on liquidity provided by the national central bank if needed to redeem their debt since), self-fulfilling debt crises are more likely. The central bank, by promising to provide liquidity in these cases, could prevent such debt crises from occurring — just as national central banks prevent bank runs (De Grauwe, 2011).

In this paper, we explore what the polar case of absence of central bank independence might mean for the survival of the euro zone. The intention in doing so is to highlight the dangers of ECB bailouts. Using a model (Debrun *et al.*, 2005; 2011) in which the central bank's decisions are purely the result of weighing together national objectives — objectives that include both financing government spending and stimulating output as well as keeping inflation low — we consider what would constitute a sustainable composition for the euro zone. In particular, the set of countries depends on incentives for euro zone members to remain in the monetary union — and for the others to want to keep them in. In this model, fiscal asymmetries are very important in determining the composition of a sustainable monetary union: a country with weak fiscal discipline would want to join a monetary union that is (somewhat) more disciplined than

---

[9]In December, 2011, euro zone countries agreed to amend the Stability and Growth Pact by applying sanctions should a country's cyclically adjusted fiscal position go into deficit, but it is as yet unclear how this would be implemented.

Fiscal Asymmetries and the Survival of the Euro Zone 267

itself, because the union delivers lower inflation, but not if the disparity is too great (since in that case the country loses too much in monetary financing). Conversely, countries that exhibit a degree of fiscal discipline would not want to have as member a country whose financing needs are too great, since this would put upward pressure on the union's inflation rate. The model also includes the benefits of a common currency as well as the usual costs that result from optimum-currency-area shock asymmetries.

In evaluating the degree of fiscal discipline, two components need to be taken into account: the government's overall spending objectives, on the one hand, and an additional amount that represents both wasteful government spending (such as outright corruption) and inefficiencies in tax collection, on the other hand. The model we use calculates the overall financing need as the sum of these two components, and the composite variable provides a measure of the pressure on the central bank to increase inflation. The euro zone at present differs greatly in the extent of fiscal discipline due to both components. Greece, for instance, has high spending commitments to its public employees because of generous benefits, while at the same time suffering from inefficient tax collection. An important part of the paper will be to estimate the asymmetries in these financing needs.

The paper provides welfare calculations using a calibrated version of the model, where welfare is assumed to depend on keeping inflation and taxes low, attaining targets for productive government expenditure, and increasing output. For each country, two cases will be considered: remaining in the euro zone (whose final composition may remain to be determined), and abandoning the union and reintroducing a national currency. At the same time, countries in the euro zone would be given the choice of expulsing a country if this would increase the welfare of the remaining members. This exercise provides insights into what configuration of countries may constitute a stable core that would be sustainable, assuming that the current political framework for the euro zone remains in place, but that the ECB is unable to maintain independence from national government budget constraints.

An important issue concerns whether some countries — in particular Germany — can guarantee the independence of their central bank, or indeed, of a narrow regional central bank that is formed around Germany and shares that independence with respect to the fiscal authorities. The controversy over current ECB policies largely reflects the unhappiness of the German government with bailouts, and a smaller euro zone with more disciplined members might be able to reestablish ECB independence. We thus consider what possible configurations might be consistent with such an independent, inflation targeting central bank.

The plan of the paper is as follows. Section 2 provides a short summary of a model of a dependent central bank, which is compared to a simple model of an inflation-targeting (IT), independent central bank that does not internalize government borrowing constraints. Section 3 deals with calibration to the euro zone — which until recently has behaved much as an independent IT central bank. Section 4 focuses on fiscal asymmetries among euro zone members. Section 5 provides welfare comparisons for individual euro zone countries of remaining in the monetary union versus reintroducing their own currencies and once again having their own monetary policies — independent or not from the fiscal authorities. In addition, an assessment is made of whether the welfare of the remaining euro zone members would be increased by that country's departure. Special attention is given to Germany, given the proven track record of the Bundesbank to deliver on a commitment to low inflation, its independence, and public support for its uncompromising position. Section 6 provides some conclusions and caveats.

2. A Model of a Dependent Regional Central Bank

Much has been written on the credibility of central banks' commitment to low inflation. It is now generally accepted that an independent central bank — with instrument independence, but not necessarily the independence to set its own goals — is best placed to achieve a rate of inflation that approaches society's optimum level (Debelle and Fischer, 1994). That level may be zero or even negative

(Friedman, 1969), while central banks that are forced by fiscal dominance to finance government budgets are likely to produce sub-optimally high inflation. A further, and related, question is whether even independent central banks can pre-commit not to use monetary policy to stimulate economic activity. Such a policy is self-defeating, since a systematic attempt to do so is built into the expectations of the private sector, and the monetary stimulus therefore has little or no effect.

The interaction between monetary and fiscal policy is made even more complicated in a common currency area grouping countries with independent fiscal policies but facing a single monetary policy decided by a supra-national central bank.[10] Fears that the monetary union would create perverse externalities for fiscal policies and free-riding behavior led the European Union to institute fiscal criteria for public deficits and debt as preconditions for membership, and to require members of EMU to subscribe to the Stability and Growth Pact (SGP) with potential penalties for those that did not comply with its provisions. In practice, there have been numerous cases of countries (including Germany and France) exceeding the 3 percent of GDP fiscal deficit ceiling and the 60 percent public-debt-to-GDP ratio, but penalties were never assessed, and the SGP was weakened in 2005. At the initiative of the German government, a reinforced SGP was agreed in December, 2011, but at time of writing it had not been ratified by euro zone members and its effectiveness remained to be demonstrated.

In this paper, we study the consequences for the euro zone of the European Central Bank internalizing the budget constraints of member governments — that is, becoming a *dependent central bank* in our terminology. Such an outcome would have seemed almost inconceivable a few years ago; after all, the Maastricht Treaty explicitly ruled out monetary financing of government budgets (Article 123 of the Treaty on the Functioning of the European Union), and

---

[10]For a recent survey of the extensive academic literature on this subject, most of which addresses the European context, see Beetsma and Giuliodori (2010).

bailing out countries in trouble[11] (Article 125). However, recent events discussed above have shown that loss of ECB independence is now an all-too-real possibility.

While independent central banks have been extensively modeled — in particular those targeting inflation[12] — the operation of a dependent regional central bank in the European context has not so far received attention. To date, pressures to finance government deficits have been thought mainly to be the lot of central banks in Africa or Latin America. The implications of internalizing governments' budget constraints in the context of African regional monetary integration have been studied by Debrun *et al.* (2005, 2008, 2011), and Masson and Pattillo (2005). Clear criteria emerge for the composition of monetary unions that are both desirable and feasible; that is, both the country joining should improve its welfare by doing so, and the existing members should be willing to accept it as a member. In addition to the usual OCA consideration that shocks should not be too asymmetric, fiscal discipline (i.e., financing needs) should not differ too radically. Countries would like to be members of a monetary union with countries that do not require much larger financing (as a proportion of GDP) than themselves — and ideally somewhat less. Nevertheless, a monetary union may be attractive when compared to independent currencies because by internalizing trade within a common monetary area, the temptation to produce counter-productive monetary stimulus is reduced (since exchange rate depreciation can occur only with respect to countries outside

---

[11] "The Union shall not be liable for or assume the commitments of central governments, regional, local or other public authorities, other bodies governed by public law, or public undertakings of any Member State, without prejudice to mutual financial guarantees for the joint execution of a specific project. A Member State shall not be liable for or assume the commitments of central governments, regional, local or other public authorities, other bodies governed by public law, or public undertakings of another Member State, without prejudice to mutual financial guarantees for the joint execution of a specific project". (Article 123.1 of the Treaty on the Functioning of the European Union).

[12] See for instance Svensson (1999; 2000), Bernanke *et al.* (1999), and Clarida, Galí, and Gertler (1999).

the monetary union). It is assumed that neither the national nor the regional central bank can pre-commit not to provide that monetary stimulus and hence the first-best outcome cannot be attained.

Specifically, national central banks are assumed to reflect the same objectives as the government (and society), namely targeting useful government spending, keeping taxes low, minimizing the deviations of inflation around its target, and increasing output. The government (including the central bank) of country i is assumed to maximize utility U_i^G given by

$$U_i^G = \frac{1}{2}\{-a(\pi_i - \tilde{\pi}(\varepsilon))^2 - b\tau_i^2 - \gamma(g_i - \tilde{g}_i)^2\} + y_i. \qquad (1)$$

The linear term in output is analytically convenient, and has the same effect as targeting a level of output that is greater than the "natural rate" in Barro and Gordon (1983). The central bank's policy instrument is assumed to be inflation π_i. The objective for inflation reflects a stabilization motive: a negative supply shock ε_i leads to a temporarily higher target for inflation. We parameterize this by making the inflation target inversely proportional to the output shock:

$$\tilde{\pi}(\varepsilon_i) = -\eta\varepsilon_i. \qquad (2)$$

The fact that the central bank internalizes the financing needs of the government leads to higher inflation, since optimal policy involves equalizing the marginal costs of raising taxes and inflation. In addition to productive spending needs, the government also engages in wasteful spending δ, linked to corruption and rewarding of supporters, as well inefficiencies in tax collection that add to financing needs. Thus, the government's budget constraint (all terms are ratios to GDP) can be written as

$$g_i = \mu\pi_i + \tau_i - \delta_i, \qquad (3)$$

where useful (i.e., welfare inducing) government spending g_i is financed by seigniorage $\mu\pi_i$ (where μ is the base for the inflation tax, assumed to be a common parameter across countries) and taxes τ_i, respectively, and reduced by wasteful spending and diversion δ_i.

272 *Paul R. Masson*

The model is built around a Barro-Gordon supply equation (Barro and Gordon, 1983), as modified by Alesina and Tabellini (1987) to include the negative effects of taxes, and extended to the open economy following Martin (1995). The log of output Y depends on inflation surprises both at home and (with negative transmission) abroad, the latter depending on the strength of bilateral trade ties between the home country i and partner country k:

$$y_i = c\left(\pi_i - \pi_i^e - \tau_i\right) - \sum_{k \neq i, k=1}^{n} \theta_{i,k} c(\pi_k - \pi_k^e) + \varepsilon_i \qquad (4)$$

Monetary expansion is negatively transmitted abroad under flexible exchange rates because it leads to a fall in the real wage, making production more competitive at home relative to that abroad; the magnitude of this effect depends on the extent of trade. In justifying this effect, Martin (1995) points to the production decisions of multinational firms with operations in many European countries; they choose to increase production in their plants with the lowest real wage costs.[13]

The central bank sets monetary policy to maximize (1) with respect to inflation, subject to Equations (2)–(4). It chooses inflation after observing the shock to output. Since it acts after private sector expectations are formed, it has an incentive to produce monetary surprises to moderate the effect of supply shocks. In the open economy, this has spillover effects on other countries as well, provided countries do not use the same currency and hence cannot change their bilateral exchange rate. The government maximizes (1) with respect to taxes and government spending, linked by the budget constraint (3).

The Nash equilibrium, found by solving the first order conditions together, gives an intuitive explanation of monetary and fiscal policies when the central bank is not independent. Optimal

---

[13]In the African context, a more plausible explanation may be that congestion in regional transportation networks means that domestic stimulus bids away intermediate inputs from other countries; see Debrun *et al.* (2005).

inflation π_i^* and taxes τ_i^* can be written in this context in terms of *Financing Need* ($FN_i = \tilde{g}_i + \delta_i$) which includes both legitimate spending objectives and wasteful spending/tax diversion. Both policy variables also depend on the shock to output:

$$\pi_i^* = \frac{\gamma\mu b}{\Lambda} FN_i + \frac{(b+\gamma)+\gamma\mu}{\Lambda} c - \frac{a(b+\gamma)\eta}{\Lambda}\varepsilon_i, \qquad (5)$$

$$\tau_i^* = \frac{\gamma a}{\Lambda} FN_i + \frac{\gamma\mu(1+\mu)+a}{\Lambda} c + \frac{a\gamma\mu\eta}{\Lambda}\varepsilon_i, \qquad (6)$$

where all parameters are assumed to be positive and $\Lambda = a(b+\gamma) + \gamma\mu^2 b > 0$. As can be seen from the first term of Equation (5), the central bank partially accommodates the financing needs of the government. The second term also contributes to raising inflation because of the inability to pre-commit. The third term embodies the use of monetary policy to offset (partially) output shocks. The reduced form for taxes also embodies the financing motive, but given positive inflation and hence seigniorage, taxes can be lower than they would otherwise be. The third term again allows for the effect of inflation on government financing, given monetary policy's stabilization role.[14]

When used to analyze currency unions, this simple model also produces some insights that extend those of the usual OCA model. The regional central bank is also assumed not to be independent of the governments of member countries: it internalizes the budget constraints of the governments weighted together according to their relative economic size ϖ_i. It maximizes

$$U_{MU} = \sum_{i \in MU} \varpi_i U_i^{\mathrm{G}} \qquad (7)$$

with respect to the common rate of inflation, subject to the same constraints as before. However, the fact that there are several

---

[14]This framework, though not dynamic and hence not suitable to explain the time series evolution of inflation, provides a reasonable explanation of the cross-sectional variations in inflation rates when calibrated to African data (Debrun *et al.*, 2011).

governments facing a single central bank affords the latter a measure of independence from countries taken individually. This in itself reduces the bias toward excessive inflation. The central bank of a grouping of countries has less of an incentive to stimulate the economy through higher inflation to the extent that it internalizes a larger proportion of the region's trade. Optimal inflation in this case is given by

$$\pi_i^* = \frac{\gamma\mu b}{\Lambda}FN_{MU} + \frac{(1-\theta_{MU})(b+\gamma)+\gamma\mu}{\Lambda}c - \frac{a(b+\gamma)\eta}{\Lambda}\varepsilon_{MU}$$

$$(8)$$

with the MU subscript indicating ϖ_i — weighted averages. This solution (which embodies the same optimization as before by governments when they set fiscal policies, taking inflation as given) has the same form as (5), with two differences: both financing needs and the shock are now averaged over all countries in the monetary union, while the bias term is reduced by the amount of trade internalized in the monetary union, θ_{MU}. The latter reflects the reduced temptation to stimulate output since the scope for beggar-thy-neighbor expansion at the expense of trading partners is reduced.

The fact that the central bank reflects the average financing need of member countries in its decision making (as well as the average shock) means that the fiscal discipline of potential members of a monetary union becomes very important. A comparison of the expected gain in welfare for a given country i of being a member versus having its own currency gives the following:

$$E_{-1}G_i = \frac{\theta_A(2-\theta_{MU})+(b+\gamma)}{2\Lambda}c^2 + \frac{\gamma\mu b(1-\psi_i)FN_i}{\Lambda}$$

$$\times \left[(1-\theta_{MU})c - \frac{\gamma\mu b(1-\psi_i)FN_i}{2(b+\gamma)}\right]$$

$$-\frac{a^2\eta^2(b+\gamma)(1-\omega_i)^2}{2\Lambda}\left[\sigma_{\varepsilon i}^2 + \sigma_{\bar{\varepsilon}-i}^2 - 2cov\left(\varepsilon_i, \bar{\varepsilon}_{-i}\right)\right],$$

$$(9)$$

where $\Psi_i = FN_{MU}/FN_i$ is a measure of the fiscal asymmetry of country i compared to the other members. The first term measures the increase in welfare due to the reduced temptation to inflate, because some of the effects are internalized; this is referred to below as the "monetary externality" term. The second term captures the effects of fiscal asymmetries on welfare; and the last term reflects the reduction in welfare due to shock asymmetries ($\tilde{\varepsilon}_{-i}$ is the average shock in the monetary union, excluding country i).

The second term is ambiguous in sign: each country would like to import fiscal discipline, that is, be part of a monetary union with somewhat lower average financing needs than its own; however, too much fiscal discipline would reduce its share of seigniorage too greatly, so there is a tradeoff here. This feature has a certain amount of relevance to the euro zone also, as the current crisis illustrates.

The dependent central bank model can be contrasted with a simple model of an independent IT central bank. Here, we once again assume that the monetary authorities cannot pre-commit not to use monetary stimulus to raise output above its "natural rate". However, they do not internalize the government's budget constraint, so that their objective function includes only inflation and output:

$$U_i^{IT} = \frac{1}{2}\{-a(\pi_i - \tilde{\pi}(\varepsilon_i)^2\} + y_i. \tag{10}$$

Optimal policy for an IT central bank is simply to target a mean inflation rate of c/a, reflecting the desire to stimulate output (the equivalent of k in the Barro-Gordon formulation, which in their model measures the attempt of the central bank to offset distortions in the economy that imply that the natural rate is too low), plus a term that involves offsetting shocks to output. Thus,

$$\pi_i^{IT} = \frac{c}{a} - \eta\varepsilon_i. \tag{11}$$

A central bank in a monetary union again would maximize a GDP-weighted average of this objective function, so would target overall inflation and output of the union — and hence respond to the average shock — but would also have a reduced temptation to stimulate the economy because of the amount of trade internalized:

$$\pi_{MU}^{IT} = (1 - \theta_{MU})\frac{c}{a} - \eta\varepsilon_{MU}. \tag{12}$$

Thus, the relevant criterion for joining a monetary union if central banks can commit to IT (including that of the union itself) involves weighing just two elements: the monetary externality versus the inability to respond to country-specific shocks. The fiscal asymmetry would not affect the attractiveness of potential monetary union partners, since the central bank does not internalize government budget constraints. In what follows, however, we evaluate Germany's incentive to remain in the euro zone versus having an autonomous, independent monetary policy using society's welfare function, Equation (1), not the more restricted objective function (10) assigned to the Bundesbank. The decomposition presented above (Equation (9)) is no longer possible in this case, since the expressions for inflation rates no longer have the same form.

3. Calibration of the Model to the Euro Zone

In this section, we describe the calibration of the model to the euro zone. In particular, the model requires estimates of output supply shocks, seigniorage, and the extent of bilateral trade among euro zone members. In addition, the weights given to deviations of inflation, taxes, and government spending from targets are estimated such as to be consistent with the euro zone's average values for key variables and those of countries before they joined.

3.1. *Shock Asymmetries*

In order to estimate shock asymmetries, we use a Blanchard-Quah[15] (BQ) identification of output supply shocks in a two-variable structural VAR, with dependent variables being the change in the log of real GDP and the change in the log of the GDP deflator. The

---

[15]Blanchard and Quah (1989), as modified by Bayoumi and Eichengreen (1992) to identify the standard deviation of the shocks.

Fiscal Asymmetries and the Survival of the Euro Zone 277

long-run effect of demand shocks was constrained not to have any effect on real output; this identification restriction is consistent with our output Equation (4), which reflects only the effect of supply shocks. Estimates were obtained with four lags[16] using SVAR in Stata, on non-seasonally-adjusted quarterly data from 1999 to 2010 (or shorter period when not available). Table 1 gives the estimated standard deviations of the supply shocks, while Table 2 presents the correlations among the shocks for euro zone countries.

As for correlations, they are typically around 0.5 or higher for core Western European countries, but are lower for some of

Table 1. Euro Zone: Standard Deviation of Annualized Output Growth, Inflation and Supply Rates of Growth and Shocks, 2000Q1–2010Q4

	Output Growth[a]	Supply Shock[b]	Inflation Rate[a]
Austria	2.74	1.07	0.25
Belgium	2.72	1.93	0.51
Cyprus	2.80	2.26	11.98
Estonia	9.29	6.21	3.19
Finland	5.35	4.69	0.96
France	2.23	1.57	0.40
Germany	3.62	3.30	0.49
Greece	5.48	3.83	1.22
Ireland	8.04	6.39	2.71
Italy	3.01	2.06	0.82
Luxembourg	16.16	7.51	4.52
Malta	6.88	6.33	9.66
Netherlands	2.80	2.14	0.99
Portugal	3.44	2.84	0.87
Slovakia	7.24	6.11	2.16
Slovenia	6.40	5.56	1.89
Spain	2.67	0.80	0.62
Euro zone	2.65	1.80	0.83

Notes: [a]400 times quarterly change in the log of GDP and in the log of the GDP deflator. [b]Residuals from Blanchard-Quah decompositions, multiplied by 400.
Sources: Eurostat data, and author's calculation of supply shocks.

---

[16]Four lags were included to account for seasonality. AIC and SBIC tests indicated that there was no need to include additional lags.

Table 2. Euro Zone: Correlation of Supply Shocks (Percent)

	Austria	Belgium	Cyprus	Estonia	Finland	France	Germany	Greece	Ireland	Italy	Luxembourg	Malta	Netherlands	Portugal	Slovakia	Slovenia	Spain
Austria	100.0																
Belgium	55.2	100.0															
Cyprus	18.6	15.1	100.0														
Estonia	23.1	33.5	34.4	100.0													
Finland	42.2	60.7	40.7	58.9	100.0												
France	37.5	41.8	38.0	43.5	60.5	100.0											
Germany	44.4	59.2	27.6	38.7	67.7	59.1	100.0										
Greece	−15.8	−6.0	20.9	23.3	11.9	17.4	7.4	100.0									
Ireland	21.9	20.1	35.8	39.7	27.2	30.8	23.5	6.7	100.0								
Italy	56.5	52.0	18.4	27.6	59.0	63.3	72.8	6.8	20.2	100.0							
Luxembourg	30.6	47.8	23.5	49.6	41.5	30.6	52.6	−13.1	14.3	48.0	100.0						
Malta	14.2	25.7	35.4	−3.5	27.0	39.3	29.9	−17.2	20.3	16.4	12.2	100.0					
Netherlands	32.1	27.0	28.3	48.3	52.1	50.7	58.0	26.4	21.2	44.6	38.6	21.7	100.0				
Portugal	36.1	33.8	17.5	37.2	52.7	36.0	52.3	−1.9	31.9	53.6	42.0	25.6	51.5	100.0			
Slovakia	18.4	21.8	25.8	29.3	29.5	5.6	36.4	13.3	26.4	10.9	22.3	6.0	40.3	32.6	100.0		
Slovenia	20.1	53.4	43.3	32.2	80.1	56.6	67.8	18.3	21.9	57.8	28.1	47.0	46.4	52.4	26.6	100.0	
Spain	52.8	36.3	28.5	40.3	39.7	30.5	32.3	−6.8	18.4	25.5	32.2	10.7	39.7	35.9	36.6	26.0	100.0

Source: Author's calculations.

Fiscal Asymmetries and the Survival of the Euro Zone

the smaller and newer EU members. Greece stands out as having several negative correlations, as well as having only small positive correlations with a number of other euro zone participants.

3.2. Base for the Inflation Tax

Though we refer to the direct effect of inflation on the government's budget constraint as seigniorage, in fact what we want is the total impact of higher inflation in financing the government. The tax rate τ in our model is assumed to be a proportional tax on income (and τ is constant for given *Financing Needs* and shocks to output, whatever the rate of inflation). In practice, tax revenues as a ratio to nominal GDP tend to increase with inflation for two principal reasons: with a progressive personal income tax system, bracket creep leads to higher marginal and average tax rates (Bailey, 1976); and in a corporate tax system in which depreciation allowances are based on historical costs, effective tax rates rise with inflation (Nichols, 1968). Thus, to the extent that tax brackets and depreciation allowances are not fully indexed, the tax take will tend to increase with inflation.[17]

The cost of servicing bonds with fixed nominal coupons will also decline as a ratio to GDP, but this is only true if the higher inflation was unanticipated. More complicated to estimate is the possible link between bailing out governments by buying their securities and future inflation. To the extent that bond purchases do not have a cost for the central bank, there would not be implications for its solvency. But if the ECB faced losses from defaults on the sovereign paper that it acquired, it might be led to finance them by higher inflation, increasing its seigniorage and that of the national central banks of the Eurosystem. This issue is not pursued here, however.

The European Central Bank provides estimates of seigniorage, but this is very small. The ECB's 8 percent share of euro zone

---

[17]This is quite separate from the Oliveira-Tanzi effect (Tanzi, 1977), which suggests that the real value of tax receipts declines with inflation, as there is a lag between the establishment of the tax liability and the actual payment of taxes. This effect is likely to be significant only at high rates of inflation, unless collection lags are very long.

seigniorage averaged about 400 million euro per year over 2006–2008 (ECB, 2010). Hence the total seigniorage of the Eurosystem (including both the ECB's share and the remaining 92 percent share divided among the national central banks) is about 5 billion euros. If we relate this to the euro zone's average annual GDP over this period (about 12,180 billion euros), seigniorage is thus only about 0.04 percent of GDP. Since actual inflation averaged 2.5 percent, if seigniorage were proportional to inflation the factor of proportionality μ would equal 0.016.

A much larger potential effect results from the non-indexation of the personal and corporate tax systems, described above. While at present we do not have detailed estimates for euro zone countries, what evidence that exists suggests that they could be sizeable. For instance, a study of the evolution of wage tax wedges over 2001–2006 estimates that fiscal drag contributed to raising them by an average of about 2 percentage points in euro zone countries (OECD, 2007). Since cumulative nominal income growth[18] in the euro zone was about 10 percent over that period, the marginal effect seems to average about one fifth. As for the effect on corporate taxes, data are hard to obtain, but Feldstein (1981) estimated that the effect of an 8 percent expected inflation rate would be to raise the real net cost of an equipment investment with a 13 year tax life by 21 percent if the firm used a 4 percent real discount rate, due to a decline in the real value of depreciation allowances.

In our preliminary simulations of monetary unions in Europe we use a figure of 0.25 for the combined effect of euro zone inflation on increased financing of government budgets: that is, one percentage point increase in inflation increases the ratio of taxes to GDP by one-quarter of a percentage point.

3.3. Euro Zone Trade

An important component of the estimated gain from a monetary union is the reduced temptation to engineer inflation surprises and

---

[18]Fiscal drag results from both inflation and real growth.

Table 3. Euro Zone Merchandise Trade, 2008

	Total Exports/GDP (Percentage of GDP)	Exports to Euro Area (Percentage of Total)
Austria	43.62	53.81
Belgium	93.52	63.49
Cyprus	6.44	37.85
Estonia	52.62	31.51
Finland	35.63	32.32
France	21.71	49.69
Germany	39.69	42.76
Greece	7.62	44.17
Ireland	47.43	40.78
Italy	23.40	44.21
Luxembourg	43.76	72.07
Malta	34.25	35.62
Netherlands	73.00	62.39
Portugal	22.67	64.75
Slovak Republic	75.03	48.35
Slovenia	62.41	50.90
Spain	17.55	56.37

Sources: IMF Direction of Trade Statistics and International Financial Statistics.

thus stimulate output. In the model, this reduced temptation is related to the amount of trade internalized in the monetary union. Thus, countries will be more apt to welcome as member of the monetary union a country which trades a lot with existing members. Table 3 gives the fraction of each euro zone member's total exports accounted for by other euro zone countries, as well as the ratio of each country's total trade to its GDP.

Most euro zone countries are very open, with a high ratio of total exports to GDP. Notable exceptions are Greece and Cyprus, and to a lesser extent, Spain. Moreover, much of that trade is with other euro zone countries — over 40 percent except for peripheral countries such as Cyprus, Estonia, Finland, and Malta.

3.4. Behavioral Parameters

The model has been adapted to the euro zone to reflect EU trade patterns and shock correlations, as well as estimated fiscal demands on the central bank (see next section). Parameters c and η were derived from the BQ decomposition to make observed variances of output and inflation relative to estimated supply shocks consistent with the responses predicted by our output supply equation and the first order condition for optimal inflation. In addition, we chose the weights a, b, γ to reflect the average data for inflation, taxes, and government spending. We use both the experience of the euro zone, assumed to be the result of inflation targeting by an independent central bank, and the data for a dependent central bank such as Italy's in the 1980s.

In particular, an independent central bank that did not internalize the government's budget but simply targeted inflation and output would produce an average inflation rate equal to c/a for a single country's central bank and $c(1 - \theta_{MU})/a$ for a regional central bank. Using a figure of 2.5 percent for average inflation in the euro zone over its first decade, and the estimate for $c = 2.208$ based on the variance of the euro area's output, gives a value for a of

$$a = c(1 - \theta_{MU})/2.5 = 2.208(1 - 0.1712)/2.5 = 0.7319.$$

As for η, it is calibrated based on the variance of inflation attributed to supply shocks by the BQ decomposition relative to the variance of supply shocks. An inflation targeting independent central bank would produce a standard deviation of inflation equal to η times the standard deviation of the average euro zone supply shock. The standard deviation of euro zone annualized inflation is 0.84, and 40 percent of the long-run variance of euro zone inflation is attributed to supply shocks by the BQ estimation. Since the central bank in the model only responds to the latter, this gives

$$\eta = \sqrt{0.4}\text{stdev}(\pi)/\text{stdev}(\varepsilon) = (0.632)(0.84)/1.80 = 0.29515.$$

The experience of non-independent central banks is needed to calibrate b and γ. As a rough stylized fact, average values for inflation, tax rates, and financing need equal to 10, 50, and 52.5 — based on Italy's experience in the 1970s and 1980s — were used to calibrate their values, conditional on the other estimates given above.

The resulting parameter estimates used in the simulations are as follows:

Parameter	Value
a	0.7319
b	0.1565
c	2.2079
η	0.29515
γ	4.0089
μ	0.25
Λ	3.0880
Θ_A	0.1712

It is not being claimed that this model captures all the features that are relevant for monetary policy in Europe. The model is not dynamic, and is thus not well adapted to explain the time series variations of inflation or of government debt accumulation. It is of interest, however, to see how such a simple framework may shed light on the possible forces at work as the euro zone faces attacks on its integrity and speculation about its disintegration or the expulsion of certain members.

4. Fiscal Asymmetries

The model identifies an important structural variable, which we call *financing need* (*FN*), which measures the pressure each country exerts on the monetary union's central bank to provide monetary financing. This variable has two components: the country's fiscal target for useful government spending, and a wedge in the government's budget constraint between government spending and tax and seigniorage revenues. This wedge results from inefficiencies in tax collection and wasteful spending that does not contribute to society's welfare — e.g., outright corruption by public officials and rewarding of government supporters.

The two components of FN_i for each country i consist of society's target for government spending, $\tilde{g}_i$, and a diversion wedge δ_i. We regress aggregate government revenues and expenditures on governance indicators to gauge directly what amounts of excess spending and tax losses are due to poor governance. We then set the governance indicators to their "ideal" levels: the resulting figure for ideal government spending gives the estimate for $\tilde{g}_i$, and the difference between the ideal and actual figures for the deficit provides the estimate for δ_i. Thus,

$$FN_i = \tilde{g}_i + \delta_i = g_i|\text{ideal} + (\tau_i - g_i)|\text{ideal} - (\tau_i - g_i).$$

This can be further simplified as follows:

$$F_i = \tilde{g} + \delta_i = \tau_i|\text{ideal} - (\tau_i - g_i) = (\tau_i|\text{ideal} - \tau_i) + g_i. \qquad (13)$$

Thus, we use the difference between ideal and actual tax revenues plus the actual government spending to compute financing need.

The effects of poor governance were captured using International Country Risk Guide indicators for the 27 EU countries and dates for which they and the other explanatory variables were available (PRS Group, 2011). For some of the 2005 accession countries, data begin in 2000; we also wanted to exclude the data from the depth of the recent crisis with its large, and hopefully temporary, widening of deficits. Therefore, we used an eight-year average (2001–2008), and assumed that this captured long-run, sustainable levels for the components of *FN*.

Some experimentation was done to find those indicators with significant effects on revenues; only governance indicators at the 5 percent level were retained. We also controlled for per capita income since revenues and expenditures seem to depend systematically on that variable. However, the relationship is not monotonic, hence we also included per capita income squared. Per capita income is assumed to affect revenues and expenditures equally, hence to have no systematic effect on the deficit. Seemingly unrelated regression (SUR) was used to estimate equations for revenues and the fiscal position expressed as ratios to GDP. Per capita income (*YPC*) is expressed in U.S. dollars, while the governance indicators are indexes ranging from 0 to 6 — for *corruption* and democratic accountability (*dem_ account*) — with in each case higher values indicating better

Fiscal Asymmetries and the Survival of the Euro Zone 285

governance. $YPCSQ$ is per capita income squared. The results of estimation are given below.

The system of equations does a reasonably good job in explaining the cross-country variation in general government revenues and fiscal positions. Revenues are positively related to per capita income, but the relationship flattens out with higher income levels, reaching a maximum at a per capita income equal to \$43,006 before turning down. Less corruption (a higher value of the variable) increases both revenues and the fiscal position (but the latter by less). Greater democratic accountability reduces the fiscal position; this can be explained in terms of the compromises reflected in the political process and the need to attract voters in order to improve the incumbents' chances of reelection.

We use the SUR estimates of the revenue equation to estimate the "ideal" revenues in Equation (13), which determines the financing need, as follows. We first put all the countries on the same footing by adjusting revenues to what they would be if all countries had the same per capita income as the EU average and ideal values for corruption. Then we add actual government spending.

Thus, using the SUR estimates of Table 4 the financing need is calculated as

$$FN = 0.289(26.98 - YPC) - 3.36 * 10^{-3}(26.98^2 - YPCSQ)$$
$$+ 3.19(6.0 - \text{corruption}) + g \tag{14}$$

where YPC is in thousands of dollars, $YPSQ$ is in millions, and \$26,980 is the mean per capita income of EU countries on average over 2001–2008.

Table 5 reports the calculated values for FN, as well as the values of the variables used in the calculation.

It can be seen that several countries have high values of FN. In particular, going in descending order, the worst performers among euro zone countries are France, Italy, Greece, and Belgium, while among the non-euro-zone members, Hungary, Poland and the Czech Republic are the highest. Among the euro-zone members, the high financing need in France is due primarily to high government

Table 4. Cross-section Estimation, Seemingly Unrelated Regressions (All EU Countries, Averages 2001–2008)

Equation	Observations	Parameters	RMSE	R-sq	Chi2
(1) Revenues/GDP	27	3	4.15299	0.5804	36.81
(2) Fiscal position/GDP	27	2	1.924414	0.4169	19.99

	Coefficient	Std. Error	z	P>z
(1) Revenues/GDP				
YPC	0.2892	0.1786	1.62	0.105
YPCSQ	−3.36E–03	1.82E–03	−1.85	0.064
Corruption	3.19187	1.228976	2.6	0.009
Constant	26.15679	2.931107	8.92	0
(2) Fiscal position/GDP				
Corruption	1.558015	0.3544836	4.4	0
Dem_account	−2.4707	1.050482	−2.35	0.019
Constant	6.863744	5.664158	1.21	0.226

spending as ratio to GDP, while in Italy and Greece, to poor values for corruption.

5. Should the Euro Zone be Shrunk or Disbanded?

The model is then applied to the euro zone in order to compare the welfare to existing euro zone members of a smaller monetary union. In turn, the welfare gain or loss for the member who leaves the euro zone is calculated (Table 6). In each case, as discussed above, several factors come into play: the extent of trade internalized in the monetary union, the size of a country, its financing need, and the asymmetry of its supply shocks when compared to the average for the monetary union. The welfare gains and losses are presented in Tables 6–8, with details concerning the factors mentioned above. In each case welfare is evaluated using Equation (1), with the same parameter values for all countries. It is measured in terms of GDP equivalents: that is, a 1 percent welfare gain corresponds to the increase in welfare that would result from a permanent increase in GDP of 1 percent.

If the European Central Bank were not independent, but instead internalized the weighted average budget constraints of member

Fiscal Asymmetries and the Survival of the Euro Zone 287

Table 5. EU Countries: Fiscal Variables and Per Capita Income (Averages, 2001–2008)

Country	FN	YPC	G	Corruption
Austria	53.65	$35,728	50.83	4.94
Belgium	56.17	$34,472	49.81	3.84
Bulgaria	52.54	$3,752	35.58	2.00
Cyprus	48.89	$21,826	41.88	4.00
Czech Rep.	57.43	$12,092	44.65	2.71
Denmark	54.43	$45,540	53.40	5.49
Estonia	46.94	$10,291	35.26	3.18
Finland	48.49	$36,470	49.09	6.00
France	60.32	$32,652	52.95	3.55
Germany	50.52	$33,030	46.34	4.53
Greece	57.37	$21,010	45.74	2.59
Hungary	61.82	$10,189	49.65	3.02
Ireland	42.23	$45,409	34.24	3.33
Italy	58.93	$29,096	48.13	2.55
Latvia	52.06	$7,681	36.37	2.10
Lithuania	49.06	$7,706	34.31	2.39
Luxembourg	48.16	$79,009	39.64	5.00
Malta	54.68	$14,567	44.34	3.31
Netherlands	47.95	$38,022	45.73	5.10
Poland	58.47	$8,053	43.51	2.30
Portugal	49.91	$17,515	41.89	3.88
Romania	48.72	$4,693	33.44	2.45
Slovak Rep.	52.05	$11,125	38.90	2.66
Slovenia	52.60	$17,627	42.10	3.10
Spain	46.23	$24,777	39.01	3.82
Sweden	53.37	$39,675	51.62	5.24
United Kingdom	44.27	$35,955	39.82	4.40

Sources: *FN* calculation as described in text; ICRG data used for corruption; IMF International Financial Statistics and World Economic Outlook data for remaining variables.

governments, then for some current member countries the euro zone would be worse than having its own currency, even if on their own their central banks would not be independent either. This is the result of considerable differences in financing needs as well as shock asymmetries. The countries with both low shock correlations (with the average shock for the euro zone) and disciplined fiscal policies (such as Estonia, Ireland, and Luxembourg) would unambiguously

288 *Paul R. Masson*

Table 6. Welfare Gain/Loss from Euro Zone Membership versus Autonomy, All Central Banks Dependent Except for the Bundesbank[a] (In Percent of GDP)

Country	GDP Share (Percent)	Shock Correlation (Percent)	FN_{MU}/FN	Welfare Gain	Decomposition of Welfare Gain		
					Monetary Externality	Fiscal Asymmetry	Shock Asymmetry
Austria	3.1	54.9	1.00	0.96	1.03	0.01	−0.08
Belgium	3.7	63.7	0.95	1.17	1.03	0.28	−0.10
Cyprus	0.2	37.4	1.10	0.38	1.03	−0.55	−0.19
Estonia	0.2	51.3	1.14	−0.78	1.03	−0.79	−1.15
Finland	2.0	77.6	1.11	0.14	1.03	−0.60	−0.39
France	20.9	76.6	0.89	1.57	1.03	0.71	−0.05
Germany	26.8	93.4	1.06	−2.62	—	—	—
Greece	2.6	17.1	0.93	0.64	1.03	0.41	−0.72
Ireland	2.0	36.7	1.27	−1.53	1.03	−1.40	−1.38
Italy	17.0	83.6	0.91	1.45	1.03	0.57	−0.05
Luxembourg	0.4	54.8	1.11	−1.25	1.03	−0.64	−1.75
Malta	0.1	32.1	0.98	−0.17	1.03	0.12	−1.30
Netherlands	6.4	68.0	1.12	0.39	1.03	−0.66	−0.09
Portugal	1.9	61.3	1.07	0.49	1.03	−0.43	−0.19
Slovakia	0.7	36.1	1.03	−0.48	1.03	−0.18	−1.36
Slovenia	0.4	73.4	1.02	0.27	1.03	−0.11	−0.66
Spain	11.8	44.0	1.16	0.20	1.03	−0.88	−0.09

Notes: [a]The ECB and national central banks except Germany's are assumed to internalize the government budget constraint; the Bundesbank on its own is assumed to be able to commit to IT.
Source: Author's calculations.

do better on their own, while smaller losses are experienced by Malta and Slovakia. Both more fiscal discipline and different shocks (it is not just the correlation that matters, but also their size) can help to explain the value of retaining the ability to design their own monetary policy rather than accepting a policy that reflects average conditions in the euro zone.

The rightmost three columns give an approximate decomposition of the welfare gain into three components.[19] This decomposition is based on the formula in Equation (9) above. The first component is the result of internalizing the Barro-Gordon temptation to generate monetary stimulus by depreciation of one's own currency

---

[19]It is not available for Germany because of the assumption that the Bundesbank targets inflation, making the decomposition not applicable.

(no longer possible in the euro zone); the second is the effect of fiscal asymmetries (a gain for countries whose fiscal policy is laxer than the average, as indicated by a value of FN_{MU}/FN less than one); and the third component is the effect of shock asymmetries. Each of the effects is important, though the third one, which is the standard OCA criterion, dominates for several countries. Perhaps not surprisingly, the largest overall net gainers are France, Italy, and Belgium. They are the only countries, with Greece, to have a significant gain from fiscal asymmetries, as the greater average fiscal discipline of the euro zone means less pressure to produce inflation relative to having their own currencies.

The case of Germany is treated differently. In particular, the historical circumstances of Germany's Bundesbank, which was at the center of the European Monetary System and the initial source of monetary policy credibility of the euro zone, as well as the constitutional protection against monetary financing in Germany, put it in a special position. Unlike other countries' central banks, the Bundesbank is assumed not to be subject to financing pressures on the part of the German government. Therefore, we compare the welfare of Germany in a euro zone having a dependent ECB to its welfare if it had its own currency, managed by an independent IT central bank. We see that under these circumstances Germany would sustain a large gain in welfare by abandoning the euro zone and reintroducing the deutsche mark. The political and administrative costs of leaving the euro zone are not considered here, however, and these would undoubtedly influence any decision to do so. Nevertheless, the welfare calculus highlights the reason why Germany has legitimate concerns about the independence of the ECB and the desirability of maintaining the euro zone in its current form.

The next exercise considers whether the welfare of the remaining countries would be improved by expelling any of the existing members individually. Table 7 summarizes these results; the difference in welfare for the country leaving can be found in Table 6. It can be seen that the departure of France, Greece, or Italy would improve welfare of all of the remaining euro zone countries. The effect of other countries' departures would be negative on all remaining

Table 7. Welfare Effects on Countries in the Stub of Dropping Countries in the Heading One-bye-One[a]

	Austria	Belgium	Cyprus	Estonia	Finland	France	Germany	Greece	Ireland	Italy	Luxembourg	Malta	Netherlands	Portugal	Slovakia	Slovenia	Spain
Austria		-0.195	-0.002	-0.004	-0.015	0.026	-0.041	0.011	-0.034	0.045	-0.014	-0.001	-0.245	-0.029	-0.020	-0.011	-0.159
Belgium	-0.061		-0.002	-0.004	-0.017	0.033	-0.405	0.012	-0.032	0.047	-0.015	-0.001	-0.229	-0.027	-0.019	-0.012	-0.142
Cyprus	-0.070	-0.210		-0.004	-0.019	0.024	-0.440	0.007	-0.042	0.063	-0.016	-0.002	-0.269	-0.031	-0.023	-0.014	-0.169
Estonia	-0.066	-0.216	0.003		0.032	0.052	-0.494	0.007	-0.053	0.085	-0.022	-0.001	-0.283	-0.034	-0.026	-0.014	-0.151
Finland	-0.065	-0.213	-0.002	-0.005		0.059	-0.517	0.015	-0.039	0.061	-0.018	-0.002	-0.266	-0.033	-0.023	-0.016	-0.137
France	-0.055	-0.166	-0.002	-0.003	-0.014		-0.350	0.007	-0.030	0.042	-0.012	-0.001	-0.212	-0.024	-0.019	-0.011	-0.130
Germany	-0.063	-0.203	-0.002	-0.004	-0.021	0.063		0.016	-0.035	0.056	-0.017	-0.001	-0.255	-0.030	-0.022	-0.014	-0.134
Greece	-0.057	-0.175	-0.002	-0.004	-0.014	0.017	-0.348		-0.031	0.055	-0.011	-0.001	-0.234	-0.024	-0.019	-0.011	-0.139
Ireland	-0.075	-0.234	-0.003	-0.006	-0.023	0.049	-0.499	0.014		0.082	-0.018	-0.002	-0.296	-0.038	-0.028	-0.015	-0.167
Italy	-0.056	-0.171	-0.002	-0.003	-0.015	0.033	-0.387	0.011	-0.029		-0.014	-0.001	-0.215	-0.026	-0.017	-0.011	-0.124
Luxembourg	-0.063	-0.216	-0.002	-0.006	-0.026	0.095	-0.571	0.031	-0.037	0.048		-0.001	-0.267	-0.035	-0.024	-0.014	-0.130
Malta	-0.060	-0.190	-0.003	-0.003	-0.019	0.013	-0.440	0.023	-0.039	0.068	-0.014		-0.238	-0.030	-0.019	-0.015	-0.133
Netherlands	-0.070	-0.213	-0.002	-0.004	-0.019	0.039	-0.469	0.009	-0.037	0.062	-0.017	-0.002		-0.033	-0.023	-0.013	-0.164
Portugal	-0.067	-0.206	-0.002	-0.004	-0.020	0.049	-0.461	0.015	-0.040	0.050	-0.017	-0.002	-0.265		-0.023	-0.014	-0.154
Slovakia	-0.063	-0.197	-0.002	-0.005	-0.021	0.086	-0.486	0.008	-0.044	0.089	-0.017	-0.001	-0.261	-0.033		-0.013	-0.150
Slovenia	-0.055	-0.195	-0.002	-0.004	-0.032	0.063	-0.512	0.012	-0.035	0.055	-0.016	-0.002	-0.243	-0.031	-0.021		-0.113
Spain	-0.076	-0.223	-0.003	-0.004	-0.018	0.028	-0.455	0.011	-0.039	0.060	-0.017	-0.002	-0.283	-0.033	-0.023	-0.013	

Notes: [a]ECB assumed to internalize government budget constraints.
Source: Author's calculation. Welfare measured in percentage points of GDP.

members. Effects are small, however, since each country has only a modest influence on the ECB's policies. The hypothetical departure of Germany would induce the largest welfare losses.

The final exercise revisits the assumption of a dependent central bank for the monetary union. In particular, it could be that a narrower monetary union centered around Germany could also effectively carry out an independent monetary policy, even if the larger euro zone were unable to do so. We therefore assume that the monetary union (whether it was called the euro zone or not) would be able to commit to an IT policy, and would not be subject to pressures to finance governments.

Three small "Germanic" monetary unions are considered: (I) a successor to the "DM zone" composed of Germany, Belgium, the Netherlands, Luxembourg, and Austria (countries whose exchange rates were stable throughout the 1992–1993 EMS crisis); (II) a wider core group that includes France as well, because France played an integral part in the process of monetary integration; and (III) a monetary union including all those countries in the current euro zone that have financing needs that are less than or equal to Germany's (see Table 5), namely Cyprus, Estonia, Finland, Germany, Ireland, Luxembourg, the Netherlands, Portugal, and Spain. We compare welfare of the hypothetical member countries of these narrower monetary unions with their welfare both as members of the present euro zone (with a dependent ECB) and as countries reverting to their own currencies — i.e., monetary autonomy, but without the ability to precommit to inflation targeting — except for Germany. As before, for Germany the comparison is with an independent Bundesbank. Table 8 summarizes those results.

Interestingly enough, all of these core monetary unions are better than the euro zone for Germany and for each of the other potential members, and the gains of welfare are sizeable, running from 1.0 to 3.5 percent of GDP. However, none of them is better than autonomy for Germany. The reason is that such a DM-based monetary union, even if it could ensure central bank independence and hence face no fiscal pressures on monetary policy, would still respond not to Germany's shock but to the average of the shocks for the member

Table 8. Welfare of "Germanic" Monetary Unions Compared to Actual Euro Zone and to Independent Currencies

	Gain with Respect to Euro Zone			Gain with Respect to Autonomy		
	I	II	III	I	II	III
Austria	1.909	1.949		2.905	2.750	
Belgium	1.639	1.650		2.817	2.661	
Cyprus			2.613			2.992
Estonia			2.925			2.146
Finland			2.730			2.875
France		1.126			2.692	
Germany	2.453	2.399	2.503	−0.165	−0.219	−0.115
Ireland			3.461			1.931
Luxembourg	2.819	2.703	2.835	1.567	1.451	1.583
Netherlands	2.660	2.682	2.750	3.047	3.068	3.136
Portugal			2.531			3.016
Spain			2.920			3.124

Source: Author's calculations.

countries. At the same time, there would be little advantage from internalizing the region's trade on monetary policy because of the narrowness of the region. The net effect would be a small loss for Germany in each case.

6. Conclusions

In sum, the basic model seems to offer considerable support for the fears that the euro zone in its current configuration is at risk, should the ECB effectively become dependent on pressures to finance its member governments. The model, of course, does not perfectly capture the complexity of the current crisis in the euro zone nor the tools at the disposal of the ECB. It could be argued, for instance, that the operations of the ECB in purchasing government bonds need not imply debt monetization and upward pressure on consumer prices, while the model assumes that ECB essentially has a single policy instrument, namely inflation. The traditional lender of last resort role for a central bank in providing liquidity to financial institutions to correct a market failure or prevent an

Fiscal Asymmetries and the Survival of the Euro Zone 293

incipient bank run need not interfere with price stability. However, the situation becomes more complicated once the ECB purchases public debt of governments that may become insolvent; if as a result the ECB makes losses and needs to be recapitalized, its independence may be put in jeopardy. The model does not analyse the complex strategic interactions between governments and the central bank that may result. Instead, it explores the consequences of assuming that the ECB might lose its independence and internalize member governments' budget constraints — with the objective of financing governments being weighed against other objectives in a way that is consistent with data for countries like Italy in the 1970s and 1980s.

Should the ECB become a dependent central bank in that sense, the departure of several of the current members with weaker regional ties, and less disciplined fiscal policies, might well be desired by the rest of the member countries. The departure of Greece — a country with fiscal problems, little trade with the rest of the euro zone, and asymmetric supply shocks and symmetric supply shocks–would make sense both on its own account and that of other members. The simulations reported here also suggest that two larger countries, Italy and France–both at the center of the European monetary unification project–are also a drag on their more fiscally disciplined colleagues whose welfare would be improved by their departure.

The idea of a narrower monetary union centered around Germany, if it had the ability effectively to carry out an IT policy and resist pressures to internalize government budget constraints, would seem to be an attractive alternative for the more fiscally disciplined members. However, the simulations presented here suggest that this may not be in Germany's interest. Rather than a full monetary union, therefore, a German-led monetary bloc might have the Bundesbank simply set monetary policy on the basis of Germany's needs, and the other countries following.[20] However, this return to the *de facto*

---

[20] As is the case in the Common Monetary Area, in which the South African Reserve Bank sets monetary policy based on conditions in that country, and Lesotho, Namibia, and Swaziland peg their currencies at a one-to-one parity with the rand and follow South Africa's monetary policy (Masson and Pattillo, 2005).

294   *Paul R. Masson*

deutsche mark zone of the 1980s and 1990s would be an enormous reverse for European integration that most European politicians as well as the general public would find difficult to accept. Thus, the likeliest outcome of the euro zone crisis may well be only a minor change in the monetary union's composition, if any, while hopefully addressing the forces that now endanger the central bank's independence.

In particular, the euro zone's institutions need to be strengthened, first, by reinforcing fiscal discipline, and second, by increasing the ability of other facilities than the ECB to provide financial assistance. In addition, creating an area-wide financial supervisor would reinforce confidence in the stability of the banking system, lessening pressures on the ECB's lender of last resort facilities. With luck, the economic and monetary union may emerge from the current crisis strengthened, not destroyed as some have feared.

Acknowledgments

The author would like to thank, without implicating, Ralph Bryant, Matt Canzoneri, Xavier Debrun, Olivier Jeanne, Paul Jenkins, seminar participants at Georgetown University, and two anonymous referees for helpful comments, and Petra Dacheva for help with data.

References

Alesina, A. and Tabellini, G. 1987. Rules and discretion with noncoordinated monetary and fiscal policies, *Economic Inquiry* 25, 619–630.

Bailey, M.J. 1976. Inflationary distortions and taxes, in H. J. Aaron (ed.), *Inflation and the Income Tax*, Washington, DC: Brookings Institution, 291–330.

Barro, R. and Gordon, D. 1983. A positive theory of monetary policy in a natural rate model, *Journal of Political Economy* 91, 589–610.

Beetsma, R. and Giuliodor, I.M. 2010. The macroeconomic costs and benefits of the EMU and other monetary unions: An overview of recent research, *Journal of Economic Literature* 48, 3 (September), 603–641.

Bernanke, Ben S., Launach, Th., Mishkin, F.S., and Posen A.S. 1999. *Inflation Targeting: Lessons from the International Experience*. Princeton, NJ, Princeton University Press.

Blanchard, O.J. and Quah, D. 1989. The dynamic effects of aggregate demand and supply disturbances, *American Economic Review*, 79(4), 655–673.

Fiscal Asymmetries and the Survival of the Euro Zone

Clarida, R., Galí, J., and Gertler, M. 1999. The science of monetary policy: A new keynesian perspective, *Journal of Economic Literature* 37(4), 1661–1707.

Debelle, G. and Fischer, S. 1994. How independent should a Central Bank be? in *Goals, Guidelines, and Constraints Facing Monetary Policymakers*, Conference Series No. 38, Federal Reserve Bank of Boston, 195–225.

Debrun, X., Masson, P.R., and Pattillo, C. 2005. Monetary union in west Africa: Who might gain, who might lose and why? *The Canadian Journal of Economics*, 38 (May), 454–481.

Debrun, X., Masson, P.R., and Pattillo, C. 2008. Modeling policy options for Nigeria: Fiscal responsibility, monetary credibility, and regional integration, Chapter 4 in Collier, Paul, Catherine Pattillo and Charles Soludo (eds.), *Economic Policy Options for a Prosperous Nigeria*, London: Palgrave-McMillan, 93–120.

Debrun, X., Masson, P.R., and Pattillo, C. 2011. Should african monetary unions be expanded? An empirical investigation of the scope for monetary integration in Sub-Saharan Africa, *Journal of African Economies* 20: ii 104–ii 150

De Grauwe, P. 2011. The European Central Bank as a lender of last resort, August 18, 2011, www.voxeu.org/index.php?q=node/6884.

Feldstein, M. 1981. Adjusting depreciation in an inflationary economy: Indexing versus acceleration, *National Tax Journal* 34 (1, March), 29–43.

Friedman, M. 1969. *The Optimal Quantity of Money and Other Essays*. Chicago: Aldine.

Martin, Ph. 1995. Free-riding, convergence, and two-speed monetary unification in Europe, *European Economic Review*, 39(7), 1345–1364.

Masson, P.R. and Pattillo, C. 2005. *The Monetary Geography of Africa*, Washington, DC, Brookings Institution.

Mundell, R. 1961. A theory of optimum currency areas, *American Economic Review* 51(4), 657–665.

Nichols, D.A. 1968. A note on inflation and common stock values, *Journal of Finance* 23 (September), 655–657.

OECD 2007. *Taxing Wages 2006/2007*, Paris: Organization for Economic Cooperation and Development.

PRS Group 2011. http://www.prsgroup.com/ICRG.aspx.

Svensson, Lars E.O. 1999. Inflation targeting as a monetary policy rule, *Journal of Monetary Economics* 43(3), 607–654.

Svensson, Lars E.O. 2000. Open-economy inflation targeting, *Journal of International Economics* 50(1), 155–183.

Tanzi, V. 1977. Inflation, lags in collection, and the real value of tax revenue, *Staff Papers — International Monetary Fund* 24(1), 154–167.

Wyplosz, Ch. 2006. European monetary union: The dark sides of a major success, *Economic Policy* 21 (April), 207–261.

Chapter 9

The Euro at 20: Lessons for Africa*

Paul R. Masson

Successive euro zone crises suggest a need for re-evaluation of currency union projects in Africa. It is argued, in this chapter, that the experience of the EU has three main lessons for Africa. *First,* regional integration is best viewed as a process rather than a linear progression, in which monetary union may abet other aspects of integration, but is not an essential component of it. *Second,* the requirements for a sustainable monetary union are not adequately captured by the optimum currency area (OCA) and macroeconomic convergence criteria (or Maastricht criteria) which are given the most attention in plans for African monetary unions. *Third,* the prerequisites for a successful monetary union require strong regional solidarity based on common approaches to policymaking that permit the creation of effective community institutions across a wide array of policy areas.

1. Introduction

Continued interest in currency union projects in Africa suggests a need for a re-evaluation of the plans for achieving them in the light of successive euro zone crises. The East African Community

---

*An earlier version of this paper, entitled "Are OCA and Convergence Criteria Enough? Prerequisites for African Monetary Unions in the 21st Century," was presented at a conference *The Future of Monetary Integration* held in Mauritius, March 8–9, 2016.

is the latest region to agree to a path to monetary union.[1] While economic benefits are expected, it is clear that the project is driven primarily by the wider objective of regional integration, with monetary union being one piece of the puzzle and a symbol of regional solidarity. Other Regional Economic Communities (RECs), including the Economic Community of West African States (ECOWAS), the Common Market of Eastern and Southern Africa (COMESA), and the Southern African Development Community (SADC) all have as one of their objectives the creation of a monetary union.

In Africa as elsewhere, many policymakers have subscribed to the "linear model of integration", which parallels the experience of Europe, at least until the recent crises. In this model, integration proceeds in stages: first, a group of countries agrees to favor trade among themselves by lowering tariffs (*preferential trade arrangement*), then a *customs union* with a common external tariff, followed by a *single market* for goods, labor and capital, and finally an *economic and monetary union* with a single currency, a common monetary policy, and some rules limiting fiscal indiscipline to prevent it from interfering with monetary policy. Later stages could involve *political union* (a federation of countries). In Europe, many view this latter objective as contentious and utopian so that even supporters of a "United States of Europe" tend to downplay this stage. EMU was thus explicitly proposed not as a stepping stone to political union but rather an objective in itself. Political union might emerge in the very distant future, or it might not, but in any case it was not viewed by its founders as a necessary component of the economic and monetary union. The Excessive Deficits Procedure of the Maastricht Treaty and the Stability and Growth Pact (SGP) agreed by countries joining the euro zone certainly impinged on national sovereignty to some extent, but the debt and deficit criteria were viewed as being in each country's interest anyway, so the loss of sovereignty was deemed to be minor. As for coordination of fiscal policies, financial regulation,

---

[1]The Monetary Union Protocol, signed by the five member countries (Burundi, Kenya, Rwanda, Tanzania and Uganda) in 2013, calls for replacing national currencies by a common currency in 2024.

or bailout mechanisms, they were given little or no attention in the Maastricht Treaty — if not actually proscribed, as in the "no-bailout clause".

Twenty years of experience with the euro zone have considerably shaken belief in the linear model and in the view that monetary union could be made sustainable without much further delegation of powers to regional authorities. Instead, community institutions to deal with financial crises, to regulate important financial institutions, and to share some of the costs of financial crises are now viewed as essential underpinnings of the euro zone. Going further, it now seems that some form of political union may be needed to support the monetary union rather than being just a distant dream, since leaving countries with complete sovereignty over their fiscal policies has failed to produce fiscal discipline, despite the SGP. Economic and monetary union, instead of being just one of the many steps in the linear progression of regional integration — with countries having the ability to stop at an intermediate stage — now seems to be a big leap that requires a whole set of other integration measures for its sustainability. The euro zone countries have been scrambling to create the necessary institutions, often in crisis mode, with France and Germany agreeing in principle to closer political integration — though what form it might take is unclear, nor whether it would be acceptable to other euro zone members.[2]

In Africa, regional integration is at an earlier stage.[3] There are a number of preferential trade arrangements, and even though customs unions have been agreed to, few of them have yet to fully implement common external tariffs. Even at these early stages, however, the linear model is not fully relevant to Africa since it emphasizes intra-regional tariff reduction, ignoring the more important "behind the border" reform measures such as improved transportation and communication links and harmonization and simplification of various

---

[2]See the communique issued after the 2011 Deauville summit between Nicolas Sarkozy and Angela Merkel.

[3]Except for the CFA franc zones and the CMA and SACU in Southern Africa, to be discussed further below.

regulations. These are likely to be at least as important as lower tariffs (WTO, 2011). Moreover, a common currency is unlikely to do much to facilitate greater regional trade since both the composition of exports (mainly primary resources) and the pull of "gravity" from wealthier countries make the latter their natural trading partners.

It is argued in this chapter that there are three main lessons for Africa in the euro zone's experience. *First,* regional integration is best viewed as a process rather than a linear progression through various stages; monetary union may abet (or hinder) other aspects of integration, but is not an essential component of African regional integration. *Second,* the requirements for a sustainable monetary union are not adequately captured by the optimum currency area (OCA) and macroeconomic convergence criteria which are given the most attention in plans for African monetary unions.[4] *Third,* the prerequisites for a successful monetary union require strong regional solidarity based on common approaches to policymaking that permit the creation of effective community institutions across a wide array of policy areas. Such regional solidarity is typically no greater in African RECs than is the case in Europe, while with a few exceptions community institutions are much less developed than in Europe.

The chapter is organized as follows. The next section briefly reviews the reasons for interest in monetary unions in Africa as well as the criteria that are used to evaluate whether they are desirable. Section 3 argues on the basis of European experience that those criteria are inadequate, and in particular criticizes the relevance of the OCA and convergence criteria. Section 4 discusses wider institutional requirements for successful monetary unions,

---

[4]The belief in more limited institutional requirements may have been influenced by the then-existing asymmetric monetary unions, which had a natural hegemon that internalized some of the costs (Cohen, 1998). This applies both to the CFA zones (where the French Treasury provides a guarantee of convertibility) and to the CMA (where South Africa's central bank sets monetary policy for the exchange rate union, the rand is legal tender in the other member countries, and the South African treasury compensates them for loss of seigniorage).

while Section 5 considers the implications of these lessons for African monetary unions. Section 6 concludes.

2. Why Monetary Unions, and What Criteria to Apply?

The seminal OCA paper by Mundell (1961) is based on the reasoning that the benefits derived from a currency increase as it circulates over a wider area, but that costs depend on the extent of shock asymmetries, since the exchange rate is not available to cushion them in a monetary union. Mobility of labor can mitigate the effects of asymmetric shocks, but labor mobility is typically limited across borders. Mundell further noted that currency areas were usually coterminous with political jurisdictions. Other potential mitigating factors include fiscal transfers between members of the common currency area (Kenen, 1969) and capital mobility.

Applications of OCA theory to assess potential multi-country monetary unions focus on the importance of asymmetric shocks, in particular shocks to the real economies of member countries. Unfortunately, OCA theory does not provide a threshold beyond which shocks are too asymmetric, since it does not assess the benefits of monetary unions. The importance of the mitigating factors — factor mobility and fiscal transfers — is also not easy to quantify.

The OCA criteria, as they came to be called, have been further criticized as preconditions for membership in a monetary union because they are endogenous: they would change as a result of membership in the monetary union in a direction that would tend to make the monetary union more sustainable (Frankel and Rose, 2002). In particular, a country joining a monetary union would be expected to increase trade with other members, and this would tend to make their real economies move more in sync, thus mitigating the asymmetry of shocks. The potential benefits from stimulating internal trade were estimated to be large, leading to a doubling or tripling of bilateral trade among members of the common currency area (Rose, 2000; Glick and Rose, 2002). These benefits would seem to make monetary unions attractive to a number of regional groupings around the world.

In Africa, OCA criteria have never been the primary motivation for interest in monetary unions. Bayoumi and Ostry (1997) showed that shock asymmetries were considerably greater than those in Europe, making African regional groupings poor candidates for monetary unions. Indeed, few African countries have a well-developed manufacturing sector. Instead, many export primary commodities, but the composition of these commodities differs greatly across countries. While there is a subset of countries for which oil production is an important source of export earnings, most African countries are oil importers, leading to great asymmetry in demand and supply shocks coming from the rest of the world and thus causing the terms of trade of the two groups of countries to behave very differently. An extensive literature on various proposed monetary union projects has concluded that they are not OCAs (see Masson and Pattillo, 2005; Tavlas, 2009, for surveys of this literature).

A second approach to evaluating fitness for membership in a monetary union is the use of convergence criteria, also known as Maastricht criteria since they play a prominent role in EMU's Maastricht Treaty. These variables measure the similarity of economic outcomes, rather than similarity of shocks as do the OCA criteria. In Europe, convergence criteria serve as preconditions for admission to the euro zone and subsequently as measures to evaluate the appropriateness of national fiscal policies when the SGP provides for sanctions for non-compliance. Convergence criteria can be justified as hurdles that countries need to jump in order to demonstrate their commitment to sound policies and hence be admitted to the single currency club (Masson, 1996), and at this stage, the Maastricht criteria include convergence of interest rates and inflation as well as government deficit and debt ratios below some critical values. After countries have joined, they need to adhere to fiscal discipline to help ensure that fiscal policy does not interfere with the European Central Bank's (ECB's) stability-oriented monetary policy aimed at low inflation, and force a bailout of profligate governments by the central bank — though whether this was in fact necessary was questioned given the statutory independence of the ECB (Eichengreen and Wyplosz, 1998). Also, the choice of ceilings for deficits and debt ratios — 3 and 60 percent, respectively — has been criticized for being arbitrary and inappropriate since they do not take account of individual country circumstances or of cyclical conditions (though the latter criticism has been addressed in recent reforms of the SGP).

Convergence criteria play an important role in the planned monetary unions in Africa, and also in the macroeconomic surveillance within the existing CFA franc zones. In all cases, some measure of fiscal deficits and debt are among the criteria, and for planned monetary unions, rates of inflation. Other criteria include balance of payments variables (months of reserves, current account deficits) and the composition of government spending or revenues. Table 1 gives details for planned and existing African monetary unions.

Monetary unions may also have benefits that are political, not economic. The monetary union should not be considered in isolation, but rather in the context of other steps toward economic and political integration. A common currency can be a symbol of regional solidarity, and may be a stepping stone toward political union. A monetary union may also provide an "agency of restraint" against imprudent policies (Guillaume and Stasavage, 2000), but the evidence of this seems slight (Masson and Pattillo, 2002). It could in principle facilitate institution-building by pooling scarce human resources and expertise, though this may not be the case if, on the European model, national central banks are allowed to coexist with the regional central bank.

In Africa, the political motive has clearly been the main driving force behind monetary union projects. African countries, with a few major exceptions, have small populations and low GDP per capita. Moreover, their borders were the result of sometimes arbitrary geographical divisions made by the colonial powers. Thus, regional integration is seen as correcting these distortions and removing some of the size disadvantages. Regional bodies also help with negotiation of partnership agreements, in particular with the European Union, and in dealing with development institutions. Continent-wide

304 *Paul R. Masson*

Table 1. Macroeconomic Convergence Criteria Applied by African Regional Groupings and EMU

WAEMU[a]	CEMAC	EAC	WAMZ	SADC[b]	EMU (Maastricht)
Primary criteria					
Fiscal balance/ GDP $\geq -3\%$	Fiscal balance[c] ≥ 0	Fiscal balance $\geq -3\%$ of GDP	Fiscal balance/ GDP excluding grants $\geq -4\%$	Fiscal balance/ GDP excluding grants $\geq -3\%$	Fiscal balance/ GDP $\geq -3\%$
Government Debt/ GDP $\leq 70\%$	Government Debt/GDP $\leq 70\%$	NPV Gross public debt $\leq 50\%$ of GDP	Central bank fiscal financing/previous year's tax revenue $\leq 10\%$	Government Debt/ GDP $\leq 60\%$	Government Debt/GDP $\leq 60\%$
	Inflation $\leq 3\%$	Inflation $\leq 8\%$	Inflation $\leq 10\%$	Inflation $\leq 3\%$	Inflation within 1.5% of 3 best
	Government arrears ≤ 0	Reserves ≥ 4.5 months of imports	Reserves ≥ 3 months of imports	Current account deficit/ GDP $\leq 3\%$	Long-term bond rates within 2% of 3 lowest-inflation countries Membership in ERM for 2 years
Secondary criteria					
Taxes/GDP $<20\%$		fiscal balance/GDP ex grants $\leq -6\%$ Taxes/GDP $\geq 25\%$	Various non-binding indicators		

Notes: [a]Criteria based on 2014 reform. See Basdevant *et al.* (2015).
[b]Criteria for 2018. See Burgess (2009).
[c]Excluding grants and foreign financed investment.

cooperation and integration are intended to increase the influence of Africa on the world stage, as well as contributing to African prosperity. Indeed, the Constitutive Act of the African Union Treaty, signed in 2000, has the following as its first four aims:

(a) achieve greater unity and solidarity between the African countries and the peoples of Africa;
(b) defend the sovereignty, territorial integrity and independence of its Member States;
(c) accelerate the political and socio-economic integration of the continent;
(d) promote and defend African common positions on issues of interest to the continent and its peoples.[5]

However, little attempt has been made to assess whether differences in economic and political objectives and institutions among countries in a region might pose problems for regional integration.

3. Inadequacy of OCA and Convergence Criteria in the Case of Europe

OCA criteria focus on one type of asymmetry — shocks to the macroeconomy — and ways of dealing with it — factor mobility and fiscal transfers. Thus, numerous critics of EMU pointed to the lack of those shock-cushioning mechanisms, which are typically present in a single country but not between them. The creation of the Single Market for goods and services and measures to enhance labor mobility were intended to mitigate potential problems. What was not well understood was the role of finance to amplify the shocks and spread them across the weaker countries (Obstfeld, 2013). Recent experience has shown that heavily indebted countries and their banks can be subject to mutually reinforcing crises, leading to higher interest rates and even greater doubts about the solvency of both sovereign borrowers and banks. With the possibility of exit from

---

[5]See http://www1.uneca.org/Portals/ngm/Documents/Conventions%20and%20 Resolutions/constitution.pdf.

306 Paul R. Masson

the currency union in play, countries start incurring exchange rate risk as well as sovereign default risk, and similar countries suffer from contagion effects.

Convergence criteria — the Maastricht Treaty and the SGP — have not been successful in achieving macroeconomic convergence, in particular, in limiting deficits and debt. In retrospect, it is clear that enforcement mechanisms were inadequate, and subsequent reforms have been made (the "two-pack" and the "six-pack") to strengthen them. However, addressing the proximate cause of the crises in Greece, Spain, Portugal and Ireland — excessive deficits, either because of over-stimulative fiscal policies or as a result of bailing out banks — would seem to require both mechanisms to enforce fiscal discipline and greater solidarity among countries so that countries can escape from the austerity rat race when problems do occur. But the solidarity part is so far still at an embryonic stage within the euro zone.

Wyplosz (2013) argues that the main problem to be addressed is the lack of a banking union with an effective lender of last resort. Financial sector issues are a euro-zone problem, not a national one, since a monetary union creates and integrated financial area. Given the size of the banking sectors in many euro-zone countries, the need for countries to bailout their own banks called into question their ability to service and roll over public debt. In his view, creation of a banking union, a decentralized model of fiscal policy in which national governments retain their sovereignty, and a credible no-bailout regime should be sufficient to break the nexus between bank and sovereign risk.

Europe's application of the Maastricht criteria was also not successful in selecting a set of countries qualifying for membership with similar approaches to economic policy. Instead, successive crises have revealed fundamental political disagreements. There are at least three reasons for this failure. *First,* the convergence criteria measure epiphenomena rather than fundamental convergence in economic philosophy and national objectives. Of course, the latter are difficult to measure, but it was not understood at the time to what extent the countries of the euro zone would have to design new institutions to make the system sustainable, making agreement on economic strategies essential. It was not enough to agree to the institutions created in the treaty, which clearly did not anticipate difficulties that arose later. Instead, a more fundamental commitment to take necessary measures in response to changing circumstances was needed. *Second,* convergence criteria can be, and were, manipulated in the short term to achieve membership. Fiscal deficits can be reduced by bringing forward revenues and postponing expenditures during the qualifying period. The Greek case is not the only example, only the most egregious one. *Third,* the convergence criteria were not applied strictly, because there was no supranational enforcement mechanism. Already in 1997 when the initial set of countries was selected, most of them exceeded the 60% debt ratio and those that met the 3% deficit ratio did so only briefly. Countries on their own had little incentive to enforce rules when deviations were treated on a case-by-case basis.

4. Institutional and Political Prerequisites for Successful Monetary Unions

The experience of the euro zone has revealed two major flaws in its operation. *First,* the institutional prerequisites for making it work are greater than previously anticipated. To prevent its collapse, the EU has gone some way to instituting a banking union, and is considering a budget union and some form of political union. *Second,* the need to respond to crises by making changes to the design of the euro zone has revealed fundamental differences in approach among member countries. This suggests that, in the absence of a regional hegemon, partner countries need to share similar objectives in order to address unforeseen circumstances if a monetary union is to work.

The euro zone was preceded by the European Monetary System, a framework of bilateral parities with margins of fluctuation (similar to the Bretton Woods System) that was intended to pave the way for a smooth transition to monetary union. Instead, the EMS was engulfed by financial crisis in 1992–1993. Ratification difficulties for the Maastricht Treaty and doubts that countries would defend parities in the light of high unemployment led to speculation against the weaker currencies, which faced very high interest rates as a result. The higher interest rates made the problem worse, as countries faced a steeper trade-off between defending and abandoning the peg (Obstfeld, 1993). In August, 1993, the EMS countries were forced to widen the margins of fluctuation greatly, thus effectively dispensing countries from the obligation to defend them. At the time, it became accepted wisdom that such systems of adjustable pegs were not sustainable, making it all the more desirable to move to a currency union where there would be no national currencies to speculate against (Eichengreen, 1994).

The early years of EMU seemed to bear this out, as interest rates on the sovereign debt of all countries converged to levels close to those paid by the German government. Such seeming absence of risk also led to an explosion of cross-border lending by banks in the euro area, which increased their exposure to consumers, firms, and governments in other countries of the zone. The global financial crisis shattered this rosy picture. Euro zone countries were led to run large budget deficits, greatly adding to the public debt/GDP ratio. Moreover, because of exposure to US subprime mortgages as well as euro area claims that were non-performing, euro area banks faced solvency problems which were expected to involve government bailouts, adding to sovereign risks of default. As a result, once again countries became vulnerable to speculative attacks. Even in the absence of currency risk, bank defaults and sovereign defaults were mutually reinforcing: higher interest rates made both more likely, opening the door to self-fulfilling expectations (Obstfeld, 2013). And in addition, sovereign defaults raised the possibility of exits from the euro zone, putting currency risk back into play.

The renewed problems faced by European monetary integration dispelled the illusion that monetary unions are not vulnerable to speculative attacks. It also led to a deeper examination of the problems faced by "incomplete currency unions" and what to do about them.[6] They are fragile because they are not accompanied by other community institutions that reduce the risk of speculative attacks and multiple equilibria.

One incompleteness that was signaled early on was the absence of a lender of last resort for the euro zone. Folkerts-Landau and Garber (1994) presciently criticized the design of EMU because the ECB was not given lender-of-last resort powers. But at the time, the architects of EMU downplayed the problem, nor was it fully appreciated by many other economists. One way of understanding the problem is the following: countries in a monetary union cannot borrow in their own currencies (since they now share a common currency), and this creates problems similar to the "original sin" faced by developing countries (Eichengreen and Hausmann, 1999). A national central bank not in a monetary union can always create unlimited liquidity to enable the government to pay its debts, but if the ECB is unwilling or unable to do so, then market sentiment can provoke a self-fulfilling liquidity crisis in a monetary union if countries are highly indebted (De Grauwe, 2013).

While it was well understood that the constraints of monetary union remove one instrument for addressing asymmetric shocks (monetary policy), what was not well understood was the effect of finance in amplifying their unfavorable effects (Obstfeld, 2013). This amplification was shown to create major credibility problems for the commitment to the monetary union.

Another issue whose seriousness was not completely appreciated was the difficulty in enforcing fiscal discipline, and the impossibility of ruling out public debt crises. Both *ex ante* mechanisms limiting deficits, and *ex post* transfers in some form to mitigate crises, are now seen by many to be necessary — though this is far from a unanimous view. It was understood that fiscal policy may be subject to moral hazard problems if countries expect that their debts to be repaid by other countries, hence the attempt to limit deficits

---

[6]The term seems to be due to Paul De Grauwe (2012).

in the euro zone through the SGP was justified (Beetsma and Bovenberg, 1999)). However, self-enforcement of the limits on public deficit and debt ratios by joint decision of the countries themselves (in the European Council) has been shown to be ineffective; some supranational enforcement mechanism is necessary. The procedures now make the recommendations of the European Commission and sanctions provided by the SGP binding unless over-ridden by the European Council. Further evidence is needed to evaluate their effectiveness.

As for *ex post* transfers to crisis countries, the original architecture did not make any provision for them; indeed, Article 123 of the Treaty on the Functioning of the European Union (TFEU) includes a draconian "no bailout" provision. But the constraints on macro policies (accompanied by the amplification effects of finance) mean that asymmetric shocks can produce very bad outcomes, as has been the case in Greece. In the view of many, some assistance in the case of severe crises is necessary to make the monetary union sustainable, though German officials have strongly resisted this view. Wyplosz (2013) argues that the no-bailout provision — which was *de facto* abandoned in the crisis — needs to be reinstated, since it is essential for the enforcement of fiscal discipline. This, and an effective banking union, would make the euro zone sustainable in his view.

The design of EMU thus seems to have been severely defective with respect to both the sanctions required to sustain macroeconomic convergence and the supporting institutions needed to make a monetary union sustainable for countries suffering extreme downturns. On the one hand, EMU included no effective enforcement mechanism, and on the other, it did not address how to help a country escape from the problems caused by a fiscal crisis. Though there is a need to limit fiscal deficits, in the absence of *ex post* assistance (either through fiscal transfers or a community-wide institution to address financial sector problems), the combination of constraints on monetary and fiscal policies may be self-defeating because it makes exits from the monetary union more likely. As argued by Drazen and Masson (1994), taking tough measures may worsen, not improve, a government's credibility because it further narrows the future room for maneuver that the government has to work with. Thus, a monetary union with just enforcement mechanisms may be less, not more, credible, since austerity measures to meet fiscal targets would make a country even more vulnerable to further negative shocks — as has amply been shown by the case of Greece.

The above problems, not generally anticipated at the time of launching by the architects of the euro zone, have led to a consensus that a monetary union needs much more institutional underpinning to be sustainable. Major new supra-national institutions have been added to the euro zone architecture, and more have been proposed. These include greater community powers in the fiscal, financial, and political areas.

While the question of greater intra-monetary-union transfers has long caught economists' attention,[7] it is only with the experience of euro zone crisis that it has appeared on policymakers' radar. A **budgetary or fiscal union** (DeGrauwe) would cushion shocks through community-wide automatic stabilizers and transfers. It could take the form of "fiscal federalism" giving to the supranational government both substantial taxing power and the ability to issue debt, or create an agency that issues debt for all national governments, sharing the risks of default across all countries. By aligning the borrower's debt servicing with the domain of the currency union, a budgetary union would remove the perverse dynamics of "original sin". However, the chances of a budgetary union seem slim for the foreseeable future; instead, the creditor countries are pushing for greater restrictions on government deficits (starting with greater scrutiny by the EU Commission) which would further restrict the ability of countries to respond to shocks, without increasing intra-euro-zone transfers. Mody (2015) argues that lack of fiscal union means that EMU is "living dangerously".

The feedback loop between bank insolvency and the risk of a sovereign default is at the root of the crises that dramatically pushed up interest rates on the debt of countries such as Spain, Italy and

---

[7]See Sachs and Sala-i-Martin (1992), Bayoumi and Masson (1995), among others.

Greece. A **banking union** (Véron, 2015) would create agencies providing common supervision, regulation and deposit insurance on the region's banking system. In Veron's view, such a banking union has largely been created through giving the ECB the responsibility to supervise the major banks, the European Stability Mechanism resources to recapitalize banks, and the creation of a European Banking Authority and Single Resolution Board. However, there are questions about whether the resources are large enough.

The lack of a central bank **lender of last resort facility** has been *de facto* remedied through the actions of the ECB to provide liquidity assistance when sovereign borrowing costs for a particular country are viewed as too high. However, this is more similar to the IMF's crisis lending to governments than to a national central bank's role of providing unlimited liquidity to the market, since it is targeted at the debt of a single country. Moreover, the ECB has required that emergency assistance be accompanied by a macroeconomic program for the country concerned (as does the IMF), getting the ECB involved in quasi-fiscal activities. The justification provided by the ECB for this facility is to level the playing field for the transmission of its monetary policy across the countries of the euro zone — not an explicit lender of last resort to sovereign borrowers, prohibited by the TFEU.

Retention of national sovereignty over fiscal policy is at the root of the failure of the SGP to discipline fiscal policies. Recent discussions suggest a desire among some countries — including France and Germany — to go some way in the direction of a **political union.** However, this ambition is contested by others, and it is hard to see whether it will be feasible given the very different political institutions and philosophies across euro zone member countries. A political union would also have to garner public support, and allow citizens greater say in community institutions. A Treaty establishing a Constitution for Europe, signed in 2004, was defeated when put to referendums in France and the Netherlands. Public support for community institutions has been waning, in part due to the recent financial crises, and notably lacking so far are measures to narrow the "democratic deficit". Increasing the power of the European

Parliament is likely to involve small and slow steps over decades, and that institution is a long way from having a role and importance comparable to those of a national parliament.

Negotiations of the latest Greek program in 2015, for instance, saw Germany, the Netherlands, and Finland taking a hard line on the need for further fiscal adjustment, while France, Italy, and a number of other countries argued for a relaxation of austerity. No consensus was reached on whether a country should be allowed (or encouraged) to exit the euro zone if it persistently exceeded the convergence criteria. While the German austerity medicine seems to have carried the day, it may be a pyrrhic victory. Asymmetries of economic philosophy (as opposed to policy outcomes) are so fundamental that they should have been taken into account in deciding whether to create a common currency in the first place, and, if so, what countries to include. They are sure to reappear in the years ahead, particularly with regard to moves toward political union advocated by France and Germany. While the architects of EMU clearly wanted to be able to use some objective, measurable, criteria, the Maastricht criteria did not do the job.

5. Implications for African Monetary Unions

Africa and Europe have important structural differences, which may affect the relative costs and benefits of monetary unions in the two regions. In addition, the institutional requirements may differ from those in Europe. In this section, we consider the relevance to African monetary union projects of the lessons drawn above for the euro zone.

An important difference between Europe and Africa is that Africa has a much lower proportion of internal trade than does the euro zone (both now and at the time of the launch of the euro). African countries' exports are more heavily weighted towards resources, which are mainly exported to other continents; there is little intra-industry trade; and the gravity model implies that in any case the richer economies will be the main trading partners of African countries, given the low per capita incomes of neighboring African countries. This suggests that gains for African monetary unions from reducing transactions costs may be limited. Of course, the scope for raising intra-regional trade from those low levels could be great, and results from Glick and Rose (2002) suggested that joining a monetary union could double or triple bilateral trade. But that estimate is now in considerable doubt, given Glick and Rose's (2015) *mea culpa*. Indeed, they find very different answers when they add the euro zone experience to the original sample in Glick and Rose (2002) and when they apply newer estimation techniques. Even assuming a doubling of bilateral trade, the estimated welfare gain for African monetary unions due to increased trade appears small (Masson, 2008).

African sub-regional institutions, despite long-standing attempts at regional cooperation, are still embryonic in most cases (exceptions are South Africa and its immediate neighbors, and the CFA franc zones). The starting point is therefore much different from that of the EU in the lead-up to the creation of the euro zone. Monetary union in Europe came after 50 years of successful measures to eliminate tariffs, improve transportation links, harmonize regulations, increase mobility, and transfer some powers (foreign policy, competition policy, etc.) and advisory roles to community institutions, including the European Commission, the European Court of Justice, Eurostat, the European Investment Bank, and the European Parliament. Despite this, the euro zone crises have shown that monetary union requires considerable further integration in other areas to make it work. If the institutional requirements of sustainable monetary unions are more onerous than was earlier thought, then the willingness and ability to create those institutions should be carefully considered before proceeding. The need for regional capacity-building in Africa should affect decisions on whether to proceed with monetary union projects and, at a minimum, lengthen the timetables for achieving them.

As was argued above, in Africa the impetus for monetary union projects has been largely political — even more so than in Europe — rather than mainly economic. As a result, neither the costs of giving up national monetary policies nor the putative economic benefits are given much attention in Africa nor factored into decision-making.

A common currency is instead viewed mainly as a symbol of regional solidarity, with little in the way of costs.

While politics may be the driving force behind a monetary union project, and political will is essential to bring about reforms needed to put it in place, political support can be fickle, and requires broader public support to be durable (Rusuhuzwa and Masson, 2012). Durable public support in turn requires that there are in fact long-term benefits from the monetary union. As discussed above, In an "incomplete monetary union" where national governments retain their sovereignty, withdrawal from a monetary union cannot be ruled out when times are bad. The Greek crisis showed, among other things, that uncertainty about the commitment to monetary union can make things worse, and contribute to a bad equilibrium. If the economic costs of membership are seen *ex post* to be great, then the political benefits (and public support) may well disappear, and monetary union could fuel regional conflict rather than solidarity.

However, the costs of abandoning monetary sovereignty may be lower in Africa. Those costs may not be very great if monetary policy has not been used wisely, as has often been the case in Africa. A regional institution, while unable to counter asymmetric shocks, might nevertheless be more able to provide low inflation and financial stability than national central banks, especially if the countries are small. However African countries have been strengthening their policymaking institutions — among other things increasing central bank independence — and inflation rates have come down markedly, making this argument less telling.

Financial development is less advanced, capital controls remain, and the banking system is much smaller in Africa than in Europe, making the nexus between bank and government solvency less tight. This makes it unlikely that African monetary unions will be subject to the same speculative attacks as the euro zone — at least for now. In particular, African countries do not borrow abroad in their own currencies so that making them borrow in a common currency would only increase their vulnerability to the extent that they were no longer able to borrow at home in their own currency.

316 Paul R. Masson

This might expose them to liquidity crises if the regional central bank were unwilling or unable to provide assistance. Moreover, it would be unwise not to allow for further financial development when designing monetary unions in Africa. In the meantime, financial infrastructure can be improved, payment systems harmonized, and greater cooperation among financial regulators can proceed within RECs and across Africa. Harmonization in these areas is a necessary precondition for creating a common currency area, but it is also valuable in itself.

African countries that are candidates to join monetary unions are more dissimilar in many dimensions than are euro zone members. Shock asymmetries among countries in many of the proposed monetary unions (ECOWAS/WAMZ, EAC, SADC, COMESA) are large. One especially important asymmetry relates to different resource endowments, in particular between oil exporters and oil importers. Table 2 lists those that produce oil; among Sub-Saharan African countries, Nigeria and Angola are significant producers on a world scale, and the CEMAC CFA franc zone countries (Cameroon, Chad, Republic of the Congo, Equatorial Guinea and Gabon), all produce oil. In ECOWAS, Nigeria stands out as a dominant producer among countries that are mainly non-producers, except Ghana and Côte d'Ivoire, which have only modest oil supplies. In fact oil constitutes over 90 percent of Nigeria's exports, and thus its terms of trade are negatively correlated with others in the region, which import oil.

Another important asymmetry concerns the objectives of fiscal policy and the ability to deliver good fiscal outcomes. Work I have done with co-authors Xavier Debrun and Catherine Pattillo uses a model that extends the OCA shock asymmetry by incorporating information about fiscal asymmetries to evaluate monetary unions in Africa (Debrun et al., 2005, 2008, 2011; Masson and Pattillo, 2005; Debrun and Masson, 2013), and I have also applied it to the euro zone (Masson, 2012). This work attempts to quantify a measure of fiscal (in)discipline that includes implicit targets for government spending and a measure of fiscal distortions (corruption, poor tax administration, wasteful spending) that drive a wedge between tax

The Euro at 20: Lessons for Africa

Table 2. African Countries and Regional Groupings: Total Oil Supply (Thousand Barrels Per Day)

	2010	2011	2012	2013	2014
Algeria	1,881	1,863	1,875	1,763	1,721
Angola	1,908	1,755	1,786	1,842	1,756
Cameroon	66	62	64	63	81
Chad	123	115	104	98	103
Congo (Brazzaville)	312	299	292	274	259
Congo (Kinshasa)	21	20	20	20	20
Cote d'Ivoire (Ivory Coast)	45	40	39	38	37
Egypt	735	718	710	694	665
Equatorial Guinea	323	299	310	291	269
Gabon	246	244	242	239	240
Ghana	8	78	79	99	106
Libya	1,785	501	1,482	983	516
Niger	0	7	20	20	20
Nigeria	2,459	2,555	2,525	2,372	2,428
South Africa	182	184	183	182	162
Sudan and South Sudan	489	455	115	250	261
Tunisia	79	67	66	64	59
Africa	10,669	9,268	9,918	9,296	8,707
Asia & Oceania	9,179	9,048	9,152	9,199	9,258
Central & South America	7,892	8,064	8,004	8,120	8,408
Europe	4,656	4,300	3,989	3,813	3,870
Eurasia	13,366	13,493	13,608	13,782	13,905
Middle East	26,221	27,674	27,880	27,472	27,836
North America	16,116	16,685	17,915	19,331	21,216
World	88,099	88,532	90,466	91,014	93,201

Source: US Energy Information Agency, downloaded December 2015.

revenues and the part of government expenditures that improves welfare.

In particular, more disciplined countries would not want to join a monetary union dominated by countries with little fiscal discipline, as the latter would likely put pressures on the common central bank to provide monetary financing. A common central bank, can, however, provide some benefits of greater monetary independence because each government's power to influence the central bank's policy is diluted in a monetary union. Moreover, the common central bank has a lower inflation bias than national central banks because it cannot use "beggar-thy-neighbor" exchange rate adjustments relative to other countries in the monetary union. Thus, there is a trade-off between having as large a monetary union as possible and only including countries that are sufficiently similar.

Empirical estimates using this model suggest that differences in fiscal discipline are at least as important as asymmetric terms of trade shocks in gauging the potential welfare gains or losses from monetary unions — using a parameterization calibrated to African data. Table 3 summarizes some of our results for existing and planned monetary unions, presenting summary statistics of the degree of shock asymmetries and fiscal asymmetries across regions.[8] It can be noted that our calibration suggests that the existing monetary/exchange rate unions, WAEMU (the West African CFA franc zone) and the Common Monetary Area in Southern Africa, are beneficial to all members. For WAEMU, it is because differences are not too great across countries — either in terms of shock or fiscal asymmetries. The CMA, despite having considerable heterogeneity, produces net gains. This is the result of having a monetary policy set by South Africa to suit conditions in that country; it is jointly beneficial because that country's fiscal discipline produces a generally stability-oriented monetary policy, and also because South Africa accounts for as much as 95 percent of the GDP of the CMA. Thus, fiscal asymmetries do not matter for the welfare comparison.

The three planned monetary unions receive a more mixed assessment. The East African Community with high shock correlations and relatively low variance of fiscal discipline is calculated to produce welfare gains, but only for four of the five member countries. A common currency for ECOWAS, because of the size of Nigeria and its dependence on oil exports, produces welfare gains only for that country, and welfare losses for all the others. A SADC monetary

---

[8]The welfare analysis was done country by country; the variance figures give a useful insight into the overall assessment, however.

The Euro at 20: Lessons for Africa

Table 3. Summary of Asymmetries and Welfare Gains Across Actual or Potential Monetary Unions

	Variance of Fiscal Discipline[a]	Average of TOT Shock Correlations[b]	Average Welfare Gain or Loss[c]	No. of Countries Gaining/Total[d]
	ACTUAL MONETARY UNIONS			
CMA	24.50%	42.65%	2.56	4/4
WAEMU	2.80%	65.75%	1.22	7/7
	PROPOSED MONETARY UNIONS			
EAC[e]	11.62%	94.13%	1.33	4/5
ECOWAS	24.04%	−1.42%	−0.06	1/11
SADC[f]	19.88%	52.44%	2.10	10/10

Notes: [a]Mean absolute deviation from average, times 100.
[b]Unweighted average of correlation with average terms of trade shock.
[c]In percent of GDP.
[d]Number of countries in calculation limited by data availability.
[e]Using historical terms of trade correlations.
[f]Asymmetric monetary union with monetary policy set by South African Monetary Authority.
Source: Masson *et al.* (2015, Tables 4.2–4.9) and author's calculations

union, while it includes major asymmetries for both fiscal policy and terms of trade shocks, nevertheless could be welfare enhancing for all members, because again South Africa is assumed to set monetary policy, as in the CMA. That might not be true for a multilateral monetary union where monetary policy reflected average conditions across the whole region (Debrun and Masson, 2013).

Of course, historical data may not be appropriate inputs into the assessment if major structural changes are in train. In the East African Community, for instance, oil and gas production has the potential to create very different movements in the terms of trade of the countries that have substantial oil and gas reserves (Tanzania, Uganda and Kenya) — assuming that they exploit them in the future — and those that do not (Burundi and Rwanda), making a single currency for the EAC problematic. Table 4 shows that their commodity terms of trade could go from large positive correlations to sharply negative ones between the first group and the

320 *Paul R. Masson*

Table 4. EAC Countries: Correlations of Commodity Terms of Trade

	Burundi	Kenya	Rwanda	Tanzania	Uganda
	Historical (2000-2011)				
Burundi	1.00	0.80	0.94	0.91	0.98
Kenya	0.80	1.00	0.77	0.89	0.84
Rwanda	0.94	0.77	1.00	0.85	0.95
Tanzania	0.91	0.89	0.85	1.00	0.89
Uganda	0.98	0.84	0.95	0.89	1.00
Memo: Net energy exports/GDP(%)	−2.74	−3.99	−1.96	−4.63	−2.99
Future (Kenya, Tanzania and Uganda become energy exporters)					
Burundi	1.00	−0.66	0.94	−0.65	−0.64
Kenya	−0.66	1.00	−0.56	0.99	0.99
Rwanda	0.94	−0.56	1.00	−0.56	−0.55
Tanzania	−0.65	0.99	−0.56	1.00	1.00
Uganda	−0.64	0.99	−0.55	1.00	1.00
Memo: Net energy exports/GDP(%)	−2.74	20.00	−1.96	20.00	20.00

Source: Masson *et al.* (2015, Tables 4.4 and 4.5).

second, if Tanzania, Uganda and Kenya become even middle-sized energy producers. In this case, a common currency would be welfare enhancing for the three energy producers but welfare reducing for Burundi and Rwanda (Masson *et al.*, 2015, Table 4.5).

Europe's experience has also highlighted the significance of political and structural differences among countries, which may make agreement on necessary reforms and institution-building difficult. ICRG data suggest that differences in governance among countries in proposed African monetary unions are great. This is especially true of SADC, which includes countries that differ in a number of dimensions (Table 5). These indicators take on values from 1 to 6, with higher values being associated with better performance. There are large differences among countries in the quality of public services and democratic institutions. These asymmetries impose further challenges on the design and operation of monetary unions, since agreement on monetary policy and on the construction of supporting institutions is essential to make it work.

The Euro at 20: Lessons for Africa   321

As in Europe, monetary union in Africa is best viewed as part of a wider process of regional integration, with various economic and political benefits but also costs. Monetary union may spur other institutional changes that increase regional solidarity and transfer

Table 5. African Regional Groupings: Selected Governance Indicators

Country	Bureaucratic Quality	Corruption	Democratic Accountability	Ethnic Tensions	Law & Order	Doing Business Ranking
EAC						
Kenya	2.0	2.0	5.5	2.5	2.0	108
Rwanda	—	—	—	—	—	62
Tanzania	1.0	2.5	4.0	4.0	5.0	139
Uganda	2.0	2.0	2.5	3.0	3.5	122
Average	1.7	2.2	4.0	3.2	3.5	
Std. dev.	0.5	0.2	1.2	0.6	1.2	
WAEMU						
Burkina Faso	1.0	2.0	2.8	4.0	3.0	143
Cote d'Ivoire	—	2.0	3.0	2.0	2.5	142
Guinea-Bissau	1.5	2.0	5.0	3.0	2.5	178
Mali	—	2.0	3.0	4.0	3.0	143
Niger	1.5	1.5	3.0	3.0	2.0	160
Senegal	1.0	2.0	2.9	3.0	3.0	153
Togo	—	2.0	2.0	2.0	3.0	150
Average	1.3	1.9	3.1	3.0	2.7	
Std. dev.	0.3	0.2	0.8	0.8	0.4	
WAMZ						
Gambia	2.0	2.5	2.0	5.0	3.5	151
Ghana	2.5	2.5	5.0	3.5	2.5	114
Guinea	2.0	1.5	2.5	2.0	2.5	165
Liberia	—	2.5	5.4	3.0	2.5	179
Nigeria	1.0	1.5	3.5	2.0	2.0	169
Sierra Leone	—	2.0	4.5	4.4	3.5	147
Average	1.9	2.1	3.8	3.3	2.8	
Std. dev.	0.5	0.4	1.3	1.1	0.6	
CEMAC						
Cameroon	1.5	2.5	2.5	4.0	2.0	172
Congo	1.0	2.0	3.0	4.0	2.0	176
Gabon	1.5	2.3	2.0	4.5	3.0	162
Average	1.3	2.3	2.5	4.2	2.3	
Std. dev.	0.2	0.2	0.4	0.2	0.5	

(Continued)

322 *Paul R. Masson*

Table 5. (*Continued*)

Country	Bureaucratic Quality	Corruption	Democratic Accountability	Ethnic Tensions	Law & Order	Doing Business Ranking
SADC						
Angola	1.5	2.0	2.5	3.0	2.5	181
Botswana	2.0	3.5	3.5	4.5	3.5	72
Congo, DR	0.0	1.5	2.0	1.0	1.0	184
Madagascar	1.0	3.0	4.3	2.5	2.5	164
Malawi	2.5	2.0	3.5	3.5	2.6	141
Mozambique	1.0	2.0	4.0	4.0	3.0	133
Namibia	2.0	3.0	4.0	4.5	5.0	101
South Africa	2.0	3.0	5.0	3.5	2.5	73
Zambia	1.0	3.0	4.0	5.0	4.0	97
Zimbabwe	1.5	0.5	2.0	4.0	3.0	155
Average	1.5	2.3	3.5	3.6	3.0	
Std. dev.	0.7	0.9	1.0	1.1	1.0	

Sources: International Country Risk Group, see http://www.prsgroup.com/about-us/our-two-methodologies/icrg, data for 2013 or latest year, and World Bank, see http://www.doingbusiness.org/rankings, downloaded December 2015.

powers to a regional authority. Nevertheless, monetary union is not an essential step in that process. Denmark, Sweden, and (for now) the United Kingdom are all members of the EU but not members of the euro zone, and do not plan to join it. Based on euro zone experience, monetary union may in fact be a source of regional discord, not solidarity. African countries should not consider that monetary union is a precondition for greater regional integration, nor should they believe that regional integration must always ultimately involve monetary union.

Behind-the-border measures are likely to have a high payoff, given widespread impediments to trade and factor mobility. An example are measures that countries can take individually to improve the environment for businesses to operate, including access to reliable power and water, simplified procedures for setting up businesses, good transportation and communication infrastructure, and transparent regulation and taxation. Improvements in these areas would themselves stimulate regional integration, even without inter-governmental agreements, and the poor ranking of Sub-Saharan

Africa in the World Bank's Doing Business survey (see the last column of Table 5) should be a call to action. A recent assessment for African countries revealed much higher transportation and communication prices relative to four developing country comparators[9] (IMF, 2015), and a deterioration of competitiveness in a number of dimensions. The cost of electricity increased markedly relative to the Asian competitors from 2011 to 2015; although relative costs of communications and transport declined, in the case of the former they remain several times those of the comparator countries (IMF 2015, Figure 2.14), and the average cost of exporting a container from Sub-Saharan Africa comes to $2,200, compared to $610 from Vietnam (IMF, 2015, p. 38). Government policies that reduce these costs are likely to be more effective in increasing trade — in particular, through integrating African countries in global value chains — than regional monetary unions.

The unexpected problems faced by the euro zone show how complex the institutional design challenge is for a successful monetary union — at least if it is not a "hegemonic" monetary union using the terminology of Cohen (1998). The successful monetary unions in Africa qualify for that label: the CFA franc zones were created and supported by France, which still has a voice in policy decisions and provides a convertibility guarantee; in Southern Africa, the Common Monetary Area is dominated by South Africa, given the size of its economy relative to its partners. McCarthy (2012) argues in any case that both currency unions are artifacts of the colonial period, hence not models for future African monetary unions. Thus, Africa should not consider that the problems of the euro area can be ignored.

An additional reason for being skeptical of the benefits from inter-governmental agreements in Africa is the danger that they may not operate as planned because government do not fulfill their commitments. Past history in Africa of not fully implementing inter-governmental agreements (for instance, to create a free-trade zone or a common external tariff) make embarking on monetary union

---

[9]Bangladesh, Cambodia, Laos and Vietnam.

324   *Paul R. Masson*

hazardous (McCarthy, 2012). Even a well-designed monetary union may fail if its provisions are not enforceable.

6. Conclusions

The experience of regional integration in Europe — in particular, recent euro zone crises — holds many lessons for monetary unions in Africa, despite differences in economic and political initial conditions. Even after decades of regional integration and preparation for monetary union leading up to the launch of the euro zone in 1999 (the Werner Report on European monetary union dates back to 1969, followed by the creation of the European Monetary System in 1979, the 1986 Delors Report, and the signing of the Maastricht Treaty in 1991), in the eyes of many today Europe got the design of the euro zone wrong. African countries would do well to re-examine their monetary union projects, and at a minimum extend the preparation period for them. In the meantime, there are other measures that have considerably greater payoff and can be implemented more quickly.

The OCA criteria suggest that there are important differences among African countries, including within regional groupings which aim to share a common currency. However, the OCA criteria are themselves seriously incomplete, since there are more fundamental asymmetries that need to be addressed when proceeding to regional integration agreements that include monetary, fiscal, and political unions. An important additional asymmetry is the degree of fiscal discipline. The euro zone crises have exhibited great differences among countries in economic philosophy in this regard that endanger the continued existence of the zone.

The experience of the euro zone has also shown the limitations of macroeconomic convergence criteria in qualifying countries for monetary union and as a basis of multilateral surveillance and enforcement. In a context where monetary union has already removed one policy instrument — monetary policy — from national hands, constraints cannot be imposed on the other macroeconomic instrument — fiscal policy — without some compensating increase in assistance at the community level or other mechanism for cushioning shocks. The jury is still out on whether Europe will be able to reconcile the different interests of the euro zone members in designing some form of fiscal union. Africa would be wise to wait for further insights from Europe in this regard.

African countries have already agreed among themselves to many preferential trade arrangements, but these have not yet been fully implemented in most cases. And these will have limited impact without "behind-the-border" measures involving harmonizing regulations, improving transportation links and border procedures, etc. These can, and should be, implemented, with undoubted economic payoffs whether or not monetary unions are created.

Political union, which remains the long-term goal for several African RECs, will doubtless run into roadblocks along the way as national leaders and the public shy away from abandoning sovereignty. But without some delegation of sovereignty and build-up of strong and effective community institutions, monetary unions are unlikely to be sustainable. A strong foundation of regional solidarity is necessary to deal with the inevitable problems as they arise.

References

Basdevant, O. *et al.* (2015). *Strengthening the West African Economic and Monetary Union*, African Departmental Paper Washington, DC: International Monetary Fund, October.

Bayoumi, T. and Masson, P.R., "Fiscal Flows in the United States and Canada: Lessons for Monetary Union in Europe," *European Economic Review*, Vol. 39 (1995).

Bayoumi, T. and Ostry, J.D. (1997), "Macroeconomic Shocks and Trade Flows Within Sub-Saharan Africa: Implications for Optimum Currency Arrangements." *Journal of African Economies*, Vol. 6(3), pp. 412–444.

Beetsma, R.M.W.J. and Bovenberg, A.L. (1999), "Does Monetary Unification Lead to Excessive Debt Accumulation?" *Journal of Public Economics*, Vol. 74, pp. 299–325.

Beetsma, R.M.W.J. and Giuliodori, M. (2010), "The Macroeconomic Costs and Benefits of the EMU and Other Monetary Union: An Overview of Recent Research." *Journal of Economic Literature*, Vol. 48(3), pp. 603–641.

Burgess, R. (2009), "The Southern African Development Community's Macroeconomic Convergence Program: Initial Performance," African Department, Staff Position Note SPN/09/14.

Cohen, B. J. (1998), *The Geography of Money*, Ithaca: Cornell University Press.

Debrun, X. and Masson, P. R. (2013), Modelling Monetary Union in Southern Africa: Welfare Evaluation for the CMA and SADC. *South African Journal of Economics*, Vol. 81, pp. 275–291. doi: 10.1111/saje.12008

Debrun, X., Masson, P.R., and Pattillo, C. (2005), "Monetary Union in West Africa: Who Might Gain, Who Might Lose and Why?" *The Canadian Journal of Economics*, Vol. 38, pp. 451–481.

Debrun, X., Masson, P.R., and Pattillo, C. (2008), "Modeling Policy Options for Nigeria: Fiscal Responsibility, Monetary Credibility, and Regional Integration." In P. Collier, C. Pattillo, and C. Soludo (eds.). *Economic Policy Operations for a Prosperous Nigeria*. Basingstoke: Palgrave-Macmillan.

Debrun, X., Masson, P.R., and Pattillo, C. (2011), "Should African Monetary Unions Be Expanded? An Empirical Investigation of the Scope for Monetary Integration in Sub-Saharan Africa," *Journal of African Economies*, Vol. 20, AERC Supplement 2, pp. 104–144.

De Grauwe, P. (2012), *Economics of Monetary Union*, ninth edition. Oxford: Oxford University Press.

De Grauwe, P. (2013), "Design Failures in the Eurozone — Can They be Fixed?" *European Economy*, Economic Papers 491, April.

Drazen, A. and Masson, P.R. (1994), "Credibility of Policies Versus Credibility of Policymakers," *Quarterly Journal of Economics*, Vol. 109 (August).

Eichengreen, B. (1994), *International Monetary Arrangements for the 21st Century*, Washington: Brookings Institution.

Eichengreen, B. and Hausmann, R. (1999), "Exchange Rates and Financial Fragility," In *New Challenges for Monetary Policy*, Proceedings of a symposium sponsored by the Federal Reserve Bank of Kansas City.

Eichengreen, B. and Wyplosz, C. (1998), "The Stability Pact: More Than a Minor Nuisance?" *Economic Policy*, 1998, vol. 13, issue 26, pages 65–113.

Folkerts-Landau, D. and Garber, P. (1994), "The ECB: A Bank or a Monetary Policy Rule", in M. Canzoneri, V. Grilli and P. Masson (eds.), *Establishing a Central Bank: Issues in Europe and Lessons from the US*, Cambridge: Cambridge University Press.

Frankel, J.A. and Rose, A. (2002), "An Estimate of the Effect of Common Currencies on Trade and Income," *Quarterly Journal of Economics*, Vol. 117(2), pp. 437–66.

Glick, R. and Rose, A.K. (2015), "Currency Unions and Trade: A Post-EMU Mea Culpa," paper presented to a conference at the Federal Reserve Bank of San Francisco, October 26.

Glick, R. and Rose, A.K. (2002), "Does A Currency Union Affect Trade? The Time-Series Evidence," *European Economic Review*, vol. 46 (June), pp. 1125–1151.

Guillaume, D.M. and Stasavage (2000), "Improving Policy Credibility: Is There a Case for African Monetary Unions," *World Development*, Vol. 28(8): 1391–1407.

The Euro at 20: Lessons for Africa

Hartzenberg, T. (2011), "Regional Integration in Africa," Economic Research and Statistics Division, Staff Working Paper ERSD-2011-14, Geneva: World Trade Organization, October.

IMF (2015), *Regional Economic Outlook: Sub-Saharan Africa*, October.

Kenen, P. (1969), "The Theory of Optimum Currency Areas: An Eclectic View." In Mundell and Swoboda (eds.). *Monetary Problems in the International Economy*. Chicago: University of Chicago Press.

Masson, P.R. (2008), "Currency Unions in Africa: Is the Trade Effect Substantial Enough to Justify Their Formation?" *The World Economy*, Vol. 31(4), pp. 533–547.

Masson, P.R. (2012), "Fiscal Asymmetries and the Survival of the Euro Zone," *International Economics*, Vol. 129, pp. 5–29.

Masson, P.R. (1996), "Fiscal Dimensions of EMU," *The Economic Journal*, Vol. 106 (July).

Masson, P.R. and Pattillo, C. (2002), "Monetary Union in West Africa: An Agency of Restraint for Fiscal Policies?" *Journal of African Economies*, Vol. 11 (September), pp. 387–412.

Masson, P.R. and Pattillo, C. (2005), *The Monetary Geography of Africa*. Washington: Brookings Institution Press.

Masson, P.R., Pattillo, C., and Debrun, X. (2015), "The Future of African Monetary Geography," in C. Monga and J.Y. Lin (eds.) *The Oxford Handbook of Africa and Economics*, Volume 2: Policies and Practices, (Oxford: Oxford University Press).

McCarthy, C. (2012), "Monetary Union: The Experience of the Euro and Lessons to be Learned for the African (SADC) Monetary Union," Stellenbosch, Tralac Working Paper S12WP02/12, March.

Mody, A. (2015), "Living (Dangerously) Without a Fiscal Union," Bruegel Working Paper 2015/03.

Mundell, R. (1961), "A Theory of Optimum Currency Areas." *American Economic Review*, Vol. 51(September), pp. 657–665.

Obstfeld, M. (2013), "Finance at Center Stage: Some Lessons of the Euro Crisis," *European Economy*, Economic Papers 493, April.

Rose, A. (2000), "One Money, One Market: Estimating the Effect of Common Currencies on Trade," *Economic Policy*, Vol. 30, pp. 9–45.

Rusuhuzwa, T.K. and Masson, P. (2012), "Design and Implementation of a Common Currency Area in the East African Community," University of Toronto Department of Economics *Working Paper No. 451*, April 4. Published in *African Journal of Business Management*, Vol. 7(35), pp. 3575–3590, September 2013 DOI: 10.5897/AJBM2013.7006.

Sachs, J. and Sala-I-Martin, X. (1992), "Fiscal Federalism and Optimum Currency Areas: Evidence for Europe from the United States," CEPR Discussion Paper No. 632.

Tavlas, G. (2009), "The Benefits and Costs of Monetary Union in Southern Africa: A Critical Survey of the Literature," *Journal of Economic Surveys*, Vol. 23(1), pp. 1–43.

Uneca (2013), *Assessing Regional Integration in Africa V*, Addis Ababa: United Nations Economic Commission for Africa.

Véron, N. (2015), "Europe's Radical Banking Union," *Breugel Essay and Lecture Series*, http://bruegel.org/wp-content/uploads/imported/publications/essay_NV_CMU.pdf.

WTO (2011), *World Trade Report 2011: The WTO and Preferential Trade Agreements: From Co-existence to Coherence*, Geneva: World Trade Organization.

WTO-IDE-JETRO (2011), *Trade Patterns and Global Value Chains in East Asia: From Trade in Goods to Trade in Tasks*, Geneva: World Trade Organization.

Wyplosz, C. (2013), "Europe's Quest for Fiscal Discipline," *European Economy — Economic Papers* 498, Directorate General Economic and Financial Affairs (DG ECFIN), European Commission.

Part III
Monetary Regimes

Chapter 10

The Scope for Inflation Targeting in Developing Countries[*]

Paul R. Masson, Miguel A. Savastano and Sunil Sharma

Inflation targeting (IT) serves as monetary policy framework in several advanced economies, where it has enhanced policy transparency and accountability. The chapter considers its wider applicability to developing countries. The prerequisites for a successful IT framework are identified as the ability to carry out an independent monetary policy (free of fiscal dominance or commitment to another nominal anchor, like the exchange rate) and a quantitative framework linking policy instruments to inflation. These prerequisites are largely absent among developing countries, though several of them could, with some further institutional changes and an overriding commitment to low inflation, make use of an IT framework.

1. Introduction

In the 1990s, a number of industrial countries adopted a framework for conducting monetary policy that has become known as inflation targeting (IT). In most cases, the adoption of this framework was a practical response to the (apparent or real) difficulties these countries had found in conducting monetary policy using an exchange rate peg or some monetary aggregate as the main intermediate target.

---

[*]This is an abridged version of IMF Working Paper WP/97/130, October 1997. At time of writing, the authors were staff members of the International Monetary Fund.

332 *Paul R. Masson, Miguel A. Savastano and Sunil Sharma*

The switch also signaled a deliberate attempt by these countries to improve their inflation record, which was generally perceived as poor by OECD standards. Improved inflation performance as well as increased accountability of the monetary authorities and transparency in their operating procedures were all intended to improve the credibility of monetary policy in these countries. In practice, inflation targeting has served as a pedagogical device to explain to the public the costs of expansionary monetary policy and the need to react preemptively to inflationary pressures. Though the actual experiences with IT are too short to form definitive conclusions, and the IT framework has generally not been thoroughly tested since the global economic environment in the 1990s was favorable to reductions in inflation, IT is widely viewed as a useful framework in countries which have practiced it.

The set of countries explicitly practicing inflation targeting at present includes only about half a dozen small- to medium-sized advanced economies. The question then rises of IT's wider applicability. This chapter addresses part of this question by examining the relevance of IT for developing countries. In order to do this, we first need to be clear on what IT involves, so as to assess whether developing countries satisfy the prerequisites for the successful implementation of such a policy framework. It is not our objective to provide an exhaustive survey or discussion of all aspects of IT. There are already a large number of papers, conference volumes and surveys dealing with various analytical and practical aspects of IT, and the body of literature continues to grow.[1] Despite this profusion of material, however, there remains some confusion about what IT is and entails, and how it differs from other frameworks for conducting monetary policy. Some authors attribute this unwelcome confusion

---

[1] A few examples are Haldane (1995a, 1995b, 1996), Leiderman and Svensson (1995), McCallum (1996a) and Svensson (1996, 1997a, 1997b). More recent studies include Bernanke and Mishkin (1997), Debelle (1997), Mishkin and Posen (1997), and most of the essays presented at the August 1996 Jackson Hole Conference (Federal Reserve Bank of Kansas City, 1996).

The Scope for Inflation Targeting in Developing Countries 333

to the misleading rhetoric often used in discussions of IT (Bernanke and Mishkin, 1997). Others ascribe it to the tendency to overplay the novelty value of lT (Haldane, 1996).

Our analysis largely draws on recent work, which reflects an emerging consensus on what IT is and is not. We focus, however, to a somewhat greater extent than other authors on institutional aspects that are taken for granted in industrial countries but may not be present in developing economies. Section 3 then briefly reviews the experiences of industrial countries, highlighting their common features. We then turn in Section 4 to the general question of the feasibility and advisability of an IT framework for developing countries. Section 5 offers some concluding remarks.

2. Conceptual Framework

The case for IT starts from the simple premise that the primary goal of monetary policy in any country ought to be attaining and preserving a low and stable rate of inflation. Until recently, this seemingly uncontroversial premise was at the center of prolonged and heated debates among monetary economists.[2] In fact, the widespread (though less than universal) support that currently exists for that premise among economists and practitioners alike owes much to the consensus around four basic propositions that were spurred by those debates.

The four propositions are as follows:

(1) An increase in the money supply is neutral in the medium to long run; i.e., a monetary expansion has lasting effects only on the price level, not on output or unemployment.

---

[2]For a glimpse at the evolution of the debates on this issue over the past four decades, see the volumes edited by Yeager (1962), Havrilesky and Boorman (1976), Campbell and Dougan (1986), and Dom and Schwartz (1987). For historical perspectives on the debate, going back to the 1800s, see Dom (1987) and Goodhart (1992).

334   *Paul R. Masson, Miguel A. Savastano and Sunil Sharma*

(2) Inflation is costly, either in terms of resource allocation (efficiency costs) or in terms of long-run output growth (breakdown of "superneutrality"), or both.[3]

(3) Money is not neutral in the short run; i.e., monetary policy has important transitory effects on a number of real variables such as output and unemployment. There is, however, at best, an imperfect understanding of the nature and/or size of these effects, of the horizon over which they manifest themselves and of the mechanisms through which monetary impulses are transmitted to the rest of the economy.[4] And, a corollary of (3),

(4) Monetary policy affects the rate of inflation with lags of uncertain duration and with variable strength, thus undermining the central bank's ability to control inflation on a period-by-period basis.

A fifth proposition that is often used by advocates of IT to provide support for the starting premise is the *inflationary bias* of monetary policy in a regime where the central bank can exercise (full) discretion in the setting of policy instruments. This "dynamic inconsistency" argument attributes the bias to the monetary authorities' inability to commit credibly to a low-inflation objective in the absence of a "commitment technology" — a behavior that is nonetheless optimal under most circumstances — and stresses the need to place some

---

[3]There remains some disagreement regarding the (approximate) rate of inflation at which these costs become "large" or "significant." The disagreements are relatively more important on the relationship between inflation and output growth. Examples of these are the fairly different estimates of the rate(s) of inflation at which the negative correlation between inflation and growth becomes statistically significant in recent cross-country studies (cf, Fischer, 1993; Barro, 1995; Sarel, 1996; Bruno, 1995a; Bruno and Easterly, 1995). Interestingly, in the case of welfare or efficiency costs of inflation, differences among the various estimates available (cf, Driffill *et al.*, 1990) have nonetheless allowed a consensus to emerge around the appropriateness, if not optimality, of aiming policy at a *low but not zero* rate of inflation (see, for example, Fischer, 1995; Freedman, 1996).

[4]For a recent list of competing explanations of the short-term real effects of monetary policy, see McCallum (1996a, 1996b). See also the symposium on the monetary transmission mechanism in the Fall 1995 issue of *The Journal of Economic Perspectives*.

The Scope for Inflation Targeting in Developing Countries 335

sort of (external or institutional) constraints on the central bank to ensure the attainment of the low inflation objective.[5] The consensus surrounding this proposition, however, is not as broad as that for the other four — see, for example, Goodhart (1994), McCallum (1995, 1996a), and Romer and Romer (1996) — but, in the end, this does not really undermine the case for inflation targeting, only changes the emphasis placed on the arguments employed to endorse its adoption. In fact, whether dynamic inconsistency is a major problem or not, it certainly seems to be true that central banks get more public criticism for raising interest rates than for lowering them and are subject to continual pressure to stimulate activity and/or pursue other objectives that may conflict with price stability. Inflation targeting, in principle, helps to redress this asymmetry by making inflation, not output or some other target variable, the explicit goal of monetary policy and by providing the central bank a forward-looking framework to undertake a pre-emptive tightening of policies before inflationary pressures become visible.

2.1. Prerequisites and Defining Features of IT

Building on the above consensus, IT is seen by many as a framework capable of improving the design, implementation and actual performance of monetary policy compared to the conventional procedures followed by central banks. It does so by providing a vehicle that is consistent both with a number of recent analytical developments in the area of monetary policy and with the four (or five) basic propositions listed earlier. In fact, the strength of the case for IT and its growing popularity are non-trivially related to the framework's ostensible capacity to take into account the main insights and/or policy implications of many strands of the recent literature on monetary policy including, *inter alia*, the "information-variables approach," advanced by Benjamin Friedman and others in the mid-1970s; the literature on "monetary policy rules," of the type

---

[5] A comprehensive presentation of the dynamic inconsistency argument can be found in Persson and Tabellini (1990); see also Cukierman (1992).

336   *Paul R. Masson, Miguel A. Savastano and Sunil Sharma*

suggested by Bennett McCallum and John Taylor in the 1980s; and the literature on central bank independence.

Notwithstanding the merits of an eclectic approach to the design and conduct of monetary policy, this encompassing feature of IT has, so far, delayed the formation of a consensus on the key distinguishing aspects and elements of the framework, especially from an operational perspective. This, added to the paucity of the data on actual experiences, has complicated the task of assessing the properties of inflation targeting (and its wider applicability) in a systematic way. The problem is apparent when one sees what the literature on the subject identifies most frequently as the main advantages of IT. Three features come at the top of the list[6]: the provision of a *nominal anchor* for monetary policy and inflation expectations, the increase in the *transparency* and *accountability* of the procedures followed by the monetary authorities (and the concomitant reduction of the inflationary bias of monetary policy), and the explicit role given to the *lags of monetary policy* in the (period-by-period) choice of instrument settings. But these features are hardly unique. It could be argued that a variety of frameworks for conducting monetary policy — for example, nominal income targeting — share, to some degree, and surely promise to deliver, similar advantages. In fact, a number of authors have stressed this point in their assessment of inflation targeting.[7] Given the focus of this chapter on the applicability of IT to developing countries, there is a need to pin down more clearly the prerequisites and defining features of this particular framework for monetary policy, and to attempt to place it more firmly in a wide spectrum of monetary regimes. We undertake this task in the remainder of the section.

The first requirement that must be satisfied by any country considering the adoption of IT is to have a central bank capable of conducting its monetary policy with a degree of independence.

---

[6]In particular, see Haldane (1995b), Leiderman and Svensson (1995), Leiderman and Bufman (1996), Svensson (1997b) and Bemanke and Mishkin (1997).

[7]Remarks along these lines can be found, for instance, in McCallum (1996a), King (1996), Summers (1996) and Taylor (1996).

This does not imply necessarily that the central bank of the country in question must be fully independent (in the sense defined by Cukierman (1992), Fischer (1994) and others) but, more modestly, that the monetary authorities ought to be able to gear (more or less) freely the instruments of monetary policy toward the attainment of some nominal objective: i.e., there should exist some reasonable degree of instrument independence, but not necessarily goal independence. Admittedly, this requirement is not specific to IT; rather, it is a precondition for formulating monetary policy separately from other financial policies, especially fiscal policy. Compliance with this requirement is generally (and justifiably) taken for granted in discussions and analyses of monetary policy in industrial countries but, as will be argued in Section 4, the issue becomes of utmost importance when trying to assess the applicability of any given monetary policy framework to less advanced economies.

In order to comply with this requirement, a country will have to exhibit no significant symptoms of *fiscal dominance* — i.e., the conduct of domestic monetary policy will not be dictated or severely constrained by developments of a fiscal nature. In general terms, this implies that the direct borrowing of public sector from the central bank (and the banking system) will be low or non-existent, that the government will have a broad revenue base and therefore will not rely systematically and significantly on the revenues from seigniorage, that domestic financial markets will have enough depth to absorb placements of public (and private) debt instruments, and that the accumulation of public debt will not give rise to explosive or "unpleasant" dynamics (Sargent and Wallace, 1981). Failure to comply with these conditions will make the country vulnerable to inflationary pressures of a fiscal origin that, if left unchecked, will often induce the creation of formal and informal indexation mechanisms (especially in labor and capital markets) and impart a high degree of persistence to the nominal variables of the economy. A fiscally driven inflation process of this type will gradually undermine the effectiveness of monetary policy to attain any nominal target, and oblige the central bank to follow an increasingly *accommodative* monetary policy. The threshold inflation

338   *Paul R. Masson, Miguel A. Savastano and Sunil Sharma*

rate at which monetary policy loses most of its role as a nominal anchor and becomes almost fully accommodative is not well defined analytically or empirically, but there is some agreement that a country that has experienced annual inflation rates in the 15–25 percent range for a number of consecutive years (say, three to five) will be unable to rely on monetary policy *alone* to target any significant and lasting reduction in the rate of inflation.[8]

A second requirement for adopting IT is the absence of any firm commitment by the authorities to *target the level or path of any other nominal variable*, such as wages or, especially, the nominal exchange rate. In fact, a country that chooses a *fixed exchange rate* system subordinates its monetary policy to the exchange rate objective and is unable to target any other nominal variable on a lasting basis, especially in the presence of capital mobility (a feature that is particularly relevant for the more advanced developing countries which are also the most likely candidates to adopt an IT framework).[9] Variants of a fixed exchange rate system — e.g., crawling pegs or target zones — relax these strictures somewhat and allow the authorities to gear monetary policy at some other nominal objective in addition to the exchange rate including, in principle, the rate of inflation. In theory, then, a nominal (non-fixed) exchange rate target could coexist with an inflation target "as long as it is clear that the inflation target has priority if a conflict arises" (Leiderman and Svensson, 1995). In practice, however, such a coexistence might well be problematic, since the authorities will typically be unable to convey *ex ante* those priorities to the public in a credible manner. Under those circumstances, the public would have to *infer* the authorities' priorities from their actual responses in those instances

---

[8]For recent analyses of the role of fiscal and monetary policies in moderate-to-high inflation episodes, and the ensuing stabilizations, see Dornbusch (1982), Dornbusch and Fischer (1993), Bruno (1991, 1993, 1995a, 1995b), and Heymann and Leijonhufvud (1995).

[9]This is not to say that pegging the exchange rate may not be inspired by the ultimate objective of price stability, but simply that the stated exchange rate objective necessarily becomes the main intermediate target of monetary policy.

The Scope for Inflation Targeting in Developing Countries   339

where the nominal exchange rate target came under pressure. But therein lies the problem: there is no assurance that either of the two main courses of action open to the authorities in situations of exchange rate pressure — i.e., adjust the instrument settings to preserve the nominal exchange rate target or allow the exchange rate to move beyond the pre-established range — would convey the appropriate signal to the public and/or increase the credibility of the authorities. Without question, the surest (and safest) way of avoiding these problems in contexts where the inflation target is the main policy objective would be to refrain from making strong commitments about the expected or desired level or time path of the nominal exchange rate.

A country that satisfies these two basic requirements could, in principle, conduct its monetary policy in a manner consistent with IT. To do so, the authorities would need to put in place a framework for monetary policy containing four essential elements[10]: (i) explicit *quantitative targets* for the rate of inflation some period(s) ahead; (ii) clear and unambiguous indications that the attainment of the inflation target constitutes the *overriding objective* of monetary policy in the sense that it takes precedence over all other objectives; (iii) a methodology ("model") for producing *inflation forecasts* that uses a number of variables and indicators containing information on future inflation; and (iv) *a forward-looking* operating procedure in which the setting of policy instruments depends on the assessment of inflationary pressures and where the inflation forecasts are used as the *main intermediate target*. The preceding list *assumes*, other than compliance with the two basic requirements, that the country's monetary authorities possess the technical and institutional capacity to model and forecast domestic inflation, have some knowledge or estimate of the time it takes for the "inflation determinants"

---

[10]Despite some differences in emphasis, a large majority of studies on IT mention these four elements as key ingredients of the framework; see Haldane (1995a, 1995b), Lane *et al.* (1995), Green (1996), Freedman (1996), Svensson (1997b) and Bernanke and Mishkin (1997).

340   *Paul R. Masson, Miguel A. Savastano and Sunil Sharma*

to have their full effect on the inflation rate,[11] and have a well-informed view of the way in which monetary impulses affect the main macroeconomic variables as well as of the relative effectiveness of the various policy instruments at their disposal.

2.2. *A Schematic Representation of Monetary Policy under IT*

The foregoing discussion implies that the policy-setting behavior of the monetary authorities in a country that follows an IT operating procedure can be usefully illustrated by the following feedback (or, more precisely, feed-forward) rule[12]:

$$\Delta R_t = \gamma({}_t\pi^e_{t+j} - \pi^*_{t+j}), \tag{1}$$

where R_t represents the preferred instrument of monetary policy, π_k is the rate of inflation in period k, ${}_t\pi^e_{t+j}$ is the authorities' expected rate of inflation in period $t + j$ conditional on information at time t (assuming no subsequent policy changes), π^*_{t+j} is the inflation target for period $t + j$ (which may, in principle, be time-varying), γ is a feedback parameter,[13] and j is the number of periods (assumed greater than zero) it takes for the policy instrument R to have its maximum effect on inflation.

Feedback rule (1) shows clearly that in order to follow an IT procedure the monetary authorities must have a well-defined inflation target π^*, a preferred policy instrument, approximate knowledge of

---

[11]The literature on IT often refers to this period as the "control lag" or "policy effectiveness interval," and typically assumes — based on available estimates for industrial countries — that its average length is in the order of 18–24 months. See, for example, Leiderman and Svensson (1995), Haldane (1996), Freedman (1996) and Svensson (1996, 1997b).

[12]The presentation in the next few paragraphs draws on Haldane (1996). In practice, the operating procedure may require following more complex feedback rules, for instance when policy instruments affect inflation with a long distributed lag.

[13]The sign of γ will depend on the choice of the policy instrument R. If R represents a price-related instrument such as the discount rate or repo rate, then $\gamma > 0$, whereas if it represents a quantity-related instrument such as credit or base money then $\gamma < 0$.

The Scope for Inflation Targeting in Developing Countries 341

j, and some view of the *expected* rate of inflation in period $t + j$. The choice and specification of the inflation target depend on a number of analytical and institutional considerations that will be discussed later. The selection of the three other components of the feedback rule, on the other hand, must be firmly based on *empirical* estimates of the inflation dynamics and of the effectiveness of monetary policy in the country under consideration. These estimates will rarely reflect the outcome of a mechanical extrapolation from a single forecasting equation or model. Instead, they will often summarize the results obtained from a number of different models of the inflation process as well as the information conveyed by a range of "off-model" indicators, including the "priors" of the authorities. In this context, it is perhaps more appropriate to interpret the expected rate of inflation in Equation (1) as a *portmanteau* for a myriad of indicators and forecasts of inflation (Haldane, 1996).

What distinguishes IT from other frameworks for conducting monetary policy, therefore, is not so much the accuracy of the forecasting techniques employed in the procedure but the fact that the setting of policy instruments relies on a *systematic assessment of expected (future) inflation*, rather than on past or current inflation developments or an otherwise arbitrary assumption about future inflation. It is because of this feature that IT is said to address one of the fundamental problems of monetary policy, namely the *imperfect control* that central banks have over the current rate of inflation — i.e., proposition (4) above.

The sources of that imperfect control are many — e.g., aggregate demand and supply shocks, instability of intermediate targets (velocity shocks), information asymmetries — and so are its manifestations — e.g., a current rate of inflation that is largely predetermined at the time policy decisions are made, uncertainty about the relative strength of policy instruments, and instances of "instrument instability". In the end, all of these factors undermine the capacity of monetary policy to deliver a steady and low rate of inflation on a permanent basis. The debates on monetary policy alluded to earlier (see footnote 2) discussed all these issues extensively. For the purpose of this chapter, however, it may be useful to recast the gist of some

342   *Paul R. Masson, Miguel A. Savastano and Sunil Sharma*

of the arguments made in those debates and illustrate their relevance for the ongoing discussion of inflation targeting.

This can be done neatly with the help of the following example taken from Cecchetti (1995).[14] Suppose that in a given country there is some agreement that inflation is actually determined by the "structural" model

$$\pi_{t+1} = \alpha(L)R_t + \beta(L)X_t + \omega_{t+1}, \tag{2}$$

where now R is a vector of policy instruments, X is a vector of inflation determinants, $\alpha(L)$ and $\beta(L)$ are lag polynomials, and ω_{t+1} is a stochastic term (a "shock") in period $t+1$ that is not known in period t.

In general, monetary policy can be characterized as the period-by-period setting of policy instruments in response to the observed realization of the determinants against the background of a given nominal objective (i.e., an inflation target) or, in terms of this particular example, as

$$R_t = \gamma(L)X_t + u_t, \tag{3}$$

where some of the terms in $y(L)$ can be zero, since policy need not react to every element in X, and u_t is a random term representing implementation errors (which may be zero as well).

Equations (2) and (3) imply that the reduced form for inflation will be

$$\pi_{t+1} = \delta(L)X_t + \varepsilon_t, \tag{4}$$

where $\delta(L) = \alpha(L)\gamma(L) + \beta(L)$ and ε_t depends on ω_{t+1} and u_t.

---

[14]The literature on IT seems to have a preference for using simple variants of the standard expectations — augmented aggregate demand/aggregate supply model to illustrate selected features of the operation of inflation targeting — e.g., Blake and Westaway (1996), Haldane (1996), Svensson (1996, 1997a, 1997b). This paper departs from that practice and instead uses a "generic" representation of the relation between monetary policy and inflation, mainly because the output gap model of inflation is not as widely accepted an analytical framework for developing countries as for industrial countries.

The Scope for Inflation Targeting in Developing Countries 343

Several aspects of the "imperfect controllability" problem of monetary policy are borne out by this simple example. First, by construction, *current* inflation is predetermined at the time the authorities choose the setting of policy instruments. Second, the relation between monetary policy and inflation is subject to lags, involves many parameters, and may not be time invariant. In particular, changes in monetary policy (i.e., changes in $\gamma(L)$, prompted, for instance, by changes in the relative weight placed on some determinant or by a change in the intermediate target) will change the correlation between X and π in Equation (4).[15] A related source of instability stems from uncertainty about the "true" coefficients of the model (Brainard, 1967). Concretely, if the parameters of $\delta(L)$ were not known with certainty, a monetary policy aimed at controlling the rate of inflation might *increase* rather than *decrease* the variance of inflation. Third, in the case where the lags in $\delta(L)$ are known (fixed) and non-zero, and shocks u_t, are uncorrelated with X_t, a monetary policy aimed at minimizing the variance of inflation around a fixed (constant) target rate will require setting the policy instruments in every period according to

$$\alpha(L)R_t = -\beta(L)X_t + \alpha(L)u_t. \tag{5}$$

Two implications of following this "optimal" policy are readily apparent. First, inflation becomes completely uncorrelated with its determinants, as its law of motion collapses to

$$\pi_{t+1} = \omega_{t+1} + \alpha(L)u_t.$$

Second, contrary to the case where the lags in $\alpha(L)$ are not known with certainty (i.e., are stochastic), it actually becomes possible to design an "activist" monetary policy that fully offsets the effects of (long) lags and past disturbances on the rate of inflation. Even so, controlling inflation through this type of activist policy may produce instances of "instrument instability", requiring ever larger changes

---

[15]This simple version of the Lucas (1976) critique captures the essence of the problems of "long and variable lags" and varying effectiveness of monetary policy.

in the policy instruments to offset their own lagged effects.[16] This can be seen clearly in (5), where nothing guarantees that the lag polynomial $\alpha(L)$ has stable roots.

Advocates of IT argue that such a procedure lessens all the problems noted above by gearing monetary policy at the expected rate of inflation some periods ahead (i.e., beyond period $t + 1$ in the preceding example) and by relying on more than one inflation forecast. These two features, the argument goes, allow the authorities to focus the public's expectations on a horizon where monetary policy can confidently influence the rate of inflation while preserving some room for a judicious smoothing of their policy instruments; also, they force the central bank to assess on a continuous basis the information content of numerous inflation determinants, thus enabling it to detect breaks in empirical relationships at an early stage. This approach to monetary policy, which has been called by some as "multiple indicators approach," suggests that, in practice, the term, $_t\pi_{t+j}^e$ in Equation (1) often summarizes a number of different forecasting procedures, some judgmental, with possibly shifting weights attributed to each measure of expected inflation.

The summary measure of the expected rate of inflation $_t\pi_{t+j}^e$ constitutes the *main intermediate target* of monetary policy under IT.[17] Operationally, the authorities will try to maintain the difference between $_t\pi_{t+j}^e$ and π_{t+j}^* in Equation (1) permanently within a target band. If at any point in time that difference is zero or (slightly) negative, the authorities will have a firm basis to assume that the inflation target remains attainable at the prevailing (and expected) configuration of the variables in X and R, and that no policy change is needed.

---

[16]The concept of "instrument instability" was developed by Holbrook (1972). Simply stated, it may occur when the current effects on the target (goal) variable of a given change in a exogenous (policy) variable are small and the lagged effects are large, creating a path for the instrument that is dynamically unstable.

[17]Svensson (1996, 1997b) argues that this summary measure, the authorities' inflation forecast, possesses features that make it the ideal intermediate target for monetary policy, since it is highly correlated with the goal, and is both easier to control and to observe than the goal.

The Scope for Inflation Targeting in Developing Countries   345

Conversely, if the difference results in a non-negligible positive number, the authorities will have strong indications that the inflation target is not likely to be attained in period $t+j$. In that case, in line with the feedback rule (1), or some variant of it,[18] the authorities will normally be expected to adjust the policy stance and change the policy instrument (ΔR_t) until the discrepancy between the updated inflation forecast and the inflation target is eliminated.[19]

2.3. *Issues in the Implementation of IT*

The simple example outlined above abstracted, on purpose, from a number of implementation issues that require explicit decisions from the authorities. Analytically, these issues can be classified in two broad categories: those that deal with the *specification* of the inflation target, and those related to the *institutional arrangements* that support the framework for monetary policy. Decisions concerning the specification of the inflation target comprise, *inter alia*, choosing on which *price index* to define the target, choosing between setting the target in terms of the *price level* or the *rate of inflation*, choosing a *numerical value* for the target, its *horizon* and its *time path* (e.g., one period or multi-period, a declining path or a flat path), deciding whether to define the target as a point estimate with or without a *band* (*tolerance interval*) and, in case they opt for one, choosing the width of the band, and deciding whether and how to specify *"escape clauses"* or *exemptions* to the inflation target in particular circumstances. Choices related to the institutional setting include deciding whether to make compliance with the inflation target(s) *a formally mandated objective* or, simply, an operational requirement of monetary policy, deciding how best to integrate IT with the

---

[18] Clearly, if the effects of the policy instrument build up over time, a trade-off may arise between changing the instrument early by a modest amount and changing it later, but more sharply.

[19] In practice, implementation of IT in industrial countries (see Table 2) has tended to be asymmetric in that monetary easing — i.e., declines in official interest rates — has not typically been prompted by the expectation that inflation would be below a target range; instead, easing seems to have been a response to weak economic activity.

country's decision making process on macroeconomic policies, and, in particular, with the *policy cycle* (which entails clarifying to the public *what, when* and *by whom* matters related to the conduct of monetary policy are decided), and choosing specific vehicles to enhance the *transparency* and *accountability* of monetary policy (e.g., periodical releases of inflation forecasts, improved means of informing the public of decisions affecting the setting of policy instruments, etc.).

The literature on IT contains long and detailed discussions on all these issues.[20] At a general level, many of those discussions revolve around a *credibility/flexibility trade-off*. Choices that are normally perceived as having the capacity of enhancing the credibility of the inflation targeting framework typically carry a cost in terms of the authorities' loss of short-term flexibility to exercise discretion in certain circumstances — though in the long run, acquiring credibility may also enhance flexibility. At an individual country level, however, the arguments used in the discussions of the various alternatives are often more elaborate and at times fairly complex (for example, on the relationship between the "escape clauses" of the inflation targets and the optimal degree of accommodation to aggregate supply shocks, or on the extent to which a particular application of inflation targeting conforms with the main requirements of an "optimal incentive contract" for the central bank). There may be an emerging consensus on some of these issues, notably on the advantages of specifying the target in terms of the rate of inflation rather than the price level and on defining the target in terms of a price index that is well known and widely used by the public such as the CPI (perhaps purged of a few items not linked to domestic demand pressures) — but the jury is still out on many others. Unfortunately, the actual experiences with this type of framework are too recent and diverse to be of use for settling any argument about the marginal contribution of a particular aspect of its implementation, so that decisions on many of these implementation issues will continue to be guided

---

[20]In particular, see Haldane (1995a, 1995b), Lane *et al.* (1995), Walsh (1995), Freedman (1996), Bemanke and Mishkin (1997) and, especially, Debelle (1997).

by pragmatic considerations. This is the view of, among others, Bernanke and Mishkin (1997), who pointedly observe that, in the cases they examine: "the (choices and) views on (these) subject(s) have been largely based on prior arguments, intuition and indirect evidence."

2.4. *IT as a Monetary Regime*

Another key aspect of the debate on IT where consensus remains elusive is on the type of monetary regime that inflation targeting represents.[21] The main themes in dispute in this area are the *novelty value* of IT (in particular, its similarities and differences with "traditional" operating procedures of monetary policy such as money targeting), the *rule-like features* of IT (or, equivalently, the scope for discretion that IT provides to the monetary authorities) and the *output-stabilizing properties* of IT (i.e., the framework's implications for the short-run behavior of output and unemployment). As several authors have noted,[22] lack of agreement on *basic terminology* has been an important obstacle in this regard. Many of the terms on which discussions on IT are cast — from "targeting" to "rules" — simply mean different things to different people.

---

[21] A "monetary regime" is a concept that goes beyond the operating procedures of monetary policy and captures as well the interactions between the authorities and the public that are consistent with the "rules of the game." It corresponds broadly to Lucas' (1976) definition of a policy — i.e., the coefficients of a system of policy reaction functions that specify how policy instruments are adjusted systematically to movements in other variables. A more complete (and simpler) definition is that of Leijonhufvud (1984), who characterizes a monetary regime as "a system of expectations governing the behavior of the public and a consistent pattern of behavior on the part of the monetary authorities that sustain those expectations." On the whole, the discussion on IT has not been carried out explicitly in these terms even though they have been used widely in the monetary policy literature to conduct comparisons across monetary standards or regimes (see, for example, Campbell and Dougan (1986) and Goodhart (1992)). It will be argued below that this shortcoming has impaired reaching a rapid consensus on the main characteristics of inflation targeting.

[22] In particular, see Haldane (1995a, 1996) and Bemanke and Mishkin (1997). See also McCallum (1996b, 1997).

348 *Paul R. Masson, Miguel A. Savastano and Sunil Sharma*

Many have argued that the confusion noted above is simply another manifestation of the embryonic stage of the debate on IT and, therefore, largely unavoidable. There is much truth in this view, especially when stated as lucidly as in McCallum (1996a): "the issues at hand concern institutional arrangements that should be judged on the basis of their effects on the operating characteristics of economies over long spans of time-the average performance, that is, over a number of cycles ... from that perspective it will be *another decade or two* before the potential advantages or disadvantages of [inflation targeting] will be clearly evident" (pages 13–14, italics added). Knowing this, however, does not make the need for a systematic assessment of inflation targeting and for a clarification of its main characteristics as a monetary regime any less pressing. Table 1, taken from Lindsey (1986), seems useful in this context. The purpose of the table is to provide a simple, albeit imperfect, vehicle where alternative monetary regimes can be classified on the basis of two central characteristics: their *policy structure* (i.e., the systematic component of the operating procedure of monetary policy)[23] and their *policy mode* (i.e., the degree of discretion granted

Table 1. Alternative Monetary Policy Regimes

Type of Policy Structure	Type of Policy Mode	
	Non-discretionary	Discretionary
Simple rules without feedback	A	B
Simple feedback rules	C	
Intermediate non-monetary targeting with feedback		D
Intermediate monetary targeting with feedback	E	
Ultimate targeting with continuous feedback to instruments		IT

Source: Lindsey (1986).

---

[23]In his paper, Lindsey actually uses the terminology of Lucas (1976) to define a policy structure as: "a general classification [that] groups together systems of reaction functions with qualitatively similar structures, despite differences among

The Scope for Inflation Targeting in Developing Countries 349

to, and exercised by, the monetary authorities). The five types of policy structures identified in the table along with the two types of policy modes form *ten general categories* of monetary regimes. Because the demarcations imply a high level of generality, each cell should be thought of as containing a large number of options aligned on imprecise metrics, both horizontally and vertically (this consideration is especially important when moving along the "policy mode" dimension since there is no simple way of measuring the degree of discretion). Thus, for example, point A in the upper-left cell (non-discretionary simple rules without feedback from other economic variables) could denote either an irrevocably fixed exchange rate (e.g., a currency board) or a *k-percent* money-growth rule *à la* Friedman. A point like B, in comparison, would represent a regime where simple rules without feedback are altered on rare occasions through discretionary actions of the authorities (e.g., a once-and-for-all devaluation of the exchange rate parity or a change in the money growth rule from k percent to $k + x$ percent).

Most (if not all) of the frameworks for monetary policy that are the subject of recent (and not-so-recent) debates have a place in Table 1. For instance, in addition to the types of regimes that could be represented by points A and B discussed above, the table has an (approximate) place for the *simple base money rules* proposed by McCallum and others in the early 1980s (say, a point like C in the second row), for the numerous proposals embodying some sort of *nominal income targeting* — *including* those advocated by Tobin (1983) and others that give a high degree of discretion to monetary authorities (and, thus, would correspond to a point like D), for the many variants of *money targeting* procedures that were in vogue in industrial countries in the 1970s and 1980s and which have since fallen in disfavor (except, perhaps, in the Bundesbank which, presumably, would still place itself at a point like E), and for the proponents of the *information variables approach*, e.g., Friedman (1975, 1994), who would advocate dispensing with all types of

---

them in the particular values of the reaction coefficients or in the particular functional forms" (Lindsey, 1986, p. 170).

formal intermediate targets and replacing them with an "engineering efficient" procedure whereby the operating instruments of monetary policy are adjusted continuously in response to information about movements in the ultimate target.

From the preceding discussion, and, especially, from Equations (1)–(5), it is quite apparent that inflation targeting belongs somewhere in the fifth row of Table 1. However, it also follows from the earlier discussion that pinning down the regime's precise location on the "policy mode" dimension is inherently difficult given the variety of technical and institutional arrangements that have underpinned this type of framework in practice. Notwithstanding these difficulties, the (admittedly light) weight of the evidence accumulated so far suggests that an inflation targeting regime would typically be located somewhere near the left border of the lower-right cell of Table 1 — i.e., a regime characterized by a policy structure of *ultimate targeting with continuous feedback* and a *mildly discretionary* policy mode (point IT). Portraying inflation targeting in this way makes it easier to reconcile many of the seemingly unrelated characterizations of the framework that one encounters in the literature, from the "constrained discretion" of Bemanke and Mishkin (1997) to Haldane's insistence on the "near equivalence" of IT with money targeting procedures that rely on information variables (Haldane, 1995a, 1995b), to the "target-rule" label proposed by Svensson (1996). More important, it provides the basic means to conduct discussions on IT from a perspective that is, arguably, broad enough to relegate the problems of terminology to a secondary plane and, thus, allows future debates to focus squarely on the main features of IT as a distinct monetary regime.

3. Common Features of the Experience with Inflation Targeting in Advanced Economies

As noted in Section 1, starting in the early 1990s a number of small- to-medium-sized industrial countries decided to conduct their monetary policy using an inflation targeting framework. The first country to explicitly adopt this type of framework was New Zealand,

The Scope for Inflation Targeting in Developing Countries   351

and its example was followed — though not replicated exactly — soon thereafter by (in chronological order) Canada, the United Kingdom, Finland, Sweden, Australia and Spain. No attempt will be made here to provide a comprehensive description and comparison of the experiences of these countries, as this ground is well covered in the existing (and growing) literature on IT, in particular in the volumes edited by Leiderman and Svensson (1995) and Haldane (1995b), and in Debelle (1997). We will simply highlight some common features of these experiences that, in our view, are particularly relevant for the discussion of the following sections. Table 2 contains information that is useful for surveying the IT experience of advanced economies.

The first common feature, which is obvious but basic, is that inflation targeting was associated with a high degree of exchange rate flexibility. Indeed, in many of the countries IT was adopted in the aftermath of a failed attempt to use the exchange rate as the main anchor of monetary policy (e.g., the UK, Sweden and Finland). In others, like Canada, it was associated with a decision by the authorities to place less emphasis on resisting exchange rate fluctuations. Spain would seem to provide an exception to this pattern, as it adopted IT while retaining its ERM central parity, admittedly with much larger bands of fluctuation after the exchange rate crisis of July 1993. However, Spain's commitment to inflation targeting has also been viewed by the authorities as a means of attaining the overriding goal of monetary union with its EU partners.

The second common feature is that all countries that adopted IT had a measure of central bank independence, at least with regard to: (i) the links between the central banks' actions and the financing of government budgets (i.e., the degree of "fiscal dominance"), and (ii) the central banks' ability to freely operate their monetary policy instruments (i.e., the degree of "instrument independence")[24] Also, in practice, the central banks of all the countries that adopted IT use short-term interest rates as their main operating instrument, and rely

---

[24]In the case of the United Kingdom, instrument independence was enhanced in May 1997 by the incoming Labour administration (see Table 2).

Table 2. Advanced Economies with Explicit Inflation Targeting Frameworks: Selected Features

Country	Date of Adoption	Target Rate and Horizon	Price Index	Other Details
New Zealand	March 1990	0–2%[a] through the 5-year tenure of the Governor of the Reserve Bank	CPI excluding interest cost components, indirect taxes and subsidies, government charges, and significant price effects from changes in the terms of trade.	Target set in Policy Target Agreements (PTA) between the Minister of Finance and the Governor of the Reserve Bank of New Zealand.
Canada	February 1991	1–3% through 1998	CPI excluding food, energy, and the effect of indirect tax changes.	Target set by the Minister of Finance and the Governor of the Bank of Canada.
United Kingdom	October 1992	2½%, plus or minus 1%.	Retail price index excluding mortgage interest payments (RPIX).	Target set by the Chancellor of the Exchequer.[b]
Sweden	January 1993	2% (with a tolerance band of ±1%) in 1996 and beyond	CPI.	Target set by the Bank of Sweden.
Finland	February 1993	About 2% in 1996 and beyond	CPI excluding indirect taxes, government subsidies, house prices, and mortgage interest payments.	The target rate has no explicit band. Target set by the Bank of Finland.

Australia	1993	Underlying inflation of 2–3%, on average, over the cycle	CPI excluding the impact of interest rates on mortgage and other interest payments, indirect tax changes, and certain other volatile price items.	Target set by the Reserve Bank of Australia and endorsed by the government in the Statement on the Conduct of Monetary Policy by the Treasurer and the Governor of the Reserve Bank.
Spain	November 1994	Less than 3% by 1997, 2% by 1998[c]	CPI.	Target set by the Bank of Spain.

Notes: [a]Subsequently increased to 1–3 percent.
[b]In May 1997, the Chancellor of the Exchequer announced that the Bank of England would be given operational independence to set interest rates in order to achieve the inflation target (which would still be set by the UK Treasury). Inflation outside the target range would require the Governor to write an open letter to the Chancellor to explain the reasons for the deviation.
[c]Announced in December 1996.
Source: IMF (1996), Box 8, updated as necessary.

on well-developed financial markets to transmit the effects of changes in the instrument to aggregate demand and inflation.

The third feature is that the inflation targets set in all the countries were forward looking, not because they involved a firm commitment to preventing any shock from leading to a deviation of inflation from its current target value, but because they represented a promise to offset the forecastable effect of shocks on future inflation over a horizon of between 1 and 2 years. It is also noteworthy that in all cases the inflation target was defined in terms of at least a notional target range or "tolerance interval" (although in the cases of Australia and Finland the range was not specified clearly) rather than as a point estimate.

Fourth, all these countries used IT as a tool for building the credibility of their macroeconomic policy framework. In most cases, this task was facilitated by the fact that inflation targets were set by mutual agreement between the fiscal and monetary authorities, thus tending to reduce the public's perception of conflicting objectives of economic policy. Moreover, IT has often been used as a pedagogical device for explaining the effects of monetary policy to the public, for instance through the release of inflation reports (notably in the United Kingdom and Canada), and for increasing the accountability of the monetary authorities (for instance by linking the terms of the "contract" for the central bank's governor to the actual performance of monetary policy, as in New Zealand). Using IT for these purposes has presupposed a non-negligible degree of initial credibility, thus enabling the central banks to influence the public's expectations through their official announcements and analyses, as well as a certain degree of economic sophistication of the public.

Finally, an important common feature is that inflation targeting was not introduced in the contexts of moderate or high inflation, but rather in situations where the inflation rate was fairly low (less than 10 percent in all the countries). This feature is likely to have contributed to the initial degree of credibility in the framework and reduced the risks of either having to announce a very drastic reduction of inflation (with possible high output costs and large margins of error) or to set targets that may have been interpreted by the public as a signal that the central bank was tolerating (or ratifying) undesirably high rates of inflation.

4. General Issues Concerning the Applicability of Inflation Targeting in Developing Countries

This section examines the feasibility and applicability of IT in developing countries. More specifically, it addresses two questions: first, under what conditions does the inflation targeting framework outlined in the preceding sections constitute a procedure that *can* be adopted by certain developing countries? And second, what aspects of the conduct of monetary policy in some of these countries are, on the contrary, *least consistent* with inflation targeting? We approach these questions from the general perspective of the prerequisites for an effective IT framework identified in Section 2, namely, the central bank's scope for conducting an independent monetary policy and the undisputed primacy of the inflation objective. We also discuss some issues related to the specification of the inflation target of particular relevance for developing countries. The section ends with a brief description of the main features of the monetary policy framework in a few developing economies.

As is customary for studies dealing with developing countries, our analysis starts from the basic proposition that these countries comprise a very heterogeneous group. On matters related to monetary policy and financial markets this proposition is more than just a neutral disclaimer. Despite some general trends toward greater reliance on indirect instruments of monetary policy, increased access to international capital markets and financial sector reform (IMF, 1995); Fry *et al.*, 1996), the diversities of monetary experiences and the differences in the degree of financial development in these countries remain wide and do not allow many generalizations. Moreover, standard indicators of interest rates, financial deepening, and the level of income have not yet produced a widely accepted classification or ranking of developing countries by degree of financial development (McKinnon, 1991; Pill and Pradhan, 1995). This state of affairs makes the task of evaluating the net benefits for these countries of adopting a monetary regime like IT extremely difficult. Besides stressing the differences across groups of countries throughout the discussion, the analysis in this section tries to deal with the problem of heterogeneity by presenting data supportive of some of our arguments and by reporting the results of a questionnaire designed to identify the main operating procedures of monetary policy in a number of developing countries that were regarded as potential candidates for adopting IT. Nonetheless, the nature of the analysis remains largely exploratory and argumentative, rather than empirical.

4.1. Scope for Independent Monetary Policy

In Section 2, we argued that the two main determinants of the scope for independent monetary policy, and thus the main prerequisites for the adoption of an IT framework, in any given country were: (i) the degree of fiscal dominance, and (ii) the absence of firm commitments by the authorities to target other nominal variables that might conflict with the inflation objective. The extent to which a developing country complies with these two prerequisites at a particular point in time normally reflects the confluence of structural and transitory elements. The fact that these elements often reinforce each other makes the task of assessing the degree of compliance quite exacting.

In a few extreme cases it is readily apparent that the basic requirements for adopting IT are not satisfied. For example, in economies where the rate of inflation has stayed in the chronic to high range (say, above 30–40 percent per annum) for a number of years, all nominal variables will tend to display a high degree of inertia and asynchronization, and monetary policy will be largely accommodative. In situations like this, as noted earlier, monetary policy will only be as good as fiscal policy and will generally have short-lived and unpredictable effects on the rate of inflation. The foremost priority of economic policy in these contexts should be attaining a lasting reduction in inflation through a comprehensive stabilization program comprising fiscal consolidation, a break in monetary financing of the government, and the choice of one or more

The Scope for Inflation Targeting in Developing Countries 357

nominal variables to anchor inflation expectations.[25] Conducting monetary policy in a manner consistent with IT will only be an option once the fiscal roots of the problem are eradicated and the rate of inflation falls to moderate levels. Another clear example where IT is not an option for the monetary authorities is given by those economies that belong to a currency union or that choose to fix their nominal exchange rate to the currency of a major trading partner. As mentioned before, these countries subordinate their monetary policy to the exchange rate objective, which becomes the main intermediate target of monetary policy and a major source of policy credibility. In these economies, the authorities implicitly accept the rate of inflation of their main trading partner(s) as their own inflation target and are committed to giving priority to preserving the parity whenever a (potential) conflict of policy objectives arises.

For the majority of developing countries, however, the degree of compliance with the basic prerequisites of IT is more difficult to assess. Fiscal dominance does not always lead to unsustainably high or rapidly rising rates of inflation; the extent to which monetary policy passively accommodates other nominal variables and shocks in the economy becomes apparent only at high rates of inflation and is influenced by a host of country-specific factors (e.g., formal and informal indexation practices); also, the middle-of-the-road exchange rate arrangements currently in place in many of these countries (i.e., managed floats, crawling bands) afford the monetary authorities considerable discretion for ranking their external and domestic objectives in a less-than-fully transparent manner, sometimes for relatively long periods.

Recent attempts to extend the research agenda on central bank independence (CBI) to developing countries have had to confront these problems.[26] A common finding of all these studies is that, despite the wide range of country experiences, central banks in

---

[25] See the references listed in footnote 8; see also Calvo and Vegh (1994) and Vegh (1992).

[26] In particular, see Cukierman (1992), Mas (1995) and Fry *et al.* (1996); see also Willett *et al.* (1995).

developing countries face environments that *differ radically* from those faced by central banks in advanced economies. In particular, the studies conclude that many of the insights and implications of the literature on CBI have limited applicability in a developing country context because the central bank's scope for conducting an independent monetary policy in these economies tends to be hampered by the presence of three related factors: heavy reliance on seigniorage, shallow capital markets and fragile banking systems.

The reliance on seigniorage is perhaps the simplest and most common manifestation of fiscal dominance. The link between the government's ability to raise revenues from conventional source and its recourse to revenues from seigniorage and the inflation tax is well documented both analytically and empirically (Phelps, 1973; Fischer, 1982). In developing countries, such a link is typically much stronger, and hence the reliance on seigniorage much heavier, than in advanced economies due to a number of structural features (e.g., concentrated and unstable sources of tax revenue, poor tax collection procedures, skewed income distribution and political instability), as well as to the proclivity of these countries to abuse this source of revenue, as opposed to issuing debt or cutting government expenditures, during times of crisis (Easterly *et al.*, 1994).

Shallow capital markets are also a common, though more subtle, manifestation of fiscal dominance. They are often a by-product of government schemes to extract revenue from the financial system through various forms of financial repression including, *inter alia*, interest rate ceilings, high reserve requirements, sectoral credit policies and compulsory placements of public debt (McKinnon, 1991; Fry *et al.*, 1996).[27] In some low-income countries, however, undeveloped capital markets may be a cause as much as a consequence of fiscal dominance. Economies that have imperfect access to international capital markets, limited fiscal flexibility, low levels of domestic wealth and a small financial system constrain the government's capacity to

---

[27]Government revenues from these sources are particularly difficult to detect and quantify, but the few estimates available suggest that they can often be sizable; see, for example, Giovannini and de Melo (1993).

The Scope for Inflation Targeting in Developing Countries   359

issue domestic debt to finance transitory revenue shortfalls, leaving seigniorage and other forms of financial repression as the only options. Regardless of the causality, however, the evidence on the adverse effects of financial repression on the development of domestic capital markets and overall economic performance are indisputable (McKinnon, 1991; Levine, 1997), and so is the fact that the conduct of monetary policy in contexts of severe financial repression becomes essentially a quasi-fiscal activity (Fry, 1993).

Fragile banking systems are one obvious consequence of prolonged periods of financial repression. But it is typically in the aftermath of financial sector reforms that they impart an *independent* influence on the conduct of monetary policy in developing countries. It is in these contexts where the conflicts between the objectives of attaining price stability and restoring (preserving) banking sector profitability reach proportions rarely observed in advanced economies. In fact, a number of recent studies have found that banking crises have been more severe in developing than industrial countries — with estimates of resolution costs reaching up to 25 percent of GDP in some extreme cases (Goldstein and Turner, 1996) — and have often been associated with balance of payments problems (Kaminsky and Reinhart, 1996). This evidence suggests that considerations of sequencing and a clear ranking of policy objectives are paramount in the early stages of financial liberalization, when central banks have *de facto* limited scope for a monetary stance based on high real interest rates (McKinnon, 1991).

Tables 3 and 4 present some evidence on the relative importance of two of the three factors just mentioned for a large sample of countries. Table 3 contains estimates of the revenues from seigniorage, the rate of inflation and the fiscal deficit for 79 countries from 1980 to 1995. For each variable, the table presents the average for seven country groups (Advanced Economies, Inflation Targeting countries, Africa, Asia, Asia excluding China, Latin America and Caribbean, and Middle East and Europe) over three periods (1980–1991, 1992–1995 and 1980–1995), as well as data for selected individual countries; each entry in the table represents the average annual estimate of the corresponding variable for the period and group (country)

Table 3. Seigniorage, Inflation, and Government balance for Selected Countries, 1980–1995[a]

	Seigniorage[b]			CPI Inflation			Govt. Balance[c]		
	1980–91	1992–95	1980–95	1980–91	1992–95	1980–95	1980–91	1992–95	1980–95
Advanced Economies (21)[d]	0.75	0.32	0.64	7.2	3.3	6.2	−3.8	−4.7	−4.0
United States	0.35	0.44	0.37	5.4	2.8	4.8	−3.5	−3.3	−3.4
Germany	0.48	0.30	0.44	2.9	3.5	3.1	−2.4	−1.6	−2.2
Japan	0.63	0.32	0.55	2.6	0.9	2.2	−3.1	−3.0	−3.1
Inflation Targeting countries (7)	*0.59*	*0.54*	*0.58*	*8.0*	*2.7*	*6.7*	*−2.4*	*−5.7*	*−3.2*
Developing and Transition Economies, by Region[d]									
Africa (19)	1.42	1.31	1.41	19.6	22.2	20.2	−5.2	−4.7	−5.1
South Africa	0.78	0.37	0.68	14.7	10.3	13.6	−3.9	−6.5	−4.6
Asia (13)	1.53	2.04	1.79	7.6	7.1	7.5	−3.2	−1.3	−2.7
China	3.54	7.75	6.52	6.5	16.1	8.9	−1.8	−1.9	−1.8
Asia excluding China (12)	*1.34*	*1.57*	*1.39*	*7.8*	*6.5*	*7.5*	*−3.3*	*−1.2*	*−2.8*
India	2.09	2.23	2.12	9.5	9.6	9.5	−8.1	−6.2	−7.6
Indonesia	0.80	1.00	0.85	9.5	8.8	9.3	−0.7	−0.3	−0.6
Korea	0.79	1.12	0.87	8.5	5.4	7.7	−1.2	0.1	−0.9
Malaysia	1.42	3.63	1.97	3.5	3.9	3.6	−6.3	0.8	−4.5
Philippines	1.40	1.39	1.40	15.0	8.4	13.3	−3.0	−1.5	−2.6
Singapore	1.57	1.22	1.48	2.9	2.3	2.8	5.2	13.1	7.2
Taiwan Prov of China	2.80	1.41	2.45	4.5	3.8	4.3	0.0	−1.9	−0.5
Thailand	0.94	1.39	1.05	5.8	4.6	5.5	−1.2	2.3	−0.3

Eastern Europe									
Hungary	0.42	4.12	2.52	12.7	23.1	15.3	−1.3	−6.1	−2.5
Poland	7.01	2.23	5.81	99.5	34.6	83.3	−2.3	−3.9	−2.7
Latin America & Caribbean (15)	3.22	2.37	3.00	251.4	110.1	216.1	−3.3	−0.8	−2.6
Argentina[e]	4.58	0.91	3.66	678.5	10.8	511.6	−5.2	0.1	−3.9
Brazil	4.35	7.46	5.13	535.9	1319.6	731.8	−0.7	−0.3	−0.6
Chile[e]	1.70	1.53	1.66	21.8	11.9	19.3	0.9	2.8	1.4
Colombia	2.20	1.97	2.15	24.5	23.3	24.2	−2.3	−0.5	−1.9
Mexico	3.72	0.69	2.96	61.7	16.8	50.5	−6.8	0.1	−5.1
Middle East & Europe (9)	2.37	1.60	2.18	22.9	13.8	20.6	−7.2	−4.3	−6.4
Egypt	6.53	3.02	5.66	17.9	12.7	16.6	−16.9	−2.8	−13.4
Israel[e]	1.92	0.53	1.57	111.1	11.3	86.1	−10.8	−3.2	−8.9
Turkey	2.98	3.14	3.02	53.3	84.0	60.9	−3.3	−4.7	−3.6

Notes: [a]Period averages, in percent.
[b]Defined as the annual change in the monetary base divided by nominal GDP, except for Argentina, Chile, Israel and Uruguay (see footnote 4).
[c]Central Government balance divided by nominal GDP.
[d]Number of countries in parentheses.
[e]Due to the presence of indexed and/or remunerated deposits in the monetary base, seigniorage was defined as the annual change in M1 divided by nominal GDP in Argentina, Chile and Uruguay, and as the change in monetary base excluding foreign currency deposits divided by nominal GDP in Israel.
Source: Authors' calculations based on IFS and WEO databases; see Appendix A.

Table 4. Central Bank Independence, Seigniorage, and Indicators of Financial Deepening in Selected Countries, 1980–1995[a]

Country	CBI Rank 1980s[b]	Seigniorage/GDP Measure		Inflation Tax Rate[e]	Real Interest Rate 1980s[f]		Money/ GDP	GDP Per Cap. (US$)[g]
		I[c]	II[d]		Average	Std. Dev.		
Denmark	1	0.50	0.22	4.8	2.7	1.4	56.9	33,034
Germany	2	0.44	0.29	3.0	2.6	0.9	59.8	29,565
United States	3	0.37	0.26	4.5	4.8	1.8	64.3	27,574
Canada	4	0.19	0.22	4.7	4.3	1.5	49.6	19,249
Norway	5	0.28	0.36	5.7	−0.2	5.1	57.9	33,490
Sweden	6	0.65	0.47	6.4	2.5	2.6	51.4	26,070
United Kingdom	7	0.20	0.25	5.7	0.7	2.1	70.0	18,986
Australia	8	0.42	0.32	5.8	3.1	2.9	49.9	19,257
France	9	0.25	0.31	*5.1*	−0.1	3.3	67.9	26,829
Hungary	10	2.52	3.69	12.7	−1.8	2.2	44.0	4,354
Spain	11	1.61	1.30	7.7	0.9	2.4	76.1	14,465
New Zealand	12	0.12	0.23	*7.5*	2.1	4.2	47.9	16,650
Greece	13	2.37	1.70	11.6	−3.1	4.1	49.9	10,947
Thailand	14	1.05	0.44	5.1	6.0	5.0	61.4	2,728
Nigeria	15	2.10	2.19	20.3	−6.1	9.2	27.S	692
Tanzania	16	3.01	3.00	23.0	n.a.	n.a.	35.S	146
Kenya	17	1.71	1.31	12.8	0.1	4.8	31.6	302
Philippines	18	1.40	*0.95*	11.1	−0.3	10.9	32.6	1,072

No.	Country							
19	Nepal	1.64	0.89	8.3	n.a.	n.a.	26.3	207
20	Ghana	2.38	2.42	26.2	n.a.	n.a.	15.4	363
21	India	2.12	1.30	8.7	−0.3	2.7	45.7	345
22	Zimbabwe	1.26	1.07	14.7	−4.6	*5.5*	28.9	541
23	Egypt	*5.66*	5.10	14.1	n.a.	n.a.	86.3	1,000
24	Israel	1.57	1.60	33.1	n.a.	n.a.	78.8	15,689
25	South Africa	0.68	0.58	11.9	*5.4*	n.a.	*55.9*	3,153
26	Indonesia	0.85	0.52	8.5	n.a.	6.1	29.8	1,034
27	Costa Rica	4.18	3.32	18.1	n.a.	n.a.	41.4	2,516
28	Korea	0.87	0.51	6.8	4.0	4.6	37.5	10,146
29	Uruguay	2.88	3.06	37.2	4.6	9.1	48.6	5,598
30	Zambia	2.86	3.04	33.8	−14.8	9.2	27.6	420
31	Peru	5.70	*5.57*	52.7	−36.9	22.6	19.9	2,363
32	Mexico	2.96	3.22	29.6	−6.2	13.3	26.1	3,164
33	Venezuela	1.82	2.00	21.8	−7.3	12.8	33.3	3,529
34	Turkey	3.02	2.98	36.5	−5.0	14.5	26.5	2,696
35	Botswana	1.81	0.95	10.7	n.a.	n.a.	26.6	2,806

(Continued)

Table 4. (*Continued*)

Country	CBI Rank 1980s[b]	Seigniorage/GDP Measure		Inflation Tax Rate[e]	Real Interest Rate 1980s[f]		Money/ GDP	GDP Per Cap. (US$)[g]
		I[c]	II[d]		Average	Std. Dev.		
Chile	36	1.66	1.34	15.9	7.8	9.6	37.0	4,868
Brazil	37	5.13	5.26	72.1	−5.2	8.3	29.3	4,370
Argentina	38	3.66	3.66	*55.5*	−16.1	15.S	19.3	8,139

Notes: [a]Period averages, in percent; unless otherwise indicated.

[b]Ranking of central banks by overall index of independence during the 1980s as reported in Cukierman (1992, Table 21.1). Countries in the list ranked from high to low overall central bank independence.

[c]Annual change in the monetary base divided by nominal GDP, except for Argentina, Chile, Israel and Uruguay (see Table 3, footnote e).

[d]Annual monetary base multiplied by the inflation tax rate and divided by nominal GDP, except for Argentina, Chile and Uruguay (where annual Ml was used) and Israel (where foreign currency deposits were excluded from the monetary base).

[e]Defined as: [CPI inflation/(100+CPI inflation)], a bounded measure of the real losses on holdings of money balances.

[f]Geometric mean and standard deviation calculated from raw series on annual *ex post* real returns on domestic currency deposits in the banking system in the period 1980–1989 reported in Easterly *et al.* (1994); raw series for Hungary, New Zealand, United States and Uruguay obtained from other sources (see Appendix I).

[g]Nominal GDP in current US dollars of 1995 divided by total population.

Sources: CBI rank from Cukierman (1992, Table 21.1); annual data on real interest rates from Easterly *et al.* (1994 Statistical Appendix, Table A.4); all other series: authors' calculations based on IFS and WEO databases.

The Scope for Inflation Targeting in Developing Countries 365

in question. Following Fischer (1982), the annual revenues from seigniorage in each country were calculated as the yearly change in the monetary base divided by nominal GDP;[28] the annual rate of inflation was defined as the percentage change in the average CPI from 1 year to the next; and the annual estimate of the fiscal deficit was computed as the overall balance of the central government divided by nominal GDP.[29]

The table reveals at least four interesting regularities: First, as expected, the reliance on seigniorage is considerably higher in developing countries than in advanced economies. Whereas in the former the average annual recourse to seigniorage ranges from 1.4 to 3 percent of GDP, depending on the region, in advanced economies annual average revenues from seigniorage in the last 16 years have been consistently below 1 percent of GDP.

Second, the aggregate relationship between average fiscal deficits, inflation and seigniorage varies considerably across regions and country groups. For example, the (average) fiscal deficits in Asia and Latin America are quite similar, but the differences in their inflation performance and recourse to seigniorage are staggering. Also, fiscal deficits in Africa are twice the size of those in Latin America, but their average inflation and reliance on seigniorage are much lower. Similarly, the average fiscal deficit in advanced economies is higher than the average for Asia and Latin America — and only 20 percent lower than the average for Africa — even though they have by far the

---

[28]Despite its shortcomings (Drazen, 1985; Fry *et al.*, 1996), this simple measure of seigniorage remains widely used. We calculated a second measure closer to the concept of government revenues from the erosion of real money holdings, but the overall picture of Table 3 did not change much. Table 4 presents the estimates of this alternative measure of seigniorage for a subset of countries. For broadly comparable cross-country evidence on the revenues from seigniorage during a similar period see Cukierman *et al.* (1992), De Haan *et al.* (1993), Flood and Mussa (1994), Easterly *et al.* (1994) and Fry *et al.* (1996).

[29]More satisfactory measures, such as the overall balance for the general government or for the non-financial public sector, were not available for many countries on a comparable basis. Use of central government data is likely to underestimate the size of fiscal imbalances, especially in federal states or in countries with large and inefficient public enterprizes.

366   *Paul R. Masson, Miguel A. Savastano and Sunil Sharma*

best record in terms of inflation and the lowest reliance on seigniorage. The apparent lack of association among these three variables is partly due to the measurement problems (especially for the fiscal deficit) but, more fundamentally, is a reflection of the nonlinearities that characterize the relationship between fiscal deficits and inflation (Bruno, 1995a; Easterly *et al.*, 1994) and, hence, of the shortcomings of these indicators as proxies for the degree of fiscal dominance.

Third, for the period as a whole, the average reliance on seigniorage in the seven countries that adopted an IT framework was similar to the average for all advanced economies, but higher than in the US and Germany. Also, as noted earlier, the improvement in the inflation performance in those countries following the adoption of IT was commensurate with the general trend toward lower inflation observed in all advanced economies in the 1990s.

And fourth, the average reliance on seigniorage and the inflation performance in a number of high-middle income developing countries (such as Indonesia, Korea, and, more recently, Israel, Mexico and South Africa) do not seem much different from the averages recorded by the seven IT countries in the period that preceded the adoption of the IT framework.

Table 4 presents data for those countries used in the calculation of the group averages of Table 3 for which Cukierman (1992) estimates an overall index of central bank independence for the decade of the 1980s.[30] Aside from the ranking of overall CBI, the table contains two alternative measures of the average annual recourse to seigniorage in each country between 1980 and 1995, a measure of the average tax rate on money holdings during the same period, and four proximate indicators of the degree of financial deepening: the average ratio of broad money to GDP, the level of GDP per capita in 1995, and,

---

[30]The index is based on the predicted values of the rate of depreciation of the domestic currency (a monotonic transformation of the rate of CPI inflation) for the 1980s obtained from regressions that included indicators of legal independence and turnover rates of central bank governors as explanatory variables. Different regressions were used for industrial and developing countries. This procedure yields an "inflation-based" overall index (and ranking) of CBI; see Cukierman (1992, Chapter 21).

The Scope for Inflation Targeting in Developing Countries   367

for 30 of the 38 countries, the (geometric) average and the standard deviation of the *ex post* real return on domestic currency deposits in the banking system in the period 1980–1989.[31]

The data presented in the table indicate that there is an inverse relationship between the degree of central bank independence, the reliance on seigniorage and the tax rate on money holdings (the coefficient of correlation between the CBI index and the two measures of seigniorage is about −0.6, while that between the CBI index and the inflation tax rate is −0.7). The sign and size of these simple correlations are not altogether surprising, however, considering that the CBI index was derived from the predicted values of regressions that used the inflation tax rate as the dependent variable (see footnote 30). The relationship between the CBI index and the indicators of financial deepening is somewhat more interesting: for this group of countries, the degree of central bank independence is *positively* correlated with the average level of real interest rates on bank deposits, the average ratio of broad money to GDP and the level of GDP per capita, and *inversely* related, and strongly so, with the volatility of real interest rates.[32] These findings are suggestive of the existence of some type of relationship between the degree of financial development and the central bank's ability to conduct an independent monetary policy or, equivalently, of the incompatibility of financial repression and central bank independence.

The above correlations can also be seen as consistent with the "political constituencies view" of central bank independence.[33] According to this view, both the rate of inflation and the degree of CBI in any given country are determined *simultaneously* by the

---

[31] The different time periods covered by the indicators of CBI and real interest rates (the 1980s) and by the other five variables in the table (averages for 1980–1995 in four cases, plus the GDP per capita in 1995) are a consequence of the lack of comparable data on the former variables for the 1990s. The results in the table were broadly similar when we used the averages for 1980–1991 for the two measures of seigniorage, the inflation tax rate and the ratio of broad money to GDP, and the level of GDP per capita in 1991.

[32] The corresponding correlation coefficients between the CBI index and those four variables are, respectively, 0.45, 0.56, 0.71 and −0.78.

[33] See Goodman (1991), Posen (1993, 1995) and Mas (1995).

interaction of political constituencies, and this equilibrium cannot be altered simply by designing legislation or institutions aimed at securing and preserving monetary stability. In particular, supporters of this view argue that the large inverse correlation between inflation and CBI commonly found in studies on industrial countries (and also apparent in Table 4) is spurious, as it is driven by a key excluded factor which they refer to as effective financial sector opposition to inflation (FOI). The essence of the argument is that financial intermediaries are strongly averse to inflation, because their main activity consists of transforming short-term liabilities into longer term largely non-marketable assets, and therefore will tend to use their political clout to oppose inflationary policies, including by lobbying for greater central bank autonomy. In the case of developing countries, the argument goes, FOI typically tends to be much weaker due to a number of structural features related to the high degree of fiscal dominance and financial repression — e.g., proliferation of inefficient public banks undertaking a variety of quasi-fiscal activities, extensive regulation of financial market transactions — and to the equally high degree of polarization and political instability.[34] These features produce a small and uncompetitive private financial sector that cannot offer an effective counterweight to competing interest groups that favor expansionary fiscal and monetary policies, hence leading to high inflation and low CBI (Mas, 1995).

Whether the fundamental determinants of CBI are to be found on the type of political-economy considerations stressed by the advocates of the FOI argument or on the more conventional view that sees the attainment of monetary stability as the end result of a drawn-out process of economic and financial market reform remains an open question. What seems clear from both the preceding discussion

---

[34]In principle, political instability may have two opposing effects: lower the incentive for banks to invest in FOI (Posen, 1993), while at the same time provide greater incentive for any administration to push for a more independent central bank to tie the hands of the successor government (Goodman, 1991). Cukierman et al. (1992) find that political instability is associated with higher recourse to seigniorage and inflation, suggesting that the former effect probably dominates.

The Scope for Inflation Targeting in Developing Countries   369

and the existing empirical evidence is that in a large number of developing countries (and transition economies) fiscal dominance and poor financial market infrastructure severely constrain the scope for an independent monetary policy. In fact, for most of these countries attainment of effective instrument independence by the central bank will most likely have to await a comprehensive public sector reform that broadens the tax base and reduces the government's reliance on seigniorage and other revenues from financial repression, the abatement of inflation to at least low double-digit levels, and the revamping of the infrastructure of the banking and financial systems (Begg, 1996; Fry *et al.*, 1996).

Nonetheless, it also follows from the previous discussion and evidence that the constraints on monetary policy imposed by fiscal dominance, high inflation and financial repression are considerably less severe for some high-middle income developing countries, especially in the 1990s.[35] For these countries, the obstacles to conducting monetary policy in a manner consistent with IT seem less related to considerations of feasibility, and more with the authorities' willingness to give clear priority to inflation reduction over all other objectives of monetary policy and with their ability to convey their policy objectives to the public in a credible and transparent manner. The discussion below elaborates on these themes.

4.2. *Conflicts with Other Policy Objectives*

In developing countries with reasonably well-functioning financial markets, moderate to low levels of inflation, and no clear symptoms of

---

[35]Paradoxically, many of the countries that would seem the most likely candidates to belong to this group are those at or near the bottom of the list in Table 4 — i.e., Chile, Brazil, Mexico, South Africa and Israel. This is largely a reflection of the fact that the CBI index used in Table 4 captures only the dismal inflation performance of these economies in the 1980s and leaves out the successful disinflation that many of them have achieved in the 1990s. More fundamentally, however, the odd ranking of these (and other) countries in Table 4 illustrates the earlier noted difficulties in trying to classify developing economies by some "objective" indicator of their scope for independent monetary policy or their stage of financial development.

fiscal dominance, the scope for conducting an independent monetary policy becomes crucially dependent on the exchange rate regime chosen by the authorities and on the extent of capital mobility. The interaction among these three factors is far more complex in practice than what is predicted by the standard Mundell–Fleming model. According to this model, the scope for independent monetary policy in a small open economy is inversely related to the degree of fixity of the nominal exchange rate and to the degree of capital mobility. For many emerging market economies, however, it has become increasingly difficult to evaluate these two basic parameters. Fixed exchange rates have become a rarity and have given way to a variety of flexible, but still managed, exchange rate arrangements (Obstfeld and Rogoff (1995)), while access to international capital markets has increased dramatically in line with a substantial rise in the volatility of capital flows (Calvo *et al.* (1995)). Since these two trends have opposite effects on a country's scope for conducting monetary policy, it is not easy to ascertain *a priori* the net effect of their joint occurrence. But the complications do not end here. The more flexible exchange rate arrangements adopted by many of these countries do not seem to have led their authorities to attach a much lower weight to exchange rate objectives (nominal or real) and/or to stop using the exchange rate to guide monetary policy settings. In addition, the processes of stabilization and financial reform undertaken by several of these countries since the mid-1980s seem to have increased money demand instability (Arrau *et al.* (1995)), hence reducing the informational content of monetary aggregates.

Taken together, the above developments have made the tasks of conducting and evaluating monetary policy in these economies quite challenging. In fact, even at a conceptual level there seems to be less agreement than before on issues as central as the scope for (and effectiveness of) monetary policy in these countries (Frankel (1994)) or the set of indicators that should be looked at to assess the stance of monetary policy at a specific juncture (Pill and Pradhan (1995); Leiderman and Bufman (1996)). Moreover, at times it is not clear whether there is consensus that the overriding goal of monetary policy for (some of) these economies should be the control

The Scope for Inflation Targeting in Developing Countries   371

of inflation over the medium term or whether the prevailing view is that the primary goal of monetary policy should be to strike some type of balance between the (potentially) competing objectives of external competitiveness and inflation reduction on a period-by-period basis.[36]

A further complicating factor has been the lack of a coherent analytical framework for assessing *empirically* the effects of monetary policy and forecasting inflation in these countries. This tends to impair both the central banks' capacity to formulate monetary policy and the external observers' ability to assess monetary developments. Judging from the studies available, the estimation of "monetary policy reaction functions" of the type developed in the 1970s for the "typical" small open economy remains, by and large, the most popular tool for gauging empirically the effects of monetary policy in developing countries.[37] However, the main purpose of these exercises is to obtain estimates of the "offset coefficient" (i.e., the fraction of the increase in net domestic credit that is offset by a contemporaneous decline in net foreign assets) and hence assess the scope for sterilization, not to model the entire monetary transmission mechanism or the process of inflation determination. Empirical research on the former is in its infancy for developing countries. For the latter, empirical studies for these countries typically rely on simple variants of the monetarist model (where inflation is essentially determined by the disequilibria in the money market), the "fiscalist" model (where budget deficits are considered an independent driving

---

[36]The role of monetary policy in dealing with the short-run trade-off between the real exchange rate and inflation has been one of the main themes of the recent (and related) debates on the appropriate response to surges in capital inflows and on the causes of currency crises in emerging markets. It is beyond the scope of this chapter to list all the important contributions to these ongoing debates. For some representative, and contrasting, views of the main issues involved, and their implications for monetary policy, the reader is referred to Schadler *et al.* (1993), Calvo *et al.* (1994, 1995), Frankel (1994), Obstfeld (1995), Dornbusch *et al.* (1995) and Leiderman and Bufman (1996).

[37]These estimates build on the seminal work by Kouri and Porter (1974); for recent applications of this methodology, see Frankel and Okongwu (1996), Fry *et al.* (1996) and Lee (1996).

force of inflation), and the Scandinavian model (where inflation is linked to wage pressures stemming from imported inflation and exchange rate changes); often, these models are amended to incorporate elements of inertia (persistence) in the inflation process.[38] None of these models commands support comparable to that obtained by natural rate models in industrial countries, where the NAIRU and the output gap are widely regarded as useful constructs,[39] or offer a clear way of testing the various possible links between instruments and targets of monetary policy.

All these factors have a bearing on the possible adoption of inflation targeting by those emerging market economies not constrained by problems of fiscal dominance and/or financial repression. As discussed in Section II, an effective IT framework requires an unequivocal indication that the inflation target takes priority over all other monetary objectives, and a forward-looking operating procedure that uses inflation forecasts as the main intermediate target of monetary policy. These conditions are difficult to satisfy in contexts where nominal or real exchange rate stability is also a stated or implicit objective of monetary policy (as is the case, for example, when the authorities announce or adopt *de facto* a target level, path, or band for the exchange rate) or where the understanding of the empirical links between instruments and targets of monetary policy is rudimentary. The first of these problems is probably the hardest to overcome. As suggested earlier, the main difficulties stem from the lack of credible means to convey to the public the authorities' ranking of policy objectives, and from the different degree of visibility of exchange rate and inflation targets. The former implies that the authorities will be able to reveal their priorities only under the

---

[38]For recent examples of the various approaches to modeling inflation in developing countries, see Bruno (1993, 1995a), Dornbusch *et al.* (1990), Edwards (1995), Fry *et al.* (1996) and Leiderman (1993).

[39]A number of recent empirical studies have re-examined the applicability of this type of models to developing countries (e.g., Coe and McDermott (1997)). The question of whether these models will (or should) become the standard approach to modeling inflation in these economies, however, remains under dispute.

The Scope for Inflation Targeting in Developing Countries 373

pressure of circumstances for instance, through their policy response to situations where the nominal exchange rate approaches an edge of the exchange rate band. The latter implies that, in "normal" times, there will be a tendency for the easily monitored exchange rate target to become the focal point of private sector expectations and public debate, to the detriment of the less visible inflation target.

The experience of Israel is instructive in this regard. For a number of years, Israel has used both inflation and exchange rate targets in the formulation of its monetary policy.[40] Specifically, since late 1991 the Bank of Israel has announced a year in advance a rate of crawl of the central parity of the exchange rate band that is approximately equal to the difference between the authorities' inflation target for that year and an estimate of the inflation rate of Israel's main trading partners over the same horizon. The *ex ante* consistency between the inflation and exchange rate targets, however, has been under severe strain on many occasions throughout the episode due, in particular, to unexpectedly large inflows of foreign capital. With limited scope for sterilized intervention, due to its high fiscal cost, the pressures for exchange rate appreciation brought about by the capital inflows have forced the Bank of Israel to confront *ex post* the trade-off between easing the stance of monetary policy to arrest the appreciation or maintaining interest rates at the levels deemed consistent with the inflation target. Most of the times, the policy dilemma has eventually been resolved in favor of the inflation target and the exchange rate band has been widened gradually, but sometimes only after a period of heavy intervention. Thus, the record so far has been mixed, both in terms of inflation reduction and of the overall credibility of the monetary policy framework. Furthermore, the potential for conflict remains. Leiderman and Bufman (1996) argue that Israel's record is partly explained by the roundabout manner in which the inflation target was adopted; in their words: "... There was considerable ambiguity in Israel about the status of the inflation target, i.e., about whether it was an official forecast

---

[40]See Bufman *et al.* (1995) and Leiderman and Bufman (1996).

or a binding policy commitment; this ambiguity may have been due in part to lack of policy transparency when the targets were first adopted" (p. 101). They go on to conclude that: "In various important cases... a conflict may develop between policies required for defending a currency band and those required for achieving the inflation target. On balance, then we would suggest treating these options as *alternatives...*" (pp. 120–121, italics added).

We agree with their conclusions. More generally, we think that as long as an inflation target coexists with other objectives of monetary policy and the central bank lacks the means to convey to the public its policy priorities and its operating procedures in a credible and transparent manner, a degree of tension between the inflation target and the other policy objectives will be unavoidable. In such circumstances, the benefits from adopting a framework akin to IT will be necessarily lower and the challenges to the conduct of monetary policy posed by the conditions currently prevailing in many emerging market economies will remain unsolved.

4.3. *Specification of the Inflation Target*

On a different level, the implementation of an inflation targeting framework in a developing country will require making the same type of decisions about the specification of the inflation target and the institutional arrangements in support of the framework that were mentioned in Section 2. As has been the case in industrial economies, most of these decisions will probably have to be based on a *pragmatic assessment* of the effects that a host of factors may have on the credibility of the IT framework under specific circumstances. However, a number of features common to many developing countries suggest that in their case such assessments would be more complex in at least four areas: the choice of the level and path of the inflation target, the choice of exemptions or "escape clauses," and the treatment of administered prices.

Choosing an inflation target for the medium term presupposes that there is some notion or consensus about the optimal inflation rate or, alternatively, the operationally relevant concept of price stability for the economy in question. These considerations have guided the choice of the medium-term inflation target in those countries that have adopted an IT framework (Table 2) and, more generally, the concepts that underlie the debate on the merits of price stability in advanced economies. In most developing countries, including those with some scope for an independent monetary policy, such a consensus simply does not exist. For a variety of reasons, the benefits of low and stable inflation in these economies have rarely been quantified or related to a precise numerical value (or range) for the inflation rate. As long as this situation persists, any choice of a medium-term inflation target for these countries is bound to be arbitrary. Nonetheless, there seems to be a general presumption that developing countries should probably aim at attaining a medium-term rate of inflation that is somewhat higher than that of industrial countries (say, between 4 and 8 percent/year), and is allowed to fluctuate within a somewhat wider band to help accommodate larger supply shocks.

Even less can be said with regard to the speed at which the medium-term inflation target ought to be attained. Some argue that once developing countries have reached a rate of inflation in the moderate to low range (say, lower than 15 percent/year), they should adopt a cautious and gradual approach to further disinflation (Dornbusch and Fischer, 1993, Dornbusch et al., 1995), but others disagree. Since the opinions on this issue are intimately linked to the earlier noted differences in views about what is (should be) the primary goal of monetary policy in these economies, there are no grounds to expect that agreement on the appropriate speed of convergence to the medium-term inflation target in developing countries can be reached quickly.

The choice of price index on which to base the inflation target is also likely to be more problematic in developing countries than in industrial economies. The fact that developing countries tend to be subject to numerous and variable supply shocks would argue in favor of removing some volatile items from the "core" (headline) inflation rate used to guide monetary policy settings. However, the need to enhance the credibility and transparency of monetary policy, and the lower quality and reliability of their statistics, would argue

376   *Paul R. Masson, Miguel A. Savastano and Sunil Sharma*

for defining the target in terms of the index that is most widely used by the public to monitor price developments and form inflation expectations (typically the CPI).

Lastly, in many developing countries administered or controlled prices are an important component of aggregate price indices and, thus, of the short-run behavior of inflation. In cases like this, a proper inflation forecasting procedure would need to incorporate explicit assumptions about the timing and magnitude of changes in those prices and, hence, demand a higher degree of coordination between monetary and fiscal authorities than in situations where the large majority of prices are market-determined.

5. Concluding Remarks

This chapter has attempted to provide an analytical basis for understanding how an inflation targeting framework is applied in industrial countries, as well as a brief review of the experience of the latter with such a framework. We then proceeded to consider the framework's applicability to developing countries.

We identified what we saw as the two major prerequisites for adopting a framework of this type: a degree of independence of monetary policy, in particular, as concerns freedom from fiscal dominance; and absence of commitment to a particular level or path for the exchange rate (or for any other nominal anchor variable such as wages). We argued that a country satisfying these two requirements could choose to conduct its monetary policy in a manner consistent with inflation targeting, defined as a framework containing an explicit target for future inflation, a commitment to that target as an overriding objective, a model for predicting inflation, and an operating procedure for adjusting monetary instruments in case forecast inflation differs from its target. In many developing countries, these requirements for an effective inflation targeting strategy are not present, either because seigniorage is an important source of financing or because there is no consensus on low inflation as an overriding objective, or both. In industrial countries, inflation

The Scope for Inflation Targeting in Developing Countries 377

targeting has only been adopted from a starting point of low (less than 10 percent) inflation, considerable exchange rate flexibility, and substantial operational independence of the central bank conditions rarely found in developing countries.

The fairly stringent technical and institutional requirements of IT and its still tentative record in just a handful of industrial countries lead us to believe that the way of improving the monetary and inflation performance of developing countries may not be through the adoption of a framework akin to IT, at least not in the near term. Over time, a strengthening of their institutions may, however, make IT an attractive option for some developing countries, especially if its robustness to shocks is demonstrated in those advanced economies that have already adopted a framework of this type. In fact, it is quite possible that inflation targeting will receive increasing consideration in developing countries as high capital mobility and instability in money demand make alternative nominal anchors less feasible.

References

Arrau, P., J. de Gregorio, C. Reinhart, and P. Wickham (1995). "The Demand for Money in Developing Countries: Assessing the Role of Financial Innovation," *Journal of Development Economics*, Vol. 44.

Barro, R. (1995). "Inflation and Economic Growth, *"Bank of England Quarterly Bulletin,"* London: Bank of England.

Begg, D. (1996). "Monetary Policy in Central and Eastern Europe: Lessons After Half a Decade of Transition," IMF Working Paper, WP/96/108, Washington, DC.

Bernanke, B. and F. Mishkin (1997). "Inflation Targeting: A New Framework for Monetary Policy?" *Journal of Economic Perspectives*, Vol. 11(2).

Blake, A. and P. Westaway (1996). "Credibility and the Effectiveness of lnflation Targeting Regimes," *The Manchester School Supplement.*

Boote, A. and J. Somogyi (1991). *Economic Reform in Hungary since 1968*, IMF Occasional Paper 83, Washington, DC.

Brainard, W. (1967). "Uncertainty and the Effectiveness of Policy," *American Economic Review, Papers and Proceedings*, Vol. LVII.

Bruno, M. (1991). "High Inflation and the Nominal Anchors of an Open Economy," *Princeton Essays in International Finance*, No. 183, International Finance Section, Princeton University.

Bruno, M. (1993). *Crisis, Stabilization, and Economic Reform: Therapy by Consensus*, Oxford: Oxford University Press.

378   *Paul R. Masson, Miguel A. Savastano and Sunil Sharma*

Bruno, M. (1995a). *Inflation, Growth and Monetary Control: Non-linear Lessons-from Crisis and Recovery*, Paolo Baffi Lectures on Money and Finance, Rome: Banca d'Italia.

Bruno, M. (1995b). "Inflation and Growth in an Integrated Approach," Ch. 9 in P. Kenen (ed.), *Understanding Interdependence: The Macroeconomics of the Open Economy*, Princeton, N.J.: Princeton University Press.

Bruno, M. and W. Easterly (1995). "Inflation Crises and Long-run Growth," *NBER Working Paper 5209*, Cambridge MA.

Bufman, G., L. Leiderman, and M. Sokoler (1995). "Israel's Experience with Explicit Inflation Targets: A First Assessment." In L. Leiderman and L. Svensson (eds.), *Inflation Targets*, Chapter 10, CEPR, London.

Calvo, G. and C. Vegh (1994). Inflation Stabilization and Nominal Anchors." In R. Barth and C. Wong (eds.), *Approaches to Exchange Rate Policy: Choices for Developing and Transition Economies*, International Monetary Fund, Washington, DC.

Calvo, G., L. Leiderman, and C. Reinhart (1994). "The Capital Inflows Problem: Concepts and Issues," *Contemporary Economic* Policy, Vol. 12.

Calvo, G., L. Leiderman, and C. Reinhart (1995). "Capital Inflows to Latin America with Reference to the Asian Experience." In S. Edwards (ed.), *Capital Controls, Exchange Rates and Monetary Policy in the World Economy*, Cambridge and New York: Cambridge University Press.

Campbell, C. and W. Dougan (eds.) (1986). *Alternative Monetary Regimes*, Baltimore and London: The Johns Hopkins University Press.

Cecchetti, S. (1995). "Inflation Indicators and Inflation Policy." In B. Bemanke and J. Rotemberg (eds.), *NBER Macroeconomics Annual 1995*, Cambridge, MA: MIT Press.

Coe, D. and C. McDermott (1997). "Does the Gap Model Work in Asia?" *IMF Staff Papers*, Vol. 44(1).

Cottarelli, C. (1993). *Limiting Central Bank Credit to the Government: Theory and Practice*, IMF Occasional Paper No. 110, Washington, DC.

Cukierman, A. (1992). *Central Bank Strategy, Credibility, and Independence: Theory and Evidence*, Cambridge, MA: MIT Press.

Cukierman, A., S. Edwards, and G. Tabellini (1992). "Seigniorage and Political Instability," *American Economic Review*, Vol. 82(3).

Debelle, G. (1997). "Inflation Targeting in Practice," IMF Working Paper WP/97/35, Washington, DC.

De Haan, J., D. Zelhorst, and O. Roukens (1993). "Seigniorage in Developing Countries," *Applied Financial Economics*, Vol. 3.

Dom, J. (1987). "The Search for Stable Money: A Historical Perspective." In J. Dom, and A. Schwartz (eds) *"The Search for Stable Money: Essays on Monetary Reform,"* Chicago: The University of Chicago Press.

Dorn, J. and A. Schwartz (eds.) (1987). *The Search for Stable Money: Essays on Monetary Reform*, Chicago: The University of Chicago Press.

Dornbusch, R. (1982). "Stabilization Policies in Developing Countries: What Have We Learned?" *World Development*, Vol. 10(9).

The Scope for Inflation Targeting in Developing Countries

Dornbusch, R. and S. Fischer (1993). "Moderate Inflation," *The World Bank Economic Review*, Vol. 7(1).

Dornbusch, R., F. Sturzenegger, and H. Wolf (1990). "Extreme Inflation: Dynamics and Stabilization," *Brookings Papers on Economic Activity*, Vol. 2.

Dornbusch, R., I. Goldfajn and R. Valdes (1995). "Currency Crises and Collapses," *Brookings Papers in Economic Activity*, 2.

Drazen, A. (1995). "A General Measure of Inflation Tax Revenues," *Economic Letters*, Vol. 17.

Driffill, J., G. Mizon and A. Ulph (1990). "Costs of Inflation." In B. Friedman and F. Hahn (eds.), *Handbook of Monetary Economics*, Amsterdam: North Holland.

Easterly, W., C. Rodriguez and K. Schmidt-Hebbel (eds.) (1994). *Public Sector Deficits and Macroeconomic Performance*, New York: Oxford University Press for the World Bank.

Edwards, S. (1995). "Exchange rates, inflation and disinflation: Latin American experiences." In S. Edwards (ed.), *Capital Controls, Exchange Rates and Monetary Policy in the World Economy*, Cambridge and New York: Cambridge University Press.

Federal Reserve Bank of Kansas City (1996). *Achieving Price Stability*, proceedings from the symposium held at Jackson Hole, Wyoming, on August 29–31, 1996, Kansas City: Missouri.

Fischer, S. (1982). "Seigniorage and the Case for a National Money," *Journal of Political Economy*, Vol. 90.

Fischer, S. (1993). "The Role of Macroeconomic Factors in Growth," *Journal of Monetary Economics*, Vol. 32.

Fischer, S. (1994). "Modem Central Banking." In F. Capie, *et al.* (eds) *The Future of Central Banking*, New York: Cambridge University Press.

Fischer, S. (1995). "The Unending Search for Monetary Salvation," In B. Bemanke and J. Rotemberg (eds.) *NBER Macroeconomics Annual 1995*, Cambridge, MA: MIT Press.

Flood, R. and M. Mussa (1994). "Issues Concerning Nominal Anchors for Monetary Policy," in T. Balino and C. Cottarelli (eds.) *Frameworks for Monetary Stability*, IMF, Washington, DC.

Frankel, J. (1994). "Sterilization of Money Inflows: Difficult (Calvo) or Easy (Reisen)?" IMF Working Paper, WP/94/159, Washington, DC.

Frankel, J. and C. Okongwu (1996). "Liberalized Portfolio Capital Inflows in Emerging Markets: Sterilization, Expectations, and the Incompleteness of Interest Rate Convergence," *International Journal of Finance and Economics*, Vol. 1.

Freedman, C. (1996). "What Operating Procedures Should be Adopted to Maintain Price Stability? — Practical Issues," in Federal Reserve Bank of Kansas City *Achieving Price Stability*, Kansas City: Missouri.

Friedman, B. (1975). "Targets, Instruments, and Indicators of Monetary Policy," *Journal of Monetary Economics*, Vol. 1.

380 *Paul R. Masson, Miguel A. Savastano and Sunil Sharma*

Friedman, B. (1994). "Intermediate Targets versus Information Variables as Operating Guides for Monetary Policy." In J.A.H. de Beaufort Wijnholds, *et al.* (eds.), *A Framework for Monetary Stability*, The Netherlands: Kluwer Academic Publishers.

Fry, M. (1993). "The Fiscal Abuse of Central Banks," IMF Working Paper, WP/93/58, Washington, DC.

Fry, M., C. Goodhart, and A. Almeida (1996). *Central Banking in Developing Countries: Objectives, Activities and Independence*, London and New York: Routledge.

Giovannini, A. and M. de Melo (1993). "Government Revenue from Financial Repression," *American Economic Review*, Vol. 83.

Goldstein, M., and P. Turner (1996). "Banking Crises in Emerging Economies: Origins and Policy Options," BIS Economic Papers No. 46, Basie.

Goodhart, C. (1995). *The Central Bank and the Financial System*, Cambridge MA: MIT Press.

Goodman, J. (1991). "The Politics of Central Bank Independence," *Comparative Politics*.

Green, J. (1996). "Inflation Targeting: Theory and Policy Implications," *IMF Staff Papers*, Vol. 43(4).

Haldane, A. (1995a). "Inflation Targets," *Bank of England Quarterly Bulletin*, London: Bank of England.

Haldane, A. (1995b). "Introduction," Chapter 1 in A. Haldane (ed.) *Targeting Inflation: A Conference of Central Banks on the Use of Inflation Targets Organised by the Bank of England*, London: Bank of England.

Haldane, A. (1996). "Some Thoughts on Inflation Targeting," Working Paper, London: Bank of England.

Havrilesky, T. and J. Boorman (eds.) (1976). *Current Issues in Monetary Theory and Policy*, Arlington Heights Ill.: Harlan Davidson Inc.

Heymann, D. and A. Leijonhufvud (1995). *High Inflation*, Oxford: Oxford University Press.

Holbrook, R. (1972). "Optimal Economic Policy and the Problem of Instrument Instability," *American Economic Review*, Vol. LXII.

International Monetary Fund (1995). *The Adoption of Indirect Instruments of Monetary Policy*, IMF Occasional Paper No. 126, Washington, DC.

International Monetary Fund (1996). *World Economic Outlook*, Washington, DC.

Kaminsky, G. and C. Reinhart (1996). "The Twin Crises: The Causes of Banking and Balance of Payments Problems," Board of Governors of the Federal Reserve System, mimeo.

Kiguel, M. and P. Neumeyer (1995). "Seigniorage and Inflation: The case of Argentina," *Journal of Money, Credit, and Banking*, Vol. 27(3), pp. 672–682.

King, M. (1996). "How Should Central Banks Reduce Inflation? — Conceptual Issues," in Federal Reserve Bank of Kansas City *Achieving Price Stability*, Kansas City: Missouri.

Kouri, P. and M. Porter (1974). "International Capital Flows and Portfolio Equilibrium," *Journal of Political Economy*, Vol. 82.

The Scope for Inflation Targeting in Developing Countries   381

Lane, T., M. Griffiths, and A. Prati (1995). "Can Inflation Targets Help Make Monetary Policy Credible?" *Finance and Development*, Washington, DC.

Lee, J.Y. (1996). "Implications of a Surge in Capital Inflows: Available Tools and Consequences for the Conduct of Monetary Policy," IMF Working Paper, WP/96/53, Washington, DC.

Leiderman, L. (1993). *Inflation and Disinflation: The Israeli Experiment*, Chicago and London: The University of Chicago Press.

Leiderman, L. and G. Bufman (1996). "Searching for Nominal Anchors in Shock-Prone Economies in the 1990s: Inflation Targets and Exchange Rate Bands," in R. Hausmann and H. Reisen (eds.,) *Securing Stability and Growth in Latin America*, Paris: OECD and IDB.

Leiderman, L. and L. Svensson (1995). "Introduction," Chapter 1 in L. Leiderman and L. Svensson (eds.) *Inflation Targets*, CEPR, London.

Leijonhufvud, A. (1984). "Constitutional Constraints on the Monetary Powers of Government," In R. McKenzie (ed.) *Constitutional Economics*, Lexington Mass.: Lexington Books, DC. Heath & Co.

Levine, R. (1997). "Financial Development and Economic Growth: Views and Agenda," *Journal of Economic Literature*, Vol. 35.

Lindsey, D. (1986). "The Monetary Regime of the Federal Reserve System," In C. Campbell and W. Dougan (eds.) *Alternative Monetary Regimes*, Baltimore and London: The Johns Hopkins University Press.

Lucas, R. (1976). "Econometric Policy Evaluation: A Critique," In K. Brunner and A. Meltzer (eds.) *The Phillips Curve and Labor Markets, Carnegie-Rochester Conference Series on Public Policy*, Vol. I.

Mas, I. (1995). "Central Bank Independence: A Critical View from a Developing Country Perspective," *World Development*, Vol. 23(10).

McCallum, B. (1995). "Two Fallacies Concerning Central-Bank Independence," *American Economic Review, Papers and Proceedings*.

McCallum, B.T. (1996a). "Inflation Targeting in Canada, New Zealand, Sweden, The United Kingdom, and in General," NBER Working Paper 5579, Cambridge MA.

McCallum, B. (1996b). "Commentary: How Should Central Banks Reduce Inflation? — Conceptual Issues," (Comment on M. King), in Federal Reserve Bank of Kansas City *Achieving Price Stability*, Kansas City: Missouri.

McCallum, B. (1997). "Issues in the Design of Monetary Policy Rules," unpublished mimeo, Carnegie Mellon University.

McKinnon, R. (1991). *The Order of Economic Liberalization: Financial Control in the Transition to a Market Economy*, Baltimore: The Johns Hopkins University Press.

Mishkin, F. and A. Posen (1997). "Inflation Targeting: Lessons from Four Countries," *Federal Reserve Bank of New York Economic Policy Review*, August.

Obstfeld, M. (1995). "International Currency Experience: New Lessons and Lessons Relearned," *Brookings Papers on Economic Activity*, Vol. 1.

Obstfeld, M. and K. Rogoff (1995). "The Mirage of Fixed Exchange Rates," *Journal of Economic Perspectives*, Vol. 9(4), Fall.

Persson, T. and G. Tabellini (1990). *Macroeconomic Policy, Credibility and Politics*, London: Harwood Publishers.

Phelps, E. (1973). "Inflation in a Theory of Public Finance," *Swedish Journal of Economics*, Vol. 5(1).

Pill, H. and M. Pradhan (1995). "Financial Indicators and Financial Change in Africa and Asia," IMF Working Paper, WP/95/123, Washington, DC.

Posen, A. (1993). "Why Central Bank Independence Does Not Cause Low Inflation," *Finance and the International Economy: 7*, The Amex Bank Review Prize Essays.

Posen, A. (1995). "Central Bank Independence and Disinflationary Credibility: A Missing Link," Federal Reserve Bank of New York, Staff Report, No. 1, May.

Rama, M and A. Forteza (1993). "Indización de Activos Financieros y Ahorro Privado: la experiencia Uruguaya," in *Indizacion de Activos Financieros: Experiencias Latinoamericanas*, CEPAL, Chile.

Romer, C and D. Romer (1996). "Institutions for Monetary Stability," *NBER Working Paper* No. 5557, Cambridge, MA.

Sarel, M. (1996). "Non-linear Effects of Inflation on Economic Growth," *IMF Staff Papers*, Vol. 43(1).

Sargent, T. and N. Wallace (1981). "Some Unpleasant Monetarist Arithmetic," *Federal Reserve Bank of Minneapolis Quarterly Review*, Fall.

Schadler, S., M. Carkovic, A. Bennett, and R. Kahn (1993). *Recent Experiences with Surges in Capital Inflows*, IMF Occasional Paper 108, Washington, DC.

Summers, L. (1996). "Commentary: Why Are Central Banks Pursuing Long-Run Price Stability?" (comment on S. Fischer), in Federal Reserve Bank of Kansas City *Achieving Price Stability*, Kansas City: Missouri.

Svensson, L. (1996). "Commentary: How Should Monetary Policy Respond to Shocks While Maintaining Long-Run Price Stability? — Conceptual Issues," (comment on J. Taylor) in Federal Reserve Bank of Kansas City *Achieving Price Stability*, Kansas City: Missouri.

Svensson, L. (1997a). "Inflation Targeting: Extensions," IIES Seminar Paper No. 625, Stockholm, February, (also NBER Working Paper No. 5962).

Svensson, L. (1997b). "Inflation Forecast Targeting: Implementing and Monitoring Inflation Targets," *European Economic Review*, Vol. 41,

Taylor, J. (1996). "How Should Monetary Policy Respond to Shocks While Maintaining Long-Run Price Stability? — Conceptual Issues," in Federal Reserve Bank of Kansas City *Achieving Price Stability*, Kansas City: Missouri.

Tobin, J. (1983). "Monetary Policy: Rules, Targets and Shocks," *Journal of Money, Credit and Banking*, Vol. 15.

Vegh, C. (1992). "Stopping High Inflation: An Analytical Overview," *IMF Staff Papers*, Vol. 39(3).

The Scope for Inflation Targeting in Developing Countries

Walsh, C. (1995). "Recent Central Bank Reforms and the Role of Price Stability as the Sole Objective of Monetary Policy." In B. Bemanke and J. Rotemberg (eds.), *NBER Macroeconomics Annual 1995*, Cambridge, MA: MIT Press.

Willett, T., R. Burdekin, R. Sweeney and C. Wihlborg (eds) (1995). *Establishing Monetary Stability in Emerging Market Economies*, Boulder, Colorado: Westview Press.

Yeager, L. (ed.) (1962). *In Search of a Monetary Constitution*, Cambridge, Mass: Harvard University Press.

Chapter 11

Are Bygones Not Bygones?
Modeling Price-Level Targeting
with an Escape Clause and Lessons
from the Gold Standard*

Paul R. Masson and Malik D. Shukayev

Like the gold standard, price-level targeting (PT) involves not letting past deviations of inflation be bygones; both regimes return the price level (or price of gold) to its target. The experience of suspension of the gold standard in World War I and resumption in the 1920s (for some countries at a different parity) is reviewed. It suggests that, in practice, PT might operate with an escape clause that would allow rebasing of the price target in the face of large shocks. Using a calibrated general equilibrium model, we show that such an escape clause can produce multiple equilibria. For some parameterizations, there is a low credibility equilibrium (with high expectation of a reset) associated with high output volatility and frequent resets. These problems reduce, or reverse, the expectational advantage PT has over inflation targeting.

---

*This chapter originally appeared in *Journal of Macroeconomics* (2011), 33(2), 162–175. At time of writing, both authors were affiliated with the Bank of Canada, Shukayev as staff member, Masson as Special Adviser to the Governor.

1. Introduction

Unlike inflation targeting (IT), price-level targeting (PT), does not let bygones be bygones. Shocks to supply or demand, even if permanent, are not allowed to have permanent effects on the price level, but have to be reversed by the central bank. In models where monetary policy is set under discretion, delegating a PT objective to the central bank gives an effective commitment device to the monetary authority. If the delegation is credible, it equips policy makers with an ability to influence private inflation expectations. This influence over inflation expectations has been identified as an advantage of PT, because it produces an extra stabilizing effect on inflation (Svensson, 1999; Vestin, 2006). A shock leading to temporarily higher inflation than target induces the expectation that inflation will be below the target in the future, since its price level effects will have to be reversed. Lower expected future inflation has a moderating effect on current inflation. Under IT, in contrast, a positive inflation shock would only induce an expectation of an eventual decline back to the target rate for inflation.

However, the PT regime is more constraining by the very fact that even temporary inflation shocks will continue to affect monetary policy until they are completely reversed. As a result of this continuing effect, it seems likely that there may be circumstances in which the regime might be temporarily suspended, or even abandoned. What might those circumstances be? Here the experience under the gold standard may provide some guidance. The peg to gold was suspended in several earlier wars and at the outset of WWI.[1] In the course of the 1920s, most of the major developed countries returned to the gold standard, in many cases at the pre-war parity, but in others — such as France and Belgium — at a depreciated rate. Finally, the world suspended the gold standard during the Great Depression, only re-establishing a link to gold in the form of the gold exchange standard after WWII, at a depreciated dollar rate.

---

[1]Bordo and Kydland (1995) also argue that the pre-1914 gold standard operated as a contingent rule under which the authorities could abandon the fixed price for gold during an emergency (such as war).

The above reasoning suggests that modeling PT as a permanent and immutable regime, with a target price chosen once and for all, may not be realistic. Because PT embodies the requirement to offset past shocks, it may be more difficult to accommodate other objectives within the regime. Therefore, it may be more important to consider the possibility the regime could be temporarily, or even permanently, abandoned, or the price-target reset. This might involve explicit or implicit escape clauses. In some countries, for instance, inflation targeting is operated subject to "caveats," so that targets do not have to be met in the case of large oil price or international financial shocks (as in South Africa). In others, e.g. the UK, the Governor of the Bank of England can explain to the government the reasons why the inflation target was not met, implicitly acknowledging that unforeseen circumstances may make it impossible or undesirable to do so. Alternatively, the government could simply override the delegation of a constant price target, writing off past overshoots. In Canada, for instance, the Minister of Finance can issue a directive to the Bank of Canada if it judges that the Bank's policy needs to be changed. Such mechanisms may be more necessary with a price-level target, because it does not allow bygones to be bygones.

The implicit or explicit escape clauses under PT are just another manifestation of our maintained assumption that society as a whole cares about the variability of inflation and not about price level variability. As a result it cannot commit fully to implementing price level targeting and thus, the credibility of the PT delegation may come under question. It needs to be understood that we are not trying to model optimal delegation, but rather considering the effect of a particular type of delegation to the central bank, namely to pursue a price-level target. This is a relevant issue, which has been advocated by Svensson and Vestin, and which is being considered in the Canadian context. We would argue on the basis of history, including that of the gold standard, that such a delegation cannot be considered irrevocable, and a natural "escape clause" exists, namely the possibility of rebasing the price target to reflect past inflation. Whether the government would explicitly establish beforehand the conditions under which that escape would be exercised is immaterial to our argument, nor is whether it is the government or the central bank that would make the decision. In the Canadian context, for instance, inflation targets are jointly agreed between the government (the Ministry of Finance) and the Governor of the Bank of Canada. In these circumstances, the central bank could internalize society's preference to let bygones be bygones, and agree with the government to rebase the price target if this seemed to be necessary to cushion large output declines.

Modeling imperfect regime credibility as involving explicit or implicit escape clauses became popular in the context of the European Monetary System crises of 1992–1993 (Obstfeld, 1996). In the EMS, changes of exchange rate parities were allowed, but discouraged. The escape clause model was based on the idea that a desirable monetary rule should have the flexibility to respond differently to large shocks (Flood and Isard, 1989). When applied to the EMS, the model included a reputational cost from abandoning the pegged rate, over and above the costs of deviating from inflation and output or employment targets. Thus, in normal times, monetary policy would ensure that the exchange rate remained within its target band. However, large positive shocks to unemployment, as occurred in many European countries in the early 1990s, gave an incentive for the authorities to abandon the peg in order to stimulate demand. An important insight from these models was that the public's expectation that a devaluation would occur exacerbated the tradeoff for the authorities, making a devaluation more likely. Thus, as Obstfeld showed, there could be self-fulfilling expectations of devaluation and indeed jumps between equilibria, depending on an exogenous change in sentiment (Obstfeld, 1996). Jeanne shows that French data support this hypothesis (Jeanne, 1997).

The implication of operating PT with an escape clause is that the stabilizing effect of the price-level target might not be so strong, since at least for a big shock there might well be some doubt as to whether the central bank would in fact reverse the price level effects. Thus, expectations of inflation would have to take into account that the central bank might suspend the price-level target, and if only temporarily, that it might adjust the price-level target to make some or all of the effect of the past shocks bygones.

In this paper, we first draw on the inter-war experience with the gold standard to argue that occasional rebasing may well accompany a target for the price level. Then we discuss in the context of PT how to model escape clauses that incorporate the possibility that the price target may be reset in the face of large shocks. The expectation that this may occur means that a strict price target is not perfectly credible, dampening some of the advantages of PT over IT (as shown by Kryvtsov *et al.* (2008) when credibility is exogenous). A model is presented where the central bank resets the targeted price level (to the latest value of the actual price level) in the face of large shocks which make it very costly to return the price-level to its unchanged target. Since the price level is an endogenous variable, the probability of resetting the target depends both on monetary policy and private expectations, and varies over the business cycle. Thus, the model endogenizes credibility. The implications of such an escape clause for PT are as follows: for a range of parameter values multiple equilibria are possible, with different levels of PT credibility. Lower credibility equilibria have a higher unconditional probability of price-target resets, raising the possibility of additional instability in inflation and output. Thus, just as in Obstfeld (1996), the public's expectation that a price target reset would occur worsens the inflation-output tradeoff faced by the Central Bank, making a price-target reset more likely. Expectations of price resets are thus self-fulfilling and jumps between equilibria are possible.

2. Gold Standard Suspension Episodes

It is useful to consider the reasons for the suspension and abandonment of the gold standard, and to assess whether they are relevant for understanding how a price-level target might work. Here we analyze the period around the time of gold standard suspension[2] at the

---

[2]Britain also imposed restrictions on the convertibility of the pound into gold in 1797, at the time of its war with France, and only resumed convertibility of specie (at the pre-war parity) in 1821 (Fetter, 1965). Bayoumi and Bordo (1998) consider the return to gold by the United States in 1879, after the Civil War,

outbreak of World War I, its resumption during the mid-1920s, and its generalized suspension during the early 1930s.

At the time of the outbreak of war in 1914, there was an increase in various controls and restrictions on the convertibility of paper currencies into gold. The war was typically financed by heavy short-term borrowing, accompanied by monetary policy easing to facilitate bond issuance. Government debt rose by a factor of 10 in Germany and the United States, relative to 1914 levels, and by a multiple of 4 in Britain and 2 in France. Thus, the threat to the gold standard became most evident after the war, when patriotic appeals and wartime restrictions could no longer keep the lid on inflation nor ensure that short-term debts would be rolled over (Eichengreen, 1992, p. 81).

European countries waited until the middle of the decade of the 1920s before resuming convertibility at a fixed gold price, the price being the pre-war parity for some countries, but not for all. Sweden was the first European country to resume the gold standard, which it did at the prewar parity in April 1924, and Britain returned to gold at its pre-war parity in April, 1925, but British prices still needed to fall and Britain suffered deflation and stagnation for the rest of the decade.

France had more severe fiscal problems than Britain, and they led France to the verge of hyperinflation (Prati, 1991). When France officially resumed the gold standard in June 1928, the value of the franc was only about 20 percent of its pre-war parity (Cassell, 1936, p. 47). By this time, all of the world's major economies were back on the gold standard, but Germany and Belgium had also depreciated relative to pre-war parities.

Starting late in 1929, the world tipped into depression, exacerbated by increasing protectionism and caused or worsened by contractionary monetary policies. Onset of severe financial crisis led countries that had remained on the gold standard to abandon it, in a desperate attempt to stave off catastrophe (Eichengreen, 1992, Chapter 9). The Credit-Anstalt crisis in Austria spread to Hungary,

---

and compare it to Britain's resumption in 1925, concluding that external factors played a role in producing different outcomes.

Germany, Britain, and Sweden in 1931. Faced with the prospect of total collapse of their banking systems, the above countries all left the gold standard in the course of the year, though it was not clear at the time that the suspension would become permanent. On April 19, 1933, President Roosevelt, in order to reflate the economy, increased the official gold price from $20.67 to $35 an ounce and suspended convertibility, which was only restored after WWII.

A major lesson from this period of operation of the gold standard is that other objectives can override the price stability target. This was certainly true when the main objective was winning a war, and restricting convertibility allowed governments to use money and short-term bond issuance as a source of war finance. The suspension of the gold standard during the Great Depression was also due to the increased importance of other objectives. Given the depths of the decline in output and the calamitous rise in unemployment, it no longer seemed essential to provide an ironclad stabilizer for prices in the form of the gold standard. It is true that this period did not see serious inflation, but nevertheless suspending the gold standard freed central banks to provide monetary stimulus in an attempt to prevent a meltdown of the financial system and to stimulate employment.[3]

3. Escape Clause Models of Price-Level Targeting

It seems intuitive that big shocks — major cataclysms like wars or a major depression — require different policy responses. How can we square this idea, and the stylized facts mentioned above, with the models that we use to evaluate policy regimes, in particular IT and PT? In the standard linear-quadratic framework, where preferences are quadratic and behavioral equations linear, the optimal feedback response to a given shock (its coefficient in a reaction function) is always the same, whatever the shock's size. That is, optimal feedback rules are also linear. This is not consistent with the stories told

---

[3]Eggertsson (2008) uses a new Keynesian model to analyze Roosevelt's policies, arguing that a regime change away from price stability to reflation of commodity prices produced a change in expectations that allowed recovery to take hold.

above, in which large shocks induce different responses compared to small shocks. Major shocks mean the essential abandonment of other objectives and a discrete change in behavior. What can explain the difference?

The convenient assumption of quadratic preferences may well be wrong. If welfare costs rise faster than the quadratic as variables deviate increasingly from their targets, then linear feedback rules would no longer be optimal. If welfare costs became very large as unemployment rose above a certain level, for instance, then other objectives like price stability would receive a zero weight at that point, thus justifying their complete neglect and the suspension of a gold standard or of a price-level targeting regime. While there are mathematical formulations that have such a property, they are often intractable. An alternative would be to introduce costs that only kick in discretely, if the policy is changed or if an endogenous variable goes outside a particular range. The escape clause models applied to the EMS have this feature. As a result, the objective function guiding the central bank is non-quadratic. A similar setup could be used to model PT.

In what follows, we introduce an escape clause into a model in which the central bank has been assigned a price-level target, but adjusts the price level path when the welfare costs of sticking to the price target exceed some particular threshold. We calculate equilibria for a range of such thresholds. Thus, we allow the CB's objective function to be non-quadratic. Society is assumed to constrain the central bank's policy discretion by assigning it a price-level targeting rule. As shown in Svensson (1999) and Vestin (2006), such a rule can increase welfare and, in some cases, approximate the first-best, commitment solution. We further assume that the CB is allowed to deviate from the delegated policy rule whenever expected welfare costs of following through with the policy rule exceed some fixed threshold. More specifically, CB is allowed to reset the price-level target (path) whenever the welfare gain from ignoring past deviations of prices from target–letting bygones be bygones–exceeds a certain threshold tolerance level. One could think of that tolerance level as parameterizing the degree of policy discretion given to the central bank. The central bank "acts in the interest of the society" when extreme circumstances call for it.

3.1. *The Dominance of PT Over IT Depends on Credibility*

Suppose, as in Svensson (1999) and Vestin (2006), that society's preferences concern the losses from variability of inflation around some constant target and the output gap, from a zero value.[4] Let

$$S_t = -\frac{1}{2}E_t \sum_{i=0}^{\infty} \beta^i \left[(\pi_{t+i} - \pi^T)^2 + \lambda y_{t+i}^2\right] \tag{1}$$

be the society's intertemporal welfare function, which is usually justified on the basis of a second-order approximation to the true welfare function. It is assumed that the central bank cannot precommit, but must operate under discretion. Society could simply delegate to the central bank the job of maximizing S_t (on a discretionary basis), which would imply certain paths for output $\{y_t^*\}$ and inflation $\{\pi_t^*\}$. This is IT. In the light of results (Svensson, 1999; Vestin, 2006), IT is dominated by a monetary policy regime in which Central Bank targets the price level to be stationary around a deterministic path given (in logs) by

$$p_t^T = \pi^T + p_{t-1}^T.$$

It would be preferable then (absent credibility issues) to assign the central bank the job of maximizing a function M_t that depends on deviations of the price level from the target price path (as well as deviations of the output gap from zero)

$$M_t = -\frac{1}{2}E_t \sum_{i=0}^{\infty} \beta^i [(p_{t+i} - p_t^T)^2 + \tilde{\lambda} y_{t+i}^2], \tag{2}$$

where $\tilde{\lambda}$ is chosen optimally by the society when assigning the objective function to the CB. This gives paths for output $\{\tilde{y}_t\}$ and

---

[4]Introducing a target greater than the natural rate introduces a suboptimal inflation bias under inflation targeting, but otherwise does not enter the analysis.

inflation $\{\tilde{\pi}_t\}$ under PT. When society's objective function S is evaluated for the IT or PT outcomes (both of them assumed to be perfectly credible and eternal), labeled by S_t^* or $\tilde{S}_t$, respectively, then it can be shown (Svensson, 1999, 2006) that

$$E_t\tilde{S}_t > E_tS_t^*.$$

However, Kryvtsov *et al.* (2008) and Yetman (2005) show that under imperfect credibility, in the sense of a non zero probability of abandonment of PT in favour of IT, the advantages of PT over IT may disappear. Let us refer to the output and price paths under imperfectly-credible PT as $\{\tilde{y}_t(\rho_t^e)\}$ and $\{\tilde{\pi}_t(\rho_t^e)\}$, respectively, where ρ_t^e is the private sector's assessment of the likelihood in period t that PT will be abandoned next period. Using a similar notation for the resulting welfare for society under imperfectly-credible PT, it can be shown that at least for some parameter values

$$E_t\tilde{S}_t(\rho_t^e) < E_tS_t^*. \tag{3}$$

This inequality would in turn justify the imperfect credibility of PT, so that $\rho = \rho^e$ could be a fixed point that was equal to both the subjective and actual probability of abandoning the regime. However, one would have to specify the circumstances under which the central bank would abandon the price-level target, and what the fallback regime would be.

3.1.1. *Delegation of monetary policy and escape clauses*

The dominance of PT over IT when there is complete credibility depends on the inability of the government or the central bank to precommit to the optimal policy. However, Rogoff (1985) proposed a partial solution to this problem, namely for society (or the government) to delegate a different rule or objective function to the central bank than society's true objective function. Thus, a more conservative central banker (in the sense of a lower welfare weight λ on the output gap in Equation (1) above), helps to correct the inflation bias in the context of a Barro–Gordon model (Barro and Gordon, 1983). A more conservative central banker produces lower mean inflation but also provides less stabilization, i.e., responds less to output shocks. On balance, this improves welfare, but as shown by Flood and Isard (1989) and Lohmann (1992), a preferable policy would be a contingent rule that kept inflation near zero except when output movements were large, since in these circumstances the need for stabilization is greater. Such a rule can be termed a "rule with an escape clause". The escape clause introduces a nonlinearity that produces an improvement relative to linear rules.

Assignment to a central banker of a welfare function weight differing from society's raises the issue of whether society has the incentive to override the delegation and fire the conservative central banker. This is the argument of McCallum (1999), who claims that delegation simply displaces the time inconsistency of the standard Barro–Gordon model, but does not change it. Alternatively, society may impose explicit costs on the central banker if she deviates from the assigned policy (such as embodied in Walsh contracts), but Jensen (1997) argues that society (i.e., the government) must also incur large costs to change the terms of the contract with the central bank. Otherwise it will have the incentive to change them and time inconsistency re-emerges.[5] Moreover, such costs cannot be arbitrarily chosen by society, but rather must correspond to some structural feature of the economy. Reputation costs can be quantified in terms of repeated games; indeed, Barro and Gordon (1983) show that a sufficiently high discount factor is sufficient to support the optimal policy in a simple version of their model.

In the current context, the problem with discretion is not the inflation bias, but rather the fact that the commitment solution, like PT but not IT, does not let inflation bygones be bygones (see Vestin, 2006, Table 1). But the advantage of PT comes through expectations reflecting the feedback of past inflation, and imperfect credibility dampens the expectations channel. We have argued, on the basis of gold standard experience, that letting bygones be bygones will sometimes be strongly preferred by society. We would argue further

---

[5]Driffill and Rotondi (2006) show that a slightly more general framework reduces the costs that society must incur to make the delegated monetary policy better than pure discretion.

that society would in some circumstances override its delegation and incur the associated costs (of reputation or otherwise). However, we will not attempt to model the delegation process nor the costs that society might incur in revoking the delegation. Instead, we will assume that the central banker, knowing that in some circumstance she will be overriden, internalizes society's desire to suspend price-level targeting when costs of doing otherwise become great.

3.2. *Rebasing the Price Target*

The above might suggest the following: society could change the delegation rule if its welfare would be improved by asking the central bank to maximize an IT-based objective function directly. It is unclear however why the reversion to IT has to be permanent; why could not society decide in the future to reverse the assignment back to PT?

An alternative setup that is both more plausible and more general would involve not abandonment of the price targeting regime, but rather rebasing the price target so that past deviations are ignored. This resembles the gold standard experience in the inter-war period, when some countries like France changed their gold parities when returning to gold after temporary suspension of the standard. It is also consistent with the suspension of gold convertibility by the United States in 1933 and its resumption after WWII at a depreciated exchange rate for the dollar. Thus, a PT regime might involve occasionally allowing bygones to be bygones, if, for the reasons argued above, reversing large shocks involves large welfare costs. In escape clause models of the EMS, this was captured by an additional term in the central bank's objective function that represented the reputation cost of abandoning the fixed exchange rate regime. However, in the current model, the central bank has no incentive to abandon the regime if it retains its objective function M_t. Instead, we assume that large enough welfare costs of returning the price level to its target trigger a resetting of the price path (letting bygones be bygones). Imperfect credibility of the price path under such PT would result from fears that the target itself would be changed to the most recent price level. Thus, the price target for period t would be

$$p_t^T = \delta_t p_{t-1} + (1 - \delta_t) p_{t-1}^T + \pi^T,$$

where $\delta_t = 0$ or 1, if the price level is maintained or reset, respectively. In deciding whether to reset the price-level target, the central bank would compare the expected value of the objective function in the two cases to judge whether the welfare costs exceeded some threshold. These two values of the objective function depend on private sector expectations regarding the possible price-target reset taking place next period: $\rho_t^e = prob(\delta_{t+1} = 1) = E_t \delta_{t+1}$. Writing the maximized values of the social welfare function S_t under each scenario we can define the conditional probability of a price-target reset in period $t + 1$ as

$$\rho_t = Pr_t\{S(\rho_t^e|\delta_{t+1} = 1) - S(\rho_t^e|\delta_{t+1} = 0) > C\}, \tag{4}$$

where C is the threshold level. In a rational expectations equilibrium, $\rho_t = \rho_t^e$.

3.3. *Implications for Policy*

Whether (4) has an equilibrium (or several) with non-zero values of ρ_t depends on the parameters, the values of the state variables, and the distribution of the shock that the central bank is assumed to react to. To be concrete, we will call this shock ϵ_t, and assume that it corresponds to a positive cost-push shock in the NKPC, so that larger ϵ_t increases the probability of abandonment. There is thus some critical value $\epsilon(\rho_t^e)$ at which the central bank chooses to reset.

$$\rho_t = Pr_t\{\epsilon_{t+1} > \epsilon(\rho_t^e)\}. \tag{5}$$

It is to be expected furthermore that greater values for ρ_t^e increase $S(\rho_t^e|\delta_t = 1) - S(\rho_t^e|\delta_t = 0)$, so $\epsilon'(\rho_t^e) < 0$. Thus, plotting the RHS of Equation (5) in (ρ_t^e, ρ_t) space gives an upward sloping curve. In this case, greater doubts about the permanence of the price level target increase the likelihood that the current shock will be greater than some critical value and the price target will be rebased. Conversely, lower ρ_t^e is self-validating, since it makes it less likely that the target price path will be abandoned. Rational expectations equilibria are given by intersections with the 45° ray from the origin.

A positive derivative of the RHS with respect to ρ_t^e with a slope greater than unity is a necessary condition for multiple equilibria for ρ_t, since the RHS must intersect the 45° ray from below. However, this is not sufficient. As shown in Jeanne (1997), the possibility of multiple equilibria depends on the position and slope of the cumulative distribution function for ϵ_t. The case of multiple equilibria then opens the door to self-fulfilling crises: if private agents doubt that the central bank will continue with the price-level target, then they can make it more costly for the bank to do so, thus bringing about a rebasing of the target. Conversely, if confidence is high, it will be easy for the central bank to continue with the price-level target, since expectations of a return to the price level path will make it unnecessary to surprise the market in order to achieve it.

4. A New-Keynesian Model of PT with Price-target Rebasing

In this section, we present a New-Keynesian model of a PT regime, in which the CB has the option of resetting the price target whenever the expected social cost of not doing so (evaluated from that point in time onward) exceeds a certain tolerance level, denoted by $C > 0$. We think of that option as the discretion given to the bank "to act in the interest of the society" if circumstances are such that trying to return the price level to the (unchanged) target is deemed too costly.

The model environment is taken from Clarida et al. (1999) and Vestin (2006). There are four types of agents in the economy: infinitely lived households, final good producers, intermediate-good producers, and a central bank.

The representative household maximizes lifetime expected utility subject to a budget constraint. The first-order conditions of the household's problem give rise to the following (log-linearized) Euler equation:

$$y_t = -\gamma[i_t - \mathbf{E}_t \pi_{t+1}] + E_t y_{t+1} + g_t. \tag{6}$$

In (6) y_t is the output gap, defined as the log deviation of actual output from the potential (flexible-price) output, i_t denotes the nominal interest rate, π_t is the period t log deviation of the inflation rate from its average level π, and g_t is a real rate shock.[6]

A competitive final good producer aggregates a variety of intermediate goods into the final good. A monopolistically-competitive intermediate-good producer faces a dynamic problem in which output prices are set to maximize the expected stream of future dividends subject to the demand conditions and Calvo-type timing restriction on price adjustments. The log-linearized first-order conditions lead to the standard New-Keynesian Phillips Curve relation:

$$\pi_t = \beta \mathbf{E}_t \pi_{t+1} + k y_t + e_t, \tag{7}$$

where β is the discount factor of the households, and $e_t = \varphi e_{t-1} + \varepsilon_t$ is a cost-push shock with normally distributed innovations, $\varepsilon_t \sim N(0, \sigma^2)$.

Given constraints (6) and (7), the central bank sets the nominal interest rate i_t to meet its policy objectives. However, as in Clarida et al. (1999) we can split the problem of the central bank into two parts. First, the central bank chooses the values of the current output gap, y_t, and the current inflation rate, π_t, that satisfy the Phillips curve constraint (7). Second, it sets the interest rate, i_t, to satisfy the constraint (6) with the chosen value of the output gap, y_t. This dissection of the problem allows us to ignore the constraint (6) altogether and assume that the central bank can directly set the output gap, y_t. It further implies that we can ignore the real rate shock, g_t.

Vestin (2006) defines price-level targeting as the optimal monetary policy under discretion with the central bank's period loss function being modified to include the deviations of the price level

---

[6]These shocks could be driven by productivity or government spending shocks. See Woodford (2003) for details.

from its target[7]

$$L_t^{PT} \equiv \frac{1}{2} \left\{ (p_t - p^T)^2 + \lambda^{PT} y_t^2 \right\}, \tag{8}$$

where p_t is the period t (log-)price level, p^T is the (log-)price-level target, and $\lambda^{PT} > 0$ is the weight on the output gap, which is chosen to minimize the unconditional expected value of the social loss function

$$\frac{1}{2} \mathbf{E} \sum_{t=0}^{\infty} \beta^t (\pi_t^2 + \lambda y_t^2). \tag{9}$$

As shown in Vestin (2006), the resulting PT policy implies the following dynamics:

$$p_t - p^T = a^{PT}(p_{t-1} - p^T) + b^{PT} e_t,$$
$$\pi_t = (a^{PT} - 1)(p_{t-1} - p^T) + b^{PT} e_t,$$
$$y_t = -c^{PT}(p_{t-1} - p^T) - d^{PT} e_t, \tag{10}$$

where a^{PT}, b^{PT}, c^{PT} and d^{PT} are strictly positive, and $a^{PT} \in (0,1)$ makes price level stationary around the target.

Vestin's contribution was to show that such PT regime attains higher social welfare (i.e., smaller social loss) by making inflation expectations change in a way that has a stabilizing effect on the economy. This is despite the fact that the central bank minimizes the "delegated" loss function L_t^{PT} on a period-by-period basis (i.e., under discretion). Vestin bypasses the issue of whether such a delegation would be credible.

In modeling PT with an escape clause we are taking a slightly different route. We assume that the central bank has the same period loss function $L_t = \frac{1}{2}(\pi_t^2 + \lambda y_t^2)$ as society's (9), but is not free to

---

[7]In what follows we assume, without loss of generality, that the average rate of inflation π^T is zero. Under PT, without escape clauses, this assumption implies that the price target p_t^T is simply a constant p^T, so $p_t^T = p^T, \forall t$.

minimize it on a period-by-period basis (which would be suboptimal given the absence of commitment, as shown by Clarida *et al.* (1999) and Vestin (2006)). Instead, we assume that the CB is *constrained* to set its policy in a way that preserves the dynamics of the price level in (10) (with the coefficients a^{PT}, b^{PT} being set optimally[8] as in Vestin (2006)), but that CB resets the target whenever the social welfare cost of not doing so exceeds a threshold value $C > 0$. So, in effect, CB has a limited discretion in choosing its target, with the degree of discretion being parametrized by C. This setup can be interpreted as one where society imposes upon the central bank a constraint on the dynamic behavior for the price level, but can only choose the values a^{PT} and b^{PT} once and for all.[9]

To formalize the policy choice we can state the central bank's problem as follows:

$$V(p_{t-1}, p_{t-1}^T, e_t|C) = \min_{p_t^T} \left\{ \frac{1}{2}(\pi_t^2 + \lambda y_t^2) + \beta \mathbf{E}_t V(p_t, p_t^T, e_{t+1}|C) \right\},$$

subject to

$$e_t = \varphi e_{t-1} + \varepsilon_t, \quad \varepsilon_t \sim N(0, \sigma^2),$$

$$\pi_t = \beta \mathbf{E}_t \pi_{t+1} + K y_t + e_t,$$

$$\pi_t = p_t - p_{t-1},$$

---

[8]In principle the optimal values of a^{PT} and b^{PT} obtained in a model without escape clauses (as in Vestin) might be suboptimal once escape clauses were taken in account. Making a^{PT} and b^{PT} endogenously determined every period would be the ideal alternative setup, but it turned out to be prohibitively hard to find numerically, perhaps because the joint endogeneity of policies and private expectations leads to instabilities due to multiplicity of equilibria. In an earlier version of the paper we tried a simpler thing. We kept a^{PT} and b^{PT} time invariant, but optimized their values to minimize the social loss function in a "high credibility" equilibrium with a given threshold. In this way we did allow for some optimization of these coefficients. However the results we computed were nearly identical to those optimized for the case without escape clauses. The reason for this similarity is that for most threshold values a high credibility equilibrium has no or almost no escapes, so the dynamics are very similar to the case without escape clauses.

[9]We are grateful to a referee for this interpretation.

$$p_t = p_t^T + a^{PT}(p_{t-1} - p_t^T) + b^{PT}e_t,$$

$$p_t^T \in \{p_{t-1}^T, p_{t-1}\}.$$

Thus, the CB's choice set in period t is either to keep the price target unchanged at its previous value, $p_t^T = p_{t-1}^T$, or reset it to the latest value of the actual price level, $p_t^T = p_{t-1}$.[10]

Let $\delta_t = 1$ if CB resets its target in period t and $\delta_t = 0$ otherwise. Further, let p_t^0, y_t^0, π_t^0 be the price level, output gap and inflation in period t, conditional on $\delta_t = 0$, while p_t^1, y_t^1, π_t^1 be the values of these variables conditional on $\delta_t = 1$. Then we can summarize the dynamics of the price-level target as follows:

$$p_t^T = \delta_t p_{t-1} + (1 - \delta_t)p_{t-1}^T,$$

where $\delta_t = 1$ if

$$\left\{ \frac{1}{2}\left((\pi_t^0)^2 + \lambda(y_t^0)^2\right) + \beta\mathbf{E}_t V(p_t, p_{t-1}^T, e_{t+1}|C) \right\}$$

$$- \left\{ \frac{1}{2}\left((\pi_t^1)^2 + \lambda(y_t^1)^2\right) + \beta\mathbf{E}_t V(p_t, p_{t-1}, e_{t+1}|C) \right\} > C, \quad (11)$$

and $\delta_t = 0$ otherwise.

The implied conditional price level values are

$$p_t^0 = p_{t-1}^T + a^{PT}(p_{t-1} - p_{t-1}^T) + b^{PT}e_t,$$

and

$$p_t^1 = p_{t-1} + b^{PT}e_t,$$

---

[10]In principle, the target could be reset to some other value. For instance it could be welfare improving to reset the price target to some convex combination between the old target p_{t-1}^T and the latest price level p_{t-1}. We do not consider such "optimal rebasing" alternatives. Our purpose is to identify the problems raised by the anticipation of rebasing on the performance of a price targeting rule. These problems would be qualitatively similar with a more complicated rebasing procedure.

while the actual price level is given by

$$p_t = \delta_t p_t^1 + (1 - \delta_t) p_t^0.$$

The corresponding inflation values are

$$\pi_t^0 = (a^{PT} - 1)(p_{t-1} - p_{t-1}^T) + b^{PT} e_t, \tag{12}$$

$$\pi_t^1 = b^{PT} e_t. \tag{13}$$

and actual inflation is given by

$$\pi_t = \delta_t \pi_t^1 + (1 - \delta_t) \pi_t^0.$$

Forwarding this one period and taking expectations we obtain expected future inflation

$$
\begin{aligned}
\mathbf{E}_t \pi_{t+1} &= \Pr(\delta_{t+1} = 1) \mathbf{E}_t \pi_{t+1}^1 + (1 - \Pr(\delta_{t+1} = 1)) \mathbf{E}_t \pi_{t+1}^0 \\
&= \rho_t b^{PT} \varphi e_t + (1 - \rho_t) \left[(a^{PT} - 1)(p_t - p_t^T)(b^{PT} \varphi e_t) \right] \\
&= b^{PT} \varphi e_t + (1 - \rho_t)(a^{PT} - 1)(p_t - p_t^T),
\end{aligned}
$$

where $\rho_t \equiv \Pr(\delta_{t+1} = 1)$ has the subscript t because it is formed as of period t.

The dynamics of the output gap y_t are determined endogenously from the Phillips curve relation (7):

$$
\begin{aligned}
y_t &= \frac{1}{K} (\pi_t - \beta \mathbf{E}_t \pi_{t+1} - e_t) \\
&= \frac{1}{K} \left(\pi_t - \beta \left[b^{PT} \varphi e_t + (1 - \rho_t)(a^{PT} - 1)(p_t - p_t^T) \right] - e_t \right).
\end{aligned}
$$

Note that the value of the tolerance level C determines how often the CB has an incentive to reset the target. If $C = \infty$, then CB never resets the target. This PT regime with no escape clauses will serve as our Fully Credible PT benchmark. Alternatively, if C is close to zero CB has an incentive to reset the target very often.

4.1. Parameterization, Computation and Results

4.1.1. Parameters

As a benchmark set of preference parameters we use the values from Woodford (2003, Table 6.1)

$$\beta = 0.99,$$
$$\lambda = 0.048,$$
$$K = 0.024.$$

We set the benchmark persistence of the cost-push shocks at $\varphi = 0.48$, halfway between the estimates of Adam and Billi (2006), $\varphi = 0$, and of Ireland (2004), $\varphi = 0.96$, and carry out a sensitivity analysis later.

The standard deviation of the cost-push shocks is pinned down by the standard deviation of inflation in the model under inflation targeting. Vestin defines inflation targeting in this environment as the optimal monetary policy under discretion, with the central bank's period loss function specified as

$$L_t^{IT} \equiv \frac{1}{2}(\pi_t^2 + \lambda y_t^2). \tag{14}$$

The resulting IT policy implies the following dynamics:

$$\pi_t = b^{IT} e_t,$$
$$y_t = -d^{IT} e_t,$$
$$e_t = \varphi e_{t-1} + \varepsilon_t, \quad \varepsilon_t \sim N(0, \sigma^2),$$

where

$$b^{IT} = \frac{\lambda}{K^2 + \lambda(1 - \beta\varphi)} = 1.86,$$

and

$$d^{IT} = \frac{K}{K^2 + \lambda(1 - \beta\varphi)} = 0.93,$$

under the benchmark parameters. It is straightforward to verify that the standard deviation of inflation under such inflation targeting is

$$\text{Std. dev.} (\pi_t) = \frac{\lambda}{K^2 + \lambda(1 - \beta\varphi)} \frac{\sigma}{\sqrt{1 - \varphi^2}}.$$

The standard deviation of quarterly CPI inflation rates in Canada during the inflation targeting period (from 1992:Q1 to 2007:Q2) was 0.4 percentage points.[11] Hence the standard deviation of the cost-push innovations in the model is

$$\sigma = \frac{K^2 + \lambda(1 - \beta\varphi)}{\lambda} \sqrt{1 - \varphi^2} \cdot 0.004.$$

With the benchmark parameter values the computed value of the standard deviation is $\sigma = 0.0019$.

Under a perfectly credible PT benchmark, we find the optimal values of the parameters a^{PT} and b^{PT} in the law of motion of the price level

$$p_t - p^T = a^{PT}(p_{t-1} - p^T) + b^{PT}e_t$$

by minimizing the unconditional expected loss[12] function

$$\frac{1}{2}E\sum_{t=0}^{\infty}\beta^t(\pi_t^2 + \lambda X_t^2) = \frac{1}{2}\sum_{t=0}^{\infty}\beta^t(var(\pi_t) + \lambda var(y_t))$$

$$= \frac{var(\pi_t) + \lambda var(y_t)}{2(1 - \beta)}.$$

---

[11] The estimated standard deviation of inflation is practically unchanged if we take a later period, e.g., 1996:1–2007:2, during which the current inflation target of 2 percent prevailed.

[12] Note that we are using the unconditional expected loss function as our welfare criterion, as opposed to the loss function which is conditional on the initial point. See Damjanovic *et al.* (2008) for the discussion of unconditionally optimal monetary policies.

Vestin (2006) shows that under (a Fully Credible) PT, unconditional variances of inflation and output gap are

$$var(\pi_t) = f^2 \frac{\sigma^2}{1 - \varphi^2},$$

$$var(y_t) = h^2 \frac{\sigma^2}{1 - \varphi},$$

where

$$f^2 = \frac{2(b^{PT})^2(1 - \varphi)}{(1 - a^{PT}\varphi)(1 + a^{PT})},$$

$$h^2 = \frac{\begin{aligned}&(b^{PT})^2 c^2 (1 + a^{PT}\varphi) + d^2 (1 - (a^{PT})^2)(1 - a^{PT}\varphi)\\ &+ 2\varphi b^{PT} cd(1 - (a^{PT})^2)\end{aligned}}{(1 - (a^{PT})^2)(1 - a^{PT}\varphi)}.$$

and

$$c = \frac{(1 - \beta a^{PT})(1 - a^{PT})}{K},$$

$$d = \frac{1 - b^{PT}(1 + \beta(1 - \varphi - a^{PT}))}{K}.$$

The resulting values of the coefficients are $a^{PT} = 0.90$ and $b^{PT} = 1.58$.

With the parameters of the model set, we can solve the model for various values of the tolerance level C. It is convenient to define an alternative measure c of the tolerance level $c \equiv \sqrt{\frac{2c}{\lambda}}$. This alternative parameter has the same units of measurement as the output gap y_t, since $C = \frac{1}{2}\lambda C^2$. Thus, if we set $c = 0.05$, for example, we could interpret it as follows: CB has the option of resetting the price-level target, whenever the cost of not doing so (in present value terms) exceeds 5 percent of potential output.

4.1.2. *Computation*

The solution procedure uses a collocation method to approximate the value function $V(p, p^T, e)$ and the inflation policy function $\pi(p, p^T, e)$

Are Bygones Not Bygones? 407

with linear splines.[13] We start by guessing the inflation rate $\tilde{\pi}(p, p^T, e)$ and the value function $\tilde{V}(p, p^T, e)$ as approximate functions of the economy's state vector (p, p^T, e). Using those functions we can evaluate $\mathbf{E}_t \pi_{t+1} = \mathbf{E}\tilde{\pi}(p_t, p_t^T, e_{t+1}|e_t)$ and $\mathbf{E}_t \tilde{V}(p_t, p_t^T, e_{t+1}|e_t)$ for any given triple (p_t, p_t^T, e_t). For a grid of values of $(p_{t-1}, p_{t-1}^T, e_t)$, we use Eqs. (12), (13) and (7) to compute the implied conditional values of inflation and of the output gap: $y_t^0, \pi_t^0, y_t^1, \pi_t^1$. With those conditional values computed, we can evaluate whether the difference

$$\left\{ \frac{1}{2} \left((\pi_t^0)^2 + \lambda(y_t^0)^2 \right) + \beta \mathbf{E}_t \tilde{V}(p_t, p_{t-1}^T, e_{t+1}|e_t) \right\}$$

$$- \left\{ \frac{1}{2} \left((\pi_t^1)^2 + \lambda(y_t^1)^2 \right) + \beta \mathbf{E}_t \tilde{V}(p_t, p_{t-1}, e_{t+1}|e_t) \right\},$$

is greater than $\frac{1}{2}\lambda c^2$. If it is greater, then $\delta_t = 1$ and thus, $\pi_t = \pi_t^1$, $y_t = y_t^1$ and

$$V_t = \frac{1}{2} \left((\pi_t^1)^2 + \lambda(y_t^1)^2 \right) + \beta \mathbf{E}_t \tilde{V}(p_t, p_{t-1}, e_{t+1}|e_t).$$

Otherwise, $\delta_t = 0$, $\pi_t = \pi_t^0$, $y_t = y_t^0$ and

$$V_t = \frac{1}{2}((\pi_t^0)^2 + \lambda(y_t^0)^2) + \beta \mathbf{E}_t \tilde{V}(p_t, p_{t-1}^T, e_{t+1}|e_t).$$

Projecting the values of π_t and V_t on the space $(p_{t-1}, p_{t-1}^T, e_t)$ we obtain the updated functions $\tilde{\pi}(p, p^T, e)$ and $\tilde{V}(p, p^T, e)$. We iterate until convergence of both functions. Once the functions converge, we use them to simulate the economy over 10,000 quarters. We use the sample means and standard deviations over these 10,000 quarters as our approximations of unconditional means and standard deviations.

---

[13]We used CompEcon Toolbox algorithms to project these functions on the space of linear splines. See Miranda and Fackler (2002) for details.

408 Paul R. Masson and Malik D. Shukayev

To assess the approximation quality in our computations we compared the average realized loss value

$$\bar{L} = \frac{1}{10,000} \left[\sum_{t=1}^{10,000} \frac{\pi_t^2 + \lambda X_t^2}{2} \right],$$

in the simulation, with the average value $\bar{V} = \frac{1}{10,000} \sum_{t=1}^{10,000} V_t$ computed using the formula

$$V_t = \frac{1}{2}(\pi_t^2 + \lambda y_t^2)\beta \mathbf{E}_t \tilde{V}(p_t, p_{t-1}^T, e_{t+1}|e_t),$$

that has the approximated value function $\tilde{V}(p_t, p_{t-1}^T, e_{t+1}|e_t)$ in it. If our computations are accurate then we must have $\bar{L} \approx (1-\beta)\bar{V}$. The difference

$$100\left(\frac{(1-\beta)\bar{V}}{\bar{L}} - 1\right),$$

was consistently below 0.15, which means that the difference was smaller than 0.15 percent of $\bar{L}$. Judging from the invariance of reported moments to changes in the number of approximating splines,[14] this level of precision seems sufficient.

4.1.3. Simulation results

As mentioned above, if the tolerance level c is very large, then CB is unlikely to ever reset the target. For example, if c is 20 percent, then CB does not reset the target unless the cost of not resetting exceeds 20 percent of potential GDP (in present value terms). As we will see, the probability of that happening is very low. Conversely, if c is very small, say 1 percent, then target resets are very likely. This is not the full story though. Our results show that for a range of values of c, there are at least two stable equilibria with different unconditional

---

[14]The quality of approximation attained in the simulations depends on the number of splines used to approximate the expectation functions. In our final simulations we used 17 linear spline segments for the price domains and 7 linear spline segments for the exogenous shock. Raising the number of splines beyond that did not change any of the reported (rounded) moments.

probabilities of price-target resets $\mathbf{E}[\rho_t]$. We call the equilibrium with high (low) unconditional price-target reset probability the "Low (High) credibility" equilibrium.

The results with the benchmark set of parameters are presented in Figs. 1–3. Figure 1 shows how the unconditional price-target reset probability changes with the tolerance level c. For very stringent escape clause rules ($c \geq 16$ percent), there is only one equilibrium, in which the computed reset probability is zero (price target resets never happen in the simulated sample). For very lax escape clause rules ($c = 0$) there also appears to be only one equilibrium with the unconditional reset probability equal to 76 percent.[15] Finally,

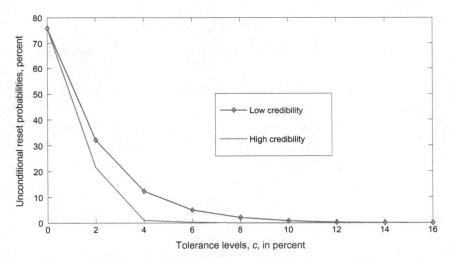

Figure 1. Unconditional Price-target Reset Probability, "High" and "Low" Credibility Equilibria

---

[15]Intuitively, it would seem that the unconditional reset probability should be 100 percent when $c = 0$, since the optimal policy under discretion is an IT regime in which the price level is a nonstationary variable. However, PT with zero reset costs is not equivalent to an IT regime. Even when the price-level target is being reset, PT implies a different response of inflation (and the output gap) to the current cost-push shock e_t. Because of that differential response, PT with resets every period attains much lower social welfare than IT. As a result, CB finds it optimal not to reset the target every period, thus retaining some influence on inflation expectations.

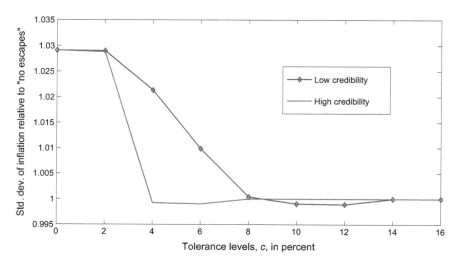

Figure 2. Standard deviation of inflation relative to Fully Credible PT

for the intermediate values of c, there are at least two stable equilibria.[16]

Figure 2 plots the standard deviations of inflation for different values of c, relative to the standard deviation of inflation in the "Fully credible" benchmark ($c = \infty$).[17] The vertical axis indicates that the volatility of inflation is barely affected by changes in the stringency of escape clauses. Thus, price target resets and low PT credibility lead to only marginally higher volatility of inflation. As we will see next, most of the action falls on the output gap.

Figure 3 plots the standard deviations of the output gap for different values of c, relative to the standard deviation of the output gap in the "Fully Credible" benchmark.[18]

From Figure 3 we can see that for very high values of c the standard deviation of the output gap is the same as in the case

---

[16]For some values of c there was also a third stable equilibrium with an intermediate reset probability. We found all these equilibria by starting with different initial guesses for the inflation function.

[17]That is $\frac{\text{std.dev.}(\pi_t(c))}{\text{std.dev.}(\pi_t(\infty))}$.

[18]That is $\frac{\text{std.dev.}(y_t(c))}{\text{std.dev.}(y_t(\infty))}$.

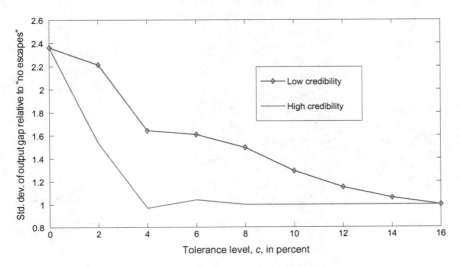

Figure 3. Standard deviation of output gap relative to Fully Credible PT

without escape clauses: i.e., the ratio of standard deviations is equal to 1. For very low values of c, the standard deviation of the output gap is twice as large with the escape clauses as without them. For the intermediate values of c, the "High credibility" equilibrium has nearly the same volatility for the output gap as in the "no escape clauses" economy. In fact, when $c = 4$ percent, the volatility of the output gap is even slightly lower. This particular example shows that a credible PT regime with "the right" escape clauses can in principle attain better stabilization results than PT without escape clauses. However, c reflects society's tolerance for the welfare loss from continuing the PT policy without resetting, and is not a choice variable. Our results for the "Low credibility" equilibria, moreover, suggest that escape clauses could also undermine the CB's credibility and lead to costly macroeconomic instability.

Figure 4 plots net welfare losses for the two equilibria relative to Fully Credible PT.[19] The dashed line shows the net welfare loss for the IT regime (also relative to PT without escape clauses). The

---

[19]These are computed as $100 * (\text{Average Loss}(c)/\text{Average Loss}(\infty) - 1)$.

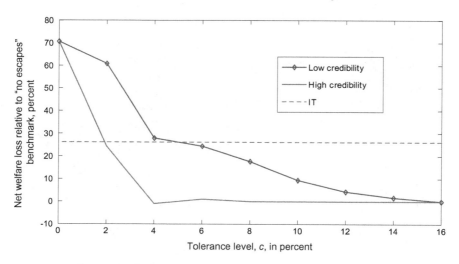

Figure 4. Net welfare loss relative to Fully Credible PT

shape of the curves is similar to those in Fig. 3, where we plotted the standard deviations of the output gap—a reflection of the fact that most welfare loss differences between PT regimes with different c levels are due to differences in the output gap volatility. It is important to note that for very lax escape clause rules, PT with such an escape clause performs considerably worse than an IT regime. Thus, low c provokes frequent resets, but the limiting value for welfare is not IT: by making policy uncertain, it deteriorates welfare relative to the IT regime. Finally, looking at the "High credibility" equilibrium with $c = 4$ percent, we can see once again, that a credible PT with the "right" escape clause can marginally improve upon PT without escape clauses. The cost of losing credibility might be high, however.

What is the intuition for these results? A credible PT has the advantage, relative to IT, of stabilizing the economy through an inflation expectation channel: an increase in the current price level relative to target implies that CB will have to lower future inflation to bring the price level back to target. Lower expected future inflation lowers the incentive to raise current prices, and stabilizes the economy by counteracting the current price increase.[20] Thus, changes in expected inflation induced by the current price change stabilize the economy even before CB has done anything to the current output gap (via changes in interest rates). This automatic stabilization mechanism is absent under IT, since it does not explicitly target any price level. Thus, the expected future inflation under IT is independent of the current price level, and there is no negative feedback effect on expected inflation. CB has to rely solely on changes in the output gap to meet its stabilization objectives.

Turning back to the PT regime with escape clauses, the positive probability of a price-target reset weakens the link between the deviation from the current price target and expected future inflation. This is precisely because CB may reset the target so that monetary policy does not have to reverse past price shocks. The consequence of a weaker link between the current price and expected future inflation is that the automatic stabilization mechanism becomes less effective. This hurts in two ways: first, since PT loses some of its automatic stabilization benefits, CB has to rely more on costly changes in the output gap to meet its objectives. Second, because of heavier reliance on output gap manipulations, it becomes costlier for CB to return the price level to an unchanged target. Price target resets look more attractive and thus, price-target resets are more likely. This further undermines CB's credibility and leads to self-fulfilling credibility problems for PT and to multiple equilibria. In other words, escape clauses may have a perverse effect on public expectations, leading to higher output volatility and a costlier PT regime.

Another important result evident from Figs. 1 and 3 is that even small unconditional reset probabilities can lead to large increases in output gap volatility. For example, when $c = 10$ percent, the unconditional probability of price-target resets in the "Low credibility" equilibrium is only 0.8 percent, but the volatility of the output gap is 30 percent higher than under PT without escape

---

[20]This negative feedback mechanism works in a symmetric way for price decreases relative to target.

414   *Paul R. Masson and Malik D. Shukayev*

clauses. This is because the conditional target reset probability changes endogenously and becomes very high when the deviation of the price level from target increases. Low PT credibility in those periods leads to big fluctuations in the output gap, which contribute disproportionately to the increase in the overall output volatility.

The volatility of the output gap is not always decreasing in c, however. For example, Fig. 3 shows that in a "High credibility" equilibrium with $c = 4$ percent, the standard deviation of output gap is lower than in a "High credibility" equilibrium with $c = 6$ percent. This non-monotonic relationship arises because there are two opposing effects of having a less stringent escape clause. On the one hand, a less stringent escape clause makes price-target resets more likely, which leads to higher volatility by destabilizing inflation expectations and the output gap. On the other hand, a less stringent escape clause lets CB act before the output gap becomes extremely large in absolute value, thus reducing the likelihood of large output fluctuations. The interaction of these two opposing effects results in a non-monotonic relationship between c and output gap volatility. Thus, while lax escape clauses moderate large output fluctuations, they also increase the frequency of medium-sized changes.

Finally, the qualitative results we presented in this section are not sensitive to the parameter values chosen. We conducted a thorough sensitivity analysis with respect to λ, κ and φ and found no remarkable differences[21] from the benchmark results. In some cases we did not find any value of c, for which PT with escape clauses dominated PT without such clauses. In particular, as Vestin (2006) has shown, when the cost-push shock is i.i.d. ($\varphi = 0$), PT without escape clauses implements the optimal policy. This means, of course, that one cannot do better. However all of our results

---

[21]We tried the following values of these parameters: $\lambda = \{0.024, 0.048, 0.096\}$, $\kappa = \{0.012, 0.024, 0.048\}$, and $\varphi = \{0.0, 0.48, 0.8\}$ (the codes were not converging for $\varphi = 0.96$). The standard deviation of the cost-push innovations, σ, was always recalibrated, as described above, to give the same volatility of inflation under IT as in the Canadian data.

regarding multiple equilibria with perverse effects of escape clauses in low credibility equilibria stayed intact.

5. Conclusions

The gold standard regime and price-level targeting have similarities in that neither lets bygones be bygones, but each requires reversing deviations from a particular nominal price. The gold standard experience suggests that in some circumstances a PT regime might also be suspended and the target rebased. While it is difficult to anticipate what those circumstances might be, nevertheless they would seem to be associated with major risks of an economic downturn or financial collapse. In our view, price-level targeting is unlikely to be implemented without an explicit or implicit escape clause that allows bygones to be bygones under some circumstances. The model presented in this paper assumes that this is the case; in particular, large enough shocks provoke abandonment of strict PT and rebasing of the price target to ignore past deviations.

In addition, this possibility may be reflected in expectations, and thus hamper the credibility of a PT regime relative to a regime like IT.[22] The latter is less constraining because it allows bygones to be bygones, and hence temporary deviations from the inflation target do not have to be corrected later. Of course, it may be that in normal times the magnitude of downturns is not so great as to affect credibility. However, history suggests that one should not ignore the possibility that large fluctuations, either derived from financial crisis, war, or fiscal indiscipline, may lead to a change of target. The inter-war period suggests that even long-anticipated resumption at pre-war parities had substantial cost in Britain in 1926, though the experience of Sweden was less severe. In contrast, France, which went back on

---

[22]The IT regime could also be subject to an escape clause, in which case a proper comparison would compare PT and IT regimes, both having escape clauses. However, following the literature, we model IT as the optimal policy under discretion. The (Markov-perfect) optimality of IT makes escape clauses redundant in such regime. Moreover, the escape clause for PT relates solely to the issue of letting bygones be bygones, which IT does in any case.

416   *Paul R. Masson and Malik D. Shukayev*

the gold standard only in 1928, at a much depreciated level for the franc, benefited from a boost to activity. Of course, a PT regime with frequent suspensions and resumptions at the prevailing price level would be similar to inflation targeting in that the price level will become nonstationary. Moreover, by introducing uncertainty about resets such a PT regime could in fact be considerably worse in welfare terms.

Acknowledgments

We would like to thank Robert Amano, Michael Bordo, Oleksiy Kryvtsov, David Laidler, Raphael Solomon, and Alexander Ueberfeldt for helpful comments.

References

Adam, K., Billi, R.M., 2006. Optimal monetary policy under commitment with a zero bound on nominal interest rates. *Journal of Money, Credit and Banking* 38, 1877–1905.

Barro, R., Gordon, D., 1983. Rules, discretion, and reputation in a model of monetary policy. *Journal of Monetary Economics* 12, 101–121.

Bayoumi, T., Bordo, M.D., 1998. Getting pegged: comparing the 1879 and 1925 gold resumptions. *Oxford Economic Papers* 50(1), 122–149.

Bordo, M., Kydland, F., 1995. The gold standard as a rule: an essay in exploration. *Explorations in Economic History* 32(4), 423–464.

Cassell, G., 1936. The Downfall of the Gold Standard. Oxford at the Clarendon Press, London.

Clarida, R., Gali, R., Gertler, M., 1999. The science of monetary policy. *Journal of Economic Literature* 37, 1661–1707.

Damjanovic, T., Damjanovic, V., Nolan, C., 2008. Unconditionally optimal monetary policy. *Journal of Monetary Economics* 55, 491–500.

Driffill, J., Rotondi, Z., 2006. Credibility of optimal monetary delegation: comment. *American Economic Review* 96(4), 1361–1366.

Eggertsson, G.B., 2008. Great expectations and the end of the depression. *American Economic Review* 98(4), 1476–1516.

Eichengreen, B., 1992. Golden Fetters: The Gold Standard and the Great Depression, 1919–1939. *NBER Series on Long-term Factors in Economic Development*. Oxford University Press, New York and Oxford.

Fetter, F.W., 1965. Development of British Monetary Orthodoxy, 1797–1875. Harvard University Press, Cambridge, Massachusetts.

Flood, Robert, Isard, Peter, 1989. Monetary policy strategies. *International Monetary Fund Staff Papers* 36, 612–632.

Ireland, P.N., 2004. Technology shocks in the New Keynesian model. *The Review of Economics and Statistics* 86(4), 923–936.

Jeanne, O., 1997. Are currency crises self-fulfilling? A test. *Journal of International Economics* 43, 263–286.

Jensen, H., 1997. Credibility of optimal monetary delegation. *American Economic Review* 87(5), 911–920.

Kryvtsov, O., Shukayev, M., Ueberfelt, A., 2008. Adopting Price-Level Targeting under Imperfect Credibility. *Working Paper 2008-3*, Bank of Canada, February 2008.

Lohmann, S., 1992. Optimal commitment in monetary policy: credibility versus flexibility. *American Economic Review* 82(1), 273–286.

McCallum, B.T., 1999. Handbook of Macroeconomics. *Issues in the Design of Monetary Policy Rules*, vol. 1. Elsevier, Amsterdam (Chapter 23).

Miranda, M.J., Fackler, P.L., 2002. Applied Computational Economics and Finance. The MIT Press.

Obstfeld, M., 1996. Models of currency crises with self-fulfilling features. *European Economic Review* 40, 1037–1048.

Prati, A., 1991. Poincare's stabilization: stopping a run on government debt. *Journal of Monetary Economics* 27, 213–239.

Rogoff, K., 1985. The optimal degree of commitment to an intermediate monetary target. *Quarterly Journal of Economics* 100, 1169–1189.

Svensson, L.E.O., 1999. Price-level targeting versus inflation targeting: a free lunch? *Journal of Money, Credit, and Banking* 31 (3), 277–295.

Vestin, D., 2006. Price-level versus inflation targeting. *Journal of Monetary Economics* 53, 1361–1376.

Woodford, M., 2003. Interest and Prices: Foundations of a Theory of Monetary Policy. Princeton University Press.

Yetman, J., 2005. The credibility of the monetary policy free lunch. *Journal of Macroeconomics* 27, 434–451.

CPSIA information can be obtained
at www.ICGtesting.com
Printed in the USA
BVHW082009260719
554489BV00003B/8/P